THE FRENCH REPUBLIC UNDER CAVAIGNAC

1848

COURTESY OF THE BIBLIOTHEQUE NATIONALE

Louis Eugène Cavaignac

THE FRENCH REPUBLIC UNDER CAVAIGNAC 1848

Frederick A. de Luna

1969

PRINCETON UNIVERSITY PRESS

PRINCETON, NEW JERSEY

L.C. Card: 68-27413

Publication of this book has been aided by the
Whitney Darrow Publication Reserve Fund
of Princeton University Press

This book has been composed in Caledonia type.

Printed in the United States of America
by Princeton University Press, Princeton, New Jersey

Acknowledgments

I am grateful to the U.S. Fulbright Commission for a grant which enabled me to do essential research in France, and to Professor Eugène Cavaignac for allowing me free access to the papers in his family archives relating to his grandfather.

For valuable advice and assistance in my research in France, I am indebted to Professors Louis Chevalier, Louis Girard, René Rémond and Emile Tersen. I wish also to thank the personnel at the Archives Nationales, the Archives Départementales de la Sarthe in Le Mans, the Service Historique de l'Armée at the Château de Vincennes, the Bibliothèque Nationale and the Bibliothèque Lavisse at the Sorbonne.

The library staffs at the British Museum, the University of Iowa, the University of Oregon and the University of Alberta were also very helpful. Among American historians, I owe a general debt of gratitude to Professors William O. Aydelotte of the University of Iowa, Samuel P. Hays of the University of Pittsburgh, Val R. Lorwin of the University of Oregon, Nicholas V. Riasanovsky of the University of California at Berkeley and Herbert H. Rowen of Rutgers University. A special word of appreciation is due to Professor Alan B. Spitzer of the University of Iowa, who offered friendly encouragement and valuable criticism. Finally, I wish to thank Mrs. Marie Griffin of Edmonton, Alberta, who typed the manuscript.

London *February 24, 1968*

Contents

THE FRENCH REPUBLIC UNDER CAVAIGNAC 1848

I · Cursed his Name

On June 26, 1848, after the last forlorn barricade of the insurgent Paris workers had fallen to the cannon and musket fire of his troops, General Louis Eugène Cavaignac issued a proclamation: "The sacred cause of the Republic has triumphed. . . . In Paris, I see victors and vanquished; cursed be my name if I consent to see victims." The general, known before 1848 only as one of the conquerors of Algeria, had assumed dictatorial powers in the midst of the fighting, and afterwards the grateful National Assembly kept him in power for six months as premier and virtual head of state in the Second French Republic. The general was also for a time the leading candidate in France's first democratic election of a president, but the extraordinary rise of Louis Napoleon Bonaparte assured his defeat in December 1848. Afterwards, while the new Bonaparte went on to create the Second French Empire, Cavaignac retired from the army and played only a minor political role until his death in 1857.

What kind of man was General Cavaignac? What was the significance of his role in the June Days? What was the nature of the government over which he presided afterwards? These are difficult questions to which simple answers have commonly been given, largely because neither Cavaignac nor his regime has been regarded as posing important or interesting problems. During that year of revolutionary upheaval throughout Europe, Cavaignac was not the only general to crush an insurrection, and some of his government's policies showed unmistakable signs of reaction. Indeed, historians customarily regard the revolution which erupted in France in February 1848 as coming to an end with the "bloody June Days," when the forces of order, through the sword of Cavaignac, suppressed the workers and destroyed the promise of a "democratic and social republic." The period dominated by General Cavaignac thus falls neatly into place as one of dreary reaction, in which the promise of February was betrayed and its few accomplishments undone. It has become almost traditional among French historians to cite either George Sand's remark that she no longer believed in a republic that began by killing its proletarians, or the anguished cry of Lamennais, "What we see is assuredly not the Republic . . . but around its blood-stained tomb, the saturnalia of the reaction."[1]

Yet the views of George Sand and of Lamennais were not very representative—most Frenchmen saw the events of 1848 in quite a different light. To them, the insurrection of June had threatened to bring civil war and anarchy to France and to undermine the very foundations of society. Cavaignac was idolized as the "Savior of society," and most of the republicans, including the socialist Louis Blanc, regarded him as the savior of the republic: he had successfully defended the sacred principle of popular sovereignty—incarnate in the first democratically elected National Assembly. Moreover, the general's conduct while in power favorably impressed some of the most astute political observers of the time. Alexis de Tocqueville thought that Cavaignac "was the only great figure to appear on the lusterless canvas of the revolution of 1848, and he will remain great in history."[2]

Cavaignac himself remained confident that posterity would honor him, and yet the curse which he rhetorically uttered has seemed to rest on his name. His dark historical reputation reflects in part the influence of Karl Marx, another great contemporary observer, whose interpretation was outlined in the *Neue Rheinische Zeitung* only three days after Cavaignac issued his proclamation: "Order! shouts Cavaignac, the brutal echo of the French National Assembly and of the republican bourgeoisie. Order! thundered his grapeshot, as it ripped up the body of the proletariat. None of the numerous revolutions of the French bourgeoisie since 1789 was an attack on order; for they allowed the rule of the class, they allowed the slavery of the workers, they allowed the bourgeois order to endure,

[1] See, e.g., Félix Ponteil, *1848* (3d edn., Paris, 1955), pp. 153-154, and Jean Dautry, *1848 et la IIe République* (2d edn., Paris, 1957), pp. 203, 206. In these and subsequent quotations from the French, the translations are my own unless otherwise indicated.

[2] From a letter to Pierre Freslon, 5 November 1857, published in Gustave de Beaumont, ed., *Oeuvres et correspondance inédites d'Alexis de Tocqueville* (Paris, 1861), II, p. 415.

however often the political form of this rule and of this slavery changed. June has attacked this order. Woe to June!"[3]

There is a strong Marxian imprint on recent French historiography of the revolution of 1848, and in any case, sympathy among historians for the insurgents of June and repugnance for the men who crushed them have permitted Cavaignac and the troubled times in which he governed to pass into a kind of opprobrious obscurity. Political interpretations of the revolution of 1848, such as the classic nineteenth century work of Pierre de la Gorce, are outmoded, and the interpretation of the revolution as a class struggle has become the prevailing orthodoxy. Yet this interpretation has always been oversimplified, and much of the evidence accumulated by recent research has brought into question this and other commonly accepted generalizations about 1848 in France.[4] Although this book does not pretend to offer a new synthesis of the entire revolution, perhaps the illumination of a neglected figure and a neglected period will suggest at least a different perspective from which to view the revolution as a whole. No qualified historian, not even in France, has previously sought to examine more than cursorily the role of Cavaignac in 1848, nor to inquire more than superficially into the activities of his government, which was not only the most durable but in some respects the most significant of the three French provisional governments of 1848. In a time of revolution, when decisive actions are taken in days or weeks, six months is a long time, and the government of Cavaignac was not idle.

This study proceeds from the conviction that the period of Cavaignac (no less than the earlier, more dramatic phases of the revolution of 1848) deserves consideration in its own right and without the presupposition that it was necessarily one of black reaction. This book is not intended to be a biography of

[3] Karl Marx, *The Class Struggles in France (1848-50)*, "Marxist Library" (New York, 1935), xxiv, p. 57.

[4] See Gordon Wright, *France in Modern Times, 1760 to the Present* (Chicago, 1960), pp. 167-170 and 264-265; and two articles by Peter Amann, "Writings on the Second French Republic," *Journal of Modern History*, xxxiv (1962), 409-429; and "The Changing Outlines of 1848," *American Historical Review*, lxviii (1963), 938-953.

Cavaignac, although it does constitute in part a political biography for 1848 and seeks to elucidate his career and attitudes before the revolution. The primary focus is on the point of view and policies of the government over which he presided. I have sought to examine the republic of Cavaignac in its historical context and to interpret it in terms of the men who governed it, the ideology sustaining it, the problems facing it, the things it did and tried or hoped to do. Cavaignac was not merely an apolitical, conservative and authoritarian general, but a man with a distinctive political and social outlook. After the fighting, he was neither a dictator nor a figurehead, but an influential and active head of government. The men of his cabinet were almost all republicans of the sort usually called moderate by historians, but they were moderates of a kind that in a sense died out after 1848, and it is misleading and anachronistic to confuse them with the conservative moderates of the Third Republic. It will be one of the objects of this work to explain the point of view of this kind of 1848 republican. In addition, I have devoted special attention to social and economic problems and policies, not only because they were central issues in 1848, but because they constitute the least known or least understood, and at the same time probably the most significant, aspects of the French republic under Cavaignac.

This study is based in part on manuscript sources, in part on published primary sources, and in part, of course, on the findings of other scholars. Of the manuscript materials, the most important are in the private papers of Cavaignac[5] and in some collections at the Archives Nationales in Paris. Of great value among the printed sources are the files of *Le Moniteur universel*, the official government newspaper, and of *Le National*, the republican daily that influenced and reflected the Cavaignac government. Although the importance of *Le National* has always been recognized, few historians have consulted it more than casually. The most valuable of the printed sources is surely the verbatim reports of the proceedings of

[5] These are now in the possession of the general's heirs at Château d'Ourne, Flée (Sarthe); most of them are now available on microfilm at the departmental archives in Le Mans.

the National Assembly. Even cursory inspection of the index to the *Compte rendu des séances de l'Assemblée nationale,* filled as it is with references to reforms and projected reforms introduced, debated, and (many of them) adopted after the June Days, is sufficient to suggest that the usual picture of reaction requires some modification.

One further kind of evidence used deserves special mention. Because the relationship of the government to the National Assembly was a central problem, it was important to know the structure of forces within the Assembly, and yet the state of knowledge on this matter was unsatisfactory. In consequence, I made my own analysis of the Assembly, based on a compilation of biographical information about the 900 men composing it. This analysis helped to clarify many important issues.

Finally, this study necessarily involves re-interpretation of some familiar events. During a successful revolution, as in July 1830, or February 1848, justice and legality seem to pass abruptly from one side of the barricades to the other: rebels become heroes and founders of a new order. This failed to occur in June, but we have become accustomed to see justice in the insurgent workers' cause, and to see only a narrow legality masking selfish class interests on the side of the victors. There can be no question that the June Days were a tragedy in which perhaps thousands of French workers lost their lives in a cause they believed just, nor that the harsh suppression served to alienate the French working classes and to prepare for the greater carnage and deeper tragedy of the Paris Commune of 1871. Yet, if we are to comprehend fully the French revolution of 1848, we must seek also to understand the victors, rather than dismiss them as bourgeois, hypocritical, and superficial democrats and republicans, or scorn them because they were not workers or socialists. The men who guided the republic of Cavaignac were, like the radicals, the socialists, and the workers, also men of 1848, inexperienced and often inept politicians forced to act in a time of revolution, when faced with bewildering new problems and painful alternatives. Implacable against the insurgents of June, bourgeois moderates to be sure, they were also men of the left, men who hoped to create a democratic society, men who looked forward to the future as well as backward to the great Revolution that had given birth to their political creed. If they were not such men, much of what they did must remain inexplicable.

II · The Republicans before 1848

THE FRENCH REPUBLICAN MOVEMENT

THE French republican tradition, to which Cavaignac and the men of 1848 looked for inspiration, was born in violence during the great Revolution. Although educated to admire the classical republics and sympathetic with the experiment launched by the American colonists, the first generation of French republicans had joyfully greeted the creation of the constitutional monarchy in 1789, and had felt compelled by circumstances to create a republic in 1792. Yet they had ready to hand, bequeathed from the Enlightenment on which all had been nurtured, a set of ideals and principles to which they could appeal in fashioning a new order without a king.

Thus the First Republic in its practices, beliefs and institutions, from the popular election of the Convention, the stillborn democratic constitution of 1793, the Terror, the "Republic of Virtue," Thermidor and beyond, was in part a pragmatic response to immediate and agonizing problems, in part an attempt to build a new and more just society. For the men of the Convention, who at great cost in blood defeated the invading armies of monarchical Europe and crushed counterrevolution at home, the Republic, "one and indivisible," became identified with the Revolution, and with the heady ideals of liberty, equality and fraternity.

Under the Directory these ideals seemed increasingly illusory, and when that dreary regime was extinguished by Napoleon Bonaparte, the Republic which Frenchmen remembered with regret or abhorrence was that of the Convention, of the high tide of the democratic revolution, and of the Terror. Bonaparte diverted the revolutionary current into strange new channels, using force when necessary to destroy the faint stirrings of republican or royalist opposition. But many former Jacobins proved willing to throw in their lot with the man who brought stability, prosperity and glory; a number of *conventionnels* sat in the assemblies or administrative offices of the Empire, and with all the resources at his command Napoleon sought for ten years "to make Frenchmen forget the Republic."[1] Yet by no means all of the surviving Jacobins and *conventionnels* forsook their ideals. A number of them kept the faith, their homes so many secret schools in which tales of the glorious days of the republic were passed on to the new generation.

Such a one was Lazare Carnot, the great Organizer of Victory, who instilled the creed in his son Hippolyte, later to become Minister of Education in 1848. "I found my political opinions in my cradle," Hippolyte recalled. "They accompanied me in the games of my childhood, in my first discussions, in my earliest reading; they became as natural to me as the love of family and the love of country."[2] Another member of the Committee of Public Safety, Prieur de la Côte d'Or, tutored the young Etienne Cabet; the Abbé Grégoire and Merlin de Thionville were other *conventionnels* who secretly propagated the republican cause.[3] Still another was Jean-Baptiste Cavaignac, regicide, *représentant en mission* and minor terrorist, who imparted his faith to his two sons, Godefroy and Eugène. Yet, such ardent republican families were few and isolated, and when the Empire fell in 1814, no one seriously proposed the revival of the republic.[4] The restored monarchy was conciliatory even toward the regicides, but growing discontent with the regime found some expression in reawakening republicanism, which Napoleon sought to captivate during the Hundred Days, when Carnot, Cavaignac and other *conventionnels* rallied to the empire of the Acte Additionnel. The vindictive second restoration witnessed the White Terror, and the *Chambre Introuvable* banished the regicides. Most fled to the Netherlands, and "it seemed that with them the republican idea abandoned France."[5]

[1] Georges Weill, *Histoire du parti républicain en France (1814-1870)* (2d edn., Paris, 1928), p. 1. Much of my discussion of early nineteenth century republicanism is based on this standard authority. Cf. John A. Scott, *Republican Ideas and the Liberal Tradition in France, 1870-1914* (New York, 1951), pp. 11-44, and John Plamenatz, *The Revolutionary Movement in France, 1815-1871* (London, 1952), pp. 1-62.

[2] MS "Mémorial," Archives Nationales, 108 AP 3 dos. 21, p. 3.

[3] Weill, *Parti républicain*, p. 8.

[4] *Ibid.*, pp. 1-2.

[5] *Ibid.*, p. 4.

But even as the regicides departed, the new generation of young republicans whom they had enflamed with the revolutionary creed was already beginning to propagandize the students of Paris and of some provincial cities. The invalidation of the election of Grégoire to the Chamber of Deputies in 1819 provoked many to put their hopes in secret societies, the most famous of which was the Carbonari.[6] Although the founders and earliest members were republicans, such as Godefroy Cavaignac and Jules Bastide, the Carbonari was not a purely republican organization; its primary aim was to overthrow the Bourbon monarchy, and it included many Bonapartists and some partisans of the Duke of Orléans.[7] The carbonarist idea spread rapidly, mostly among students, soldiers and petty bourgeois youth, until there were cells or "ventes" in some sixty departments with a total membership of perhaps 30,000 to 40,000.[8] Before attempting an uprising, the young republicans in the Carbonari persuaded the Marquis de Lafayette and other veterans of the revolution who sat with the left opposition Independent faction in the Chamber of Deputies to join the secret leadership in the "Supreme Vente." The series of uprisings in 1822 were all tragic or ludicrous failures. Although Lafayette and other prominent men escaped incrimination, many young Carbonari were arrested and a few were executed, notably the "four sergeants of La Rochelle," promptly hailed as martyrs to the revolution.

Thus far, the republicans had little in the way of doctrine, which amounted to a cult of the Revolution in its republican rather than its liberal or Bonapartist phase. The one significant work of doctrine was Destutt de Tracy's *Commentaire sur l'esprit des lois* (1819), in which the author offered, in contrast to Montesquieu, a theory of republican government based

[6] A. Calmette, "Les Carbonari en France," *La Révolution de 1848*, IX (1912-13), pp. 401-417, and X (1913-14), pp. 52-73, 117-137, 214-230. The French Carbonari are the subject of a forthcoming work by Alan B. Spitzer.

[7] *Ibid.*, X, p. 53.

[8] G. de Bertier de Sauvigny, *La Restauration* (2nd edn., Paris, 1963), p. 180. Other estimates range from a few thousand to 800,000, but the latter figure is improbable, as the Carbonari scarcely penetrated the masses.

on universal suffrage. In the 1820's the republican cause also benefited from the historical works of Adolphe Thiers and others, who tended to rehabilitate the Revolution as a whole. The songs of Béranger also contributed to a revival of sympathetic memories of the First Republic. "If they helped to create the Napoleonic Legend, they were also the first popular apology for the republican armies."[9]

After the fiasco of 1822, the Carbonari were moribund, and the young republicans shifted to other kinds of organizations, such as the Francs-Parleurs, which collaborated with the liberal society, Aide-toi, le Ciel t'aidera, during the elections of 1827. In street demonstrations following their electoral victory, barricades went up in Paris for the first time since the Fronde, but the uprising was quickly suppressed. Afterwards, in the atmosphere of impending crisis following the appointment of the reactionary Polignac ministry in 1829, some republicans began to prepare secretly for another insurrection.[10] It was in 1829 also that newspapers of a vaguely republican cast began to appear. The most important was the *Tribune des départements*, supported financially in 1830 by Lafayette and Destutt de Tracy. But the most famous to appear on the eve of the revolution was *Le National*, which then supported the Orleanist cause but which would later become the most influential republican newspaper.

The traditional view that the revolution of 1830 was made by the republicans before being captured by the Orleanists has recently met serious criticism, notably from David H. Pinkney, who suggests that it "may have come close to being a Bonapartist revolution."[11] Pinkney has found little evidence of specifically republican opinions among the insurgents, but rather

[9] Weill, *Parti républicain*, p. 17.

[10] *Ibid.*, p. 22.

[11] "The Myth of the French Revolution of 1830," in *A Festschrift for Frederick B. Artz* (Durham, N.C., 1964), p. 68. Other important articles by Pinkney on 1830 are "A New Look at the French Revolution of 1830," *Review of Politics*, XXIII (1961), 490-506, and "The Crowd in the French Revolution of 1830," *American Historical Review*, LXX (1964), 1-17. The importance of the Bonapartists in 1830 also has been emphasized by J. Lucas-Dubreton, *Le Culte de Napoléon, 1815-1848* (Paris, 1960), pp. 271-297.

a strong hostility to the Bourbons combined with vague revolutionary sentiments; the most important leaders were not students or former Carbonari, but veterans of the revolutionary and imperial armies.[12] Nevertheless, there is good reason to believe that young republicans were involved from the outset, and that contemporaries regarded them as a redoubtable force. On the final day of combat, July 29, Jules Bastide, Godefroy Cavaignac and others led a group of insurgents from the Panthéon across the Pont-Royal and against the Tuileries Palace, where they raised the tricolor.[13] Moreover, in the famous placard advocating the Duke of Orléans, Thiers and Mignet thought it important to reject the Republic but not the Empire as an alternative ("The Republic would expose us to frightful divisions; it would embroil us with Europe"). Lafayette, the nominal leader of the republicans, played a crucial role by rallying to the Orleanist solution. There can be little doubt that the "republican kiss" at the Hôtel de Ville helped make a king. Although Lafayette later protested that he had never called Louis Philippe "the best of republics," he did tell him that "what the people need today is a popular throne, surrounded by republican institutions."[14]

Yet Pinkney's conclusion that the insurgents were animated mostly by anti-Bourbon sentiments, with the implication that the republicans were weak, seems borne out in a statement made by Godefroy Cavaignac. To an Orleanist who commended the republicans for "sacrificing their republican ideal in the interests of France," Cavaignac replied: "You are wrong to thank us. We gave in only because we were not strong enough. It was too difficult to make the people who had fought with the cry of '*Vive la Charte*' understand that their first act after the victory should be to arm themselves to destroy it. Later, it will be different."[15] Moreover, the republicans were at

[12] "The Crowd in the French Revolution of 1830," pp. 13, 15-16.

[13] Weill, *Parti républicain*, p. 24, and Calmette, "Les Carbonari en France," x, p. 230.

[14] S. Charléty, *La Restauration (1815-1830)*, "Histoire de France contemporaine," ed. Ernest Lavisse (Paris, 1921), IV, p. 382. Cf. Bertier de Sauvigny, *La Restauration*, p. 452.

[15] Prosper Duvergier de Hauranne, *Histoire du gouvernement parlementaire en France, 1814-1848* (Paris, 1871), x, pp. 651-652.

first satisfied with the results of the insurrection, for they were most concerned with removing Charles X and had only vague ideas about the regime that should replace him. It was only after the public appearance of the duke with Lafayette that they drew up the so-called program of the Hôtel de Ville, which was compatible with a monarchy that accepted popular sovereignty.

Some republicans demanded the convocation of a constituent assembly, but most were willing to accept the regime of the amended Charter, with the promise of future reforms. For the first six months of the July Monarchy, the republicans remained an ill-defined faction within the "party of movement," and associated with the liberal monarchists in Aide-toi, le Ciel t'aidera.[16] The new regime was at first solicitous, even timid in its relations with the republicans, and Lafayette remained commander of the National Guard until the end of the year. The government was permissive about new disorders, such as those in December 1830, attending the trial of Polignac and other former ministers, and the sack of the archbishopric of Saint-Germain l'Auxerrois in February 1831. But as the regime became consolidated, the republicans gradually grew disillusioned and began to adopt a stance of opposition. The appointment of the Casimir Perier ministry in March 1831, signaled the victory of the "party of resistance" and led to a definite rupture between the July Monarchy and the republicans.[17] At a trial of republican leaders in April for alleged complicity in the disorders attending the Polignac affair, the accused boldly defended their ideals in what amounted to a public declaration of war against the regime.

"My father," declared Godefroy Cavaignac, "was one of those, in the National Convention, who proclaimed the Republic. . . . It was for that reason that he died in exile. . . . My father and his colleagues suffered alone for the great cause that so many others betrayed. . . . This cause, Gentlemen, is bound up with all my filial sentiments; the principles that it embraces are my heritage. Study has fortified this direction given naturally to my political ideas, and now that the occa-

[16] Weill, *Parti républicain*, pp. 53, 56.
[17] *Ibid.*, p. 65.

sion is finally offered to me to pronounce a word that so many others proscribe, I declare it without affectation and without fear, from my heart and my conviction: I am a republican."[18] Cavaignac's eulogy of the Convention was wildly applauded, and the testimony of Lafayette and others also moved the jury, which acquitted all of the accused. Casimir Perier nevertheless continued his fight against the republicans, in particular by arresting the editors of their newspapers. Many republicans who fought on the barricades in July demonstrated their disgust with the regime that they had helped to create, by refusing "medals of July" because acceptance required an oath to the new king.[19]

The republicans did not as yet form a coherent party, but were a loose assortment of men diverse in backgrounds and in their conception of the republic. Heinrich Heine observed that in 1830 middle-aged men were rare among the republicans, most of whom were old men or youths.[20] The older men, veterans of the revolution such as Lafayette, were mostly ideologues who held republicanism as a distant ideal but were resigned to the July Monarchy. But there was also a tiny but influential group of older democrats who carried a more revolutionary message to the younger generation. The most important of these was Filippo Michele Buonarroti, who had participated with Babeuf in the "conspiracy of the equals" in 1796, and who had been in prison or exile ever since, conspiring anew, and writing his book, *Conspiration pour l'égalité dite de Babeuf*, which appeared in Brussels in 1828. He returned to France after the revolution of 1830, one of the few survivors of the First Republic in whom the Jacobin fire still burned brightly. Despite his association with Babeuf and his belief in a "community of goods and labor," Buonarroti regarded himself as primarily a Robespierrist and his aims were more political and moral than economic and social.[21] In the

[18] S. Charléty, *La Monarchie de juillet*, "Histoire de France contemporaine," ed. Ernest Lavisse (Paris, 1921), v, pp. 64-65.

[19] Weill, *Parti républicain*, p. 65.

[20] *Ibid.*, p. 33.

[21] See Elizabeth L. Eisenstein, *The First Professional Revolutionist: Filippo Michele Buonarroti (1761-1837)*, (Cambridge, Mass., 1959), esp. pp. 26 and 130-133.

early years of the July Monarchy, Buonarroti was very active in influencing many young republicans, such as Raspail, Cabet, Godefroy Cavaignac, Louis Blanc and probably Blanqui.[22]

Some of the youthful republicans were bred to their political faith by family tradition, others were inspired by the vogue of romantic and nationalistic adulation of the Revolution. A humanitarian concern for the poor moved some of them to advocate the democratic republic as the form of government most likely to improve their condition. One was Ulysse Trélat, who knew the misery of the working classes from his experience as a physician: "His propaganda was a long cry of pity, inspired by the sufferings of the poor."[23] Quite a different attitude led Armand Carrel, an editor of *Le National,* to shift from Orleanism to republicanism by 1832. His primary concern was for a vigorous foreign policy, and he was an admirer of Bonaparte. For France, he offered a moderate and even conservative republicanism which helped to divorce it from implications of violence and Terror. With Lafayette, Carrel admired 1789 and the American republic rather than the Convention.[24] But most republicans focused their vision on the First French Republic and the Convention of 1793 and repudiated Bonapartism. Lafayette's influence had greatly diminished by the time of his death in 1834.

During the early years of the July Monarchy, the republicans began to organize and to develop a body of doctrine. Popular sovereignty, not fully accepted by the Orleanists, became their basic principle. The only other doctrinal point common

[22] *Ibid.*, pp. 99, 124, 155, 187. Cf. Weill, *Parti républicain*, pp. 35-36; Leo A. Loubère, *Louis Blanc: His Life and His Contribution to the Rise of French Jacobin-Socialism* (Evanston, Ill., 1961), p. 17; and Alan B. Spitzer, *The Revolutionary Theories of Louis Auguste Blanqui* (New York, 1957), pp. 126-129.

[23] I. Tchernoff, *Le Parti républicain sous la monarchie de juillet: formation et évolution de la doctrine républicaine* (2d edn., Paris, 1905), p. 250.

[24] *Ibid.*, pp. 130-137; Weill, *Parti républicain*, pp. 45-48; Lucas-Dubreton, *Culte de Napoléon*, pp. 320-321. Carrel's semi-Bonapartism was not typical of the republicans, particularly during the 1840's, nor was Emile Ollivier, who was influenced by Carrel, a typical republican of 1848, as Theodore Zeldin seems to imply in *Emile Ollivier and the Liberal Empire of Napoleon III* (Oxford, 1963), pp. 4-25.

to them was universal manhood suffrage, as the sole electoral system compatible with popular sovereignty, and republicanism became virtually synonymous with democracy.[25] Beyond these fundamentals, republicans differed widely. Some spoke of an American School as opposed to a School of the Convention, and within the latter, Girondin as opposed to Jacobin or Montagnard factions. Pierre Leroux even sought to explain one internecine conflict in terms of three rival sects, the "queue de Danton," representing Liberty, the "queue de Robespierre," representing Equality, and a middle group representing Fraternity.[26]

In an attempt to organize their discussions of French republicanism under the July Monarchy, some historians have adopted other classifications. For example, the English writer John Plamenatz speaks of four varieties of republicans: "(1) the moderate republicans, (2) the Jacobins or radicals, (3) the social reformers, and (4) the revolutionaries."[27] Although such schemata are suggestive, they are artificial and misleading, implying clearer distinctions than actually existed. It is with good reason that the principal French authorities, Georges Weill and I. Tchernoff, speak of a single republican "party" embracing a diversity of individuals, groups and ideas, but sharing fundamental principles and aspirations. In the early 1830's, one real distinction had to do with method, some advocating new insurrections while others preferred peaceful propaganda; another distinction derived from the importance assigned to social as opposed to political questions. These and other differences were reflected in various organizations that took shape in those years.

At first, republicans worked mainly through legal or semilegal associations, such as Aide-toi, le Ciel t'aidera, which, however, was soon surpassed in importance by a purely republi-

[25] Weill, *Parti républicain*, p. 30.

[26] Gabriel Perreux, *Au Temps des sociétés secrètes: la propagande républicaine au début de la monarchie de juillet* (Paris, 1930), p. 260; and Eisenstein, *Buonarroti*, p. 123. For interesting comments on the "American school" and its decline after the death of Lafayette, see René Rémond, *Les Etats-Unis devant l'opinion française, 1815-1852* (Paris, 1962), II, pp. 660-667.

[27] Plamenatz, *The Revolutionary Movement in France*, pp. 38-39.

can organization called the Amis du peuple. To Heinrich Heine, their meetings had "the smell of an old, worn and much-read copy of the *Moniteur* of 1793,"[28] but the Amis du peuple also reflected the new interest in the condition of the workers. As yet they had few proposals to offer, but except for the Saint-Simonians, they were the first group to realize that they must grapple with a new social question.[29] The social orientation of the Amis du peuple led them to propagandize among the workers, a policy which so alarmed Casimir Perier that he had the officers arrested. They were prosecuted in what was called the "Trial of the Fifteen" in January 1832, but as there was no evidence of conspiracy, all were acquitted.[30]

Another type of organization which flourished in 1831 was the National Association, which was not purely republican, but which was notable in that it sought to organize in the provinces as well as in Paris.[31] At the peak of the movement in 1831 there were National Associations in forty-one departments, and although they declined soon thereafter, they helped lay the groundwork for the republican movement in the provinces. Casimir Perier fought the republicans with all the legal weapons at his command, and "never in the time of the Villèle ministry had there been such a series of press seizures and trials."[32] The *Tribune* in particular, where the young Armand Marrast defended the right of revolutionary action against an unjust government, "was always involved in at least one trial."[33]

The death of Casimir Perier in May 1832, opened a period of crisis in which some of the revolutionary activists, united with Bonapartists and even with some Legitimists in a secret society, prepared to rise.[34] The occasion was the funeral of

[28] Weill, *Parti républicain*, p. 62.

[29] *Ibid.*, p. 31. Cf. Ernest Labrousse, *Le Mouvement ouvrier et les théories sociales en France de 1815 à 1848*, "Les Cours de Sorbonne" (Paris, n.d.), p. 120.

[30] Weill, *Parti républicain*, p. 68.

[31] Perreux, *Au Temps des sociétés secrètes*, p. 5.

[32] Weill, *Parti républicain*, p. 66.

[33] *Ibid.*, pp. 66-67, and Tchernoff, *Parti républicain sous la monarchie de juillet*, p. 150.

[34] Weill, *Parti républicain*, p. 69.

General Lamarque, a popular orator of the left, on June 5, 1832; following a clash between demonstrators and cavalry, barricades went up in eastern Paris. After some hesitation, the republican leaders decided against a general insurrection, and the insurgents were defeated at considerable cost in casualties on June 6. Later, in December, the government sought to destroy the Amis du peuple on charges of violating the law prohibiting unauthorized associations of more than twenty persons. Although the leaders were acquitted, the court declared the association dissolved. But already a stronger and more militant group was replacing it. This was the Société des droits de l'homme et du citoyen, which was a partly secret organization consisting of many small sections of fewer than twenty members. But it had a larger overall membership than the Amis du peuple and made a stronger appeal to the workers. The Société also fostered daughter organizations in a number of provincial cities, some of which began to publish republican newspapers. The Société des droits de l'homme was subject to the usual factional conflicts, chiefly over the problem of methods. At one point, several of the more radical sections went so far as to condemn to death the man who was seeking to reconcile the factions, Godefroy Cavaignac. He was compelled to hide for a month until the sentence was revoked, but in November 1833, the "Montagnard" faction, influenced by Buonarroti, came to power in the central committee, which chose Cavaignac as president.[35]

Among the new committee members was Athanase Recurt, a physician much esteemed in the Faubourg Saint-Antoine, where he treated the poor free of charge.[36] The new committee adopted as its own the Declaration of Rights which Robespierre had presented to the Convention in April 1793. More "advanced" than the original declaration of 1789, it put greater emphasis on equality and the right of insurrection, and contained some "social" articles such as Number 11: "It is the duty of society to provide a living for all its members, either by procuring them work, or by assuring the means of sub-

[35] Eisenstein, *Buonarroti*, pp. 122-125, and Weill, *Parti républicain*, pp. 88-89, 93.

[36] Weill, *Parti républicain*, p. 93.

sistence to those who are unfit to work."[37] In addition, the central committee also drew up a republican program, including an elective and temporary national executive, a single national assembly elected by universal suffrage, a centralized administration, a democratized National Guard, an improved educational system, freedom of association, and some "social" principles such as state credit and a state role in "industrial organization."[38]

In response to the militancy of the republicans, the government first unsuccessfully prosecuted the leaders in the "Trial of the Twenty-Seven" in December 1833, and then introduced a rigorous new law in March 1834, which prohibited all unauthorized associations, no matter how small. Many republican leaders regarded this as a provocation to insurrection. Nevertheless, a new insurrection occurred first in Lyon, following a trial of leaders of a strike which had taken place earlier in the year. Troops suppressed the insurgents in four days of fighting; the Paris republicans agreed to rise in sympathy, but after the government arrested 150 leaders, the others sought unsuccessfully to prevent a doomed uprising. Barricades went up on April 13, but the insurgents were easily defeated, and the "massacre" of the Rue Transnonain soon followed.[39]

The abortive insurrections of 1834 marked the end of the militant republicanism aroused by the revolution of 1830. The government sought to destroy the republican movement by prosecuting 164 leaders for conspiracy. During the "Monster Trial" before the Chamber of Peers, they brought discredit upon themselves by quarrelling publicly, and when conviction seemed certain, twenty-eight of the accused, including prominent leaders such as Godefroy Cavaignac and Armand Marrast, escaped to England. The others were condemned to deportation or imprisonment, and the Société des droits de l'homme was dead.

[37] J. M. Thompson, *Robespierre* (Oxford, 1935), II, pp. 43, 52-53. Maxime Leroy, in his *Histoire des idées sociales en France* (Paris, 1962), II, p. 411, sees this article as a virtual proclamation of "le droit au travail."

[38] Weill, *Parti républicain*, p. 94, and Tchernoff, *Parti républicain sous la monarchie de juillet*, pp. 276-277.

[39] Weill, *Parti républicain*, p. 101.

In 1835 the republican movement was further weakened by other events. One was the expiration of the *Tribune*, after its editors had undergone 111 trials and suffered twenty convictions.[40] Another was the attempted assassination of King Louis Philippe by Fieschi, who proclaimed himself a republican and whose two accomplices had been members of the Société des droits de l'homme.[41] Finally, the government followed up its attack by the passage of the so-called September laws of 1835, which provided for rigorous control of the press. Preliminary money bonds for national dailies were quadrupled—to 100,000 francs—and it was now forbidden to criticize the king or the regime, or to adhere to any other form of government: the republicans were no longer permitted publicly to call themselves republicans. A number of Parisian and provincial newspapers were compelled to suspend publication, and those which managed to survive had to resort to cautious self-censorship. To comply with the law, the republicans began to call each other "radicals" and "democrats," but everyone knew what was meant.[42]

Thus, by the end of 1835 the republican movement, which had seemed a dangerous threat ever since 1830, had been brought under control by the July Monarchy. Thereafter the surviving partisans of revolutionary methods, a small minority, were driven to completely secret societies, while the republican party as such repudiated revolutionary methods and sought to exist as an opposition group within the law, disseminating its views through discreet publication and seeking the election of republicans to the Chamber of Deputies. The only major republican newspaper to survive the September laws was *Le National*, which had been moderate enough in its views and now had to be even more circumspect, remaining so after the death of Carrel in 1836.

Thereafter the sole remaining republican leader of any prominence besides the aging Dupont de l'Eure was Etienne Garnier-Pagès, who sought to rebuild the party as a moderate,

[40] *Ibid.*, p. 115.

[41] *Ibid.*, p. 108, and Charléty, *Monarchie de juillet*, p. 120.

[42] Weill, *Parti républicain*, p. 124, and Tchernoff, *Parti républicain sous la monarchie de juillet*, p. 173.

pacific and legal movement, but without forsaking the fundamental aspiration to a democratic republic. With universal suffrage now seemingly a chimerical goal, the republicans hoped to achieve something by seeking at least a broadening of the electorate, an aim in which they could collaborate with the dynastic left group led by Odilon Barrot. As *Le National* argued in 1837: "All of the genuine opposition must be concentrated in the area permitted by law, and the fight for sovereignty of the people be waged under the flag of Electoral Reform. *Hoc signo vinces.*"[43] The republicans supported an unsuccessful movement for electoral reform in the National Guard in 1838.

An amnesty in 1837 permitted some republican leaders to return to public life, but those who had fled abroad remained exiled until 1840. As for the secret societies, they flourished briefly in the late 1830's. Buonarroti died in 1837, but a new generation of conspirators was coming into its own, spreading "communist" doctrines in some of the workers' districts of Paris and Lyon and organizing for combat. Blanqui had founded in 1834 a secret "Society of the Families," which was discovered and destroyed by the police, but after a brief imprisonment he, along with Armand Barbès and Martin Bernard, created another, "The Society of the Seasons."[44] This group, with a membership of only about a thousand, attempted an insurrection during a period of economic and political crisis in Paris in May 1839. It failed to win mass support and was easily crushed; the three leaders were captured and imprisoned. The public was alarmed, for many believed that the day of insurrections was past; even the republican newspapers disapproved of this resort to violence. Thereafter a few secret societies continued a precarious existence, but with little contact or influence either with the workers or with the republican party.

[43] Cited in Weill, *Parti républicain*, p. 141.

[44] Barbès had been strongly influenced by Godefroy Cavaignac, whom he called "my master in democracy." Tchernoff, *Parti républicain sous la monarchie de juillet*, p. 361.

THE REPUBLICANS DURING THE 1840's

During the 1840's, the republican movement regained its vigor, developed new doctrines, and split into two rival factions. Such factionalism was, of course, nothing new, but the stability of the July Monarchy gave a certain stability to republican politics. There was still no highly organized party of the modern type, and there continued to be doctrinal and tactical differences to which the new issue of socialism added complexity, but in these years the dominant pattern was that of a majority wing, to be called simply republican, and a minority radical wing.[45]

[45] The dominant faction was that usually called moderate in 1848, but there is little justification for identifying under the July Monarchy two distinct parties, the "Moderates" and the "Radicals." (But cf. George W. Fasel, "The French Moderate Republicans, 1837-1848," unpublished Ph.D. dissertation, Stanford University, 1965.) I follow most French authorities in viewing the republican movement as a single one, marked by sometimes virulent factionalism. Contemporaries did not speak of a "Moderate Republican Party," nor did the dominant faction refer to themselves as "moderates," but rather applied that term disdainfully to the dynastic left group of Odilon Barrot. The term "radical" offers further complications, having had several distinct meanings in the period. The word appeared as early as 1819 in France, but was not often used until after the September laws of 1835 outlawed the term republican. (See Jacques Kayser, *Les Grands batailles du radicalisme, des origines aux portes du pouvoir, 1820-1901* [Paris, 1962], pp. 6-10.) Thereafter it was most often used as a simple euphemism, along with the word "democrat," for the word "republican," so that all republicans in this sense were "radicals." However, beginning around 1837 the term also was used to refer to a few deputies slightly to the right of the republicans, who admired the English radicals whom Armand Marrast in his dispatches from exile depicted as ideological brothers of the French republicans. (See Weill, *Parti républicain*, p. 123, and Tchernoff, *Parti républicain sous la monarchie de juillet*, p. 129.) "Radical" in this sense meant "an attenuation rather than an intensification of the word republican," recalled the Count d'Alton-Shée, himself a convert to republicanism in 1847. (See his *Souvenirs de 1847 et de 1848, pour faire suite à mes mémoires (Oeuvre posthume)* [Paris, 1879], pp. 5, 53.) Conscious of this ambiguity, the left-wing republicans sometimes referred to themselves as "ultra-radicals." In view of all the verbal confusion, to which the revolution of 1848 would add, I have settled on the practice of referring to the dominant wing as simply republican, and the left wing as radical.

In the absence of any permanent organization, the offices of *Le National* served as headquarters for the Paris republicans and for broader committee meetings, while the newspaper itself functioned as a kind of nationwide bulletin for this "central committee" of the republican party.[46] *Le National* was a truly national newspaper, though on a limited scale, for most of its circulation of between 4,000 and 4,500 copies was distributed in the provinces.[47] Throughout the 1840's, *Le National* retained its moderate tone, even after Armand Marrast assumed the editorship following his return from exile. Previously an advocate of violent insurrection, Marrast had learned the virtues of moderation in England, where he admired the methods of the English radicals and the Chartists. Through a spirited, satirical opposition on the margin of what seemed possible under the September laws, Marrast "sought to disarm the aversion of the middle classes for the republicans"; circulation improved, and although the editors were frequently prosecuted, juries often acquitted them.[48]

The republicans also sought to intervene as effectively as possible in legal opposition politics. In 1840, *Le National* became virtually "the official newspaper of the reform campaign,"[49] and republicans were also willing to collaborate with the Legitimists against the regime. It was with Legitimist support that Etienne Garnier-Pagès had been elected to the Chamber of Deputies in 1837 and 1839.[50] He was virtually the only spokesman for the republicans in the chamber until his death in 1841. The republicans also sought in 1840 to create a nationwide organization of committees of correspondence under Parisian leadership. In February 1841, *Le National* claimed that 200 local committees were in existence, but the figure was undoubtedly exaggerated, and the system declined

[46] See Fasel, "The French Moderate Republicans," pp. 65-72.

[47] Jean-Pierre Aguet, "Le Tirage des quotidiens de Paris sous la monarchie de juillet," *Schweizerische Zeitschrift für Geschichte*, x (1960), 273. Cf. also Irene Collins, *The Government and the Newspaper Press in France, 1814-1881* (Oxford, 1959), p. 94, and the tables in Charles Ledré, *La Presse à l'assaut de la monarchie, 1815-1848* (Paris, 1960), pp. 244-245.

[48] Weill, *Parti républicain*, pp. 139-140.

[49] *Ibid.*, p. 141. [50] *Ibid.*, p. 121n.

COUNCIL OF MINISTERS

GOUDCHAUX *Finances* · SENARD *Interior* · VAULABELLE *Public Instruction* · TOURRET *Commerce* · CAVAIGNAC *Chairman* · MARIE *Justice* · LAMORICIERE *War* · VERNINHAC *Marine* · BASTIDE *Foreign Affairs* · RECURT *Public Works*

and disappeared by 1842.[51] In preparation for the elections of 1842, the republicans formed still another committee, led by François Arago, which met at the offices of *Le National*. The republicans were remarkably successful, sending ten deputies to the chamber, five of them for the first time.[52]

Among the newcomers were Louis Antoine Garnier-Pagès, the younger brother of the celebrated orator, and two men who had won renown as lawyers for republican defendants, Alexandre Marie and Eugène Bethmont. Republican electoral strength was considerable in Paris, which elected three deputies, and also in several isolated departments. In the republican stronghold at Le Mans, Etienne Garnier-Pagès was replaced by a new man who had made a great impression by taking a strongly radical posture and dissociating himself from the other republicans. This was Alexandre Auguste Ledru-Rollin. The electoral committee disappeared after the elections, and the majority republicans depended on *Le National* for leadership.

In 1842, the republicans sought to present their views more fully in a *Dictionnaire politique* of 944 pages, a work that went into several editions and was regarded as authoritative. The editors included a cross section of republican opinion, from Armand Marrast and the publisher Pagnerre, to Martin de Strasbourg, Thoré and even Louis Blanc. Here national or popular sovereignty was affirmed to be the "fundamental dogma," from which the other doctrines derived.[53] For basic political institutions, the editors advocated a single national assembly elected by universal manhood suffrage and a temporary but strong executive. They were hostile to Legitimism and to Bonapartism, and implicitly critical of the existing regime.

In some respects, the *Dictionnaire* belied the "moderate" appeal of the republicans.[54] In historical articles it eulogized the

[51] Fasel, "The French Moderate Republicans," pp. 65-66, 69.

[52] *Ibid.*, p. 69.

[53] *Dictionnaire politique: encyclopédie du langage et de la science politiques, rédigé par une réunion de députés, de publicistes et de journalistes, avec une introduction par Garnier-Pagès* (2d edn., Paris, 1843), pp. ix, 893.

[54] Although it has been argued that the dictionary was designed to facilitate a closer collaboration with the dynastic left. See Robert Balland, "Une Interprétation du Dictionnaire politique de 1842," *Actes du*

pre-Thermidorian Convention and the Montagnards and was critical of both Girondins and Hébertists. It was scornful of "Moderates," the current representative of which was the Barrot dynastic left, and highly critical of the "Bourgeoisie," which was the ruling "nobility of the nineteenth century."[55] Although Etienne Garnier-Pagès in his posthumous introduction justified insurrection against despotic regimes, he opposed it in a regime such as the July Monarchy, except as a last resort, but the article on Revolution seemed to justify in advance the revolution that was to come in February 1848: "A Revolution is legitimate when it is provoked by a long resistance by the constituted authority to a reform imperiously demanded by the public . . . when it is desired and accomplished by a majority."[56] Garnier-Pagès had also considered the problem of insurrection once the democratic republic was achieved and concluded: "In countries where the sovereignty of the people is established in law and in fact, conspiracies and insurrections are the greatest of all crimes."[57]

The *Dictionnaire politique* also reflected to a slight degree a significant development within republicanism in the 1840's, that is, a renewed interest in social questions as opposed to the previous almost exclusive concern for political issues such as electoral reform. The changing orientation was signalized in 1840 during the reform campaign itself, when several republicans, such as François Arago and Michel Goudchaux, took up the slogan "organization of labor," recently popularized by Louis Blanc.[58] In the *Dictionnaire politique*, Etienne Garnier-Pagès also indicated a social aim for the republicans: "In countries governed by the sovereignty of all, we need concern ourselves only with social reforms."[59] But the reforms suggested were few and often vague. The editors were critical of the ideas of Saint-Simon and Fourier, but also of "individual-

---

soixante-seizième congrès des sociétés savantes, Rennes, 1951 (Paris, 1951), pp. 244-261.

[55] *Dictionnaire politique*, p. 165.

[56] *Ibid.*, pp. 846-847.

[57] *Ibid.*, p. xxiii.

[58] Fasel, "The French Moderate Republicans," pp. 61-62.

[59] Introduction, p. xxiii.

ism," and greeted favorably the idea of "association" among workers and employers. The most concrete proposal offered was for a drastic tax reform, including the end of most consumption taxes and the introduction of a progressive income tax.[60] Another specific proposal that was to find partial fruition in 1848 was the suggestion that the canton could serve as an effective unit for dealing with unemployment and other social ills.[61]

Le National also began to reflect the new point of view. Under the editorship of Carrel it had been narrowly political in its aims and conservative in its economic views; Carrel systematically deleted the word "proletarian" from articles submitted. Under his successors, the term began to appear with some frequency,[62] and after Marrast assumed the editorship in 1840, *Le National* "posed the social question and outlined a social program."[63] Although *Le National* continued its hostility to the various socialist theories which also found increasing expression in the 1840's, and although its social program was mild and its chief preoccupation remained political, nevertheless there was a wide gulf between its position and that of the dominant economic theorists of the day, along with the Orleanists who dominated the legislature; not even the dynastic left had any social program. Most liberals refused to recognize the existence of a social problem, or held Malthusian views as the sole remedy, resisting on principle any intervention of the state in social and economic matters.

Le National was sympathetic to the plight of the working classes and critical of what it termed a new "industrial feudalism," but instead of seeking to destroy capitalism and revolutionize the social order, it wanted to remove abuses and improve the condition of the working classes through legislation dealing with specific issues. This could be expected to follow as a matter of course once the battle for political democracy was won; indeed, in 1844 Marrast in *Le National* went so far as to insist that the political aims were only a means to social

[60] *Ibid.*, p. 281.
[61] *Ibid.*, p. 184.
[62] Weill, *Parti républicain*, p. 118.
[63] Labrousse, *Mouvement ouvrier*, p. 138.

reform: "If the political institutions towards which we aspire would not have the result of ameliorating the condition of the lower classes . . . we would cease to be involved in politics."[64] Yet the specific proposals offered were few, including the right of labor to organize, the suppression of the *livret*, and equal representation for workers in the *conseils de prud'hommes*, courts which adjusted minor labor disputes. *Le National* also looked with favor on experiments in workers' cooperative associations.[65] In addition, it proposed a serious tax reform and the improvement of the general condition of the workers through free and compulsory primary education.[66]

Despite the body of doctrine built up by the republicans during the 1840's, it never found a completely coherent and systematic expression. Republicanism was no longer simply a cult of the Convention, and the republicans had no intention of resorting to "terror," establishing a "Republic of Virtue," or even reviving the constitution of 1793. What they wanted was a representative democracy, which they felt would be better than the democracy of the ancient republics and better than the experiments of the great Revolution; moreover, democracy would inevitably improve the condition of workers. They had high ideals, but once they had rejected any recourse to violence to achieve them, they were condemned to a war of words and collaboration with ideological enemies to achieve reforms which fell far short of their professed goals, and which proved to be unattainable within the political context of the July Monarchy. The republicans were more successful in making the idea of the republic acceptable to Frenchmen, though this would not be apparent until after the February revolution. But during the 1840's, if they helped to dissociate the notion of "terror" from the republic, their mild policies provoked the appearance of a vigorous radical wing.

One of the leading critics was Godefroy Cavaignac, who on his return from exile in 1840 was astonished "to see the republicans pacified and soft," and directed his wrath against his old

[64] Issue of 6 December 1844, cited in Weill, *Parti républicain*, p. 142n.
[65] Tchernoff, *Parti républicain sous la monarchie de juillet*, p. 153, and Weill, *Parti républicain*, pp. 143-144.
[66] Labrousse, *Mouvement ouvrier*, p. 138.

companion Marrast.[67] Godefroy Cavaignac was not simply the champion of an old cause; he had been one of the first to take a serious interest in the condition of the workers, and this interest became more pronounced during the 1840's. Although critical of Saint-Simon and Fourier, Cavaignac was very sympathetic to the view of another socialist, Pierre Leroux, who argued that true republicanism must involve socialism, and George Sand wrote that at his death in 1845 Godefroy was "almost a socialist."[68] This was an exaggeration, for Godefroy Cavaignac's ideas went little beyond a desire to "emancipate the proletariat." Nevertheless, his new social concern and his radical temperament led him to repudiate the *National* wing of the republicans.

With several others he sought to transform *Le Journal du Peuple* into a daily to rival *Le National*; this was accomplished by early in 1842, and under Godefroy's editorship it published a manifesto declaring that the true aim of politics must be the amelioration of the condition of the lower classes.[69] The *Journal du Peuple* expired after only a few months as a daily, despite desperate attempts to win financial support, to which Godefroy's brother contributed out of his salary as an army officer in Algeria. By this time, however, another influential member of what was now the radical wing of the republicans came to the fore. This was Ledru-Rollin, who had been a deputy since 1841. The wealth of his wife provided the funds necessary to found another new daily which was destined to play a historic role, *La Réforme.* Godefroy Cavaignac served for a time as editor of *La Réforme*, and later the chief editor was Ferdinand Flocon. Although it was the voice of the radicals, *La Réforme* differed from *Le National* largely in rhetoric and tone. In its first issue, it advocated "electoral reform as a point of departure, with universal suffrage as the goal."[70] Yet in the pages of *La Réforme* there was much greater emphasis

[67] Weill, *Parti républicain*, p. 145, and Fasel, "The French Moderate Republicans," p. 91.

[68] Tchernoff, *Parti républicain sous la monarchie de juillet*, p. 238. See also pp. 107-109, 239-240.

[69] Weill, *Parti républicain*, p. 145.

[70] Cited in Weill, *Parti républicain*, p. 146.

on social questions. It borrowed from the Fourierists and popularized the slogan, "the right to work,"[71] and occasionally published articles by Louis Blanc and other socialists. *La Réforme* also opposed *Le National's* policy of collaboration with the dynastic left, and sought to remain an organ of pure republican propaganda.[72]

Although the two leading republican newspapers often quarreled over specific issues, they agreed in fundamental aims and even on many particulars. Both had as their ideal the democratic republic, but both eschewed violence and conspiracy, preferring to work within the law. Both were revolutionary in theory but reformist in practice. Both agreed that political reform was a necessary preliminary to social reform which both regarded as desirable. Both demanded free, compulsory primary education by the state as the very basis of democracy. Both agreed that the state, rather than private companies, should construct and operate the new railway network. Both favored a radical tax reform, both advocated the abolition of the practice of *remplacement* whereby wealthy individuals conscripted for military service could hire substitutes. Both strongly advocated the suppression of slavery in the colonies.[73]

Both wings of the party were strongly nationalistic in foreign policy and supported the national aspirations of the Germans, Italians and Poles. Traditional hostility to England remained strong, but hatred of Russia was diminishing, and the possibility of an alliance with Russia was considered. In general, the republicans favored democratic movements against the monarchies and envisioned a general disarmament after the triumph of the Revolution in Europe.[74] The French republicans of both wings were staunchly imperialistic with respect to Algeria, favoring its complete conquest, but advocated civil administration rather than the military colonies proposed by Bugeaud.[75]

With respect to socialism, the republican movement also was more united than has sometimes been suggested. It is true that a few republicans were also socialists, Louis Blanc being

[71] *Ibid.* [72] *Ibid.*, p. 147. [73] *Ibid.*, pp. 148-154.
[74] *Ibid.*, pp. 152-153. [75] *Ibid.*, p. 154.

the prime example. But the radical wing of the party was but slightly more hospitable to the socialists than was *Le National*, and *La Réforme* was not socialist in policy. In general, the republican and socialist movements were quite distinct before 1848. Both Saint-Simon and Fourier had been indifferent to political forms, as was Proudhon before 1848. Louis Blanc and a few others aside, the republicans repudiated socialism while favoring some measure of social reform. Yet by the eve of the revolution the republicans had come to adopt the Saint-Simonian doctrine that society must "ameliorate the condition of the most numerous and poorest class." As Paul Bastid observed, "most of the republicans felt the influence, direct or indirect, of the socialist schools."[76]

The most important differences between the two wings of the republican movement had to do with tactics and personal rivalries. *Le National* had a well-entrenched team of writers led by Marrast, and *La Réforme* was often considered the private newspaper of Ledru-Rollin. The most persistent point of conflict was over *Le National's* policy of collaboration with the liberal Orleanists; *La Réforme* championed instead a policy of isolated purity.[77] In sum, as Weill put it, "If we consider fundamentals, and set aside the superficial disagreements, *La Réforme* and *Le National* defended a common program, that of the republican party as a whole."[78]

Indeed, in the peculiar conditions of the July Monarchy, with politics confined to a narrow electorate and with important groups of even wealthy *notables* refusing to accept the regime, the only political differences of much real significance were those involving commitments to mutually antagonistic ideals and systems of government. The republicans, despite their renunciation of violence and their legal and pacific behavior, were an inherently disloyal opposition; they remained revolutionary in theory and represented the political extreme left. The counterpart of the republicans on the extreme right were the Legitimists, another inherently disloyal opposition

[76] *Doctrines et institutions politiques de la seconde république* (Paris, 1945), I, p. 50.

[77] Weill, *Parti républicain*, p. 147.

[78] *Ibid.*, p. 148.

which renounced violence and hoped for the fall of the regime. The revolution of February and subsequent events down to the final decades of the nineteenth century would reveal how deep and lasting these political differences could be.

What was the strength of the republicans on the eve of the revolution? As a political group within the *pays légal*, it was a tiny, weak and divided minority; in the Chamber of Deputies, the republicans numbered only ten in 1842 and declined slightly thereafter. The two great Parisian dailies had in 1845 a combined circulation of only 5,760 and most of the subscribers lived in the provinces.[79] The party, however, was of considerable importance in Paris, where in 1846 it triumphed in its electoral alliance with the dynastic left, while losing in the country as a whole. Lyon, Lille, Le Mans, Clermont-Ferrand and Strasbourg also had strong republican factions. There were also clusters of republicans in many other cities and towns, particularly in Burgundy, Alsace, part of Lorraine, the villages of the lower Rhône valley, and in the Mediterranean coastal departments.[80] But large areas of France had but a few isolated knots of republicans, particularly the west and southwest. In the Alpine region, only Grenoble was able to sustain a republican newspaper.[81] Some masonic lodges were also sympathetic to republicanism, and there were a few republicans in the army; officers such as Louis Eugène Cavaignac acquired notoriety, but were too few to be dangerous.[82]

The republican movement before 1848 was almost exclusively urban in character; with the partial exception of the Mediterranean regions, there were virtually no links between it and the peasants who constituted about 75 percent of the population.

Even in the cities and towns, conscious republicanism was

[79] Aguet, "Le Tirage des quotidiens de Paris," p. 273.

[80] See Weill, *Parti républicain*, pp. 188-201, and Louis Girard, *Le Liberalisme en France de 1814 à 1848: doctrine et mouvement*, "Les Cours de Sorbonne" (Paris, 1967), Part II, pp. 117, 128-129.

[81] Philippe Vigier, *La Seconde république dans la région alpine: étude politique et sociale* (Paris, 1963), I, pp. 176-177.

[82] Weill, *Parti républicain*, p. 196.

almost entirely bourgeois and petty bourgeois in character. Although the republicans claimed to speak on behalf of the workers, actual links with the popular milieux were few. Neither *Le National*, whose circulation in 1845 was 4,062, nor *La Réforme*, with only 1,698, followed the lead of Emile de Giradin's *La Presse* (22,000) in winning a wider audience by lowering the subscription rate from the prevailing 60 francs to 40 francs. Nevertheless, the republicans had maintained some contacts with the workers, particularly in Paris. *La Réforme's* more pronounced social program theoretically appealed more strongly to the workers, but some men associated with *Le National* also had considerable influence among the workers—Recurt and Bastide in particular, but also Goudchaux and Marie. Moreover, the most important Parisian periodical actually written and published by workers, *L'Atelier*, supported the views of *Le National* rather than those of *La Réforme*. It repudiated socialism and sought concrete reforms such as minimum wage and hour legislation, its most insistent demands being for reform of the *conseils de prud'hommes* and for state encouragement to producers' cooperatives.[83] But most of the time *L'Atelier* was a monthly of small circulation, which appealed primarily to artisans and was virtually unknown among unskilled laborers.[84]

It is difficult to assess the strength of republican sentiment in the working classes before 1848. Links with the "party" after 1835 were few, but the secret societies which recruited members largely from the working class also had a republican character. Yet following the abortive insurrection of 1839 and the strikes of 1840, revolutionary republicanism and "communism" were weaker than ever, with Blanqui and Barbès in prison, and police spies such as Lucien de la Hodde infiltrating the movement. "Composed of several hundred men, the secret societies formed a force small in numbers, poorly led, little to be feared."[85] Moreover, these activists represented only a tiny

[83] Armand Cuvillier, *Un Journal d'ouvriers: L'Atelier (1840-1850)* (Paris, 1954), pp. 24, 137-139, 144-151.

[84] Collins, *The Government and the Newspaper Press*, p. 93.

[85] Weill, *Parti républicain*, pp. 164-165.

minority within the developing workers' movement, which in general aimed at progressive reforms.[86] There seems to have been a slight resurgence of the societies in the working class districts in Paris and some provincial towns around 1846, according to Marc Caussidière, but they were little interested in doctrine—socialist, communist or even republican.[87] On the eve of the February revolution, the revolutionary communist movement still constituted only an "infinitesimal phalanx" among the workers.[88]

In the middle 1840's, with the July Monarchy seemingly secure and prospering, the republican party was regarded as weakening. Some of its most renowned leaders, such as Etienne Garnier-Pagès and Godefroy Cavaignac, were dead, and others, such as Trélat and Raspail, had left politics.[89] A few republicans seemed to weary of the struggle and to hint at rallying to the monarchy; in 1847, Hippolyte Carnot published a conciliatory work called *Les Radicaux et la Charte* which embarrassed *Le National* and aroused the bitter opposition of *La Réforme*.[90] Emile Ollivier later recalled the sense of resignation on the eve of the revolution: "At that time I frequented Ledru-Rollin and his friends. There was not a single one whom I did not hear say many times that before the death of Louis-Philippe there was nothing to attempt or to hope for the Republic."[91] The last major republican activity before the revolution was the collaboration with the liberal Orleanists in the reform campaign of the banquets in 1847.

In sum, on the eve of the revolution the republicans constituted a tiny minority party of the extreme left. Hippolyte Castille estimated that there were 100,000 republicans in the population of around thirty-six million,[92] but Lucien de la

[86] Labrousse, *Mouvement ouvrier*, pp. 176-177.

[87] Marc Caussidière, *Mémoires de Caussidière, ex-préfet de police et représentant du peuple* (3d edn., Paris, 1849), I, pp. 34-35.

[88] Labrousse, *Mouvement ouvrier*, p. 182.

[89] Weill, *Parti républicain*, pp. 198-199.

[90] Fasel, "The French Moderate Republicans," p. 126.

[91] *L'Empire libéral, études, récits, souvenirs* (Paris, 1895-1918), I, p. 470.

[92] *Histoire de la seconde république française* (Paris, 1854-56), II, p. 4.

Hodde thought that the total number of republicans of all factions, from *Le National* to the secret societies, numbered at most 4,000 in Paris and 15,000 to 16,000 in the provinces, or 5 percent of the adult male population.[93] Yet, the revolutionary tradition, the events of 1830 and the general intellectual mood of the 1840's had generated among many Frenchmen who took no part in politics an awareness of and sympathy for the ideal of "la République." This was true in particular of the working classes of Paris, as the events of February would demonstrate.

[93] *Histoire des sociétés secrètes et du parti républicain de 1830 à 1848* (Paris, 1850), pp. 402-403.

III · "The General of the Republic"

THE REPUBLICAN AS *MILITAIRE*

BEFORE 1848, Louis Eugène Cavaignac was a general of no more than the second level in Algeria, a man with an excellent reputation as commander of the zouaves and as a regional administrator, but lacking the immense prestige of Bugeaud and the dash of a Lamoricière. However, he was slightly notorious as one of the few republican officers, but for years he had been inactive in politics and was known to the republicans in France only as the brother of the late and esteemed Godefroy. Yet General Cavaignac was by no means simply a nominal republican. His convictions were rooted in the same family heritage as Godefroy's, in his youth he had participated to some extent in republican conspiratorial politics, he remained a lifelong friend and admirer of Godefroy, whose views he claimed to share, and he defied pressure on him to renounce his republicanism after Godefroy's death. But his long years in the army had also left their mark, and when Cavaignac wielded power both of these often incompatible influences were reflected in his behavior.[1]

The Cavaignacs came of a bourgeois family that had been of considerable prominence in the Rouergue since the sixteenth century. The father of Godefroy and Eugène, Jean Baptiste Cavaignac, an *avocat* attached to the Parlement of Toulouse,

[1] There is no satisfactory biography of Cavaignac. Several slight and popular ones appeared in 1848 and during the following few years; the first full-length biography was that of Auguste Deschamps, *Eugène Cavaignac* (2 vols., Brussels, 1870), an uncritical eulogy based on published materials. The only other full-length biography is that of a General Ibos, *Le Général Cavaignac, un dictateur républicain* (Paris, 1930). Ibos did consult the Cavaignac papers, but his work, though accurate in many factual details, lacks documentation and is strongly tendentious. For Cavaignac's adult life, I have relied almost exclusively on primary materials, in particular the collection of his letters to his mother and to his brother as preserved in the family archives. Of relatively little value are the letters of Cavaignac to his uncle, as published in *Les Deux généraux Cavaignac, souvenirs et correspondance, 1808-1848* (Paris, n.d. [1899]).

enthusiastically supported the revolution of 1789, and in 1792 was elected to the Convention. A fiery Montagnard, Cavaignac was prominent enough by October 1792 to become a member of the first Committee of General Security.[2] He voted without qualification for the death of Louis XVI, and in the spring of 1793 went as a *représentant en mission* to the armies of the west coast and of the Pyrenees. At Bayonne, Cavaignac organized an extraordinary investigating committee that won "a bloody renown" by condemning sixty-two persons to death during a period of seven weeks,[3] and the bitter memories of the Terror associated with Cavaignac *père* were to be revived against Eugène in the presidential campaign of 1848. Cavaignac rallied successfully to the Thermidorian republic; in 1795 he helped direct the defense of the Convention during the uprisings of Prairial and of Vendémiaire. He was one of the "perpetuals" elected to the Council of 500, but soon lost his seat by lot.

Shortly thereafter, in 1797, he married Julie Marie Corancez, daughter of a prosperous Parisian publisher of strong republican views. The Corancez family had long moved in Enlightenment circles; they knew La Place, Turgot and other philosophes, and during the Revolution Corancez hid Condorcet for a time shortly before his death.[4] Brought up in this atmosphere, Julie Marie received a good education for a female by the standards of the time. Rousseau in particular made a profound impression on her; she would read *Emile* every two years throughout a long life, toward the end of which she wrote her own emotional if innocuous confessions, published posthumously under the title, *Mémoires d'une inconnue.*[5] Madame Cavaignac also was a staunch partisan of the Revolution, and remained so even when she became an ardent admirer of Napoleon and embraced Catholicism. The cult of the

[2] Jacques Godechot, *Les Institutions de la France sous la Révolution et l'empire* (Paris, 1951), p. 220.

[3] Henri Wallon, *Les Représentants du peuple en mission et la justice révolutionnaire dans les départements en l'an II (1793-1794)* (Paris, 1889-1890), II, pp. 408-409.

[4] [Julie Marie Cavaignac], *Les Mémoires d'une inconnue, publiés sur le manuscrit original 1780-1816* (Paris, 1894), pp. 157-160.

[5] She died in 1849, and the book was published anonymously in 1894.

Revolution was thus transmitted to their sons by both parents. Godefroy was born in 1800, and two and one-half years later, on October 15, 1802, Louis Eugène was born in Paris.

Cavaignac *père* had difficulty making his way under Bonaparte. He refused the offer of a prefecture after Brumaire, but accepted two minor positions before his brother, Jacques Marie, who had advanced rapidly in the French army until he was aide-de-camp to Joseph Bonaparte, persuaded him to go to the Kingdom of Naples. When his friend Murat replaced Joseph as king in 1808, Cavaignac *père* became a councillor of state. Madame Cavaignac, then still in France, has left an interesting portrait of Eugène at that time (he was about six years old), comparing him with Godefroy, who already was the stronger, more independent personality:

> Eugène, unlike his brother, was very obedient and more affectionate, more demonstrative than the elder. He was usually gentle and easy to manage, but on rare occasions had fits of stubbornness in which I had to pacify him, because he would break before he would give in. Eugène had perseverence, tenacity in everything that he began, in whatever he decided to do, whether it be amusement or some task, and showed more than his brother a desire to please, to make himself agreeable. With his pleasant manner and his shrewdness, he gave promise of becoming a man of spirit, with an affectionate nature and self-possession, a promise that was realized. Living habitually with older children, he was, as was customary, the butt of the group (for children are not fair-minded), but he never complained. One day, at Brive, Godefroy was singing to his grandmother some couplets written by my father, and Eugène wanted to sing with him. When Godefroy opposed this, little Eugène cried, "But let me be your echo." In sum, he was a good boy, like his brother. I saw in them the seeds of two distinguished men, and I was not mistaken.[6]

It was during this separation from her husband that Madame Cavaignac was converted to Catholicism. When she rejoined

[6] *Mémoires d'une inconnue*, pp. 213-214.

her husband in Naples, he accepted her new religiosity but remained a rationalist himself and refused to permit his sons to have any religious training. He arranged for a private tutor, and soon replaced Madame Cavaignac as the dominant influence in their lives. "They loved him even though they feared him, because he loved them very much himself and was a good father to them. . . . I knew that I counted for much less with my children than their father, and I feared that I was less loved."[7]

The years in Naples from 1808 to 1812 were the most prosperous and successful in the life of Cavaignac *père*. He was a close associate of the king, and although Madame Cavaignac shunned court life, young Godefroy and Eugène sometimes played with the Murat children. When a third Cavaignac child was born in 1811, a daughter, she was named Caroline after Napoleon's sister, who as Murat's wife was queen of Naples.[8] In the same year, the old Montagnard Cavaignac accepted the imperial title of Baron of Lalande. In 1812, a series of reverses began. Cavaignac *père* and his brother were compelled to return to France in order to avoid losing French citizenship, and Jean Baptiste suffered serious financial losses in disposing of property he had acquired. Always solicitous of his sons' education, he enrolled them in the renowned Collège Sainte-Barbe in Paris.

In the spring of 1814, with the defeat of Napoleon imminent, Cavaignac and other regicides sent representatives to seek a promise of amnesty from the brother of Louis XVI, and the declaration of Saint-Ouen, as well as the Constitutional Charter, did contain a pledge not to molest anyone for his "opinions and votes."[9]

Although Cavaignac *père* was left undisturbed by the restored monarchy, he felt ostracized, even by some relatives, but Madame Cavaignac affirmed her complete devotion to him

[7] *Ibid.*, pp. 287-288.

[8] *Ibid.*, pp. 232, 304.

[9] Madame Cavaignac says that it was her suggestion to add the word "votes" to the "too vague" word "opinions," in order to include the regicides expressly, and "thus I had my phrase in the Charter." See *Mémoires d'une inconnue*, pp. 363-364.

and to his "past, present and future."[10] Toward the end of 1814, Cavaignac *père* departed somewhat mysteriously for Naples, where Murat was still king. Napoleon's dramatic return from Elba brought him back to France. He was eager, along with other republicans, to respond to Napoleon's appeal as a man of the Revolution. Madame Cavaignac's own response was more emotional: "Napoleon has landed in France! What a dawn! What a deliverance!"[11] Cavaignac sought a position as prefect through Carnot, the most renowned of the republicans to throw in his lot with Napoleon during the Hundred Days. Napoleon obliged by appointing him prefect of the Somme, but scarcely a month later Waterloo brought ruin.

Banished by the Second Restoration, Cavaignac *père* went to Brussels early in 1816, leaving his wife and children in Paris. Although the Cavaignacs were not destitute, their resources were limited, for Cavaignac had also lost his property in Naples as a result of the fall of Murat and the restoration of the Bourbons there. Godefroy and Eugène corresponded with their father, and visited him annually during school vacations.[12] Both parents continued to instill in them hatred for the Bourbons, but the boys absorbed the republicanism of their father, and were remarkably untouched by the emotional Bonapartism of their mother. In later years they would chide her for her admiration of the Emperor.

Cavaignac *père* chose careers for his two sons. The more articulate Godefroy was to study law, while Eugène was to attend the Ecole Polytechnique and thereafter probably serve in the army corps of engineers. From the beginning, Godefroy was more deeply enflamed with revolutionary zeal than was Eugène. Upon graduation from the Collège Sainte-Barbe, he joined the milieux of the regicides in Brussels, and on his return became involved in the secret revolutionary societies among the students of Paris, enlisting Eugène as a propagandist while he was still at the Collège Sainte-Barbe.[13]

It was apparently because of these youthful activities that

[10] *Ibid.*, p. 371.

[11] *Ibid.*, p. 372.

[12] Ibos, *Le Général Cavaignac*, p. 14.

[13] *Ibid.*, p. 15.

in 1820 Eugène was temporarily barred from the Ecole Polytechnique, on the ostensible ground that he was the "son of a regicide." The objection seemed spurious, because the brother of the same regicide, Jacques Marie, had rallied to the Restoration, been made a baron, and was about to be appointed inspector general of cavalry. Fearing to compromise Jacques Marie by asking him to intervene in Eugène's favor, Madame Cavaignac instead prevailed upon the influential Abbé Frayssinous, who had converted her to Catholicism, to persuade the Minister of War that Eugène's activities were a passing childish fancy. As a result, Eugène was admitted to the Ecole Polytechnique on October 1, 1820.[14]

The Ecole Polytechnique had a justified reputation as a center of liberal political opposition, and Eugène apparently helped to organize a *vente* of the Carbonari there.[15] Neither Cavaignac brother seems to have been involved directly in the series of abortive Carbonarist uprisings in 1822, perhaps because according to plan the *ventes* in Paris were to await the results of the uprisings in the East and the West.[16] But the nervous authorities dismissed a group of students at the Ecole Polytechnique, and were about to bar Eugène from the army upon the completion of his training at the school in October 1822 when his uncle successfully interceded for him, arguing

[14] *Ibid.*, pp. 15-16. Cf. Pierre Chalmin, *L'Officier français de 1815 à 1870* (Paris, 1957), p. 170.

[15] The evidence for Eugène Cavaignac as a Carbonaro is sparse, but seems convincing. The Count de Montalivet, a classmate at the Polytechnique, recalled seeing Cavaignac at secret meetings of the *vente.* See his *Fragments et souvenirs*, ed. Georges Picot (Paris, 1899-1900), I, pp. 22-25. The only evidence that I have found in the Cavaignac papers is a reference by him, in a letter to his brother Godefroy dated October 7, 1837, to another man as "my former co-charbonnier." Archives Départementales de la Sarthe (Le Mans), microfilms de complément (1955), "Documents des archives privées de M. Eugène Cavaignac, concernant la famille Cavaignac, XVIIIe-XIXe siècle (archives privées de M. Cavaignac, chez Mme Paul-Dubois, Château d'Ourne, Flée)," 1 Mi 2, Reel 28. G. Pinet, *Histoire de l'école polytechnique* (Paris, 1887), p. 118, says that Etienne Arago was the leader, but that Eugène Cavaignac won "many of his comrades" to the cause.

[16] Calmette, "Les Carbonari en France," X, p. 217.

that he had been misled by "agitators."[17] Cavaignac's record at the Ecole Polytechnique was mediocre, for he ranked forty-ninth in a class of sixty-eight, and fourteenth among the seventeen planning to enter the corps of engineers.

During two more years of studies at the Ecole d'application at Metz, Eugène maintained his correspondence with his father in Brussels, and he defied the advice of his uncle to rally to the monarchy. He was grateful for his uncle's aid, and he declared his intention to fulfill his responsibilities as an officer but resolved that "the day when my duties as an officer and as a citizen came into conflict would be the last of my military career."[18] After graduating from the school at Metz, Eugène spent several years in provincial posts, and in 1828 served with the French expeditionary force sent to support the Greek revolutionists in the Morea. He returned to France in 1829, shortly after learning of the death of his father. Although Godefroy was intimately involved in republican conspiratorial politics, Eugène's own political interests had waned. On the eve of the revolution of 1830, Eugène's chief concern seemed to be an impending visit by his mother and sister to his post at Arras.[19]

Yet the revolution itself, in which Godefroy was among the most prominent of the insurgents, reawakened Eugène's republican ardor and opened a period of political involvement. Eugène sent Godefroy his warm congratulations: "You are the soldier now. I only regret that I was unable to do anything for the good cause. However, my dear friend, if the fighting in Paris had lasted another twenty-four hours, perhaps I also might have rendered an important service."[20] Indeed, Lieutenant Cavaignac did organize, in defiance of his superiors, a force of several hundred men to march in support of the revolution, but this proved to be unnecessary.[21] Although

[17] See letters of 25 November, 2 December, and 4 December 1822, in Cavaignac's military dossier, 1207 G.D., Service Historique de l'Armée, Château de Vincennes (hereafter cited as S.H.A.). Cf. Pinet, *Histoire de l'école polytechnique*, p. 117.

[18] Letter to Madame Cavaignac, 15 September 1823, Cavaignac family archives, 1 Mi 2, Reel 27 (hereafter cited to Reel No.).

[19] See *ibid.*, 26 July 1830, Reel 27.

[20] Letter to Godefroy, 3 August 1830, Reel 27.

[21] *Ibid.*, 3 and 11 August 1830, and to Madame Cavaignac, 9 August

the crisis seemed to be over when Louis Philippe assumed the throne, Cavaignac had misgivings. "This is a time for firmness on the part of you Parisians," he wrote Godefroy, "for already I see that false friends want to stop the movement, and would be content with the Charter as it is as the price of all the blood spilled. Let us hope that clear-sighted men will obtain better guarantees, and that after having been so brave you will not be so foolish."[22] He believed that a popularly elected National Assembly should have been called, and the monarchy maintained only "if the majority wanted it."[23]

In August 1830, perhaps owing to Godefroy's influence, Eugène was transferred to Paris, where he was soon promoted to captain. However, he seems to have abstained from political activity during late 1830 and early 1831, when other republicans began to manifest their growing disillusionment. His one political affiliation apparently was with the National Association. As he was about to return to Arras in 1831, his commanding officer warned, "This officer has very extreme views, and he is awaited with impatience by the Patriotic society."[24] Accordingly, he was assigned instead to Thionville, where he felt isolated, most of his fellow officers being "Carlists." In the town itself, however, he attracted sympathetic attention after his brother's dramatic political trial and acquittal in 1831. Captain Cavaignac wrote amusingly of one encounter with a citizen:

> "Sir," he said to me, "I am happy to tell you how much your speech . . ."
>
> "Sir, it is not I, it is my brother."
>
> "Sir," said the other, "I am not completely of your opinion, but you have made a great impression on me and on my friends."
>
> "Sir, it is my brother."

1830, Reel 27. Cf. the official reports of 1 September 1831 and 15 June 1832, Cavaignac dossier, S.H.A. 1207 G.D.

[22] Letter to Godefroy, 3 August 1830, Reel 27.

[23] Letters to Madame Cavaignac, 9 August 1830, and to Godefroy, 11 August 1830, Reel 27.

[24] Letter of 31 March 1831, Cavaignac dossier, S.H.A. 1207 G.D.

"Oh, you are only the brother! It's all the same, Sir. I want to present you to my whole family."[25]

Captain Cavaignac soon was transferred to Metz, where his colonel was reluctant "to see me, a dangerous man and a republican, in command of a company,"[26] but after Cavaignac challenged the colonel to denounce him formally, the colonel became conciliatory. When the silk workers of Lyon arose in November 1831, Cavaignac openly expressed his sympathy. As Marshal Soult marched on that city at the head of a sizable army, Cavaignac wrote his mother: "For a week now, I've heard nothing but denunciations against the good workers of Lyon. I have no need to tell you that not only do I defend them with words, but that I would defend them in another manner if necessary. . . . The workers were foolish to become reconciled with their enemies, to come to terms with the prefect, who after having had them shot down, calls them his children. That will cost them dear."[27] Cavaignac's attitude on this occasion placed him among the most "advanced" republicans, for as Louis Blanc noted sadly, other republicans fought against the workers at Lyon.[28]

The climax of Cavaignac's early political activity came in June 1832, following the abortive insurrection in Paris occasioned by the funeral of General Lamarque. In his post at Metz, Cavaignac was already suspected of being the leader of a group of twenty-two officers who were "declared enemies of the present political order" and affiliated with the National Association in the town.[29] Hearing reports that Cavaignac and the other republican officers had planned, then canceled, a simultaneous uprising in Metz, his colonel raised directly the question of Cavaignac's loyalty: "If the regiment had to fight against the Carlists, would you fight? If it had to fight against

[25] Letter to Madame Cavaignac, 15 August 1831, Reel 27.

[26] *Ibid.*, 9 September 1831, Reel 27. Cf. the report of 1 September 1831, Cavaignac dossier, S.H.A. 1207 G.D.

[27] Letter to Madame Cavaignac, 3 December 1831, Reel 27.

[28] See Louis Blanc, *Histoire de dix ans, 1830-1840* (11th edn., Paris, 1848), III, p. 62.

[29] Confidential letter from the commandant at Metz to the Minister of War, 15 June 1832, Cavaignac dossier, S.H.A. 1207 G.D.

the republican party would you fight? To the first question he replied affirmatively, to the second negatively."[30] Although Cavaignac denied that his oath required him to fight against republicans, the commandant was unwilling publicly "to declare war against his opinions," but advised that Cavaignac and the other politically dangerous officers be dispersed.[31] Accordingly, Captain Cavaignac was hastily ordered to a place where the issue of marching against republicans would not arise—to Algeria. He embarked from Toulon August 8, 1832.

CAVAIGNAC IN ALGERIA

Cavaignac would spend much of his mature life in Algeria, his active service there coinciding closely with the period of conquest. He went as a captain in 1832, and when he returned definitively to France in 1848, he was a divisional general. In between these two dates, the life in Algeria, fighting a brutal war against a native people with no other justification than military discipline and the right of conquest, left its mark on Cavaignac as it did on all of his comrades in arms. "As humane as though he had not waged war in Africa for eighteen years," wrote Tocqueville of another general, Bedeau; Cavaignac by implication fell among those who were no longer humane.[32] Cavaignac's enemies in 1848 would sometimes throw the charge of ingrained brutality at him, and historians have sought to explain his behavior in June by reference to his Algerian ex-

[30] *Ibid.* Cf. Cavaignac's letter to Madame Cavaignac, 12 June 1832, Reel 27. The exchange was cast in the form of a conversation in a biographical article that was published with Cavaignac's approval in *Le Moniteur de l'Armée* in November 1848. See Count Boniface de Castellane, *Journal du Maréchal Castellane, 1804-1862* (Paris, 1897), IV, p. 109. In Deschamps, *Eugène Cavaignac*, I, p. 16, the incident is described as perhaps apocryphal, and is dated 1831. Clearly the story was not apocryphal. The error in date is repeated in the *Dictionnaire de biographie française*, VII (1956), col. 1485. For an interesting comparison of June 1832, with June 1848, but without reference to Cavaignac, see Georges Duveau, *1848* (Paris, 1965), pp. 180-185.

[31] Letter from commandant at Metz to Minister of War, 13 June 1832, Cavaignac dossier, S.H.A. 1207 G.D.

[32] *The Recollections of Alexis de Tocqueville*, tran. Alexander Teixeira de Mattos, ed. J. P. Mayer (New York, 1959), p. 43.

perience. The influence of that experience is undeniable, but Cavaignac was not simply another "Africain."

When he arrived in Algeria in 1832, the French held little more than Algiers, Oran and a few other towns. The conquest was proceeding in a desultory, uncertain fashion against an Arab resistance that was also scattered and disorganized. But Cavaignac's career in Africa was to coincide almost precisely with that of the great Algerian leader Abd el-Kader, who was accepted as Emir and leader of a holy war against the infidel invaders in November 1832, and who did not surrender until December 1847. At first, Cavaignac served as an engineer officer, proving his resourcefulness by introducing a kind of prefabricated blockhouse, for which he was made a knight of the Legion of Honor in 1833.

The young captain turned his attention to political events in France during the crisis of 1834 and 1835. Now the issues seemed to him much more personal, associated with the fate of his brother more than anything else. The news that Godefroy was safe after the insurrection did not console him. "How long must that kind of life last?" he wrote his mother. "And when this crisis is over, it will be necessary to undergo another. . . . The time will come when they will hunt us down like wild animals. . . . I find in myself no other grief but the dangers of my brother, no other courage than, when it becomes necessary, to devote to him my rather useless life as he has devoted his to a good and just cause."[33] Comparing Godefroy's role—as a political prisoner—with his own, troubled Eugène, and he considered leaving the army.[34] But he was politically disillusioned, too. "It seems to me that everything is stagnant in France right now. . . . If I were with Godefroy sharing his fate and his emotions, perhaps I would be, like him, preoccupied above all with the future of our poor country, but from here, I must admit, such ideas most often recede to the last place."[35] When the mass trial of the 164 accused, including Godefroy, was finally arranged in 1835, Eugène sought a two-month's leave to visit his brother, but was prevented from doing so by

[33] Letter to Madame Cavaignac, 27 April 1834, Reel 27.
[34] *Ibid.*, 18 July 1834, Reel 27.
[35] *Ibid.*, 13 October 1834, Reel 27.

a delay in the trial and by the renewal of fighting in Algeria.[36] After Godefroy escaped to England, Eugène once more became engrossed in the military conquest.

In 1836 and 1837, Captain Cavaignac participated in his first major operation, as commander of 500 soldiers isolated in a town within territory which was under the control of Abd el-Kader. The arduous sixteen-month "siege" of Tlemcen gripped the imagination of the French public. From London, Godefroy wrote, "it is a great joy to see one of us serving our country, apart from the scoundrels who govern it."[37] Although cut off most of the time, Eugène was able to exchange a few letters, and once read a letter from Godefroy to a Moor. " 'Why doesn't your brother come to Africa?' he asked me. 'Our books say that the French ought to govern this country justly.' I had some difficulty in making him understand that the men who fight for justice had things to do in our country."[38] The siege finally ended in July 1837 when Tlemcen was evacuated in accordance with the Treaty of Tafna, whereby the French made peace by giving Abd el-Kader control of most of the provinces of Oran and Algiers. For his able defense of the town, Cavaignac won praise, promotion to the rank of major, and his long-desired transfer to the infantry, as commander of a new battalion of zouaves made up primarily of his volunteers at Tlemcen.

The privations of the siege so weakened his health, however, that he spent most of the following three years on inactive duty in France. He also visited Godefroy in England, and on his return renewed his acquaintance with some of the Paris republicans. But he found *Le National* too mild for his taste, and wrote Godefroy that "it is a pity that you are not here to keep the thermometer hot."[39] Suffering from chronic bronchitis, despondent over the death of his sister and the exile of his brother, pessimistic about his prospects in the army, Cavaignac

[36] Letter to his sister Caroline, 8 June 1835, Reel 28.

[37] Letter to Madame Cavaignac, 30 May 1836, Reel 16. Some official letters from Cavaignac at Tlemcen are reproduced in Marcel Emérit, *L'Algérie à l'époque d'Abd-el-Kader* (Paris, 1951), pp. 104-134.

[38] Letter to Godefroy, ? 1837, Reel 28.

[39] Letter to Godefroy, 26 September 1837, Reel 28.

considered resigning his commission and pursuing a civilian career.[40] He resolved not to return to active duty "except for another '92."[41] Yet he had spent too much time in Algeria to turn his mind from it, and in 1839 he published a book on the subject, *De la Régence d'Alger: Notes sur l'occupation.* A brief, unpretentious work which aroused little interest among the many published in those years by French "Africains," it was, in the opinion of André Julien, "the most original . . . containing penetrating views" on the Algerian people and on Abd el-Kader.[42]

As it turned out, another '92 was not required to revive Cavaignac's military ardor. When Abd el-Kader resumed hostilities late in 1839, Cavaignac immediately asked to return to active duty, and did so, bringing to an end a period in which, he confessed to Godefroy, "I was no longer good for much. . . . I await the first puff of gunsmoke to awaken me."[43] He did not wait long. As commander of an infantry battalion, he was wounded for the first time during a skirmish in April 1840, at Cherchell. For his successful defense of that town, he won the admiration of Marshal Valée and of the Duke of Orléans; promotion, and the command of a regiment of zouaves, soon followed. During the next three years, Cavaignac was involved in numerous battles and *razzias*, was wounded once more and promoted to colonel. In 1843, he took command of the new military outpost of Orléansville, named for the duke who had recently died. In 1844 he became brigadier general (*maréchal de camp*), and returned triumphantly to take command of the new subdivision of Tlemcen, where he had first won renown. From Tlemcen, Cavaignac participated in much of the fighting against the Arabs in 1844 and 1845, but thereafter was engaged mostly in administrative work.[44] He took a leave of several months in France in 1847,

[40] *Ibid.*, 29 May 1837, 7 and 17 October 1837, Reel 28.

[41] *Ibid.*, 5 February 1839, Reel 28.

[42] *Histoire de L'Algérie contemporaine, la conquête et les débuts de la colonisation (1827-1871)*, (Paris, 1964), p. 162.

[43] Letter of 30 March 1840, Reel 28.

[44] Some historians erroneously state that Cavaignac fought at the battle of Isly (Morocco) in 1844. They have confused Eugène Cavaignac with

returning to Algeria in time to witness the formal surrender of Abd el-Kader in December 1847. In January 1848, he was appointed temporary commandant of the province of Oran, a position he held when the revolution erupted.

What kind of a soldier was Cavaignac? After his early difficulties over politics, he had an excellent record. In the view of General Bugeaud, Cavaignac had proved himself at Tlemcen, and despite his republican views he was a first class officer of great value to the army. "Competent for all duties," wrote another superior, "but above all for war."[45] But war as it was fought in Algeria was of a particularly sordid and savage kind, and virtually all of the French officers who fought there were brutalized by it. The Arabs, pitiless warriors who decapitated their victims, massacred colonists and burnt their farms, provoked the French to a fierce retaliation. "In combat with a foe who gave no quarter," writes Julien, "enflamed by stories of tortures inflicted on their brothers in arms, they came to believe that they should not shrink from any means to prove the might of the conqueror."[46] In the end, as Tocqueville observed in 1841, "We were waging war in a manner much more barbarous than the Arabs themselves."[47] The most characteristic practice was the "razzia," or punitive destructive raid on Arab villages; employed sporadically during the early years, it was systematized and vigorously defended by Bugeaud after 1840 as a means of compelling submission, but it often degenerated into mere theft of livestock for army supply or even simple pillage, sometimes involving the massacre of inhabitants. Virtually all of the French commanders, in the grip of what Julien has called a "psychosis of repression," accepted

---

a cousin, Antoine Louis Stanislas Cavaignac, who fought at Isly and afterwards was promoted to brigadier general in September 1844, ten days after Eugène reached that grade.

[45] See Bugeaud's annual reports of 1837 and 1841, and his letters of 9 February 1839 and 15 September 1843, Cavaignac dossier, S.H.A. 1207 G.D.; and the report of General Fabvier, 1842, Cavaignac dossier, S.H.A. 1207 G.D.

[46] Julien, *Histoire de l'Algérie*, p. 321. This work, pp. 315-323, is the authority for most of this general discussion.

[47] Cited in *ibid.*, p. 316.

and justified the *razzia*.[48] Cavaignac disapproved of the *razzia* in principle, but practiced it without protest.

In his one public statement on the matter, in *De la Régence d'Alger*, published before the *razzia* was systematized or degenerate, Cavaignac strongly disapproved of this method of repressive action taken against the Arab population as immoral and tending to perpetuate hostilities. Customarily, villages that submitted to the French after a raid were subject to later reprisals by Abd el-Kader. "Placed between two enemies who fight over them," wrote Cavaignac, "they expect only ruin and misery from both."[49] Cavaignac argued that the French should seek to defeat Abd el-Kader militarily, but should try to win over the Arab population by offering a just and tolerant rule that would foster prosperity and weaken the Emir's appeal. "It would no longer be, as has too often been said in criticism, a war of pillage and of massacres." Cavaignac urged his fellow officers to "see the Arabs, not as enemies who must be destroyed, but as men who must be convinced; to forget the past which encourages reprisals, and to think of a future worthy of France, worthy also to occupy the life of a soldier."[50] Although Cavaignac, along with most of his contemporaries in France (and including both wings of the republican party), assumed the superiority of the French and justified the conquest, he was rare among the *Africains* in regarding the Arabs, not as barbarians, but as a people with a proud past who had been able to conquer and rule by the very methods that he advocated, tolerance of differing religious views and justice.[51]

Despite these views, Cavaignac by 1842 had come to believe that the *razzia* was justified by its success in compelling the submission of many villages; although "hardly brilliant or

[48] *Ibid.*, p. 321. Julien seems to overlook Cavaignac's views.

[49] *De la Régence d'Alger*, p. 211.

[50] *Ibid.*, pp. 227-228. He expressed similar views in letters, e.g., to Godefroy, 4 December 1839, Reel 28.

[51] See his remarkably sympathetic discussion of the Muslims, in particular of their conquest of Spain, in *De la Régence d'Alger*, pp. 162-195. I must differ with Julien, *Histoire de l'Algérie*, p. 315, who says that "not one" of the French officers understood the nature of the Arab resistance. Cavaignac did to a remarkable extent.

civilized," he wrote, the method of the *razzia* "has produced more than battles would have done, and practically without bloodshed."[52] Not only did he practice the *razzia*, but Cavaignac also was apparently the first to employ the method that most shocked public opinion, the *enfumade* or asphyxiation by smoke of Arabs who took refuge in caves. The one instance that aroused angry debate in France was carried out by Colonel Pélissier in 1845, but the year before a similar action involving Cavaignac had gone unnoticed, and at least two others are known to have occurred. The Pélissier "affair of the grottos of Dahra" was particularly shocking because of the large number of Arabs—between 500 and 1,000, including many women and children—who died horrible deaths even though they had offered to surrender.[53]

Although the evidence is sparse and contradictory, the Cavaignac affair of June 1844, was probably on a much smaller scale. Cavaignac ordered the use of smoke to try to compel surrender of a part of the Sbeah tribe; his circumspect report noted that the Arabs finally submitted after "about twenty" women and children had died of asphyxiation. Years later, however, other *Africain* officers suggested that many Arabs had died in the Cavaignac *enfumade*.[54] The number, however, was probably not very large, because whereas Dahra shocked the whole region into submission, the Sbeah remained rebellious. In 1845 the official Algerian newspaper, *L'Akhbar*, sought to justify Pélissier by invoking the previous example of Cavaignac, "whose humanity no one will contest."[55]

[52] Letter to his mother, 15 June 1842, published among a number of others by his son, Godefroy Cavaignac, in *Carnet de la sabretache*, No. 100 (1901), p. 221. The original is in the Cavaignac papers, Reel 27.

[53] Julien, *Histoire de l'Algérie*, pp. 320-321. For details, see Raoul Busquet, "L'Affaire des grottes du Dahra (19-20 juin 1845)," *Revue africaine*, LI (1907), 116-168.

[54] Cavaignac's report is in the journal of Orléansville for June 1844, S.H.A. H 210. In the 1854 edition of his *Annales algériennes* (Paris), III, p. 126, E. Pellissier de Reynaud mentioned "several hundred" victims. Canrobert, who participated in the expedition, implied there were many victims, in his memoirs first published in 1898: Germain Bapst, *Le Maréchal Canrobert, souvenirs d'un siècle* (7th edn., Paris, 1909), I, pp. 418-419.

[55] Cited in *Le Moniteur universel*, 2 August 1845. Another report in the

Curiously, the Cavaignac *enfumade* does not seem to have aroused much comment, nor was his reputation tarnished as was Pélissier's. Despite the furor over Dahra in the opposition press and in the Chamber of Peers, Marshal Bugeaud vigorously defended Pélissier and justified the *enfumade* as necessary under Algerian conditions; even Tocqueville, persuaded along with most of his countrymen of the French right of conquest, accepted Bugeaud's arguments, "and suppressed from his consciousness the brutality of the conquest."[56] Cavaignac undoubtedly did the same, for he retained his reputation for moderation among Arabs and French officers alike. Although some of the *Africains*, such as Pélissier and Lamoricière, had a reputation for severity and even cruelty toward the Arabs, Cavaignac was by some regarded as a "roseau peint en fer,"[57] literally, a reed painted like iron. Cavaignac was unusual among the *Africains* in insisting on just treatment of Arab prisoners. Though summary executions were commonplace, Cavaignac once in 1845 astounded a colonel by imprisoning him for such an act—but only for four days! The colonel, Montagnac, wrote contemptuously of Cavaignac's policy of "moderation pushed sometimes to absurdity."[58] Yet Cavaignac expected no mercy from the Arabs, and commented philosophically on a massacre of French prisoners that enflamed public opinion in 1846: "Because the enemy has declared that he will give no quarter, ought we abstain from war? . . . War is something anti-human; everything that occurs in it is translated into bloodshed. If we make war, we must accept the consequences."[59]

Although Cavaignac shared with the other *Africains* a de-

---

same issue referred to the "small number of victims" in the Cavaignac affair. (pp. 2244-2245.)

[56] Melvin Richter, "Tocqueville on Algeria," *Review of Politics*, xxv (1963), 377-398.

[57] *Les Deux généraux Cavaignac*, p. 67.

[58] F. J. L. de Montagnac, *Lettres d'un soldat, neuf années de campagne d'Afrique* (Paris, 1885), pp. 452-456, 481-482. For the anomaly of Cavaignac's attitude, see Julien, *Histoire de l'Algérie*, p. 322.

[59] Letter to Madame Cavaignac, 6 July 1846, Reel 27. For the incident, see Julien, *Histoire de l'Algérie*, p. 203.

termination to crush Abd el-Kader, he also had great respect for the Arab leader and a singular understanding of the nature of the Arab resistance. He denied that Abd el-Kader was simply a religious fanatic or motivated by a thirst for personal power. As the leader of the fight against oppression, his position was analogous to that of Spartacus, the Gracchi, or Sertorius, "who with the goal of liberation gave the signal of revolt." Indeed, Cavaignac also compared him with the great Gallic chieftain and French national hero, Vercingétorix: "He is an admirable personality and he will not have his historian. We will write his history as Caesar wrote that of Vercingétorix."[60]

Yet Cavaignac later felt no more compassion for the defeated Arab than Caesar had felt for Vercingétorix. "The sight of that man reminded me of my poor soldiers, and I have only one joy, and that is to think that he is going to live out his beastly life in a sound citadel in France."[61] It is significant also that though Cavaignac placed a high premium on honor, he did not believe the French were bound to honor the conditions under which the great Arab chieftain had surrendered. Abd el-Kader had submitted only after Lamoricière gave his solemn word that he would be permitted to go to Alexandria or Saint Jean d'Acre, and yet the government of Guizot ordered his imprisonment in France. After the revolution brought Cavaignac to power with Lamoricière as his Minister of War, the Emir was confident that the pledge woud be honored at last, but they failed to answer his letters, and it was finally left to Louis Napoleon Bonaparte to keep the word of the African generals.[62]

The dishonorable treatment of Abd el-Kader did not seem to affect Cavaignac's reputation for military virtue. He had acquired in the army "a pure and uncontested renown,"[63] and he was universally respected despite his cold aloofness and his republican taint. Canrobert called him "a soldier full of energy

[60] Letters to Madame Cavaignac, 24 April 1846 and 10 March 1847, Reel 27.

[61] *Ibid.*, 16 January 1848, Reel 27.

[62] Julien, *Histoire de l'Algérie*, pp. 207-208.

[63] Ferdinand Hugonnet, *Français et arabes en Algérie* (Paris, 1860), p. 125.

and abnegation whom all esteem," who had "the most upright and the most loyal heart I have ever seen."[64] Cavaignac impressed Le Flô more than anyone else he knew in a long military career. He was "an admirable soldier" and "the greatest and most noble figure" among all the commanders of the zouaves.[65] Cavaignac's accomplishments were solid rather than brilliant, and the strain of obstinacy which his mother noted in the child was also observed in the man by Pierre de Castellane. In addition, there was something studied about his qualities of leadership. "Absolute in command, energetic in action, slow to decide, because he is slow to understand, but concealing this laborious work under a solemn silence and speaking only when he has decided, General Cavaignac was esteemed by all, loved by some, feared by many. . . . Moreover, General Cavaignac never avoided war, when war offered him the opportunity to plunge into danger and battle."[66]

Although Cavaignac appeared to be the epitome of the professional officer, it is interesting that throughout his career he had periodically and privately expressed misgivings about his métier. As a young officer, he had mused, "When I see all these men working and learning to get themselves killed according to the rules, I begin to question a social order which makes war necessary," and delivered himself of a judgment that would be belied by most of his life's work: "Truly a war which is not waged for the defense of the (national) soil is an immoral thing."[67] On two separate occasions in 1834 he seriously considered leaving the service, but was dissuaded by his mother and brother. "I think that a *militaire* has little chance of reconciling himself with his profession, and that his best hope if he is an honest man is to be able to say one day that he has done nothing evil."[68] During his long period of inactivity he also considered leaving the service.

[64] Bapst, *Canrobert*, I, pp. 411, 424.

[65] Undated manuscript, Cavaignac dossier, S.H.A. 1207 G.D.

[66] Comte Pierre de Castellane, "La Vie militaire en Afrique," *Revue des deux mondes*, IX (1851), 1071. See also letters to his uncle, 4 August 1843, and to his mother, 9 March 1846, Reel 27.

[67] Letter to Madame Cavaignac, 3 October 1841, Reel 27.

[68] *Ibid.*, 27 April 1834, Reel 27. See also letters of 4 March 1834 and 18 July 1834, Reel 27.

Although he returned eagerly to Algeria in 1840, and took pride in his military successes if not in the *razzias*, flashes of discontent reappeared. In 1843 he wrote his mother that he remained in uniform only to provide economic security for her. "The soldier's life is a life contrary to nature. Everything in it is artificial, everything is violent. . . . The right to kill his fellowman, and with honor; submission sometimes toward a man you despise; obedience sometimes to orders that are revolting to our minds. . . . Truly, if one considered our profession only in its daily aspect, one could not endure it."[69] Shortly after the *enfumade* he wrote, "The years have only strengthened in me the belief that war is a miserable pastime when it is only that. . . . If after twenty years of Africa I had no other memories but of *razzias*, I would think that I had spent my life pitifully indeed."[70] In 1845 he affirmed that if he could relive his life, he would not enter the military again, nor would he wish any son of his to do so.[71] Cavaignac's misgivings derived not only from the kind of warfare waged in Algeria, but also from his difficult relations with Bugeaud and his contempt for the careerism of many officers. Seemingly lacking insight into his own obsessive interest in advancement (as indicated in letters to his mother and uncle), Cavaignac offered one ironic observation on this theme that is almost worthy of Stendhal:

> A brigadier general is a man who wants to become a divisional general, and that's all there is to it. For that purpose he has six thousand men, a dozen cannon, some powder and lead. He puts all of this to work, and he becomes a divisional general. He has caused the deaths of three or four hundred men, spent one or two hundred thousand francs, but a star on his epaulette is well worth that.[72]

He was often critical of officers for their petty intrigues and their selfishness: "People say that the military man is selfless. The soldier yes, the officer no. He is capable, doubtless, of generous sentiments, of devotion, of abnegation, but towards

69 *Ibid.*, 11 August 1843, Reel 27.
70 *Ibid.*, 19 November 1844, Reel 27.
71 *Ibid.*, 28 January 1845, Reel 27.
72 Letter to his sister Caroline, 26 July 1835, Reel 28.

only one thing, duty. Beyond that he is egoistic and selfish. It would be difficult perhaps to determine how many minutes and seconds pass between the moment when the lieutenant sees his captain fall and the moment when he thinks that he will be able to replace the captain in his rank."[73] Yet, at a time when French soldiers were professionals conscripted almost exclusively from the poorest classes, Cavaignac never imputed inferiority to enlisted men, but often praised them and expressed sympathy for their hard lot. As a young company commander, Cavaignac declared himself a "partisan of a regime of kindness and indulgence for the soldier," and Bugeaud noted that during the siege of Tlemcen, "In order not to succumb, he imposed on his battalion the most severe privations, and not a man complained."[74] A physician who accompanied an expedition led by Cavaignac into the Sahara in 1847 was impressed with the soldiers' esteem for Cavaignac and with his marked solicitude for their welfare.[75]

If the democratic and humanitarian values associated with republicanism had but slight influence on his attitude toward the Arabs, Cavaignac's political ideals do seem relevant to his attitude toward the common soldier, and also to his views on colonization. He was critical of Bugeaud's proposal for exclusively military colonies, and also of the "official" plan whereby the state subsidized colonists if they had capital of their own. For the frontier region, Cavaignac did advocate military colonies, with land given over to veterans capable of defending themselves. He indignantly opposed any plan that would "ex-

[73] Letter to Madame Cavaignac, 11 August 1843, Reel 27.

[74] Cavaignac's letter to Madame Cavaignac, 3 October 1831, Reel 27; Bugeaud's letter of 9 February 1839, Cavaignac dossier, S.H.A. 1207 G.D.

[75] Felix Jacquot, *Expédition du général Cavaignac dans le sahara algérien en avril et mai 1847* (Paris, 1849), pp. 162, 322, 332-334. There is no basis in fact, to my knowledge, for a hostile cartoon that appeared in France in 1848, depicting Cavaignac, standing with hands bloody against a background of soldiers being subjected to severe punishments, as saying, "Now that I have learned to discipline men in Africa, I leave for France to apply my system against those good Parisians who say they have a Republic." The picture is reproduced in Julien, *Histoire de l'Algérie*, opposite p. 336. The allusion was to published accusations made in 1845 about brutal treatment of soldiers in Algeria. See Julien, *Histoire de l'Algérie*, pp. 280-281.

clude colonization by the poor man." After all, it was the poor who, as soldiers, were winning Algeria; without them, "where would they be, all these future ministers, future marshals, future governments (monsters of ingratitude and of selfishness)? Exclude the poor man from his share! Are there not moments when one feels sympathy for the tribune who seeks the agrarian law?"[76]

Cavaignac regarded the granting of land to army veterans as in part a recompense for their years of hard service. "We have made and seen the soldier suffer a great deal; in no other army, perhaps, has he suffered more. . . . It is only just that they possess a piece of this land on which they have worked so hard in all ways."[77] During his second period at Tlemcen, Cavaignac had an opportunity to put these ideas into practice on a small scale, creating a colony of army veterans which by 1847 numbered about 100. The settlement was so prosperous that many of the old soldiers brought relatives and wives over from France. "No memory of Africa," wrote Cavaignac, "will remain more precious."[78] Except for the frontier, Cavaignac favored colonization by civilians. His chief concern was to prevent their exploitation by capitalists. "If we give the colonist over to the capitalist, we will be doing in agriculture what in France we do in industry, where the factory worker is a serf."[79]

[76] Letter to Madame Cavaignac, 29 May 1847, Reel 27.

[77] Letter to his uncle, 26 March 1847, copy in Reel 27, also published in *Les Deux généraux Cavaignac*, pp. 239-254. For a discussion of the appalling conditions in which the soldiers lived, see Julien, *Histoire de l'Algérie*, pp. 279-294. In addition to his early views published in *De la Régence d'Alger*, Cavaignac developed his ideas on colonization in the letter to his uncle, cited above, in response to his uncle's request. Knowing that General Jacques Marie Cavaignac planned to show the letter to Guizot as proof of his brilliance, and wishing to prevent this, Cavaignac deliberately included "several idiotic remarks" (as he told his mother in a letter of 28 March 1847, Reel 27), but the uncle sent the letter to Guizot anyway. In another letter to his mother, on 29 May 1847, Cavaignac offered further clarification of his views, expressing more hostility to "capitalists" and more sympathy for the "poor man" than in the letter to his uncle.

[78] Letter to his uncle, 26 March 1847, Reel 27, and *Les Deux généraux Cavaignac*, p. 254. See also letters to Madame Cavaignac, 21 January 1847, and 20 December 1847, Reel 27.

[79] Letter to Madame Cavaignac, 29 May 1847, Reel 27.

There was the danger of creating a new "feudalism, quite as bad as the old," of "founding here a new Ireland, of having here a population reduced to a hard life only to fatten the *absentees*."[80] Cavaignac also drew on current republican criticism of French railway policy, suggesting that capitalistic exploitation of Algeria would result in similar speculative abuses.[81] All of these dangers could be avoided if the state took charge of the civilian colonization. Private capital could be permitted to establish commercial and industrial enterprises, as in France, but should not be permitted to dominate agriculture. Instead the state should, on simple request, establish colonists on farms of 100 to 500 hectares, at its own expense.[82]

THE *MILITAIRE* AS REPUBLICAN

Despite his long years in Algeria, Cavaignac remained self-consciously a republican. After his visit to Godefroy in 1837, the two brothers maintained a frequent correspondence; Eugène's chief interest was Algeria, but while he was in France he also reported on the activities of some of the Paris republicans. In late 1839 and early 1840, before returning to Algeria, Eugène was involved in some kind of venture concerning Godefroy and Latrade, a former army officer who had become an editor for *Le National*—a mysterious undertaking that the two brothers kept hidden even from their mother.[83]

When Godefroy received amnesty in 1840, Eugène invited him to Algeria, "so that no one will get the idea that you are not my brother and my friend."[84] Godefroy eagerly accepted, and although the government uneasily ordered him kept under surveillance, no difficulties arose, and he was well-received by Eugène's fellow officers.[85] In 1841 Godefroy suggested that

[80] Letter to his uncle, 26 March 1847, Reel 27, and *Les Deux généraux Cavaignac*, pp. 247-248.

[81] Letter to Madame Cavaignac, 29 May 1847, Reel 27.

[82] Letter to his uncle, 26 March 1847, Reel 27, and *Les Deux généraux Cavaignac*, p. 249.

[83] The collection of letters from Eugène to Godefroy is in Reel 28.

[84] Letter to Godefroy, 8 August 1840, Reel 28.

[85] See letter from the Minister of War to the Governor-General of Algeria, 22 September 1841, Cavaignac dossier, S.H.A. 1207 G.D., and

his brother seek election to the Chamber of Deputies, but Eugène indignantly refused. "To take the oath to the present government in order to be able to serve in Africa is permissible, I believe . . . but the community of heritage and duty bequeathed by the memory of our father will never permit me to accept a political position that you would reject."[86]

In 1842, Godefroy's attempt to create a new, more socially oriented newspaper to rival *Le National* was strongly supported by Eugène, who contributed 2,000 francs to sustain it. Nevertheless, the paper, *Le Journal du Peuple*, failed after a few months. "Politically," wrote Eugène, "I would be very distressed to see the journal end, but fraternally, I would rather lose an eye."[87] Through Godefroy's influence, he also subscribed to the mildly socialist *Revue Indépendante*.[88] Eugène shared Godefroy's scorn for *Le National*, but he seemed most concerned with its views on Algeria when he referred to that "animal of a *National*."[89] In 1842, two republican notables, Charles Ledru and Martin de Strasbourg, visited Cavaignac in Algeria, and the following year Godefroy returned to spend another three months there. Once more he charmed the officers,[90] and exerted his powerful influence on Eugène.

"I am engaged in *high politics*," the latter wrote his mother. "Godefroy gives me good ideas, and then afterwards I begin to believe that they are mine. What a shame that such a man is unable to conduct affairs."[91] Although Cavaignac did not often discuss political or social ideas in his letters, clearly he was sympathetic to his brother's point of view, and on one occasion, commenting on an article of Godefroy's in the *Revue Indépendante*, indicated that he had a good grasp of the social question that was arousing so much interest:

---

letters from Eugène to Madame Cavaignac, 16 October 1841 and 15 December 1841, Reel 27.

86 Letter to Godefroy, 14 May 1841, Reel 28.

87 *Ibid.*, 25 April 1842, Reel 28.

88 *Ibid.*, 13 April 1843, Reel 28.

89 *Ibid.*, 25 December 1842, Reel 28.

90 See Bapst, *Canrobert*, I, pp. 413-412.

91 Letter of 4 October 1843, Reel 27.

> The modern economists had always seemed absurd to me in considering production and all economic matters solely from an arithmetical point of view, in accepting the principle of absolute liberty which seems to me dangerous, completely *anti-social*, society having for a primary purpose and duty precisely the contrary task of regulating those things that only society can control. They have deserted their responsibilities, it seems to me, in seeking to avoid interfering with instead of regulating economic activity. As you say, it is appalling to think that production should become for mankind a bane instead of a benefit, that the machines which ought to give comfort to the worker in offering him a greater return for smaller effort should be, on the contrary, nothing but a source of even greater misery and servitude. I did sense that there was something absurd in this theory of laisser-faire.[92]

Cavaignac's affection for his brother was unusually strong, and when Godefroy died in 1845, Eugène grieved deeply. He wrote to several republican leaders concerning public honors for Godefroy, and was chagrined that Ledru-Rollin failed to reply;[93] he was careful, however, to avoid giving any impression that he was estranged from the republicans.[94] His reputation as a republican had posed problems for his military career from the beginning, and although he and Godefroy easily reconciled his profession with his political views, his superiors remained suspicious. After 1832, Cavaignac carefully refrained from political activity within the army; he even avoided talking politics with his colleagues, but he did nothing to change his reputation for republicanism and never openly rallied to the regime.

In general, the policy adopted toward him was that expressed by Bugeaud in 1839, that he was simply too good an officer for the army to lose.[95] Yet Bugeaud, a staunch con-

[92] Letter to Godefroy, 13 April 1843, Reel 28.

[93] Letters to Madame Cavaignac, 9 November 1845, and 5 February 1846, Reel 27.

[94] *Ibid.*, 15 March 1846, Reel 27.

[95] Letter of 9 February 1839, and report of 1841, Cavaignac dossier, S.H.A. 1207 G.D.

servative who detested anything that smacked of revolutionary politics, later turned against Cavaignac, who, he believed, "has fundamentally the same opinions as his brother."[96] Cavaignac was watched closely during the visits of Godefroy, and on one occasion he narrowly missed compromising himself when, sitting next to the Duke d'Aumale, he decided at the last minute to follow protocol in drinking the health of the king.[97] Actually the Duke d'Aumale, as well as another son of Louis Philippe, the Duke of Orléans himself, both of whom served with the Army of Africa, had a high regard for Cavaignac, and Ibos argues that their influence helped him win his promotions to colonel and to brigadier general.[98]

"Cavaignac's behavior," wrote Aumale to the king, "is perfectly correct and honorable; he is too young and too spirited for us to consider obstructing his career. We would only delay his advancement, and that would be, in my opinion, awkward. In seeming to give him unwillingly the ranks that everyone knows he has earned, we would absolve him of all gratitude and would render him more dangerous. He has a real popularity in the army."[99] Cavaignac's promotion to brigadier general followed not long afterwards, and it was the Duke d'Aumale who, as governor-general of Algeria, appointed Cavaignac to the command of the province of Oran in January 1848.

It is difficult, particularly in light of such interventions in his favor, to determine the extent to which, if at all, his republicanism hurt Cavaignac's professional career. He often complained to his mother and brother about obstructions to his advancement, but it is impossible to disentangle the political from personal factors. His rate of advancement was actually faster than that of many officers serving in Metropolitan France, but slower than regulations allowed, and considerably slower than that of some other officers in Algeria,

96 Letter to Minister of War, 15 September 1843, Cavaignac dossier, S.H.A. 1207 G.D.

97 Letter to Madame Cavaignac, 31 March 1843, Reel 27.

98 See Ibos, *Le Général Cavaignac*, pp. 74, 78-82.

99 Pierre Athanase Larousse, *Grand dictionnaire universel du XIXe siècle français* (Paris, 1866-90), III, p. 636.

"the promised land" of "rapid careers."[100] Lamoricière, who had been four years behind Cavaignac in the Ecole Polytechnique, became divisional general in 1843 while Cavaignac was still a colonel, and Cavaignac did not reach that grade until after the revolution of 1848. To be sure, Lamoricière had a more brilliant career, and Cavaignac had had almost three years of inactivity, but probably a still more important factor was "favoritism and nepotism," which in Algeria played a more important role than merit in advancement.[101]

Cavaignac was unusual among the *Africains* in refusing to join any coterie or become anyone's protégé. Bugeaud's later hostility apparently resulted in part from this attitude, as well as from Cavaignac's refusal to marry his daughter.[102] Cavaignac believed that Bugeaud, as governor-general, was hindering his career by assigning him to routine duties, and a fellow officer noted that "It was a sort of destiny for Cavaignac to have to undertake tasks that were difficult yet lacking in brilliance and even thankless. . . . These trials, as well as his poor health, undoubtedly helped to give to Cavaignac that sad and severe appearance which was habitual with him."[103] Cavaignac also complained that Lamoricière was obstructing his career, but he made these complaints privately to his relatives, for in Africa he remained proudly aloof and taciturn.

"I have become attached to silence as a system after having adopted it through modesty," he wrote.[104] "The silence in which the general lived," recalled Pierre de Castellane, "and the isolation that he pleased to create around him, chilled his imagination, and the dark fire of his glance indicated a man who has believed himself all his life dedicated to sacrifice.

[100] Julien, *Histoire de l'Algérie*, p. 300. See also Raoul Girardet, *La Société militaire dans la France contemporaine* (*1815-1939*), (Paris, 1953), pp. 68-69. The opinion of Chalmin in *L'Officier français de 1815 à 1870*, p. 256, that "his family and his opinions had not hurt him in anything," is an exaggeration based on little evidence. The military historian of Algeria, Paul Azan, believed that Cavaignac's republican views did hinder his advancement. (*Les Grands soldats d'Algérie* [Orléans, 1931], p. 98.)

[101] Julien, *Histoire de l'Algérie*, p. 300.

[102] Ibos, *Le Général Cavaignac*, pp. 75, 135.

[103] Hugonnet, *Français et arabes*, p. 128.

[104] Letter to Madame Cavaignac, 15 December 1843, Reel 27.

. . . He received his promotions, but his pride was too great to go after them."[105]

After Cavaignac finally received his general's star in 1844, he was in a more sensitive and conspicuous position, and with Godefroy's influence gone after 1845, he felt increased pressures to renounce his republican identity, or at least to adopt a more sympathetic attitude toward the July Monarchy. The pressure came from various sources, from some of his fellow officers, among whom he was known derisively as "the general of the Republic,"[106] from the government, to some extent from his mother, and in particular from his uncle, General Jacques Marie Cavaignac. Jacques had switched loyalties easily again after 1830, and Louis Philippe had made him a peer in 1839. He and Eugène corresponded fairly frequently, but mostly on military matters, for Eugène always felt the barrier of political principles between them.[107]

In 1846, General Jacques Marie Cavaignac sought to influence the government to appoint Eugène to the temporary command of the province of Oran, and suggested that he might accept the title of Count of Tlemcen, a notion that Eugène indignantly rejected.[108] Despite even Bugeaud's support at this point, the government declined to appoint Cavaignac, ostensibly on grounds of lack of seniority in his grade.[109] Yet an agent of Guizot let Cavaignac know that the commander of the province "should be a man of the government," but instead of making any such declaration, Cavaignac merely invoked his twenty-seven years of faithful service in the mili-

[105] Castellane, "La Vie militaire en Afrique," IX, 1071.

[106] Letter to Madame Cavaignac, 28 March 1847, Reel 27.

[107] Some of these letters appear in *Les Deux généraux Cavaignac.* Cavaignac was relaxed and candid in his letters to his mother and brother, but not in those to his uncle.

[108] He wrote a long letter to Eugène, apparently hinting that he should make a gesture to the government, and sent a copy to the Minister of War, according to the reply dated 24 June 1846, Cavaignac dossier, S.H.A. 1207 G.D. Cavaignac's polite reply to his uncle, 6 July 1846, is reprinted in *Les Deux généraux Cavaignac*, pp. 233-235. The reference to the title is in a letter to Madame Cavaignac, 6 July 1846, in which he complains of the "ridiculous" intervention of his uncle (Reel 27).

[109] Letter from the Minister of War to General Jacques Marie Cavaignac, 24 June 1846, Cavaignac dossier, S.H.A. 1207 G.D.

tary. "You may be assured that the award of one or ten or a hundred stars will not make me serve this cause otherwise than I would believe that I should and could do it."[110]

At the same time, Cavaignac was cautious enough to refuse to return to France to attend public honors for Godefroy, fearing that the action might ruin his career.[111] But he contemptuously rejected the suggestion by his uncle to ingratiate himself with Guizot,[112] as well as his uncle's insinuation that he was less firm in his political convictions than Godefroy had been. "I have never considered this distinction as anything but a criticism, and every time that anyone calls it to my attention, he will only incline me in the direction from which he thought I had strayed. Tell that to the general."[113] To his mother, who hinted that a "capitulation of conscience" would improve his position, Cavaignac responded, "One can with honesty be a *militaire* such as I have been, but one can be a politician only as our Godefroy was. Fortunately I have no desire to become such."[114] Eight months before the revolution, Cavaignac set out his political attitudes in a long letter to his mother:

> I have never been a politician, and if my reason has always told me that goodness, justice, honesty and the future were in my brother's camp, I have never felt the same strong impulses that would have led me to emulate him. . . . What sad satisfaction would my uncle find in persuading me to make an approach that would be an error? Tell him that if all my life I must bring a sad heart to the tomb of our Godefroy, at least let me bring it always unburdened and without regret. . . . I have no desire to engage in politics, he can be assured on that score. . . . I will make war as much as they like, but politics, never. That of the government I find detestable, that of the opposition in all its forms I find incoherent, lacking grandeur, very often without good faith.[115]

110 Letter to Madame Cavaignac, 13 September 1846, containing copies of letters between de la Rue and Cavaignac, Reel 27.

111 *Ibid.*, 9 September 1846, Reel 27.

112 *Ibid.*, 28 March 1847 and 7 June 1847, Reel 27.

113 *Ibid.*, 28 March 1847, Reel 27.

114 *Ibid.*, 17 November 1846, Reel 27.

115 *Ibid.*, 29 May 1847, Reel 27.

What kind of man was Cavaignac on the eve of the revolution? In appearance, he was moderately tall and slender, and wore the mustache and short beard common to many of the *Africains.* A brigadier general impatiently awaiting promotion, he was well respected, but lived an austere, proud and lonely life, although he had a few close friends and was capable of relaxing occasionally in the evenings.[116] He was still a bachelor, like most of the French officers in Algeria, owing to the difficult conditions there,[117] and perhaps also for psychological reasons of his own.

His relationship with his mother was unusually close; although on a number of occasions he expressed a desire to marry and asked her and his uncle to find a wife for him, these efforts were not serious, and he would remain a bachelor until after the death of his mother in 1849. Both felt more lonely after the death of Godefroy, and relied on each other for emotional comfort. Cavaignac wrote her regularly, about once a week, and visited her as often as he could; he was able to express candidly to her the frustrations and uncertainties which he concealed behind his cold and aloof manner. "I have a sad heart," he wrote in January 1847, "sad as are the hearts seared by all of the evil passions that develop under the sun of Africa. Ah! What need I have to go to you, my mother, in order to become better again."[118]

Cavaignac was also drawn closer to his mother because of his changing views on religion. Previously he had been a freethinker, mildly Voltairean, but in the 1840's he began to turn for consolation to Thomas à Kempis and to Pascal; in his grief over Godefroy, he had his mother send him a Catholic medallion, and once wrote gloomily of becoming a Trappist monk.[119] But his spiritual outlook still had predominantly humanistic and even political overtones. "I believe in martyrs since the martyrdom of my brother," he wrote, and he now looked

[116] Bapst, *Canrobert,* I, p. 413, and Castellane, "La Vie militaire en Afrique," IX, 1071.

[117] Julien, *Histoire de l'Algérie,* p. 311, relates that some of the married officers found it advisable to leave their wives in France.

[118] Letter of 20 January 1847, Reel 27.

[119] Letter to Madame Cavaignac, 4 August 1845, Reel 27.

upon religion not as an enemy, but as an agent of human progress.[120] Cavaignac's new sympathy for the church corresponded with a trend within the republican party and did not involve any profound conversion; indeed, Cavaignac remained uncertain whether or not to call himself a Catholic.[121]

As a general, Cavaignac lived comfortably enough in his own house in Algeria, kept a flower and vegetable garden, and at various times had as pets chickens, a goat, gazelles and an ostrich. Although neither intellectually brilliant nor profound, he was probably more bookish than most of the *Africains*—he even thought it a weakness that Bugeaud could not appreciate poetry.[122] He did a considerably amount of reading, and classical or other literary allusions are not uncommon in his correspondence. Among modern authors he read Voltaire and the *Histoire de dix ans* of Louis Blanc, which moved him deeply,[123] but his favorite author was Plutarch, whom he reread many times, and who seems to have helped form his own self-image.

Although he published only the book on Algeria, Cavaignac did make copious notes for projected works of a military and historical character. He had studied the Thirty Years' War and the campaigns of Napoleon, and planned histories of France from Merovingian times to 1789, and of Europe from 1610 to 1661.[124] Cavaignac possessed a good, and remarkably critical, sense of history, as was revealed in his sympathetic discussion of the Arab conquest of Spain in *De la Régence d'Alger*. The many evidences of Roman civilization in Algeria also excited his imagination; he was among the few French officers who sought to preserve, rather than wantonly to destroy, Roman remains, in particular the ancient town of Castellum Tingitanum, near Orléansville.[125]

[120] *Ibid.*, 9 May 1846, Reel 27.

[121] *Ibid.*

[122] Charles de Rémusat, *Mémoires de ma vie*, ed. Charles H. Pouthas, *Les dernières années de la monarchie, la révolution de 1848, la seconde république (1841-1851)*, (Paris, 1962), IV, p. 349.

[123] Letter to Madame Cavaignac, 2 March 1847, Reel 27.

[124] This material is still in the family archives at Château d'Ourne.

[125] Julien, *Histoire de l'Algérie*, pp. 305-306.

Cavaignac on the eve of the revolution was a forty-five-year-old man who had been shaped by many influences, but chiefly by two different value systems, two different traditions that in some respects were diametrically opposed, but which seemed to act as mutually reinforcing influences in others as well: republicanism and the military. Despite occasional misgivings, he was a professional officer committed to the army, hardened by years of cruel warfare and habituated to a hierarchical and authoritarian system. Tocqueville, during an official investigation, was alarmed by the violent and autocratic habits acquired by the French officers in Algeria, and wrote in 1841: "God help us from ever seeing France governed by one of the officers of the Army of Africa!"[126] Yet Tocqueville himself would help vote Cavaignac into power in 1848, and vote for him again in preference to Louis Napoleon Bonaparte as president. Cavaignac was aware that "the exercise of this nearly unlimited authority has gotten into my blood a little, but to say that I find satisfaction and comfort in this, No."[127] Yet he shared the *Africains'* distaste for criticism from Metropolitan France, and to some extent Bugeaud's contempt for the civilian officials who appeared in Algeria following the reorganization ordinance of 1845.[128]

Cavaignac's commitment to republicanism was emotional and familial more than intellectual, deriving from the heritage of his father and sustained by the stronger commitment of a brother whom he reverenced. He had no developed political ideas of his own, but his faith in the democratic republic was more than simple loyalty or duty. Although he remained aloof from the republicans in France, and abstained from political activity during the 1840's, his interest in social and economic questions paralleled developments within the republican movement, and his hostility to Bonapartism was strong despite the authoritarian habits acquired in the military.

General Cavaignac liked to believe that his own version of

[126] *Alexis de Tocqueville: Oeuvres complètes,* ed. J. P. Mayer (Paris, 1962), III, p. 236.

[127] Letter to Madame Cavaignac, 8 December 1844, Reel 27.

[128] *Ibid.*, 16 November 1846, Reel 27. See also Julien, *Histoire de l'Algérie*, pp. 216-221.

republicanism was no different from that of Godefroy, and according to Hippolyte Carnot, "Godefroy often spoke to me of his brother as a republican as sure as himself,"[129] but clearly Godefroy belonged in the radical wing of the republicans, whereas Eugène in 1848 would find himself more at home with the moderate republicans. Moreover, the revolution would thrust him more fully into the political arena than Godefroy had ever been and force him to face problems of power that Godefroy had been spared.

[129] MS "Mémorial," dos. 15, p. 2.

IV · The February Revolution

THE ESTABLISHED ORDER

THE February revolution took nearly everyone by surprise: the king, Guizot, the men of the banquet campaign, undoubtedly most of the insurgents themselves, the republicans who would assume power, and even Alexis de Tocqueville, who actually prophesied revolution in a speech on January 29, 1848, but who later confessed that he had not really expected what happened in February.[1] There were sound reasons for the confidence of Louis Philippe and for the complacency of the possessing classes. Paris had been tranquil since the great strikes of 1840; republican, Legitimist, and Bonapartist opposition seemed cowed, and even the problem of ministerial instability had been solved with the Soult-Guizot cabinet. The government had won all of the elections since 1830, and 1846 had witnessed its greatest victory. Moreover, the July Monarchy had given France almost two decades of peace and, until 1846, of relative prosperity and real economic growth. Although Guizot was increasingly under attack for his immobility, the regime was by continental standards a liberal and even progressive one.

Yet to say that revolution was unexpected is not to revive the old thesis that it was an accident. There were profound weaknesses in the regime that seemed so stable and confident in the 1840's, and when Parisians were once more impelled into insurrection in 1848, Louis Philippe would surrender more readily than had Charles X, and in falling would release the profoundly revolutionary force of political democracy.

[1] *Recollections*, pp. 11-13, 15. See also Edward T. Gargan, *Alexis de Tocqueville: The Critical Years, 1848-1851* (Washington, D.C., 1955), pp. 55-58; Emile Ollivier, *Empire libéral*, I, pp. 467-470; and Elsbeth Spring, "Tocquevilles Stellung zur Februarrevolution," *Schweizer Beiträge zur allgemeinen Geschichte*, XII (1954), 50-98. Although the literature on the revolution of 1848 is enormous, there is no standard synthesis incorporating recent scholarship. For valuable discussions of recent research and new lines of interpretation, see the two articles by Peter Amann, "Writings on the Second French Republic," and "The Changing Outlines of 1848."

To the end, the so-called bourgeois monarchy was dominated by the landed *notables.*[2] The electorate of the revised Charter, which reached 241,000 by 1846, was still much narrower than that of the *unreformed* British House of Commons in 1830,[3] and consisted overwhelmingly of owners of agricultural property.[4] Most of the ruling *notables* were Orleanists in politics, not through any intense loyalty to Louis Philippe, but because they were committed to the political and social institutions of the settlement of 1830 and 1831.[5] Some Orleanists derived from long established bourgeois families, others from families that had won prominence in the revolutionary and imperial epochs. Most of their wealth was in land, but business and commercial interests were also predominantly Orleanist, and Orleanism was hospitable to new men such as Adolphe Thiers. "Orleanism, with its doctrine of the *juste milieu,* represented rule by the *notables,* by the managerial classes, by all the aristocracies—those of birth, wealth and intelligence."[6] Orleanism reflected a narrow kind of liberalism that was essentially conservative, and there was little difference

[2] The best recent additions to the literature on the nature of the July Monarchy are Vigier, *La Seconde république dans la région alpine*; André-Jean Tudesq, *Les Grands notables en France (1840-1849): étude historique d'une psychologie sociale* (Paris, 1964); and Adeline Daumard, *La Bourgeoisie parisienne de 1815 à 1848* (Paris, 1963). See also two recent articles in *French Historical Studies,* v (1967): Alfred Cobban, "The 'Middle Class' in France, 1815-1848," pp. 41-52; and Patrick L. R. Higonnet and Trevor B. Higgonet, "Class, Corruption, and Politics in the French Chamber of Deputies, 1846-1848," pp. 204-224. For some recent versions of the traditional emphasis on the bourgeois character of the regime, see Emmanuel Beau de Loménie, *Les Responsabilités des dynasties bourgeoises* (Paris, 1943-54), I, *De Bonaparte à Mac-Mahon,* and Jean Lhomme, *La Grande bourgeoisie au pouvoir, 1830-1880: essai sur l'histoire sociale de la France* (Paris, 1960).

[3] See the tables in Anthony Wood, *Nineteenth Century Britain, 1815-1914* (London, 1960), pp. 449, 453.

[4] See Sherman Kent, *Electoral Procedure Under Louis Philippe* (New Haven, 1937), pp. 36-54, 58.

[5] For complementary analyses of Orleanism and the Orleanists, see Tudesq, *Les Grands notables,* I, pp. 237-378, and René Rémond, *The Right Wing in France; from 1815 to de Gaulle,* trans. James M. Laux (Philadelphia, 1966), pp. 99-124.

[6] Rémond, *The Right Wing in France,* p. 117.

between Guizot's majority and the center left led by Thiers. However, there was a genuinely liberal if antidemocratic wing of Orleanism, represented in the Chamber by a group of sixty to eighty deputies led by Odilon Barrot, which expressed the aspirations of the middle and petty bourgeoisie seeking a place for themselves in the *pays légal.*[7]

The 1840's were the golden age of the French *notable,* but it was remarkable that a large minority of those who exercised such powerful social and economic domination were hostile to the political regime. These were, of course, the Legitimists, consisting mostly of the nobility of the Ancien Régime, now the party of loyalty to the Bourbon dynasty, of militant Catholicism, and of a generally prerevolutionary system of values.[8] The Legitimist nobility was still so entrenched that it owned an estimated five-eighths of the agricultural property in France in 1841, and in some regions they had a strong popular following, not only among peasants but also in some workers' districts, chiefly in the south.[9] But their influence was weakened by a deliberate abstention from politics out of contempt for Louis Philippe, that "interior emigration" described by René Rémond. The Legitimist delegation in the Chamber of Deputies was accordingly small, representing those willing to take the oath required even to vote. There were factions within Legitimism as within republicanism, including one significant but small group defining a new "social Catholicism," but Legitimism in general looked to the past, even though some hoped to bring about a restoration of Henry V through universal manhood suffrage.

Besides Orleanism, Legitimism, and republicanism, there was one other political force during the 1840's that was at best a potentiality, having but a few scattered adherents, and a sole deputy (Narcisse Vieillard). This was Bonapartism, which had

[7] Tudesq, *Les Grands notables,* I, p. 348. See also Daumard, *La Bourgeoisie parisienne,* pp. 599-600.

[8] For complementary analyses of Legitimism, see Tudesq, *Les Grands notables,* I, pp. 130-236, and Rémond, *The Right Wing in France,* pp. 79-98.

[9] Tudesq, *Les Grands notables,* I, p. 186; Theodore Zeldin, *The Political System of Napoleon III* (London, 1958), pp. 157-158.

animated many of the insurgents in 1830 but which had lost what little practical significance it had thereafter with the death in 1832 of Napoleon's son, the Austrianized Duke of Reichstadt. The young Louis Napoleon, nephew of the emperor, assumed leadership of the cause and collected a few dedicated followers, but his attempted uprisings at Strasbourg in 1836 and at Boulogne in 1840 were sorry failures, which evoked no popular response.[10]

So little did King Louis Philippe fear the Bonapartist pretender that he had sought to win popularity for himself by catering to the popular adulation of the emperor, most obviously by negotiating the return of his remains from Saint Helena. The immense crowds that watched the procession in the bitter cold of December 1840, a few months after the Boulogne uprising, indicated the strength of the Napoleonic legend, but this sentiment was quite different from political support for Louis Napoleon, who sat ignored in the fortress of Ham.

Yet it was the Napoleonic legend rather than Louis Philippe that benefited from the return of Napoleon's remains, and the 1840's witnessed its full flowering.[11] The many books, songs and plays about the emperor testified to the growing interest of the reading public, but among the population at large the legend was perpetuated mostly by direct oral tradition, most families having had members who fought in the imperial armies.[12] Imprisoned comfortably at Ham, Louis Napoleon did not lose heart, but continued to develop and to publish his views, which took the legend as a point of departure. Universal suffrage (as well as heredity) was basic to his system, and he sought to ally himself with the republicans, who rejected his overtures. His *Des Idées napoléoniennes,* published

[10] See Adrien Dansette, *Louis Napoléon à la conquête du pouvoir* (Paris, 1961), pp. 125-126, 174, and Lucas-Dubreton, *Le Culte de Napoléon*, pp. 343-344, 373. See also Tudesq, *Les Grands notables*, II, p. 549. For another discussion of Bonapartism, see Zeldin, *Political System of Napoleon III*, pp. 3-6.

[11] A. Tudesq, "La Légende napoléonienne en France en 1848," *Revue historique*, CCXVIII (1957), 64-65. See also Ollivier, *Empire libéral*, I, pp. 400-409.

[12] Tudesq, "Légende napoléonienne," p. 75. See also Daumard, *La Bourgeoisie parisienne*, pp. 633-641.

in 1839, went into four editions, and six editions of his *L'Extinction du pauperisme* (1844) had been issued before 1848. But after his two abortive coups and his imprisonment, Louis Napoleon was no longer regarded seriously as a pretender, and his escape to England in 1846 aroused little interest.[13] Popular idolatry of the emperor would not be translated into political support for Louis Napoleon until the February revolution created the appropriate conditions.

Beneath the world of the *notables* (the great and the merely wealthy who ruled French society), lived most of the population. The upper and much of the middle levels of the bourgeoisie were included in the *pays légal*, but many whose style of life marked them as bourgeois were disenfranchised though not lacking in influence.[14] For the urban working classes, this period of burgeoning industrialization was an arduous one, marked by diminishing real wages, lengthening workdays (reaching fourteen hours in some of the newer factories) and chronic unemployment in time of crisis.[15] Organization was weak, with the old *compagnonnages* in decline, with the newer mutual aid societies and the more militant *sociétés de résistance* hampered by legal restrictions and governmental surveillance. The older handicrafts still predominated and were best organized; the last major wave of strikes in Paris in 1840 had created virtually a general strike atmosphere.[16] Workers in the newer mechanized industries, drawn mostly from the peasantry, were too docile to engage in much strike activity.[17] The worker movement was weak, finding only limited and indirect expression through their organizations, but the condition of workers was attracting increasing attention, in particular from the socially tinged republican movement.

Despite the growing importance of the urban working classes, France remained a rural and agricultural society, with

[13] Lucas-Dubreton, *Le Culte de Napoléon*, p. 394.

[14] For Paris, see Daumard, *La Bourgeoisie parisienne*, pp. 31-58.

[15] See Labrousse, *Mouvement ouvrier*, pp. 6, 33-39.

[16] *Ibid.*, p. 174.

[17] See Peter N. Stearns, "Patterns of Industrial Strike Activity in France during the July Monarchy," *American Historical Review*, LXX (1965), 371-394.

peasants constituting about 75 percent of the population.[18] Yet the peasantry was not organized, and none of the political groups took an interest in their problems. They themselves, as Engels noted, seemed ignorant of "everything that lies outside the village."[19] At best, the peasantry seemed to share a few deep-seated attitudes, inherited from the revolutionary and imperial periods: "distrust of complete domination by the priests, fear of a revival of 'feudalism,' unlimited admiration for 'the Napoleon of the people.' "[20] In many regions, however, an agricultural revolution was creating distress and social tensions; indeed, Soboul suggests that the situation of the peasantry before 1848 resembled that on the eve of 1789.[21]

If France was still rural and agricultural, Paris ruled France, and Paris was sick. The increase in the population of the country during the first half of the nineteenth century had been steady, from twenty-seven million to thirty-five million, but that of Paris was rapid beyond all precedent. Here the population almost doubled, from 548,000 in 1801 to 1,054,000 in 1846. Most of the increase occurred during the July Monarchy, and was largely the result of immigration from the provinces. Paris was a monster city, with more than five times the population of the second city, Marseille.[22] Moreover, most of the workers flocking to Paris in search of higher earnings and better opportunities came from departments of the east and north, with revolutionary traditions of their own to mingle with those of the old quarters such as the Faubourg Saint-Antoine.

The rapid influx of immigrants was not the result, however, of the coming of the industrial revolution to Paris; rather the traditional artisan trades remained dominant, most workers

[18] For the peasantry before and during 1848, see Albert Soboul, "La Question paysanne en 1848," *La Pensée*, 18 (1948), 55-65; 19 (1948), 25-37; and 20 (1948), 48-56.

[19] Cited in Gordon Wright, *Rural Revolution in France: The Peasantry in the Twentieth Century* (Stanford, 1964), p. 10.

[20] Philippe Vigier, *La Monarchie de juillet* (Paris, 1962), p. 52.

[21] Soboul, "La Question paysanne," 18 (1948), 65.

[22] See Charles H. Pouthas, *La Population française pendant la première moitié du XIXe siècle* (Paris, 1956), pp. 143-174, and Louis Chevalier, *La Formation de la population parisienne au XIXe siècle* (Paris, 1950).

being employed in small shops, making basic commodities and luxury items for consumption within Paris itself.[23] It was the typographers who took the lead in seeking to coordinate efforts of the Paris workers' "corporations" around 1845, a prelude to the remarkable activities of 1848.[24] Although Paris lacked a true industrial proletariat, contemporaries in the 1840's increasingly used the term "proletariat" to refer to the Paris workers, in particular the poorest, those "classes laborieuses et classes dangereuses" whose physiognomy has recently been described by Louis Chevalier.[25] While Chevalier's picture of several hundred thousand men, women and children living in appalling poverty and degradation may seem exaggerated, it is clear that living conditions for the Paris workers were bad even in good times. Other recent research into the social conditions in the Twelfth (roughly the present Fifth) *arrondissement*, which Balzac called the poorest in Paris, confirms the existence of widespread misery; conditions deteriorated between 1820 and 1847, and about three-quarters of those in the area possessed at death nothing but their clothing.[26]

Paris had another sickness. In the highly centralized administrative structure of France, control of the capital since the revolution had meant control of the country, and in Paris the revolutionary tradition was most alive. The calm since 1839 and 1840 was deceptive, for successful recourse to violence was a recent memory. Marshal Gérard had worked out a plan for effective deployment of military forces against an insurrec-

[23] Chevalier, *Population parisienne*, pp. 104-109.

[24] See Paul Chauvet, *Les Ouvriers du livre en France de 1789 à la constitution de la fédération du livre* (Paris, 1964), pp. 129-135, and Rémi Gossez, "Les Ouvriers de Paris, 1848-1851. Livre premier: l'organisation ouvrière," unpublished *thèse de troisième cycle*, University of Paris, 1963, p. 2058.

[25] *Classes laborieuses et classes dangereuses à Paris pendant la première moitié du XIXe siècle* (Paris, 1958), esp. pp. 456-458. Chevalier, by combining evidence from literary and statistical sources, suggests a near-identity between the working and criminal classes. This thesis is intriguing but only partially persuasive; certainly the respect for property shown by the workers after the February revolution would seem to belie it.

[26] See Adeline Daumard, "Une Source d'histoire sociale: l'enregistrement des mutations par décès: le XIIe arrondissement de Paris en 1820 et 1847," *Revue d'histoire économique et sociale*, xxxv (1957), 52-78.

tion, but it depended upon the cooperation of the National Guard, and many guardsmen, though bourgeois, were growing increasingly disgruntled over their seemingly permanent exclusion from the *pays légal.*

The plight of the working classes drew increasing attention from writers during the 1840's. It was evoked in novels by Eugène Sue, whose *Mystères de Paris* appeared in 1842, by Victor Hugo, who began writing *Les Misérables* at about the same time, by George Sand, and many others. The poet Lamartine, whose politics evolved from royalism to liberalism and was democratic by 1848, also was one of the earliest politicians of the July Monarchy to take an interest in the social question. He was one of the first writers to use the new word "socialism" (although he identified it with charity),[27] and in 1834 he spoke of organizing a "parti social." During his years in the Chamber of Deputies, despite his political aloofness, Lamartine was an eloquent champion of popular causes.

But beyond his speech-making and the interest in social questions emanating from the republicans, the July Monarchy also witnessed a brilliant efflorescence of socialist thought, albeit of a pre-Marxian and largely utopian variety. Given the disillusion following the "trois glorieuses," the obvious and deepening gulf between the ruling elites and the suffering poor, the Romantic idealization of "le peuple," and the failure of the government to take cognizance of social distress, this was not surprising. In the face of problems attending the beginnings of industrialization and of more traditional social ills exacerbated by population growth and migration to the cities, the July Monarchy was content to follow its laissez-faire inclination to do nothing. The only piece of social legislation adopted, and over considerable opposition, was the law of 1841 prohibiting the employment of children under eight in factories, and limiting the workday for older children, a law that was never adequately enforced.

The socialist thinkers issued morally outraged criticisms of the social and economic system that produced such misery, and elaborated brilliant if often unrealistic remedies, usually

[27] David O. Evans, *Social Romanticism in France, 1830-1848* (Oxford, 1951), p. 81.

substituting some kind of collectivized economic and social organization for individualism and competitive capitalism. Adherents of the early Saint-Simonian school soon dispersed, though some would come to power in the Second Republic and Second Empire. Fourierism remained a more coherent movement under the leadership of Considérant, who during the 1840's popularized the master's ideas on "le droit au travail" and on the virtues of association. Another socialist school, that of Etienne Cabet, whose *Voyage en Icarie* appeared in 1840, was the only one to win much support from the working classes.[28] Cabet had developed his communitarian theories after an early association with the republican movement.

Others who elaborated their own doctrines while remaining active among the republicans were Philippe Buchez, the co-editor of the voluminous *Histoire parlementaire de la Révolution française*, who developed a kind of Christian socialism based on producers' cooperatives, and Louis Blanc. The latter won attention for his *Histoire de dix ans*, and above all for his *Organisation du travail*, which popularized a phrase already current. Blanc also advocated producers' cooperatives, and in addition envisaged a larger role for the state than did most of the other socialists, in particular to subsidize the "ateliers sociaux."[29] Proudhon also began writing under the July Monarchy, his *Qu'est-ce que la propriété?* appearing in 1840, but his doctrine then was essentially critical. French socialism before 1848 was not a coherent doctrine, but consisted of a number of quite diverse competing ones. It remained bourgeois from the point of view of the social origins of all its exponents except Proudhon, and had little impact on the working-class movement,[30] although, as we have seen, it did influence the republicans to some extent.

Beyond the profusion of social criticism, there was a growing mood of dissatisfaction with the July Monarchy. The crude materialism of the possessing classes, the interest-based petty politics of the Chamber of Deputies, the hypocrisy of the *juste*

28 Weill, *Parti républicain*, p. 161.

29 Labrousse, *Mouvement ouvrier*, p. 151. See also Loubère, *Louis Blanc*, pp. 31-48.

30 Labrousse, *Mouvement ouvrier*, pp. 143-164.

milieu were scornfully depicted in the flourishing opposition press, in the cartoons of Daumier, in the novels of Stendhal and Balzac. The unholy union between political institutions and private interests was apparent, and it is significant that the same image occurred to both Marx and de Tocqueville. For Marx, "The July Monarchy was nothing other than a joint stock company for the exploitation of French national wealth, the dividends of which were divided amongst ministers, Chambers, 240,000 voters and their adherents."[31] And de Tocqueville mused, "Posterity . . . will never, perhaps, know to what extent the government of that day, towards its close, assumed the ways of an industrial enterprise, which conducts all its transactions with a view to the profits accruing to the shareholders."[32]

Dissatisfaction was also reflected in the mystique of revolution which informed so much of the literature, art and historical writing of the time. The July Monarchy could neither persuade men that it did indeed represent the revolution, nor could it offer a very attractive alternative principle of loyalty or authority. By opposing "an ideal to a tawdry reality," in the words of Leo Gershoy, the mystique of revolution "helped undermine active acquiescence in Louis Philippe's monarchy," and the histories that Lamartine, Louis Blanc, and Michelet published in 1847 contributed to this mood.[33] Among the sources of discontent in the late July Monarchy also must be included the generally pacific and inglorious foreign policy, and such events in the late 1840's as that involving Pritchard in Tahiti, followed by the affair of the Spanish marriages and Guizot's increasing rapprochement with Metternich in 1847.

Nevertheless, despite the discontent and the inherent weaknesses in government and society, there was no overtly revolutionary movement of any strength. What brought down the regime and released social forces previously inert or suppressed was insurrectionary action in Paris resulting from the conjunction of a political and an economic crisis. Although it

[31] *Class Struggles in France*, p. 36.

[32] *Recollections*, p. 3. Cf. Tudesq, *Les Grands notables*, I, pp. 369-376.

[33] "Three French Historians and the Revolution of 1848," *Journal of the History of Ideas*, XII (1951), 131-146.

is not here suggested that revolution must inevitably result from such a combination, clearly that of 1848 did.[34]

The French economy under the July Monarchy had serious flaws. Although the period witnessed the beginnings of an industrial revolution, it is perhaps not surprising that this "bourgeois monarchy" dominated by rural magnates should be but mildly hospitable to business. The ruling *notables* maintained the system of protection of both agricultural and industrial products at rates which probably retarded economic growth; industry tended to remain family-centered and cautious, and a climate of hostility toward aggressive enterprise inhibited new ventures, as did the outmoded banking structure.[35] However, the government supported canal and road-building projects, and though it discouraged for a time the construction of a railway system, a law finally adopted in 1842 provided for a mixed scheme of state aid for construction plus favorable concessions to private companies. For a few years, France experienced a wave of speculative "railroad mania," but the economic crisis starting in 1846 ruined many companies, and although 1,921 kilometers of rail had been laid by 1848, France was still far behind Great Britain and even Prussia, which had more than 3,000 kilometers.

The economic crisis of the mid-century, European-wide in scope, began in 1846 with poor grain and potato harvests. Commercial, industrial and financial crises followed, resulting in widespread unemployment, near-famine conditions in some regions, business failures and a large budgetary deficit. In

[34] Some of the most important contributions to current emphasis on the social and economic context of the revolution have been made by Ernest Labrousse. See in particular his "1848—1830—1789: Comment naissent les révolutions," in *Actes du Congrès historique du centenaire de la révolution de 1848* (Paris, 1948), pp. 1-20, and the collection of articles that he edited, *Aspects de la crise et de la dépression de l'économie française au milieu du XIXe siècle* (Paris, 1956). For a criticism of these views, suggesting the endemic nature of economic recession during the July Monarchy, see Douglas Johnson, *Guizot: Aspects of French History, 1787-1874* (London, 1963), pp. 230-240.

[35] See Bertrand Gille, *La Banque et le crédit en France de 1815 à 1848* (Paris, 1959), and also the illuminating discussions in Charles P. Kindleberger, *Economic Growth in France and Britain, 1851-1950* (Cambridge, Mass., 1964).

Paris, commerce was stricken more severely than in other cities, but the lower classes suffered most critically.[36] Although the harvest of 1847 was good and the crisis in other sectors also seemed to be terminating by the close of the year, social distress remained serious. Worsened by seasonal layoffs, unemployment continued on a large scale, wages had declined, and food prices were still high, at a time when savings were depleted by the long crisis. There were scattered peasant disturbances and even some bread riots in Paris.

Opposition spokesmen were quick to blame the government for the economic crisis, but their attention in 1847 was fixed on the more familiar issues of electoral and parliamentary reform. Although a previous reform movement had failed, there was a growing mood of frustration with the general immobility of the Soult-Guizot government and increasing demands for an end to the apparent corruption at the base of its majorities. The defeat of the opposition parties in the elections of 1846 led them to embark the following year on the banquet campaign which was to culminate, to their astonishment, in revolution.

When reform bills were rejected by Guizot's majority, the opposition groups laid plans for a campaign to publicize the issues through a series of huge public banquets.[37] Although Thiers gave oblique support, the leadership was taken by the republicans and by the dynastic left. The campaign was in no sense revolutionary; the republicans were hoping at most for a broadening of the suffrage that might eventually lead to a democratization of the regime. During the campaign, additional fuel for the charges of "corruption" was given by several well-publicized scandals: the Teste-Cubières affair, the murder involving the Duke de Choiseul-Praslin, and finally,

[36] A. J. Tudesq, "La Crise de 1847, vue par les milieux d'affaires parisiennes," *Aspects de la crise*, p. 27.

[37] The most recent works on the campaign are by John J. Baughman. See his article, "The French Banquet Campaign of 1847-48," *Journal of Modern History*, XXXI (1959), 1-15, and also his unpublished doctoral dissertation, "The Political Banquet Campaign in France, 1847-1848," University of Michigan, 1953. See also Jean Vidalenc, "A propos de la campagne des banquets (1847-1848)," *Actes du quatre-vingt-unième congrès national des sociétés savantes* (Paris, 1956), pp. 679-689.

in January 1848, "l'affaire Petit," which touched Guizot himself.

In addition to parliamentary and electoral reform, the issue of social reform also entered the campaign; indeed, a toast to the ameliorating of the conditions of the working class was offered at the very first banquet, at Château Rouge in Paris in July.[38] The *La Réforme* faction at first was contemptuous of the campaign, but in November joined it, while seeking to remain aloof from the chief organizers. Now toasts and speeches of a vaguely social nature became more common (toasts on this issue were offered at more than half the fifty-nine banquets), but the campaign still remained limited in appeal, being addressed almost exclusively to the *pays légal.* Not even the radical republicans either sought or obtained mass support during the campaign.[39] Despite the economic depression and the widespread evidence of lower class suffering and despite the rhetoric of the banquets, the republicans, whether of the majority or radical factions, remained essentially what they had been since 1835—advocates of peaceful and gradual reform rather than revolutionary activists.

When the banquet campaign seemed at an end in December 1847, the republicans prepared for the battle of words and votes in the Chamber of Deputies, which reconvened December 27. After having tolerated the entire campaign in silence the king himself brought up the reform issue immediately by denouncing in his speech from the throne the "hostile or blind passions" expressed in the campaign.[40] The opposition angrily bent their efforts toward removing Guizot, but the adoption of the address by a large majority on February 12, 1848, revealed the bankruptcy of the campaign of the banquets.

THE FEBRUARY REVOLUTION

The events of February 22 to 24 are too well-known to need recounting here, but the role of the republican leadership re-

[38] Baughman, "French Banquet Campaign," p. 3.

[39] Baughman, "Political Banquet Campaign," pp. 215, 222-232.

[40] Baughman suggests, in "French Banquet Campaign," pp. 12-13, that the change in policy resulted from the fear of a new type of banquet, "revolutionary and communistic," such as that planned at Limoges on January 2.

quires some clarification.[41] The decision to hold a banquet in the working-class Twelfth *arrondissement* of Paris did not emanate from either wing of the republican party, but from officers of the National Guard in that area. It was governmental prohibition of the banquet that stirred the republican and other opposition deputies into action, but they so feared arousing popular agitation that they insisted on shifting the banquet to the bourgeois First *arrondissement*, and even made an agreement with the government to disperse peacefully upon demand of the police, leaving the issue of freedom of assembly to be settled in the courts.

The new banquet had created an unusual amount of interest, however, and in an atmosphere of growing tension in Paris, republican leaders began to consider the possibility that the banquet might lead to an insurrection. A few republicans met secretly before February 21 in the home of Michel Goudchaux; although, true to their policy of legality, they did not actually plan an uprising, they went so far as to discuss the composition of a provisional government. Marie agreed to become a member, Louis Blanc and Ledru-Rollin were rejected, and the list seems to have been the basis of the one drawn up on February 24 at the offices of *Le National*.[42] But Marie later insisted, "that no one then wanted a revolution, that there was no preparation in this sense. In a word, no conspiracy. Wishes, desires, hopes perhaps, nothing more."[43]

A more influential action was taken by Armand Marrast, editor of *Le National*, who drew up a manifesto designed to provoke a mass, albeit peaceful, demonstration to precede the

[41] The best monograph on the February revolution is still Albert Crémieux, *La Révolution de février, étude critique sur les journées des 21, 22, 23, et 24 février 1848* (Paris, 1912). See also Louis Girard's recent *Etude comparée des mouvements révolutionnaires en France en 1830, 1848 et 1870-71 (1830-1848)*, "Les Cours de Sorbonne" (Paris, n.d.), and Fasel, "The French Moderate Republicans," pp. 141-196.

[42] See the testimony of Goudchaux in *Rapport de la commission d'enquête sur l'insurrection qui a éclaté dans la journée du 23 juin et sur les événements du 15 mai* (Paris, 1848), I, p. 288; Aimé Cherest, *La Vie et les oeuvres de A.-T. Marie* (Paris, 1873), pp. 94-95, and Crémieux, *La Révolution de février*, pp. 367-368.

[43] Cherest, *Marie*, p. 94.

banquet. This "Reformist manifesto" appeared on February 21 not only in *Le National*, but also in *La Réforme* and in liberal opposition papers such as *Le Siècle* and *Le Constitutionnel.* It appealed to students and to National Guardsmen to gather along with the banqueteers at La Madeleine, and to march via the Place de la Concorde to the banquet site off the Champs-Elysées. *La Réforme*, which previously had stood aloof, now came out in favor of the demonstration, announcing, "The Revolution and Counter-Revolution are face to face. On one side, law, on the other, arbitrary government. . . . We will join the demonstration and summon there all our friends."[44]

The call for a demonstration was the first time, except for a minor affair in Limoges, that the reform campaign had threatened to harness mass discontents, and it was accompanied by a thinly veiled usurpation of the government's powers to call up the National Guard. The government replied with a new prohibition, and the opposition deputies, meeting on the evening of February 21 at the home of Barrot, decided not to attend the banquet. With the exception of Marrast and Marie, most of the republicans voted with the majority of eighty to seventeen on this issue. Thinking the government to be in a strong position, they were afraid that the demonstration might turn into a massacre.[45]

The attitude of the radicals of *La Réforme* was little different. At a meeting in the offices of the newspaper, a few, such as Lagrange and Caussidière, favored fomenting an insurrection, but Ledru-Rollin opposed this, fearing a massacre. Louis Blanc declared, "You may decide on insurrection if you wish, but if you take this decision, I will go home, put on mourning clothes, and weep for the ruin of democracy."[46] The radical group decided to try to call off the demonstration and to await further developments. Much the same pessimistic hesitation

[44] *La Réforme*, 21 February 1848, p. 1. Hereafter citations to newspapers will be to p. 1 unless otherwise indicated.

[45] See Crémieux, *La Révolution de février*, p. 73, for a discussion of Marrast's views, about which there has been some disagreement.

[46] Crémieux, *La Révolution de février*, p. 86. Cf. d'Alton-Shée, *Souvenirs de 1847 et de 1848*, pp. 224-226.

was expressed by the radical regiments of the National Guard and by the secret societies, but some Fourierist socialists and a group of students from the Twelfth *arrondissement* were determined to demonstrate.[47]

The decision of the republicans to abandon the demonstration and the banquet was made too late to be disseminated widely, and on the morning of February 22 Parisians began to gather in large numbers, despite a cold rain, at La Madeleine. Lacking leadership, the crowds seemed at first to consist mostly of onlookers, many of them bourgeois, but they were galvanized by a group of about two hundred students who marched from the Panthéon across the Pont-Neuf and appeared singing "The Chorus of the Girondins." The demonstrators moved to the Place de la Concorde, where they were joined increasingly by workers. Some crossed over the bridge and demonstrated in front of the Chamber of Deputies in the Palais Bourbon. After some clashes with the Municipal Guards and troops, the crowds dispersed around 3 P.M. and barricades began to go up in many quarters. The National Guard was called out, but few responded. This should have been taken as an ominous sign, but as yet neither the king nor his advisers were worried. The Minister of the Interior calmly held a small dinner party that evening. "What a charming riot," said his daughter-in-law of the day's events. "I certainly hope the spectacle resumes tomorrow."[48]

Resume the next day it did, a spontaneous and popular insurrection now beyond the inspiration or control of the republicans. Although the revolution had begun with demonstrations in the center and west of Paris, it was now developing mostly in the working-class east, where barricades were erected in large numbers. Once again the National Guard was called out. This time the guardsmen appeared, but most of the regiments, even those from the most bourgeois quarters, were infected with the demand for reform. "A bas Guizot!" they cried, "Vive la Réforme!" The king was at last alarmed, and by afternoon agreed to surrender Guizot. The news

[47] Crémieux, *La Révolution de février*, pp. 75-85, 93-94.
[48] Fasel, "The French Moderate Republicans," p. 166n.

cheered some of the insurgents, but those in the east, fearing a ruse, remained suspiciously in arms.

Most of the republicans were still uncertain about what to do. Some thought the dismissal of Guizot was all that could be accomplished for the present; Carnot even went among the insurgents to try to convince them that they should put up their arms now that they had won. On the evening of February 23, Marie, dining with a few friends who asked if a republic would result, replied, "I love it too much to wish that it be born prematurely."[49] Some republicans, however, made a few feeble efforts to provide leadership. One group, a self-styled Democratic Electoral Committee, including men as diverse as the banker Goudchaux and the socialist Louis Blanc, drew up during the same evening a manifesto which, far from demanding a republic or even abdication and a regency, merely called for the democratization of the National Guard, the dissolution of the Municipal Guards, and a prohibition on the use of the army to suppress civil disorders.[50]

But the crowds now began to demand guidance from the republicans. Around 9 P.M. on February 23, a large group of demonstrators appeared in front of the offices of *Le National*, on the Rue Lepelletier, near the Boulevard des Capucines. In a brief but fiery speech, Marrast urged them to remain armed until they had compelled the indictment of the Guizot ministry, the dissolution of the Municipal Guards, and the acceptance of electoral and parliamentary reform.[51] Marrast clearly had dropped his previous opposition to the use of violence and was hoping now to force the abdication of the king and the establishment of a regency together with a Barrot-Thiers ministry.[52] Although there was still no demand from the crowds for a republic, this was the strongest position yet taken by any of the republican leaders. But within half an hour even Marrast was overwhelmed by the "massacre" of the Boulevard des Capucines.

[49] Cherest, *Marie*, pp. 97-98.

[50] It was published in *Le National* on February 24, by which time demands for the republic were beginning to issue from the crowds. It is also reprinted in Crémieux, *La Révolution de février*, pp. 177-179.

[51] Crémieux, *La Révolution de février*, pp. 184-185.

[52] Fasel, "The French Moderate Republicans," p. 168.

The massacre involved the same column of demonstrators that Marrast had addressed. After leaving the offices of *Le National*, they proceeded down the Boulevard des Capucines, but were stopped by troops in front of the official residence of Guizot, the Ministry of Foreign Affairs. There the apparently accidental discharge of a musket produced panic among the troops, who fired wildly and indiscriminately, occasionally even at each other, but mostly into the crowd of demonstrators. In the end, some fifty-two lay dead, and at least seventy-four others were wounded.[53]

The insurrection, which had shown signs of weakening after the fall of Guizot, was instantly reanimated by this incident. Infuriated demonstrators piled sixteen corpses on a wagon which they drew in a torch-lit procession through the city, spreading the information that the massacre had been deliberate. More barricades went up during the night, and the National Guard, hesitant after the fall of Guizot, now turned definitely against the king.[54] During the night also, the king made two significant decisions. First, he indicated his determination to crush the insurrection by giving the supreme command of the armed forces to General Bugeaud, the tough conqueror of Algeria and a staunch conservative, reputed (erroneously) to have carried out the "massacre of the Rue Transnonain" in 1834. Second, with Molé unable to form a ministry, he called on Thiers, who persuaded him that Barrot also must be included. The political concession to the left was more than counterbalanced by the military shift to the right; the insurgents, and even Thiers, remained unconvinced of the sincerity of the king.

By the time Bugeaud commenced his assault around 5:30 A.M. on February 24, the streets of Paris, from the working-class east to the bourgeois west, were clogged with barricades. Bugeaud sent out three columns from the Place du Carrousel, but in the face of the immensity of the insurrection and lacking the support of the National Guard, the troops were demoralized and reluctant to fire on the populace. By 8 A.M.,

[53] Crémieux, *La Révolution de février*, pp. 191-196.
[54] *Ibid.*, p. 207.

Bugeaud felt compelled to order a humiliating retreat, during which many of the troops were disarmed.[55]

Meanwhile, on this same morning of February 24, the republicans at last began to seek to guide events, in particular through discussions in the offices of *Le National* and *La Réforme.* By shortly after 9 A.M., Marrast was rejecting the Thiers-Barrot ministry as insufficient, and demanding the abdication of the king by noon.[56] At the offices of *La Réforme,* Proudhon used his old skill as a typographer to draw up a placard declaring: "Citizens, Louis-Philippe assassinates you as did Charles X; let him join Charles X."[57] Shortly after 11:30 A.M., a group of republicans and demonstrators gathered in the offices of *Le National* and decided to name a provisional government, which at first was referred to obliquely as a *Comité de direction.* After an agitated discussion, in the course of which Louis Blanc pleaded in vain for his own inclusion, the group drew up a list of six names, copies of which were tossed to crowds of insurgents outside. It was the first of several lists from which a provisional government was to be drawn. It reflected primarily the point of view of *Le National,* comprising four well-known republicans, Marrast, Marie, Garnier-Pagès and François Arago, the independent left-wing poet Lamartine, and Odilon Barrot. Protests arose from the crowd over the inclusion of Barrot and the exclusion of Ledru-Rollin, and soon new lists appeared.[58]

Around 11 A.M. the king made a final effort to rally support by reviewing some troop and National Guard regiments in the Tuileries grounds, but the hostile cries of "Vive la Réforme!" shattered his resolution. He agreed to remove Bugeaud, and to replace Thiers with Barrot, but almost immedi-

[55] For a recent discussion of these events, in which they are compared with the March events in Vienna and Berlin, see William L. Langer, "The Pattern of Urban Revolution in 1848," in *French Society and Culture Since the Old Regime*, eds. Evelyn M. Acomb and Marvin L. Brown, Jr., (New York, 1966), pp. 89-118.

[56] Crémieux, *La Révolution de février*, p. 369. Cf. Weill, *Parti républicain*, p. 207.

[57] *Ibid.*

[58] Crémieux, *La Révolution de février*, pp. 369-372.

ately afterwards, at a few minutes past noon, with the sound of surging crowds in his ears, the old king abdicated in favor of his grandson, the nine-year-old Count of Paris.

By mid-day of February 24, demands for "La République" began to supplant those for "La Réforme" among the insurgents. One last effort to save the monarchy was made at the emergency session of the Chamber of Deputies which began at 12:30 P.M., when Louis Philippe was already in ignominious flight. Delegates from the offices of *Le National* arrived to inform Marie and other deputies of the nomination of a provisional government. Marrast and several other republicans sought the support of Lamartine. "You know what we are," said Marrast, "and what we want. We are republicans, and it is the republic that we want." He went on to say that since the immediate proclamation of the republic might lead to civil war, he and his colleagues would be willing to accept the regency temporarily, with Lamartine as premier. The poet astonished Marrast by arguing that not even a regency was possible in view of events and by coming out in favor of a provisional government.[59] Around 1:30 P.M., the Duchesse d'Orléans entered the Chamber, accompanied by her two young sons; ominously, a few insurgents entered at the same time.[60] In the agitated session that followed, the Chamber loudly applauded the proclamation of the regency of the duchess, but Marie took the floor and demanded instead the immediate creation of a provisional government.[61] Disordered debate was interrupted when noisy crowds flooded the Chamber. Ledru-Rollin and Lamartine spoke in favor of a provisional government, and when more insurgents entered the Chamber, most of the deputies fled, together with the duchess.

With insurgents in the seats of the departed deputies, Dupont de l'Eure and Ledru-Rollin read out names for the proposed provisional government, and shouted demands for the

[59] For somewhat variant versions of this episode, see Louis Antoine Garnier-Pagès, *Histoire de la révolution de 1848* (Paris, 1861-72), II, pp. 196-198, and Alphonse de Lamartine, *Histoire de la révolution de 1848* (Paris, 1849), I, pp. 160-171. Cf. Henri Guillemin, *La Tragédie de quarante-huit* (Paris, 1948), pp. 32-36.

[60] Crémieux, *La Révolution de février*, p. 379.

[61] *Ibid.*, p. 385.

proclamation of the republic. The list approved by acclamation consisted of Dupont de l'Eure, Arago, Lamartine, Ledru-Rollin, Garnier-Pagès, Marie, and one monarchist, Crémieux. All then departed for the Hôtel de Ville. At the same time, a group of republicans sought to win Barrot's support for the new government, but he refused, saying, "What is happening goes beyond all my desires, all my expectations. I cannot follow you; I would be only an obstacle for you."[62] Barrot then advised the Duchesse d'Orléans to flee Paris, but to remain in readiness to profit from the dissensions which undoubtedly would break out among the republicans.[63] Thus did revolution split the reform coalition.

While these dramatic events went on in the Chamber of Deputies, other groups of insurgents and republicans, reflecting more strongly the opinions of the radicals of *La Réforme*, chose a rival provisional government. After the first list had been drawn up at the offices of *Le National*, Martin de Strasbourg, who for some weeks had been trying to reconcile the republican factions, had accompanied Louis Blanc to the offices of *La Réforme*, in hopes of winning support for the list.[64] Although even Louis Blanc spoke in favor of Barrot's inclusion, as a necessary concession to the National Guard, the crowds rejected the name but accepted all the others on the list of *Le National*, to which they added Ledru-Rollin, Louis Blanc, Flocon and a worker named Alexandre Martin and called Albert. The group also designated Caussidière to assume direction of the Prefecture of Police, and Etienne Arago, brother of the astronomer, to take over the central Post Office.[65]

At the Hôtel de Ville during the afternoon of February 24, there were several confused and competing movements aimed at establishing a revolutionary government. After the failure of an attempt to create a new Commune, a group of insurgents proclaimed Garnier-Pagès mayor of Paris.[66] Around 5 P.M., the men designated in the Chamber began to arrive. Encumbered by the crowds, they were in the process of organizing a government when, around 8 P.M., the journalists chosen at the offices of *La Réforme*—Marrast, Flocon and Louis Blanc—

[62] *Ibid.*, p. 415. [63] *Ibid.*, p. 416. [64] *Ibid.*, p. 421.
[65] *Ibid.*, pp. 422-424. [66] *Ibid.*, p. 435.

arrived and sought to join the Provisional Government. The deputies chosen in the Chamber received them coolly, but realizing that they too had been chosen by insurgents and were strongly supported by those still milling about the halls of the Hôtel de Ville, finally agreed to accept them, along with the absent Albert, as "secretaries"; soon thereafter, however, the distinction was abandoned, and all were functioning as full members of the government.[67]

The first problem facing the new rulers of France was whether or not to proclaim the republic. Lamartine and others argued that the decision must be that of France, through a popularly elected assembly. Louis Blanc, supported by Ledru-Rollin and Flocon, argued for immediate proclamation to meet the demands of the insurgents. After confused debate and attempts at compromise, the Provisional Government shortly before midnight agreed to declare that they desired the republic, subject to ratification by a National Assembly. But the qualification was ignored by the insurgents; two workers had already anticipated the decision by unfurling through a window of the Hôtel de Ville a makeshift flag announcing in large charcoal letters: "La République une et indivisible est proclamée en France."[68]

THE REPUBLICAN SPRING

Thus, the revolutionary crowds of Paris had, in three confused days, brought down the July Monarchy and created a second republic in France. Eight of the eleven men whom they thrust into power had long been republicans, and the others had been close to the party in different ways. The eighty-one-year-old Dupont de l'Eure had sat in the Council of Five Hundred, and had been an elder statesman of republicanism since the 1830's. He was chosen president of the Provisional Government, but was too infirm to play an active role. Other veteran republicans were François Arago, the distinguished astronomer, Alexandre Marie, Armand Marrast, Louis Antoine Garnier-Pagès, Ferdinand Flocon, Louis Blanc and Ledru-Rollin.

[67] *Ibid.*, p. 452.
[68] *Ibid.*, p. 464.

Albert had been a member of a vaguely republican secret society.

Lamartine had followed a haughtily independent political career, but on February 24 had come out for the republic even before most of the republicans. He charmed the insurgents many times with his oratory, and his aristocratic origins and experience made him acceptable to the *notables*; he soon became the most prominent member of the government.[69] The only member of the government who was obviously not a republican was Albert Crémieux, who had been associated with the dynastic left; but he had spoken out in favor of a provisional government in the Chamber on February 24, and when Ledru-Rollin read out his name, the crowds had accepted him.

Most members of the government also assumed ministerial portfolios, the most significant assignments being Lamartine to Foreign Affairs and Ledru-Rollin to Interior. Hippolyte Carnot became Minister of Education, Michel Goudchaux, Minister of Finance, and Eugène Bethmont, Minister of Agriculture and Commerce. For the Ministry of War, the group first thought of General Eugène Cavaignac, but on deciding that it was necessary to choose a general already in Paris appointed Cavaignac governor-general of Algeria. The Ministry of War was offered to Lamoricière and to Bedeau, but on their refusal it went to a General Subérvie, seventy-two-year-old veteran of the armies of the Convention. In the provinces, the prefects were replaced by new "commissaires," most of whom were republicans, although a few liberal Orleanists were also appointed.

The Provisional Government from the beginning was weak and divided, and it is astonishing that it was able to hold together unchanged during more than two months of agitation in Paris and revolutionary upheaval in Europe. Although the original division had been between the deputies and the journalists, within a few days a different grouping emerged, reflecting largely the two major prerevolutionary factions. The

[69] For a good recent discussion of Lamartine's role, see Gordon Wright, "A Poet in Politics: Lamartine and the Revolution of 1848," *History Today*, VIII (1958), 616-627.

men of *Le National,* supported now by Lamartine and Crémieux, formed a majority of seven, as against a radical wing consisting of Ledru-Rollin, Flocon, Louis Blanc and Albert. In the circumstances of successful revolution, with the entire political spectrum shifted drastically leftward, the governmental majority could now justly be called moderate republican, but only in relation to the left in the government and to the still more radical attitudes that began to be expressed in Paris following the reappearance of released prisoners such as Barbès and Blanqui, and the rapid efflorescence of clubs.

Yet it is a seriously misleading oversimplification to divide the Provisional Government—and the men of 1848 in general—into two distinct and opposing factions, as did, for example, Donald McKay: "the 'moderates,' who favored a political revolution pure and simple; and the radical republicans, who welcomed a political revolution as the vestibule to a profound reorganization of society."[70] Some of the reasons why such a dichotomy is inaccurate have already been suggested. Certainly the moderate republicans favored something more than a purely "political" revolution, and many of those Frenchmen who presently began to call themselves "moderates" were hostile to the political regime as well as to social reorganization. As for the radicals, Flocon was often with the majority, and Ledru-Rollin was no more a socialist than was Armand Marrast. Louis Blanc and perhaps Albert were the only members of the Provisional Government who favored a "profound" reorganization of society, and yet Louis Blanc shared most of the moderates' political views and even to a large extent their apprehension about the revolutionary crowds of Paris. Moreover, Lamartine's attitude was always idiosyncratic, and Ledru-Rollin occupied a kind of intermediate position. In sum,

[70] *The National Workshops: A Study in the French Revolution of 1848* (Cambridge, Mass., 1933), p. 3. This dichotomy has been common in the historiography of 1848 in France. See, e.g., the influential Charles Seignobos, *La Révolution de 1848—Le second empire (1848-1859),* "Histoire de France contemporaine," ed. Ernest Lavisse (Paris, 1921), VI, pp. 3-4. It is sometimes incorporated into a class analysis of the revolution, the moderates representing the bourgeoisie and the radicals representing the workers. See, e.g., Ponteil, *1848,* pp. 64, 101, 105-106.

then, although the bipartite division within the Provisional Government had some significance, neither group was purely political or purely socialist in its aims.

If the proclamation of the republic on February 24 was political in the change of regimes, it soon became apparent that this revolution, unlike that of 1830, had a marked social character. The attitude of the bourgeois National Guard had been crucial, but by the end the insurrection had assumed a popular, working-class aspect. Tocqueville was struck by the "uniquely and exclusively popular character of the revolution . . . the omnipotence it had given to the people properly so-called—that is to say, the classes who work with their hands." The great theorist of democracy compared the emotions of the possessing classes of Paris with "that which the civilized cities of the Roman Empire must have experienced when they suddenly found themselves in the power of the Goths and Vandals."[71] Conscious of their power, the worker-insurgents remained for a time in arms, and soon began to exert pressures of various kinds on the government and to demand "la République démocratique et sociale." Yet the revolution had been accomplished in the name of simply "la République," and that slogan had appeared only on the last day. Moreover, the men whom the insurgents had put into power were all bourgeois except for the ineffectual Albert, and only one, Louis Blanc, was a socialist.

The men of the Provisional Government were partisans of social reform, but according to their republican creed they gave first priority to the awesome task of introducing republican institutions and political democracy to France. The government adopted as its own the hallowed revolutionary trinity, Liberty, Equality, and Fraternity; abolished royalty in all its forms, as well as titles of nobility; proclaimed the end of the death penalty for political offenses (to assuage fears of a new Terror); opened the National Guard to all adult citizens; and decreed universal and direct manhood suffrage for elections to a National Assembly to be held April 9.

At the same time the Provisional Government responded to some of the demands of the revolutionary crowds. On the

[71] *Recollections*, pp. 73-75.

morning of February 25, some armed workmen had interrupted a session of the new government to demand "the organization of labor, the right to work guaranteed," and Louis Blanc hastily drew up a decree whereby the government implicitly endorsed "le droit au travail."[72] The majority accepted this socialist principle only reluctantly, but in succeeding days they sought to give substance to the decree by the creation of "National Workshops" for the unemployed and of a special *Commission du gouvernement pour les travailleurs*, presided over by Louis Blanc and Albert. Although the origin of this "Luxembourg Commission" was perhaps in part a political maneuver to divert Blanc and his socialist supporters into "innocuous paths," Blanc himself took it seriously, and the closest student of the Paris workers, Rémi Gossez, regards the creation of the Luxembourg Commission as the decisive step in fostering workers' organizations in 1848.[73] The Provisional Government, partly through the oratory of Lamartine, was able to resist demands that the red flag replace the tricolor, but bowed to crowd pressure on March 2 to abolish an exploitative labor practice called "marchandage," and to set a maximum working day of ten hours in Paris and eleven in the provinces. To help some of the poor in distress, the government also decreed that articles worth 10 francs or less should be returned free of charge from the *Monts de Piété*, or state pawnshops.

Meanwhile, France was absorbing the news of the revolution. In many towns where there were strong republican factions, the republic was proclaimed amid rejoicing, and quiet municipal revolutions were carried out. But even where the republicans were weak, the news was received calmly; once more France accepted a revolution made by Paris, and no one rose to defend the fallen monarchy; the bureaucracy, the army hierarchy, and the powerful *notables* meekly accepted the republic. Many Legitimists exulted in the demise of the false king; the clergy and the "Catholic party," who had had

[72] F. Henry, "Le Droit au travail," in *1848, Révolution créatrice* (Paris, 1948), p. 44. Cf. Loubère, *Louis Blanc*, pp. 74-75.

[73] Loubère, *Louis Blanc*, pp. 78-81; Gossez, "Les Ouvriers de Paris," pp. 26-38; Chauvet, *Les Ouvriers du livre*, p. 186.

their difficulties with Louis Philippe, welcomed the republic apprehensively but hopefully. When the mania for planting trees of liberty spread across the land, priests were there to bless and to pray.[74] The calm acceptance of the revolution in the provinces revealed more the moral bankruptcy of the July Monarchy than enthusiasm for the republic. The moderate attitude of the Provisional Government persuaded Frenchmen that no new Terror was at hand, and Lamartine's early announcement of a pacific foreign policy also had a soothing effect, although the shock waves of revolution were already being felt throughout Europe.

In France, beneath the demeanor of calm acceptance, the world of the *notables* was also profoundly shocked by the February revolution.[75] Physical fear for lives and property soon dissipated, but a deep current of "social fear" remained. Many *notables* quietly fled Paris, and in the country at large the anxiety of the *notables* was expressed by what Tudesq has called the "sacrifice of convictions." Monarchists of both varieties hastened to rally publicly to the new regime. As a republican *commissaire* wrote from Limoges on March 4: "All the philippists proclaim themselves republicans today. It must be recognized, however, that the rich classes have in general little sympathy for this new form of government, which alarms them, and it is evident to me that fear, the impossibility of resistance, and the need to give support to the Provisional Government in the interest of order and tranquillity, have created this sudden manifestation of an artificial unanimity." To avoid seeming hostile to the regime, *notables* participated in republican demonstrations, eulogized workers and even wore emblems of social revolution; one worker at Lyon observed that the largest red cockades were worn by royalists.[76] As

[74] R. Aubert, *Le Pontificat de Pie IX (1846-1878)*, (Paris, 1952), pp. 41-44. But the revolution also stimulated in some regions a wave of popular anticlericalism. See C. Marcilhacy, "Les Caractères de la crise sociale et politique de 1846 à 1852 dans le département du Loiret," *Revue d'histoire moderne et contemporaine*, VI (1959), 18-20.

[75] Most of this discussion is based on Tudesq, *Les Grands notables*, II, pp. 989-1072.

[76] *Ibid.*, pp. 1012, 1014.

Marx put it, "All the royalists were transformed into republicans and all the millionaires of Paris into workers."[77]

The revolution also shocked the slowly recovering economy into a new and deeper depression, an "economic paralysis without precedent," according to Ernest Labrousse.[78] Values on the Paris Bourse plunged, there was a run on the banks, commerce and industry stagnated, prices fell, unemployment spread. Panic in the business community belied the seeming enthusiasm for the republic. In Paris and some other regions, labor unrest exploded into violence of a "Luddite" nature, including destruction of some newly constructed railroad lines, and peasant discontent continued to boil over in riots and attacks on forestry officials.

Social unrest was most pronounced in Paris, where the atmosphere still crackled with revolution. The secret societies emerged as clubs, and hundreds of others sprang up, reflecting mostly but not exclusively a more radical and socialist outlook than that of the Provisional Government. Those organized by Barbès and Blanqui, now bitter rivals, were the most influential, but in many clubs and newspapers, radical agitators offered competing interpretations of "la République démocratique et sociale," and sometimes advocated further revolutionary action if necessary against the Provisional Government.[79] Distinct from, but often allied with, the radical activists and club members were the Paris working-class corporations, which showed remarkable vigor after February, encouraging a wave of strikes that added further to the economic stagnation and exerting pressure on employers and on the Provisional Government.[80]

[77] *Class Struggles in France*, p. 44.

[78] Labrousse, *Aspects de la crise*, p. xx. See also T. J. Markovitch, "La Crise de 1847-1848 dans les industries parisiennes," *Revue d'histoire économique et sociale*, XLIII (1965), 256-260.

[79] An old but standard work on the clubs is Suzanne Wassermann, *Les Clubs de Barbès et de Blanqui en 1848* (Paris, 1913). See also Peter Amann, "A French Revolutionary Club in 1848: The *Société Démocratique Centrale*: A Document from the Archives Nationales, Edited and Translated," unpublished Ph.D. dissertation, University of Chicago, 1958.

[80] Gossez, "Les Ouvriers de Paris," pp. 3-720. See also Chauvet, *Les Ouvriers du livre*, pp. 171-211.

With the municipal police dissolved and Paris abandoned by the army, with all adult male Parisians now members of the National Guard and rapidly arming themselves, with Caussidière enjoying a certain autonomy at the Prefecture of Police, with the National Workshops attracting unexpected thousands of unemployed, the Provisional Government was for a time defenseless. As early as February 25, however, they began the creation of a new force designed to offer some protection, the Garde Mobile. It was to be recruited from among the young insurgents of February, who would be paid at the favorable rate of 1.50 francs per day, and maintained by the state. But the Garde Mobile took time to organize, and until the June Days it was felt to be unreliable.

In March and April, the government had to face several hostile demonstrations without adequate means of defense; first, that of the old bourgeois units of the National Guard on March 16; then a more threatening demonstration of club members and workers on March 17, which was an attempt to enforce a delay in elections for the National Assembly. Since the decision to hold national elections on April 9, many of the radicals had become disturbed by the possibility that they would yield a conservative result. Blanqui and Louis Blanc in particular pleaded for postponement to permit the republican education of the electorate. The moderate majority, supported by recommendations from *commissaires*, favored early elections to benefit as much as possible from the wave of popular enthusiasm for the republic. On March 17, Louis Blanc indicated his solidarity with the majority in the Provisional Government, however, and the demonstration remained peaceful; shortly thereafter the elections were delayed, but only for the relatively insignificant period of two weeks, to April 23. Another demonstration on April 16 seemed for a time seriously to threaten a possible purge of moderates in the government, but in the end Ledru-Rollin called out the National Guard and again the demonstration remained peaceful. The general impression was that the Provisional Government had won a victory, and that the popular revolutionary forces had suffered a defeat.[81] The government immediately thereafter recalled

[81] Seignobos, *La Révolution de 1848*, pp. 70-71; Gossez, "Les Ouvriers de Paris," pp. 533-542.

five regular army regiments to Paris, where they paraded in a great fraternal celebration on April 20.

Thus, despite the divisions and rivalries within the Provisional Government, in each successive crisis they remained solidly together in the face of hostile demonstrations. There was among them no real distinction between bourgeois and moderate "men of order," and men of the revolution. Once the February revolution had been successful, all of the men put in power then recognized the need to restore and preserve order in Paris. On February 28, Louis Blanc himself had proposed as the motto of the republic, "Order in Liberty," and the minutes of the Provisional Government reveal how constant was their concern to preserve "order."[82]

The Provisional Government continued to adopt measures reflecting the new spirit of innovation. Since the February days, a de facto freedom of press and of assembly existed in Paris, as was evident from the profusion of clubs and from the scores of new and often ephemeral newspapers. The government on March 6 suspended the "September laws" of 1835, but indicated that a new press law would have to be enacted by the National Assembly. On March 4, the Provisional Government created a special commission to prepare for the abolition of slavery in the colonies, which was proclaimed April 27. Imprisonment for debt was suspended on March 9, and Louis Blanc decided to use the emptied debtors' prison at Clichy for an experiment in workers' association, in which nearly 1,600 tailors, organized according to Blanc's model social workshop, made uniforms for the National Guard.[83] In the Ministry of Education, Carnot introduced a number of reforms, especially in the Collège de France, and appointed a committee to draw up a general reform of the system of primary education.

Economic and financial problems continued to demand serious attention. Government finance was already in grave

[82] See the *Procès-verbaux du gouvernement provisoire et de la commission du pouvoir exécutif, 24 février-22 juin 1848*, ed. Charles Pouthas (Paris, 1950), pp. xv and passim. The citation from Louis Blanc is in *Pages d'histoire de la révolution de février 1848* (Paris, 1850), p. 32.

[83] Loubère, *Louis Blanc*, pp. 86-88.

difficulty, and Goudchaux sought to maintain confidence by paying off *rente* coupons early, but state securities fell rapidly. Goudchaux resigned after only a week in office, protesting that his efforts to reassure the financial community were being hampered. His successor was Garnier-Pagès, who pursued much the same traditional policies, while Marrast succeeded him as mayor of Paris. In an attempt to deal with the continuing economic slump, the Provisional Government in March created several new credit institutions, in which the state supplemented private and municipal credit to aid businessmen. The government responded to a demand of the workers by abolishing productive labor in prisons. To give employment to textile workers in Lyon, the government placed orders for thousands of flags and sashes. To deal with the cessation of railway construction work, it proposed nationalization of the entire network.

The Provisional Government also gave much thought to the problem of taxation. The tax program worked out by the republicans before the revolution had contemplated the reduction of the indirect taxes in favor of a tax on income, but the Provisional Government decided that in the existing crisis it would be impossible to introduce such drastic reforms. They contented themselves with promising to end the indirect taxes, particularly those on salt and wine, in the future, but the only concrete measures taken were the abolition of the stamp tax on newspapers and of the duty on meat entering Paris. The only substantial tax policy of the Provisional Government was the fateful decision to avoid innovations by resorting to the traditional expedient of a temporary addition to the existing direct taxes. This was the famous 45-centime surtax, which was decreed on March 16. In response to protests, the government decided to exempt the poor, but this policy was difficult to apply, and the 45-centime tax was to have fatal political consequences later in the year.[84]

[84] See R. Schnerb, "Les Hommes de 1848 et l'impôt," *1848 et les révolutions du XIXe siècle*, No. 176 (1947), pp. 5-51, and Rémi Gossez, "La Résistance à l'impôt: les quarante-cinq centimes," *Etudes*, "Bibliothèque de la révolution de 1848," xv (1953), pp. 89-132.

V · The National Assembly

THE ELECTIONS

THE most revolutionary action taken by the Provisional Government had nothing directly to do with social or economic matters—it was the introduction of universal manhood suffrage for the elections to a national and constituent assembly. Manhood suffrage was the most radical political doctrine current in the middle years of the nineteenth century, and France in 1848 was the first country in modern history to organize its political life on the basis of representative democracy.[1] All Frenchmen twenty-one years of age and older, including servants and soldiers, could vote for representatives who would be paid at the rate of 25 francs per day. Representation was to be one deputy for every 40,000 inhabitants, each voter to cast a ballot for the entire departmental delegation. The resultant assembly would consist of 900 members, including those from Algeria and other colonies; it was necessary to construct for its sessions a huge temporary building in the courtyard of the Palais Bourbon, a project that also had the merit of giving jobs to workers in the stricken building industry.

The elections of April 23 and 24, 1848, have yet to be subjected to exhaustive analysis for all of France, but recent research, in particular studies of certain regions by French historians, has done much to illuminate them.[2] The sudden

[1] Universal manhood suffrage existed in only a few of the newer states in the United States, and in any case, no country tolerating human slavery within its borders in the nineteenth century can any longer be considered democratic. Switzerland followed the lead of France in 1848 in adopting universal manhood suffrage; England in the same year rejected with horror the democratic program of the Chartists. See J. A. Hawgood, "Liberalism and Constitutional Development," *New Cambridge Modern History* (Cambridge, 1960), x, pp. 189-196. The Convention of 1792 had been elected by nearly universal but indirect manhood suffrage; the Constitution of 1793 had provided for universal and direct manhood suffrage, but it was never put into effect.

[2] For aspects of the elections as a whole, see Tudesq, *Les Grands notables*; two articles by Alfred Cobban, "The Influence of the Clergy

expansion of the electorate from 240,000 wealthy and socially prominent Frenchmen to include the entire male population of almost ten millions, the majority of them illiterate and lacking political experience, completely upset traditional patterns of electoral practice. None of the existing "parties," not even the republicans, had any experience in appealing to a mass electorate. Some immediate circumstances, in particular their monopoly of national political power, favored the republicans, but they had been a small minority in most of the country, and while enough able republicans were found to replace most of the prefects and subprefects, many Orleanist officials in positions of electoral influence on the local level had to be retained for lack of republican successors.[3] Although the republicans also had in their favor the enthusiastic reception of the revolution and the apprehensive unwillingness of the monarchists to challenge the republican form openly, these conditions created confusion and ambiguities about political affiliation which gave the republicans a superficial victory that was in reality a defeat.

The acceptance of the republic by the great *notables* in February had been the result of stupefaction, resignation and social fear rather than genuine conversion, and many of them

---

and the '*Instituteurs Primaires*' in the Election of the French Constituent Assembly, April, 1848," *English Historical Review*, LVII (1942), 334-344, and "Administrative Pressure in the Election of the French Constituent Assembly, April, 1848," *Bulletin of the Institute of Historical Research*, XXV (1952), 133-159; and the unpublished doctoral dissertation of Fasel, "The French Moderate Republicans." In addition, my own study of the political composition of the Assembly is helpful in understanding the election. The most important regional studies are are those of Louis Chevalier, "Les Fondements économiques et sociaux de l'histoire politique de la région parisienne (1848-1870), tome I (février 1848-décembre 1851)," unpublished doctoral thesis, University of Paris, 1950; Vigier, *La Seconde république dans la région alpine*; André Armengaud, *Les populations de l'Est Aquitain au début de l'époque contemporaine: recherches sur une région moins développée (vers 1845-vers 1871)*, (Paris, 1961); and Georges Dupeux, *Aspects de l'histoire sociale et politique du département de Loir-et-Cher, 1848-1914* (Paris, 1962). For an appraisal of these and other regional studies, see Amann, "Writings on the Second French Republic," pp. 421-425.

[3] Cobban, "Administrative Pressure," pp. 140-143.

began almost immediately to adopt a covert counterrevolutionary attitude.[4] Above all, they sought to revive their authority by intervening in the elections to the National Assembly, but for the most part they felt compelled to do so indirectly, without affirming their real political ideals or objectives. With all Frenchmen now ostensibly republican, the prerevolutionary republicans identified themselves as *républicains de la veille*, and the converts as *républicains du lendemain.* In the first difficult weeks, the Provisional Government had joyfully accepted the support of former monarchists, and even though Ledru-Rollin as Minister of the Interior replaced most of the prefects with *républicains de la veille* as *commissaires*, he felt compelled to appoint more than a dozen men formerly attached to the dynastic left.[5] But the task of preparing for the elections led the republicans to emphasize the differences between those who had long advocated the republic and the *hommes du lendemain.* In circulars sent to the *commissaires* in early March, Ledru-Rollin advised them to purge local officials who were not tried republicans, and to seek the election of men who were. After the demonstration of March 17, he also sent out a new group of *commissaires généraux* who were all radical *républicains de la veille.*

Although the republicans were thus in the best position to give national leadership in the elections, in fact local conditions usually played a crucial role in determining the results. The electoral procedures, whereby voters had to cast ballots for all seats in their department, gave great influence to those groups able to distribute, for use as ballots, complete lists of attractive candidates. Everywhere electoral committees sprang up, some purely republican, most representing influential groups of *notables. Commissaires* in all of the departments drew up lists, but these were often revised by local republican committees, and radicals sometimes offered rival lists. The moderate republicans of Paris also sought to give guidance through a national committee and through lists of candidates

[4] Tudesq, *Les Grands notables*, II, p. 989.

[5] See V. Haury, "Les Commissaires de Ledru-Rollin en 1848," *La Révolution française*, LVII (1909), pp. 438-474.

published in *Le National.* In the new circumstances, the moderate republicans normally refused to follow their prerevolutionary policy of collaboration with the dynastic left, but rather sought to make a common front with the radicals as *républicains de la veille.*[6] Thus in Paris *Le National* advocated the election of all of the members of the Provisional Government, including Louis Blanc and Albert. *La Réforme* did not offer a rival list until the very day of the election, but the socialists and organized workers of Paris prepared for the elections through the Luxembourg commission and the clubs. The list of the Luxembourg commission advocated the election of only the left wing of the Provisional Government, together with twenty workers and ten socialists. Those organizations collaborating in the "Club des clubs" also sent out, supported by funds supplied by Ledru-Rollin, some 400 delegates to influence the voting in the provinces.[7] Despite the mild interventions by the government, there was virtually no corruption involved, and the elections were probably the freest in the nineteenth century.[8]

The *notables* intervened very effectively, if often indirectly. Where the republicans were most powerful, as in Paris, the *notables* abstained from offering their own candidates, but instead supported the least objectionable of the republicans or liberal Orleanists. Most of the Orleanist and Legitimist newspapers in the capital felt it wise to advocate the election of the entire Provisional Government, to assure the success of Lamartine and to oppose the radicals. However, a new and influential newspaper, representing Legitimists and Orleanists mak-

[6] See *Le National*, 2 May 1848; Garnier-Pagès, *Histoire de la révolution de 1848*, II, p. 303; Fasel, "The French Moderate Republicans," pp. 283-285; and Vigier, *La Seconde république dans la région alpine*, I, pp. 228-259.

[7] Cobban, "Administrative Pressure," p. 138. These club delegates had some influence in the Paris region, but not in the Alpine area. See Chevalier, "Les Fondements économiques et sociaux," pp. 208-220, and Vigier, *La Seconde république dans la région alpine*, I, p. 244. For the workers' electoral committee, see Chauvet, *Les ouvriers du livre*, pp. 186-187; and Gossez, "Les Ouvriers de Paris," pp. 573-616.

[8] Cobban, "Administrative Pressure," p. 159.

ing common cause, *L'Assemblée nationale*, supported only the seven moderate members of the government, together with a number of former deputies of the dynastic left.[9]

At the other extreme, in some departments where the republicans were virtually nonexistent, the *notables* put forward their own candidates, making obeisance to the revolution only by withholding those most compromised by association with Guizot and by silence on dynastic claims behind affirmations of republicanism *du lendemain.* The Orleanist great *notables* sometimes backed Legitimists, more often former liberal Orleanists, and sometimes moderate *républicains de la veille,* depending on local conditions. In some regions, the Legitimists sought to win over the peasantry by implying that in the National Assembly they would repeal the 45-centime tax, but in general this was not yet the important issue that it later became.[10]

Clerical influence also was strong on the side of the Legitimist candidates, particularly in Brittany, and in general for conservatives who agreed to support the aims of the "Catholic party" with respect to education.[11] In some cases, Legitimists refused to make the "sacrifice of convictions," but few of those who failed to present themselves as republican converts were successful. For example, in the department of Maine and Loire, where the monarchists collaborated on a single list, the Comte de Falloux disgusted many of his friends by seeking election as a *républicain du lendemain,* but he was the only Legitimist elected, whereas his friend Quatrebarbes, who was on the same list but neglected to make a republican *profession de foi,* was defeated overwhelmingly.[12] On the other hand, the reputed leader of the Legitimists, Pierre Antoine Berryer, was one of the very few to be successful despite his refusal to proclaim himself a republican. "The new revolution has not

[9] Tudesq, *Les Grands notables,* II, p. 1055.

[10] Gossez, "La Résistance à l'impôt," pp. 97, 125-126.

[11] See Cobban, "The Influence of the Clergy," and also "Administrative Pressure," pp. 147-148, 158.

[12] See Albert Houtin, "Le Clergé et la noblesse d'Anjou aux élections de l'Assemblée nationale constitutante de 1848," *La Révolution de 1848,* VIII (1911-12), pp. 149-161, 208-218, 289-299.

made a new man of me," he stated. "My sentiments and my opinions are known to you."[13] In general, the Legitimist and Orleanist *républicains du lendemain* sought to present themselves, not as opposition candidates against the republic, but as defenders of order and of liberty, of the will of the majority of the people against a revolutionary minority represented by the radicals and revolutionaries of Paris.

The elections took place in an atmosphere of calm enthusiasm, and a massive 84 percent of those eligible cast ballots. With virtually all of the successful candidates claiming to be republicans, it was difficult to interpret the outcome. Yet some of the results were unmistakable. The democratic electorate repudiated the majority in the last Chamber of the July Monarchy, very few of whom were elected. Guizot himself was not a candidate, Thiers stood but was defeated, Barrot was elected, but as a *républicain du lendemain.*[14]

The elections were also a crushing defeat for the radicals, the socialists, the clubbists, and the organized workers of Paris, who were repudiated not only by provincial France, but in the revolutionary capital itself. Of the candidates of the Luxembourg, only six were elected, and these apparently only because they were also on other lists. Albert and Louis Blanc were successful, but ranked only twenty-first and twenty-seventh among the thirty-four elected. Barbès gathered only 64,000 votes in Paris, but was successful in his home department of the Aude. Thus the Luxembourg list apparently did not have the support of a majority of the approximately 204,000 adult male workers of Paris.[15]

The elections were most generally seen as a triumph for moderation, although it remained unclear how republican a triumph it was, for many Legitimists and many men of the former dynastic left were successful. Lamartine was personally triumphant, not only in Paris, where he led the list with

[13] The full *profession de foi* is reprinted in Charles de Lacombe, *Vie de Berryer* (Paris, 1894-95), II, pp. 541-543.

[14] Charles Alméras, *Odilon Barrot, avocat et homme politique* (Paris, 1951), pp. 194-195.

[15] For a somewhat different assessment, see Loubère, *Louis Blanc*, pp. 114-115. See also Gossez, "Les Ouvriers de Paris," pp. 617-641.

259,800 votes, but also in nine other departments. The elections were also a victory for the Provisional Government, all of whom were elected in Paris, the moderates at the top with Lamartine, the radicals near the bottom. Several members also won in other departments.

The attitude of the Paris republicans toward the results of the election ranged from the guarded enthusiasm of *Le National* to dismay and alarm among the club members. Though pleased with the success of its candidates in the capital, *Le National* was not overjoyed with the results in the provinces. While expressing the "firm hope" that the majority would be devoted to the republic, it noted that the "reaction" was stronger than anticipated, and blamed the delay in holding the elections.[16] *La Réforme* was less oblique: "We had counted on very bad elections, but the event, it must be conceded, has passed our expectations. . . . The tree of monarchy, which we had only pruned, has borne its fruit."[17] As further returns became available, *La Réforme* lamented: "Let us not fool ourselves: the elections were made against the men who prepared and proclaimed the Republic."[18] The club of Barbès urged the Provisional Government to retain power "dictatorially" until it was certain that the National Assembly "merits the confidence of the true republicans,"[19] and some of the socialist newspapers in Paris threatened violence against the Assembly if it proved too conservative.[20]

For the moment, however, Paris remained calm as it waited to see what the Assembly would do. But in a few provincial towns, workers rose in violence following the defeat of their candidates. At Rouen in late April bitter street fighting broke out, in which soldiers and National Guardsmen restored order after killing twenty-three workers and wounding many others. The Paris activists, in particular Blanqui, were enraged at this "massacre" of proletarians.[21]

[16] *Le National*, 30 April 1848.

[17] Issue of 29 April 1848.

[18] Issue of 2 May 1848.

[19] Wassermann, *Les Clubs*, p. 157.

[20] Daniel Stern [the Comtesse d'Agoult], *Histoire de la révolution de 1848* (new edn., Paris, 1878), III, p. 8.

[21] See Seignobos, *La Révolution de 1848*, pp. 80-82, and the more recent and thorough study by André Dubuc, "Les Emeutes de Rouen et

It was the world of the *notables* that greeted the election results most favorably. *L'Assemblée nationale* took cheer from the fact that it had supported a majority of those elected in Paris, and many provincial newspapers echoed the *Courrier de la Gironde* in regarding the elections as a "triumph of moderation," which made the "extremist agitations" in Paris seem those of a minority. Yet the very approval of elections which, though moderate, were also ostensibly republican, indicated that even the great *notables* were still gripped by "social fear," for they "considered as a success the election of a Chamber which would appear to them, several months later, as too revolutionary."[22]

THE ASSEMBLY

The social position of the vast majority of the deputies also was a source of satisfaction to the *notables* and of dismay to the militant radicals of Paris. Most were drawn from the provincial bourgeoisie, and many would have qualified for election under the July Monarchy.[23] Despite the democratic suffrage and the apotheosis of the worker, more noblemen than workingmen were successful, including seven peers of France and sixty-eight other noblemen, among them two Bonapartes: Pierre, son of Lucien, and Napoleon, son of Jérôme.[24] Seventeen workers and seven foremen were elected, only four of them in Paris, of whom only Albert and Agricol Perdiguier had been on the Luxembourg list. Anthyme Corbon of *L'Atelier* was elected on the list of *Le National*. Moreover, in a year of considerable agrarian unrest, when elsewhere, as in

d'Elbeuf (27, 28 et 29 avril 1848)," *Etudes d'histoire moderne et contemporaine* (Paris, 1948), II, pp. 243-275.

[22] Tudesq, *Les Grands notables*, II, pp. 1068-1071.

[23] This discussion is based partly on the articles by A. Chaboseau, "Les Constitutants de 1848," *La Révolution de 1848*, VII (1910), pp. 287-305, 413-425, and VIII (1911), pp. 67-80, and partly on my own research, which corroborates and amplifies Chaboseau. Cf. also Tudesq, *Les Grands notables*, II, pp. 1065-1068.

[24] Louis Napoleon did not pose his candidacy in April. He was elected in the by-election of June 4, but declined his seat, and assumed it only after winning in another by-election in September.

Germany, peasants often elected peasants to represent them, not a single French peasant was chosen.[25]

The deputies included a large number of agricultural landlords—about 160—but professional men made up the majority, the most common being that of *avocat* (176). There were also a number of magistrates, army officers (including thirteen generals, among them Cavaignac), government functionaries (including seventy-seven of Ledru-Rollin's *commissaires*), physicians, professors, writers, and sixteen ecclesiastics, of whom three were bishops. Men drawn from commerce and industry were in a small minority, but Alexis de Tocqueville, himself a deputy, was very mistaken in his impression that the Assembly had more noblemen and landlords than the Chambers of Deputies of the July Monarchy, in which recent research has shown that noblemen held from 25 to 33 percent of the seats.[26] The first experiment in political democracy had produced an Assembly neither of proletarians nor of great *notables*, but rather of bourgeois and lesser provincial *notables*.

Thus, both socially and politically the New Assembly seemed moderate, but contemporaries had difficulty in assessing the relative strength of different political groups, and historians have reflected their puzzlement. One problem was the novelty of democratic suffrage and the absence of real party organizations. Another, was the fact that the basic political issue of the republic had been held by virtually all candidates to be not at issue. All seemed to accept the republic, but few observers were willing to take these conversions at face value. The *républicains de la veille* were on their guard when it came to prominent Legitimists such as Larochejaquelein and Falloux, and even liberal Orleanists such as Barrot, but the real problem was that most of the deputies were new

[25] In the Austrian assembly of 1848, there were 92 peasants in a total of 383, and in the Prussian diet, 68 out of 402. See Lewis Namier, *1848: The Revolution of the Intellectuals* (Oxford, 1946), p. 20.

[26] See *Recollections*, p. 112, and the recent articles by Jean Bécarud, "La Noblesse dans les chambres (1815-1848)," *Revue internationale d'histoire politique et constitutionnelle*, new series, No. 11 (1953), 189-205; and by the Higonnets, "Class, Corruption, and Politics," p. 207.

to national politics; fewer than one-quarter of the almost 900 deputies, or 190, had sat in previous parliaments, although some had been active on the departmental or municipal level.

It was a combination of strong suspicions about the conversions of known politicians, uncertainty about the many new deputies, and undoubtedly political tact that led *Le National* to offer only a vague assessment. Just before the Assembly convened, *Le National* confessed itself ignorant "of the spirit that will animate the majority."[27] It is noteworthy that *Le National* made no systematic analysis of the election results, not even bothering to report on the number of its candidates who proved successful. Perhaps this was because the number was relatively small, 355 out of 853, and not all of these were *républicains de la veille.* Most contemporary observers seem to have been content with general impressions or rough estimates of forces.[28] Tocqueville had the impression that the majority consisted of men of the former dynastic left, elected as *républicains du lendemain.*[29] Louis Blanc considered that only about half the deputies were republicans, in addition to 300 Orleanists and 150 Legitimists.[30] The estimates of other contemporaries varied widely, but the most common belief was that the moderate republicans had a majority, although few attempted to distinguish consistently between those of *la veille* and of *le lendemain.*[31]

[27] Issue of 3 May 1848.

[28] It is possible that some contemporary analysis has escaped my notice, for I make no claim to an exhaustive study of the elections. In the course of 1848, a number of handbooks were published offering biographical sketches of all or most of the deputies, but these were all biased, and most were carelessly and incompletely done. For a discussion of some of them, see E. N. Curtis, *The French Assembly of 1848 and American Constitutional Doctrines* (New York, 1917), pp. 116-117. The solid information gleaned from these and other sources after critical examination appears in the standard *Dictionnaire des parlementaires français, comprenant tous les membres des assemblées françaises et tous les ministres français depuis le 1er mai 1789 jusqu'au 1er mai 1889*, eds. Adolphe Robert, Edgar Bourloton, and Gaston Cougny (Paris, 1889-91), which was the major source of information for my study of the deputies.

[29] *Recollections*, p. 105.

[30] *Histoire de la révolution de 1848* (Paris, 1870), II, p. 67.

[31] For a discussion of some of the estimates, see Curtis, *The French Assembly of 1848*, pp. 50-54.

Historians writing from quite different perspectives, from Karl Marx to Pierre de la Gorce, thereafter commonly expressed the view that the National Assembly had a moderate republican majority, and this belief seemed corroborated by an analysis published in 1921 by Charles Seignobos in the influential Lavisse series, *Histoire de France contemporaine.* According to Seignobos, the elections of April produced an Assembly of approximately 500 "républicains modérés," less than 100 "partisans de la République démocratique et sociale," almost 200 "orléanistes ralliés," and 100 Legitimists.[32]

Although many historians have adopted these figures, it seems that the Seignobos analysis was never sound, and the evidence suggests quite a different political composition of the Assembly. The Seignobos analysis was based on an unpublished essay written by one of his students, J. Tournan, critical examination of which reveals serious systematic flaws that virtually invalidate the conclusions.[33] Tournan failed to apply uniform criteria, classifying some of the deputies according to campaign statements and others according to two parliamentary votes. Moreover, he ignored the fact that virtually all candidates stood as republicans, accepting such self-designations at face value. By such methods, he concluded that no less than 687 of 876 seats were held by moderate republicans, a figure so fantastically high that Seignobos felt obliged to reclassify some of these (according to some unexplained principle), as "rallied Orleanists" in order to attain the figure of only 500 moderate republicans. Even this figure is too high, for it still obscures in many cases the very real distinction between *républicains de la veille* and those *du lendemain,* almost all of whom called themselves *républicains modérés.*

This very distinction suggests a more fruitful way of analyzing the Assembly, and that is according to the prerevolutionary affiliations of the deputies. This procedure is implicit in

[32] *La Révolution de 1848,* pp. 82-83.

[33] This 34-page essay entitled "Etat des partis en France au commencement de la seconde république d'après les élections du 23 avril 1848," was written for the *Diplôme d'Etudes supérieures,* and now may be found among the papers of Seignobos, Archives Nationales (hereafter cited as A.N.) AB xix 2842.

any estimate that includes Legitimists and Orleanists; but it should be applied consistently to all the deputies. Once all are classified in this fashion, quite a different pattern emerges.[34] The major task is to identify all of those deputies who before 1848 were known or reputed to be republicans. The majority of the others, but by no means all, can also be classified as Legitimists, Orleanists, or, in a very few cases, Bonapartists. Although this "biographical" method yields some precise figures, these should be understood rather as approximations subject to some margin of error, and subject to change should additional information come to light, particularly in the case of some of the more obscure deputies whose sole venture into politics was in 1848. Nevertheless, such a procedure provides a much better understanding of past political orientation than do the impressions of contemporaries or the analysis of Tournan. Some figures from Chevalier's study of the Parisian region indicate the gross inaccuracy of Tournan's conclusions: In the six departments concerned, Tournan found forty-three moderate republicans and three socialists among the fifty-three deputies, whereas Chevalier found only seventeen *républicains de la veille*.[35]

For France as a whole, the total number of men elected in April who were known or reputed to be republicans before the revolution was only 285, even including Lamartine on the basis of his conversion of February 24. Thus, the *républicains de la veille* of all nuances, from General Cavaignac to Louis Blanc, constituted only a third of the 851 deputies chosen at that time.[36] Of these, about 55 were radicals and socialists,

[34] The political analysis offered here is my own, resulting from the application of "biographical" and quantitative techniques similar to those employed by Lewis Namier, J. E. Neale, W. O. Aydelotte and others to the study of British parliaments. Biographical information on all of the deputies was collected from numerous sources, in particular reference works such as the Robert and Cougny *Dictionnaire des parlementaires*, and standard works on the republicans such as Weill and Tchernoff. In addition, I have made use of many recent regional studies, those of Chevalier and of Vigier being of greatest value.

[35] See "Fondements économiques et sociaux," pp. 290-292.

[36] The figure is slightly higher if the multiple elections of Lamartine and others are counted rather than the individuals; thus, Seignobos uses

and 230 were republicans of the majority wing, less than half the number of "moderate republicans" suggested by Seignobos, and far short of a majority.[37]

What of the political background of the others, virtually all of whom may be regarded as *républicains du lendemain*? Very few had been strong supporters of the government of Guizot, whether in the Chambers, in the administration, or on the departmental or municipal level. Only 19 such men were elected in April, although a few more would be returned in by-elections during the year. But there were a large number of deputies—231—who had reflected, to one degree or another, the loyal, dynastic opposition, from some men of the left center to many expressing the nuance of Odilon Barrot. In addition to these liberal Orleanists, 56 of the deputies can confidently be identified as Legitimists. Thus, the men who were known to be monarchists of one or the other persuasion before the revolution numbered 306, or slightly more than the number of republicans. In addition, evidence strongly suggests that another 133 deputies were also monarchists, even if their precise

---

the figure of 880. A total of 915 was ultimately elected to the Assembly in colonial and by-elections during the year, but these produced no important changes in the relative sizes of the groups. The English writer J. F. Corkran was one of the few contemporaries to declare flatly that the *républicains de la veille* were in a minority. See his *History of the National Constituent Assembly from May 1848* (London, 1849), I, p. 11.

[37] This figure is arrived at by subtracting the number of radicals and socialists from the total. Except for the most prominent, it is difficult to distinguish these from the ordinary *républicains de la veille* by any objective test. The figure 55 represents those who signed the manifesto published November 9, 1848 in *La Réforme*, together with Albert, Louis Blanc and Caussidière, who by then were in prison or exile. A somewhat larger total for the moderate republicans, between 310 and 320, is suggested by Fasel in "The French Moderate Republicans," on the basis of the successful candidates among the 853 supported by the Paris *Comité central des élections générales pour l'Assemblée nationale*, but this method, although yielding the same general conclusion as my own, namely, that the moderate republicans were in a minority in the Assembly, still suffers to some extent from a failure to distinguish consistently between *républicains de la veille* and those who were "sincerely *républicains du lendemain*." (See pp. 298-305.)

orientation is unclear in the sources.[38] Thus, the total number of former monarchists is better conceived of as 439, or slightly more than half of those elected in April.

At best a handful of deputies could be regarded as Bonapartists before 1848, and doubt remains on some of these. Neither of the two Bonapartes elected had had much to do with advancing the cause of their cousin, Louis Napoleon, and neither would be a very reliable supporter even under the Empire. Two of the other deputies elected from Corsica also perhaps should be counted as Bonapartists, Casabianca and Conti.[39] Lucien Murat was not known as a Bonapartist before 1848, but Narcisse Vieillard, the tutor and faithful correspondent of Louis Napoleon, was regarded as a Bonapartist when he sat in the Chamber of Deputies from 1842 to 1846.

For 122 of the deputies, not enough information is available to permit their classification in any of the categories. Most were men new to politics, even on the local level. There is no evidence suggesting that they were *républicains de la veille*; rather, the relatively high proportion of magistrates, *militaires* and landlords among them would suggest a conservative background. Lacking strong political commitments under the July Monarchy, they perhaps should be regarded as acquiescent Orleanists.

It was not yet clear how much substance there was to the mass rallying to the new regime of the *républicains du lendemain.* The conversions of many of the known monarchists were obviously tactical, or cynical, or resigned, but undoubtedly many were possessed of the exhilarating spirit of the spring of 1848 and felt sincerely that they had become republicans. Even the most sincere of the new republicans, however, differed from the *républicains de la veille* in their lack of a long commitment to a radically democratic point of view at a time when it was regarded as dangerous, and when

[38] Many of them are simply identified as "conservateurs" in the *Dictionnaire des parlementaires,* and 66 became members of the Réunion de la Rue de Poitiers, which was recognized as the stronghold of the combined monarchists in the Assembly.

[39] On these men, new to politics, the *Dictionnaire des parlementaires* and other authorities conflict.

certain expressions of it were illegal. Assuredly some of the conversions were genuine and lasting, such as those of Crémieux, and of Armand Dufaure; but in the case of other liberal Orleanists who ostensibly rallied to the republic in 1848, men such as Rémusat and Thiers (the latter elected in a by-election on June 4), and even Tocqueville, the experience of 1848 was but one step in what Louis Girard has called their "slow discovery of the Republic, that is, of a Republic that would be as durable and as stable as a monarchy."[40] Even though they accepted the republic in 1848 as a de facto government with no immediately realizable alternative, they were still separated from the *républicains de la veille* in their distrust of universal manhood suffrage and of its social implications.[41]

Only if the *républicains du lendemain* are assumed to be identical with the *républicains de la veille* could it be said that the "moderate republicans" had a majority, and in that case the majority would be much larger than 500, or even Tournan's 687, for it would embrace virtually the entire Assembly except for the radicals and socialists. But if the political orientation of the deputies before the revolution is taken into account, then it seems clear that the majority of the deputies were formerly monarchists or at least nonrepublicans, a conclusion that would seem to accord with the picture of the Assembly as largely a collection of lesser provincial *notables.*

In sum, then, the elections of April had produced the unstartling result of a crushing defeat for the previous governing groups by the combined opposition forces—dynastic left, Legitimists, and republicans. The return of the Legitimists from their "interior emigration" to reflect something akin to their actual strength was a matter of considerable importance, obscured by the fact that most were posing as republicans and were ready to collaborate with their erstwhile Orleanist foes in what would come to be called the Party of Order. The republicans triumphed in two senses, first in that, as *Le National* observed, the monarchists of all varieties had felt com-

[40] "Political Liberalism in France, 1840-1875," trans. Joseph N. Moody, in *French Society and Culture Since the Old Regime*, p. 120. See also Rémusat, *Mémoires de ma vie*, IV, pp. 249-251, 483.

[41] Girard, "Political Liberalism in France," p. 123.

pelled to parade under the banners of the republic,[42] and second, in that universal suffrage had inflated their parliamentary strength beyond their fondest hopes of 1847. Yet the elections were a defeat in that the *républicains de la veille* had failed to win a majority; the magnitude of this defeat was not realized at first, because no one could be sure how many of the conversions of the *républicains du lendemain* were genuine, profound, or lasting.

The opening session of the Assembly on May 4 revealed that the deputies, however monarchist their past, were determined to perpetuate the myth of the electoral campaign—that all were now republicans. Although some radicals and club members had feared that the National Assembly might fail to proclaim the republic, and had considered what action to take in the event,[43] the assembled deputies cried "Vive la République!" no less than seventeen times, once before large crowds outside of the great hall, and then unanimously resolved that "The Republic, proclaimed on the 24th of February 1848, is, and shall remain, the form of government of France."

One radical newspaper, the *Vraie République* of Thoré, bitterly commented: "Do you believe in conversions? The whole National Assembly has cried together: *Vive la République*! We watched carefully the hands which have for so long weighed down upon us; all were raised today for the Republic. . . . Not a single man was met who had sufficient conscience to declare that he was not and that he had never been a republican. Even Berryer cried, "Vive la République!"[44]

For its officers, the Assembly chose men who were all *républicains de la veille*. Indeed, it acknowledged the social aspect of the February revolution by choosing as the first of its monthly presidents the Christian socialist Philippe Buchez, and by electing Corbon of *L'Atelier* as one of six vice presidents. Yet the moderate cast of the Assembly became apparent when

[42] Issue of 30 April 1848.

[43] Wassermann, *Les Clubs*, p. 157.

[44] See Corkran, *National Constituent Assembly*, I, pp. 4-6, and Curtis, *The French Assembly of 1848*, pp. 58-59. For the discomfort of one who was not a republican, see Rémusat, *Mémoires de ma vie*, IV, pp. 292-293.

in creating an Executive Commission to supplant the Provisional Government, it eliminated the socialist left. Arago, Garnier-Pagès, Marie, Lamartine, and Ledru-Rollin formed the new executive, Ledru-Rollin owing his position to the fact that Lamartine refused to serve without him. Ledru-Rollin did lose his Ministry of the Interior, however, but to the staunch republican Recurt. Carnot and Crémieux retained their portfolios, and *républicains de la veille* were assigned to other ministries. Blanc and Albert were the only members of the Provisional Government who formed no part of the new one.

These and other early actions of the National Assembly enflamed the radical activists of Paris, whose emotions exploded on May 15 in the most serious of the demonstrations since February. Although the events of that day were confusing and although some aspects of them remain puzzling, the climax of the drama was incontrovertible—large crowds of demonstrators, some armed, swarmed into a session of the National Assembly, disrupted it for more than two hours, accepted the declaration of a club leader that it was dissolved, and thereafter proclaimed a new Provisional Government.[45] The original purpose of the demonstration was a petition in favor of aid to Poland, but after marching from the Place de la Bastille the demonstrators crossed the river and invaded the Assembly. Blanqui and Barbès, originally dubious, now dis-

[45] There is no standard account of this "journée," but most historians have treated it as a spontaneous movement. The somewhat puzzling roles of Blanqui and others have been considered by their biographers. Some contemporaries saw conspiracy behind the affair, and recently a French historian revived and elaborated one of these views, charging Marrast, Recurt and a few other colleagues with having instigated the demonstration through an *agent provocateur* (Huber) in order to crush the revolutionary "clubbists." See Guillemin, *La Tragédie de quarante-huit*, pp. 237-257, and cf. Fasel, "The French Moderate Republicans," pp. 330-346. The conspiracy thesis does not seem persuasive. See also the older articles by L. Lévy-Schneider, "Les Préliminaires du 15 mai 1848: La Journée du 14, d'après un document inédit," *La Révolution de 1848*, VII (1910), pp. 219-232; and by Gabriel Vauthier, "La Journée du 15 mai 1848," *La Révolution de 1848*, XXV (1928), pp. 242-251. Peter Amann effectively refutes the charge that Huber was a police agent in "The Huber Enigma: Revolutionary or Police Spy?," *International Review of Social History*, XII (1967), 190-203.

puted the leadership of the crowds, both making speeches while the deputies listened in shocked silence. The call for dissolution by Huber took the other club leaders by surprise, but the deputies and most of the demonstrators then dispersed, Barbès and Albert with a crowd to the Hôtel de Ville, where they proclaimed a new Provisional Government. Soon thereafter National Guardsmen scattered the demonstrators and arrested Barbès and Albert.

Although the aims of the demonstrators were confused, the day had become a February 24 that failed, and constituted a serious defeat for the clubs and for the radical working-class movement in Paris. The governing republicans were aghast. "The sovereignty of the people has been violated in the person of its representatives," wrote *Le National*. "It is a crime . . . of *lèse-majesté* nationale."[46] To Carnot, "the violation of a power born of universal suffrage is in my eyes the greatest of outrages. . . . It is one of those wounds from which a republic can die."[47]

The affair of May 15 also had a strong impact on the world of the great *notables*, who regarded the outcome as a victory for conservatism, "a revenge for February 24," and many criticized not only the demonstrators but also the Executive Commission.[48] Those of provincial France were jubilant and began to resume the posture of dominance which they had lost in February, but the great *notables* of Paris remained apprehensive.[49]

The government took strong action against those who seemed to be the authors of the invasion of the Assembly. Albert was imprisoned at Vincennes, as were Barbès, Raspail and Blanqui: the clubs lost their most popular leaders. Moreover, Louis Blanc was accused of complicity as was Caussidière, who was finally divested of the Prefecture of Police. The Luxembourg commission ceased to function, and the clubs

[46] Issue of 16 May 1848. See also *Le Moniteur* of the same day for the official declaration of the Executive Commission that it was a criminal assault on the Assembly.

[47] MS "Mémorial," A.N. 108 AP 3 dos. 15, p. 10.

[48] Tudesq, *Les Grands notables*, II, pp. 1076-1081.

[49] *Ibid.*, pp. 1084, 1107.

of Blanqui and of Raspail were suppressed, although that of Barbès and others continued to exist. The workers of the National Workshops, hitherto regarded as a moderate counterweight to the Luxembourg, became more restive. The clash between the government and the socialists and activists of Paris had been serious but not decisive. About 130 of the demonstrators were arrested,[50] but most were still at liberty. General Courtais, who had faltered in the crisis, was removed from the command of the Paris National Guard, and although the Executive Commission remained, its prestige was seriously wounded by its ineffectual behavior.

After May 15 the Executive Commission was preoccupied with preparing adequate defenses against any new insurrection,[51] and they had already chosen the man to whom they wanted to entrust that defense—General Cavaignac.

THE RISE OF CAVAIGNAC

On February 24, 1848, as the Second Republic was born in Paris, General Cavaignac in Algeria thought that his career was coming to an end, and he looked forward to a quiet life in retirement.[52] The news of the revolution electrified him. His first thought was regret that Godefroy was not alive "to experience the only real joy that he could feel and that seemed due him. With him dead . . . whatever may happen I have some duty to fulfill but I am not sure what it is."[53]

He was certain, however, that he would be most useful in Paris, and contemplated seeking election to the new National Assembly. "The only thing that I don't want," he wrote his mother, "is to remain in Africa, no matter what the position."[54] But when he learned that the Provisional Government had appointed him governor-general, he accepted, believing that a refusal would have been misunderstood; he was still deter-

[50] Stern, *Histoire de la révolution de 1848*, III, p. 329.

[51] See the *Procès-verbaux du gouvernement provisoire*, pp. 267-268, 270-271, 275, 301-303, 307-309.

[52] See letters to Madame Cavaignac, 28 March 1847, 29 May 1847, 12, 13 and 20 December 1847, 24 February 1848, Reel 27.

[53] Letter to Madame Cavaignac, 5 March 1848, Reel 27.

[54] *Ibid.*

mined to return to France at the earliest opportunity.[55] It was only as an afterthought that the Provisional Government gave Cavaignac the promotion to divisional general that he had so long awaited, considering it more appropriate to his new position.[56]

The Provisional Government soon began to reconsider its action and named Cavaignac to be Minister of War. At this point, the general's mother intervened personally in a decision for which Cavaignac was severely criticized: his refusal of that position. As early as March 7, Madame Cavaignac on her own initiative had informed Ledru-Rollin that she thought her son would refuse.[57] At the same time, she intimated to her son only a vague reluctance to see him accept, hinting at her distrust of some members of the Provisional Government. Cavaignac himself was delighted at the prospect of becoming Minister of War; not only would it enable him to return to Paris, but "in good conscience, I believe that they need me. . . . In the present frame of mind in the army, there is hardly anyone but I who could reorganize it and keep it good for the republic . . . to republicanize an army which is not republican, while maintaining discipline and good order."[58]

Nevertheless, because Cavaignac knew little of the situation in Paris, he decided to rely on his mother's judgment.[59] She argued that Cavaignac would be foolish to align himself with a government that would soon be superseded. The general agreed to refuse until the convocation of the National Assembly; confident that he would himself be elected, he would be able to reconsider the matter in Paris.[60] On March 21, Madame Cavaignac again informed the Provisional Government

[55] *Ibid.*, 10 March 1848, Reel 27.

[56] *Procès-verbaux du gouvernement provisoire*, pp. 23, 27.

[57] See the text of her letter in Alvin R. Calman, *Ledru-Rollin and the Second French Republic* (New York, 1922), p. 420, and the discussion p. 82. Calman wrongly assumed that the letter, which was signed J. (for Julie) Cavaignac, was from General Jacques Cavaignac, and because the letter referred to "mon fils," proceeded to the erroneous conclusion that Eugène was not the son of the *conventionnel.*

[58] Letter to Madame Cavaignac, 12 March 1848, Reel 27.

[59] *Ibid.*

[60] *Ibid.*, undated, but between 12 and 21 March 1848, Reel 27.

that Cavaignac would refuse the portfolio if it were offered to him.[61] Nevertheless, on the same day, before or despite this second warning, the Provisional Government formally appointed Cavaignac Minister of War.[62] By this time, Cavaignac thought he had real grievances against the Provisional Government: Ledru-Rollin had wounded his pride and aroused his prejudices as an African general by indicating an intention to send civilian officials to Algeria;[63] moreover, Cavaignac had heard rumors that the Provisional Government planned to reduce the size of the army and would otherwise intervene directly in military affairs.[64] Finally, he was angered because "The government, in appointing me although it knew in advance that I would not accept, has embarrassed me in the eyes of the country."[65] Madame Cavaignac thought her son would not dare to refuse the actual offer, but he did so immediately, in a long letter which indicated clearly that, for the moment, the *militaire* was ascendant in Cavaignac over the republican:

> As a soldier, I will always be ready to shed my blood for the Republic. . . . As a politician, if I were condemned to become one, I would never sacrifice my convictions as a soldier well advanced in his career. The Republic needs its army. Far from my country, I am ignorant today of what the army is, where it is; but this I know, that if unfortunately the army were deeply wounded in its conditions of existence, it would be necessary to reassure it; if its head were bowed, it would be necessary to raise it. That is my conviction.
>
> Thus, in order to be a minister, I must know the thinking, the will of the Republic; I must be certain that I would not

[61] Madame Cavaignac to the Provisional Government, 21 March 1848, Reel 27.

[62] *Procès-verbaux*, p. 84.

[63] Letters to Madame Cavaignac, 18, 22, 25, 27 March 1848, Reel 27.

[64] *Ibid.*, 27 March 1848, Reel 16, and 30 March 1848, Reel 27.

[65] Letter to Flocon, 1 April 1848, Reel 22. Flocon, one of the radicals in the Provisional Government, was a friend of Cavaignac and of his mother. This letter is included among documents that Cavaignac preserved from his later term as War Minister.

have to mutilate the army with the very hand and sword with which I have served it for almost thirty years.[66]

The members of the Provisional Government were astonished and angered by Cavaignac's "ill-concealed arrogance. . . . The citizen disappeared behind the soldier."[67]

So Cavaignac remained for six more weeks as governor-general of Algeria. There he sought to further republican policies, but soon found himself in conflict with both the radical republicans and the conservative elements of the population, foreshadowing his later difficulties in France. The civilians in Algeria had greeted the revolution enthusiastically, hoping that the republic would free them from control by the military. Although Cavaignac was a republican, his appointment was received coolly, because he was also an African general.[68] In Algiers, Cavaignac officially proclaimed the republic, exhorting the army to rally loyally to the new regime, and promising the civilian population that republican principles would soon be introduced into the colony.[69] The Provisional Government made a point of congratulating him on the tone and content of these proclamations.[70] He also lent encouragement to the public demonstrations that accompanied the birth of the republic in Algeria as in France, such as the planting of "trees

[66] Letter to the Provisional Government, 27 March 1848, Reel 27. The letter was published in Stern, *Histoire de la révolution de 1848*, II, pp. 389-390. See also Cavaignac's letter to Madame Cavaignac, 29 March 1848, Reel 27.

[67] Louis Blanc, *1848: Historical Revelations: Inscribed to Lord Normanby* (London, 1858), p. 475. Cf. Lamartine, *Histoire de la révolution de 1848*, II, p. 298, and Carnot, MS "Mémorial," dos. 15, p. 1. As Ledru-Rollin recalled the incident in the bitterness of exile in 1850, the refusal "took the form of an insolent protest against the revolution," but no other member of the Provisional Government makes such an accusation, and nothing in the letter would seem to support it. See Calman, *Ledru-Rollin*, p. 81.

[68] Pierre Boyer, "La Vie politique et les élections à Alger," *La Révolution de 1848 en Algérie: Mélanges d'histoire.* (Paris, 1949), p. 44. See also Julien, *Histoire de l'Algérie*, p. 347.

[69] The proclamations were published in *Le Moniteur*, 19 March 1848, p. 638.

[70] S.H.A. H 263—5, letter to Cavaignac, 21 March 1848.

of liberty."[71] Even such symbolic gestures, however, put Cavaignac in difficulties, and he revealed a certain irresolution that would later manifest itself in his participation in politics on the national level. He approved plans to remove the statue of the Duke of Orléans from in front of the government building in Algiers, but retreated in the face of loud protests and allowed the statue to remain. He watched approvingly as a red Phrygian cap was placed atop the "tree of liberty" in the same public square, but had the cap removed in response to protests.[72]

In more concrete matters, Cavaignac gave less equivocal support to revolutionary developments. By decree he introduced complete freedom of the press in Algeria, announcing that the old system of censorship was incompatible with republican principles.[73] He encouraged the formation of clubs,[74] and supported the "democrats" of Algiers in general;[75] he dissolved the Orleanist municipal government in Algiers and approved the formation of a new one in which "the workers hold a strong position."[76] His support of the radical republican groups soon alienated much of the population. Cavaignac also showed a willingness to act in the face of the social and economic crisis that gripped the colony as well as the *métropole*, but he accomplished little before he departed. He approved the proposals of businessmen to create emergency public credit institutions (*comptoirs d'escompte*) of the sort already created in Paris.[77] He favored priority payment of workers' wages in the event of bankruptcy by employers, but offered no real proposals

[71] Marcel Emérit, "L'Esprit de 1848 en Algérie," *La Révolution de 1848 en Algérie*, p. 17.

[72] Boyer, "La Vie politique à Alger," pp. 45-46, has the most coherent account of these incidents.

[73] J. Bonnardot, "La Presse algérienne sous la seconde république et le second empire," *1848 et les révolutions du XIXe siècle*, No. 180 (1948), pp. 27-28.

[74] Emérit, "L'Esprit de 1848 en Algérie," p. 17. Cavaignac said that when he was first appointed Minister of War "all the clubs came to ask me not to leave." (Letter to Madame Cavaignac, 30 March 1848, Reel 27.)

[75] Boyer, "La Vie politique à Alger," p. 45.

[76] Letter to Madame Cavaignac, 27 March 1848, Reel 16.

[77] Emérit, "L'Esprit de 1848 en Algérie," p. 20.

to cope with unemployment, preferring to await the suggestions from the special committee on labor questions that was meeting at the Luxembourg under Louis Blanc.[78]

Cavaignac's major difficulties were political. After his initial anger at the idea, he accepted calmly enough three civilian officials sent from France,[79] but a special *commissaire* embroiled him in conflict with the Provisional Government and increased his difficulties with segments of the population in Algeria. Cavaignac took the arrival in early April of the *commissaire*, Couput, as a reprisal for his refusal of the ministry,[80] but actually Couput seems to have been the Algerian representative in the second wave of *commissaires*, more radical than the first, sent out by Ledru-Rollin.[81] The general complained bitterly to Arago and to Ledru-Rollin about Couput's activities, which aroused considerable opposition,[82] but felt compelled in the interests of republican unity to defend Couput publicly: "I had to choose between that and an attitude of glaring opposition."[83]

Cavaignac's defense of Couput increased his difficulties with the local population, and even with many army officers and other officials,[84] while at the same time the incident deepened his distaste for Ledru-Rollin and for the methods of the radicals in general: "I am convinced that there is reaction in France, and that Ledru-Rollin is fighting against it, but if he has been as completely maladroit in France as he has been here, if he has used the same men, if these men have employed the same means, then I say that he has served the cause badly

[78] *Ibid.*, pp. 18-19.

[79] Letter to Madame Cavaignac, 29 March 1848, Reel 27.

[80] *Ibid.*, 15 April 1848, Reel 27.

[81] See Haury, "Les Commissaires de Ledru-Rollin en 1848," pp. 438-474. However, Haury neglects to deal with Algeria.

[82] Letter from Arago to Cavaignac, 27 April 1848, Reel 22; letter from Cavaignac to Ledru-Rollin, 27 April 1848, Bibliothèque Thiers, Papiers Jules Baroche, MSS Thiers 1241. Cavaignac's letters do not indicate very clearly the nature of Couput's policies, nor do the standard works, although some writers, including Ibos, associate him with the incident of the statue. (*Le Général Cavaignac*, p. 124.)

[83] Letter to Madame Cavaignac, 30 April 1848, Reel 27. See also that of 15 April 1848, Reel 27.

[84] *Ibid.*, 30 April 1848, Reel 27.

indeed."[85] Cavaignac's problems also fortified his desire to leave Algeria. Eager from the first to seek election to the National Assembly, in March he had asked his mother to pose his candidacy in the department of Lot, because that department had sent his father to the Convention.[86]

He sent a campaign *profession de foi* to his cousin Firmin Cavaignac, asking him to publish it. In this document, Cavaignac emphasized his lifelong republicanism: "I have accepted all my life, as our cherished Godefroy did with greater devotion and abnegation, the heritage of our father."[87] But he also presented himself as a partisan of order, offering the characteristic republican argument that the democratic republic, against which no revolution was justified, offered the best guarantee for order of any political regime. He assured electors also that the republic would respect property, and indeed would seek to generalize property holding. These views, together with silence on the popular social slogans of *le droit au travail* and *association*, stamped Cavaignac unmistakably as a moderate. Although the general sought election only in Lot, *Le National* supported his candidature in Paris also. In the election of April 23, Cavaignac was successful in both areas. Lot chose him at the top of its departmental list;[88] in Paris, he was fourteenth of thirty-four, ahead of some of the more prominent but more radical republicans, including Ledru-Rollin and Louis Blanc.[89]

As General Cavaignac prepared to take up his Assembly seat, he was hopeful once more of becoming Minister of War. Following his earlier refusal, Arago and Flocon had reassured him concerning the army, and asked him to reconsider.[90] La-

85 *Ibid.*

86 *Ibid.*, undated, March 1848, Reel 27.

87 Letter to Firmin Cavaignac, 20 March 1848, Reel 28.

88 A.N., F 1C III—5. See also F. Vallès, "Le Suffrage universel dans le département du Lot," *La Révolution de 1848*, II (1905), pp. 106, 146-160.

89 It is interesting that Cavaignac won few votes from soldiers, who gave Lamartine twice as many. Rémi Gossez, "Notes sur la composition et l'attitude politique de la troupe," *L'Armée et la seconde république*, "Bibliothèque de la révolution de 1848," XVIII (1955), p. 94.

90 Letters from Arago to Cavaignac, 7 and 9 April 1848, Reel 22.

martine also had become a stout partisan of Cavaignac after seeing the general's *profession de foi* in a newspaper. He told Madame Cavaignac of his desire "to see the army return to Paris under the republican guarantee of the name of her son,"[91] and Cavaignac indicated on April 19 that he was ready to accept a renewed offer of the War Ministry.[92] Delighted, Lamartine promised that he would be appointed as soon as the National Assembly convened.[93] Cavaignac departed from Algeria on May 11 and arrived in Paris on May 17, shortly after the abortive popular invasion of the National Assembly; the same day he was appointed Minister of War.[94] Hippolyte Carnot has left an interesting sketch of the impression Cavaignac made on joining the ministry: "After his famous letter to the Provisional Government, I expected to see a very arrogant and rugged man. To the contrary, he has the engaging vivacity of the French officer, with a friendly manner. A pleasant smile tempers the gravity of his countenance and betokens a man of feeling. But his speech is jerky, his gestures are somewhat abrupt and nervous."[95]

Cavaignac had assumed office on the morrow of the invasion of the Assembly, and he immediately took steps to prepare against the possibility of another such attack. First, he sought to create unity of command under himself, a policy that led to the resignation of the conservative General Baraguey d'Hilliers, who had been appointed to defend the National Assembly.[96] Strongly encouraged by Lamartine, Cavaignac also began to strengthen army garrisons in and near Paris. As late as May 1, the Provisional Government had been dependent for defense only on the National Guard and the Garde Mobile, for

[91] *Histoire de la révolution de 1848*, II, pp. 298-300.

[92] Letter to Lamartine, through Madame Cavaignac, 19 April 1848, Reel 27.

[93] Lamartine to Cavaignac, 29 April 1848, Reel 28. Cf. Lamartine, *Histoire de la révolution de 1848*, II, p. 301.

[94] *Le Moniteur*, 18 May 1848, p. 1075.

[95] MS "Mémorial," dos. 15 p. 21.

[96] *Compte rendu des séances de l'Assemblée nationale; exposés des motifs et projets des lois présentés par le gouvernement; rapports de MM. les représentants* (Paris, 1849-50), I, pp. 380-381, 23 May 1848. See also Cavaignac's speech of 29 May, *ibid.*, pp. 523-524.

troops in Paris then numbered only 9,822, as against 37,800 on February 24.[97] In early June, the Executive Commission decided that 25,000 regular troops were to be concentrated in Paris.[98]

Cavaignac also was beginning to assume a role of political importance. The National Assembly as early as May 6 had chosen him to be one of its six vice-presidents. During June, dissatisfaction was growing in the Assembly toward the Executive Commission, there was much talk of replacing it with a single executive, and Cavaignac's name was prominently mentioned as a candidate.[99] An open conflict between the commission and the Assembly occurred in mid-June, concerning the election of Louis Napoleon as a deputy. The commission opposed his admission to the Assembly, but the Assembly voted to accept him. In consequence, some members of the commission, notably Lamartine and Ledru-Rollin, considered resigning.[100] At this point, Cavaignac, to whom many looked as the successor to the commission, played an important role in preserving it, for it was he who opposed most vigorously any resignations, and the Executive Commission decided to remain.[101]

The next day, however, rumors circulated in Marseille that the Executive Commission had resigned in favor of a triumvirate composed of Cavaignac, Armand Marrast, and one Berger. A sea captain carried the rumor to Algeria, and Algiers was then also placarded with the news, a fact that some newspapers later cited as evidence of complicity by General Changarnier, who was then governor-general, in preparing the way to Cavaignac's dictatorship.[102] The rumors were false, but

[97] *Rapport de la commission d'enquête*, II, pp. 49-51.

[98] See the depositions of Lamartine and Ledru-Rollin, *ibid.*, I, pp. 306, 312.

[99] Pierre de la Gorce, *Histoire de la seconde république française* (4th edn., Paris, 1904), I, p. 296.

[100] Calman, *Ledru-Rollin*, pp. 194-199.

[101] *Ibid.*, p. 199.

[102] Changarnier, no friend of Cavaignac's, denied the charge. He said the placards were put up by a civilian prefect. See his *Mémoires: campagnes d'Afrique, 1830-1848*, ed. Henry d'Estre (Paris, 1930), p. 309. *Le National* mentioned the report on July 2, p. 2, professing ignorance of

Cavaignac continued to be considered seriously as a successor to the Executive Commission. Nevertheless, it was not until the midst of the formidable insurrection of June that the National Assembly decided to put the fortunes of the republic in the hands of a general who happened to be a republican.

---

its origin. In 1850 Ledru-Rollin also referred to it. (Calman, *Ledru-Rollin*, p. 199n.)

VI · The June Days

"IF IT COMES TO A FIGHT, YOU WILL ALL PERISH"

On the morning of June 23, a vast new insurrection began in Paris, much larger in scope than that of February, and after four days of bitter fighting in which several thousands were killed and wounded, the government forces were victorious. These were the bloody "June Days," which have since then been universally regarded as a major turning point in the French revolution of 1848, and to which Karl Marx attributed worldwide historical significance as the first great struggle between the revolutionary proletariat and the bourgeoisie. What did this extraordinary event mean to contemporaries, in particular to the governing republicans?[1]

In the first place, Marx was by no means the only one to see a class character in the insurrection. Tocqueville's observa-

[1] There is no satisfactory monograph on the June Days, although the French scholar Rémi Gossez has done extensive research on the subject for a *thèse pour le doctorat ès lettres* at the University of Paris, which is to be a companion work to "Les Ouvriers de Paris." A few conclusions about the insurrection appear there and in other writings by Gossez, in particular "Diversité des antagonismes sociaux vers le milieu du XIXe siècle," *Revue économique*, vi (1956), 439-458.

Another French scholar, Witold Zaniewicki, has recently revealed much about the military aspect of the repression in "L'Armée française en 1848. Introduction à une étude militaire de la deuxième république (22 février-20 décembre 1848)," unpublished *thèse de troisième cycle*, University of Paris, 1966. My own research also throws light on the subject, although I have not attempted an exhaustive investigation.

The standard older work is Charles Schmidt's brief and undocumented *Les Journées de juin 1848* (Paris, 1926), and the best detailed contemporary account appears in the history by Madame d'Agoult, originally published in 1850-53. A recent Soviet study by A. I. Molok, "Problèmes de l'insurrection de juin 1848," was published in the collection, *Questions d'histoire*, ii (Paris, 1954), pp. 57-100. Claude Levy offers a brief survey of recent writings in "Les Journées parisiennes de juin 1848 d'après des études récentes," *Bulletin de la société d'études historiques, géographiques et scientifiques de la région parisienne*, xxxv (1961 [1963]), 19-26. Two recent long narratives that contribute little are by Pierre Dominique: *Les Journées de quarante-huit* (Paris, 1948), pp. 139-285; and *Les Journées de juin* (Paris, 1966).

tions are well known: "It was not, strictly speaking, a political struggle, . . . but a struggle of class against class, a sort of Servile war . . . the whole of the working class was engaged, either in fact or in spirit, in the struggle."[2] Less perspicacious Frenchmen were at first puzzled and alarmed at an uprising that seemed to have no clear political objective and no recognized leaders. Although some viewed the insurgents as criminals and madmen, "anarchists" bent on pillage, demonstrators bought by British or Russian gold, or supporters of Louis Napoleon or even Henry V, many in Paris soon realized that it was the workers who had risen. The barricades flew banners with a variety of legends, but the most common demand seemed to be for "la République démocratique et sociale," or simply, "Bread or Lead." Men and banners from the National Workshop were numerous, and some contemporaries thought erroneously that the workshops furnished the bulk of the insurgents.[3]

"It is said that the proletariat is giving battle," observed *Le National*, and this impression was shared among others by the London *Times*, by Madame d'Agoult, and by Cavaignac and other government officials, who issued proclamations to "the workers."[4] The class character of the uprising, in contrast with earlier insurrections, also seemed apparent from the virtual absence of bourgeois leadership and from its localization in the eastern half of the city, unlike the situation in February when barricades went up also in the more bourgeois central and western *arrondissements.*

However, given the traditional nature of the Parisian working classes, the insurrection was by no means that of a modern proletariat in the Marxian sense. In the Faubourg Saint-Antoine and other artisan quarters at the heart of the insurrection, there was no clear distinction between small employers and workers.[5] Rémi Gossez's recent research confirms the im-

[2] *Recollections*, pp. 150-157.

[3] McKay, *National Workshops*, pp. 145-150.

[4] *Le National*, 25 and 26 June 1848; Stern, *Histoire de la révolution de 1848*, III, pp. 145-242; *The Times*, 27 and 29 June 1848, p. 5; *Le Moniteur*, 25-27 June 1848.

[5] Chevalier, *Population parisienne*, p. 28.

pression that it was primarily an uprising of the working classes, although some insurgents came from other classes in eastern Paris; there was a scattering of "*déclassés* from all the social *milieux*,"[6] but very few students. Some came from the poorest "classes dangereuses," but instead most had been among the more prosperous workers whose living conditions and expectations were severely affected by the economic crisis. Only a minority came from the newer mechanized industries; most were artisans in the traditional crafts, particularly cabinetmakers and workers in the building trades. Yet the workers' corporations did not arise as groups, nor did the militants of worker organization do much fighting.[7] Finally, most of the insurgents were apparently recent immigrants to Paris, chiefly from turbulent regions of the east and the north,[8] and the insurrection in one sense was the final explosion of the great demographic phenomenon of the first half of the nineteenth century, the "monstrous growth" of Paris, which then stagnated during the mid-century years of crisis.[9]

In recent historical works, the insurrection has commonly been interpreted from a point of view strongly sympathetic to the insurgents. It has been suggested that the bourgeois republicans were motivated by selfish class interests, frightened by the threat of social revolution into deserting their professed ideals and becoming reactionary champions of "order." To this interpretation there has often been added, following Marx, a charge that the bourgeois National Assembly deliberately provoked an uprising of the workers in order to crush them. "*Il faut en finir*! This situation must end! With this cry the National Assembly gave vent to its determination to force the proletariat into a decisive struggle."[10]

[6] "Diversité des antagonismes sociaux," pp. 450-452.

[7] "Les Ouvriers de Paris," pp. 806-810. Gossez studied the individual dossiers of some 11,000 prisoners arrested during and after the insurrection.

[8] Chevalier, *Population parisienne*, p. 17.

[9] See Pouthas, *La Population française*, pp. 143-174.

[10] Marx, *The Class Struggles in France*, p. 55. The thesis of provocation appears in Georges Renard, *La République de 1848*, "Histoire socialiste," ed. Jean Jaurès (Paris, n.d. [1906?]), IX, pp. 74-77; Georges Duveau,

The fact that a conflict was foreseen by many on the side of the government seems to support the thesis of provocation. Lamartine, for example, regarded a final struggle as inevitable, and from early June he urged speed on Cavaignac in bringing troops to Paris: "Prepare yourself for a battle; the battle is imminent."[11] Rémusat also thought a conflict inevitable, as did Tocqueville, who even believed that "it would be well to seize the first opportunity to deliver it."[12] The writer Maxime du Camp, who as a young National Guardsman fought against the insurgents, recalled that Michel Goudchaux told him that the government had resolved to hasten the dissolution of the National Workshops "in order to engage the combat immediately and to vanquish the insurrectional army before it was completely organized."[13]

But if Tocqueville and others were led to advocate a kind of preventive war, it was precisely because there was good reason to believe that the radical activists would themselves attack. Although popular sovereignty as expressed through universal manhood suffrage had long been a dogma for the republicans, the old Jacobin belief in the revolutionary superiority of the people of Paris had been implicit in the demand for adjournment of the elections, and on April 5, the influential Club of Clubs declared that if the National Assembly was too moderate, then "insurrection would be the most sacred of duties."[14] Moreover, a similar injunction had even emanated from the Provisional Government, in the form of the famous Bulletin of April 15 (written by George Sand but issued over the name of Ledru-Rollin, who disavowed it), which advocated a new resort to the barricades in the event the elections should produce a "false national representation."[15]

1848: Le Livre du centenaire (Paris, 1948), pp. 72-73; Gaston Martin, *La Révolution de 1848* (Paris, 1948), p. 99; Dautry, *1848*, pp. 167ff.; Emile Tersen, *Quarante-huit* (Paris, 1957), p. 154; and McKay, *National Workshops*, p. 134.

[11] *Histoire de la révolution de 1848*, II, p. 453. Cavaignac recalled the statement on November 25: *Compte rendu des séances*, V, p. 822.

[12] *Recollections*, p. 108; Rémusat, *Mémoires de ma vie*, IV, p. 325.

[13] Maxime du Camp, *Souvenirs de l'année 1848* (Paris, 1876), p. 234.

[14] Seignobos, *La Révolution de 1848*, p. 62.

[15] Stern, *Histoire de la révolution de 1848*, III, pp. 292-293.

The invasion of the Assembly on May 15 had been serious enough, and afterwards many residents of Paris, workers and bourgeois as well as deputies, expected another crisis. Men from the National Workshops had been prominent among the demonstrators on May 15, and thereafter sentiment grew in the government and Assembly that this costly foyer of a hundred thousand potential insurgents must be ended, if necessary by dissolution. The Executive Commission decided to stop enrollments, and to give young bachelors the option of enlisting in the army or facing dismissal, but it proceeded warily.[16] Enrollments were restricted but not completely ended, and the alternative of army service was quietly if temporarily shelved. Further preparatory measures were drawn up, but resistance by Emile Thomas, the workshops' director, led on May 26 to his dismissal and forced exile to Bordeaux. Alarmed at the removal of the popular Thomas, many workers protested, and rumors spread of an impending insurrection.

The National Assembly on May 30 adopted a number of proposals anticipating gradual dissolution, notably one to send nonresidents back to the provinces through transportation allowances. But the Executive Commission, fearful of the possible results, delayed in applying the new policies. From the beginning of June, the atmosphere in Paris was tense, and a new factor was added by the popularity of Louis Napoleon Bonaparte, who was elected to the National Assembly on June 4. The continued street disorders impelled the Assembly a few days later to adopt a law forbidding gatherings of men bearing arms, but despite numerous arrests, agitation increased.

There were some indications that workers and club members looked forward confidently to a new insurrection. Michel Chevalier predicted to Nassau Senior on May 24 that there would be another battle in the streets soon, for the "anarchists" had been near success on May 15, and thought themselves nearer now.[17] Some clubs adopted a threatening attitude; the Club des Monts de Belleville began to make musket balls, and all "awaited the shooting." In Paris, many workers began to

[16] McKay, *National Workshops*, p. 77.

[17] W. Nassau Senior, *Journals Kept in France and Italy, from 1848 to 1852* (London, 1871), I, p. 114.

look to the *Comité central des ouvriers* for leadership in "the resumption of the armed struggle," and one delegate affirmed, "When the time is ripe, all of us will then be able to arise as one man, to crush them all without mercy. . . . *Il faut en finir.*"[18]

Rumors circulated that the signal for a new uprising would be another banquet, a huge and proletarian 25-centime affair, originally scheduled for June 4, then postponed finally to July 14.[19] Two weeks before the uprising, Tocqueville was startled to hear George Sand, whom he met for the first time at a dinner party, tell him in great detail of the workers' preparations. As a self-styled spokesman for them, she warned: "Try to persuade your friends, Monsieur, not to force the people into the streets by alarming or irritating them. I also wish that I could instil patience into my own friends; for if it comes to a fight, believe me, you will all perish."[20]

If a battle was anticipated on both sides, there is no real evidence that it was intentionally provoked, that Tocqueville's theory of preventive war was actually adopted. Indeed, the evidence suggests that the government was apprehensive, eager to avoid a conflict. Madame d'Agoult observed that everyone foresaw a battle, but that the republicans "feared it as the greatest peril that the republic could face."[21] On June 21, the mayor of Paris, Armand Marrast, opposed immediate municipal elections in the capital because he feared they would spark an uprising.[22]

It would have been extremely rash for the government, four months after the successful insurrection of February, to insti-

[18] Gossez, "Les Ouvriers de Paris," p. 721. For the clubs, see Gustave Geffroy, "Les Journées de juin 1848," *La Révolution de 1848*, I (1904), pp. 22-29. However, Wassermann, *Les Clubs*, pp. 216-217, says that the clubs did not plan an insurrection.

[19] See Peter Amann, "Prelude to Insurrection: The Banquet of the People," *French Historical Studies*, I (1960), 436-444.

[20] *Recollections*, p. 149. See also some testimony suggesting a planned uprising in *Rapport de la commission d'enquête*, I, p. 183. One deputy who was a former worker said that several days before the insurrection he had received passwords which he successfully used to cross barricades. (*Ibid.*, p. 298.)

[21] *Histoire de la révolution de 1848*, III, p. 120.

[22] A.N., C 926, minutes of the Committee on Departmental and Communal Administration, p. 89.

gate a battle in the streets that they stood a good chance of losing. Louis-Philippe had had a force of about 84,000 in Paris in February, including the National Guard and some 37,000 regular troops, and yet the insurgents won; the republican government had only 25,000 regular troops in Paris on June 23, and the new democratized National Guard could easily prove no more reliable than Louis-Philippe's had been. It was now theoretically 237,000 strong, but in the event of a real class conflict, a defection of armed National Guardsmen in the eastern working-class legions was at least as likely as the crucial defection of the bourgeois Guardsmen in February. The Garde Mobile was also unreliable. This force, which numbered some 15,000 in June, had been recruited from among the insurgents of February, mostly from youths sixteen to twenty years of age. To contemporaries the Garde Mobile seemed drawn from the same social milieux which threatened a new insurrection, and even though it had proved loyal during the demonstration of May 15, the belief remained strong both among workers and bourgeois that in the feared crisis "the Garde Mobile would be found on the side of the insurrection."[23]

Despite appearances, Gossez has found that there were some social differences between the insurgents and the Garde Mobile, the latter being younger, native-born Parisians drawn mostly from the "classes dangereuses" and chronically unemployed social outcasts.[24] Marx, too, had distinguished the Garde Mobile from the workers by describing them as the "lumpenproletariat." These *gamins*, well paid, owed all they had to the government that employed them, and contrary to expectations, they fought loyally and even enthusiastically in June. Madame d'Agoult believed that if they had fought on the other side, the insurrection would have triumphed, a con-

[23] Commandant P. Chalmin, "Une Institution militaire de la seconde république: la garde nationale mobile," *Etudes d'histoire moderne et contemporaine*, II (1948), p. 61. However, Peter Amann has found evidence that delegates to the Club des clubs had predicted in April that the Garde Mobile would fight loyally for the government in the event of a new uprising. See "Writings on the Second French Republic," pp. 415-416.

[24] "Diversité des antagonismes sociaux," p. 446.

clusion shared by Gossez.[25] The thesis of provocation rests on the unhistorical assumption that the triumph of the government was inevitable, when in fact the issue was in doubt for some time, and in the end four days of difficult combat were necessary to defeat the insurgents.[26]

The abrupt manner in which the National Workshops seemed about to be liquidated has been interpreted as intentionally provocative, for the incident usually credited with touching off the insurrection was the publication, on June 22, of the decree offering the alternatives of dismissal or army enlistment. Donald C. McKay, author of the standard study of the workshops, observed that the decree "could scarcely be viewed by the workers as other than an outright provocation. . . ."[27] But McKay himself gives no evidence that the government intended the decree to be provocative; indeed, his evidence tends to refute the idea of deliberation. The workshops were a real dilemma; it was feared that an insurrection might result from the huge concentration of idle men, and also that insurrection might result if they were dispersed. The Executive Commission resisted pressure from the Assembly for the dissolution, fearing, in the words of Marie, "agitation . . . one rising after another."[28] The government adopted the forced enlistment policy on June 16 but delayed publishing it until June 22. Even then it acted not in confidence, but in fear, and apparently out of a desire to revive its prestige with the Assembly.

Was the Assembly seeking to be provocative? To the contrary, for on June 23, when the insurrection was just beginning, the Assembly went out of its way to avoid giving this appearance by refusing to discuss a proposal by the Comte de Falloux for dissolution within three days.[29] Was it then Falloux? McKay and others imply that he, as chairman of a special committee on the National Workshops, deliberately sought by

[25] Stern, *Histoire de la révolution de 1848*, III, p. 164; "Diversité des antagonismes sociaux," p. 447.

[26] For the mood of fear and uncertainty, see also Rémusat, *Mémoires de ma vie*, IV, p. 335.

[27] *National Workshops*, p. 134.

[28] *Ibid.*, p. 112.

[29] *Ibid.*, pp. 143-144.

his hasty introduction of his committee's proposal to provoke an uprising that would assure the triumph of the "forces of order."[30] Madame d'Agoult imputes political rather than social motivations to Falloux, charging him with fomenting a proletarian insurrection in order to undermine the republic and prepare for a Legitimist restoration.[31]

There seems little basis for either allegation. Falloux was one of the small and advanced group of Catholic Legitimists who had a "sincere desire for social reform."[32] Moreover, his proposals included a number of reforms of benefit to workers, and his own explanation to the Assembly of his haste in advocating dissolution makes sense. The fighting had already begun, and "if the misguided workers who attack us are defeated tomorrow, I will never consent to sponsor a measure which they regard as disastrous to them. . . . I will not allow them to think that I awaited their defeat to proclaim here what you have for a long time believed desirable and necessary."[33]

THE INSURRECTION

No single incident touched off the insurrection, but agitation increased after June 19, when Ulysse Trélat, now Minister of Public Works, announced the government's intention to start sending men from the National Workshops to projects in the provinces. "The immediate origins of the insurrection," says McKay, "are to be found in a meeting held in the Faubourg Saint-Marceau on June 21."[34] Here men from the workshops and some of the clubs apparently decided to resort to barricades should the government fail to respond favorably to a protest over the impending dissolution of the National Workshops. As planned, several hundred men from the work-

[30] *Ibid.* See also his article, "Le Vicomte de Falloux et les ateliers nationaux," *La Révolution de 1848*, xxx (1933), pp. 30-42; Renard, *La République de 1848*, pp. 74-75, and Guillemin, *La Tragédie de quarante-huit*, pp. 301-313.

[31] *Histoire de la révolution de 1848*, III, p. 120.

[32] J. B. Duroselle, *Les Débuts du catholicisme social en France (1822-1870)*, (Paris, 1951), pp. 444-445.

[33] Cited in McKay, *National Workshops*, p. 143.

[34] *Ibid.*, pp. 132, 136. Gossez questions this view; see "Les Ouvriers de Paris," pp. 803-806.

shops gathered early on the following morning, June 22, at the Place de la Bastille and marched to the Petit Luxembourg, seat of the Executive Commission.

A decree published in *Le Moniteur* of that day further enflamed the demonstrators: it was the one giving workers between eighteen and twenty-five years of age the option of enlistment in the army, or dismissal.[35] A group of demonstrators led by one Louis Pujol held a stormy interview with Marie, a member of the Executive Commission, who gave them no satisfaction but threatened to use force if necessary to carry out the decisions. Scattered demonstrations occurred throughout the day, the workers shouting, "Bread or lead! Lead or work! We will not depart!" At a mass meeting that evening at the Panthéon, Pujol cried, "The people have been deceived! You have done nothing more than change tyrants, and the tyrants of today are more odious than those who have been driven out. . . . You must take vengeance! And to avenge yourselves, you have an invincible weapon in the barricades!"[36] Pujol called for another gathering early the next day.

Around noon on June 22, in the face of the turmoil, General Cavaignac as Minister of War had ordered the First Military Division (Paris) into a state of alert.[37] Moreover, sentiment within the National Assembly was mounting to supplant the Executive Commission with Cavaignac as single executive. On June 22 *La Presse* of Emile de Girardin published a satirical dialogue in which the republicans were portrayed as seeking to maintain themselves in power by "rendering necessary the

[35] *Le Moniteur,* 22 June 1848, and 23 June 1848 for correction of the minimum age from the previously stated seventeen to eighteen years. McKay, *National Workshops,* p. 133n., pointed out that previous writers who spoke of a decree of June 21 concerning army enlistments or work in the provinces had confused two separate announcements. On June 19, the policy of shifting workers to the provinces was announced; the notice in *Le Moniteur* of June 22 referred only to the decision on military enlistments, "worded in such a way that it seemed to refer to an earlier decree, actually adopted June 16 but never published."

[36] McKay, *National Workshops,* pp. 140-141.

[37] General Doumenc, "L'Armée et les journées de juin," *Actes du congrès historique du centenaire de la révolution de 1848* (Paris, 1948), p. 262.

dictatorship of Cavaignac."[38] That same evening, delegates from the most important group of republican deputies, the Réunion du Palais National, visited the general and asked if he were willing to assume power. He said that he would, provided the Executive Commission fell and the National Assembly wanted him.[39] A spokesman for the monarchist faction, the Réunion de la Rue de Poitiers, also told Cavaignac of support within that group. There the matter rested for a time.

At 6 A.M. on Friday, June 23, thousands of workers began to assemble as planned in the Place du Panthéon. After another speech by Pujol, they proceeded to the Place de la Bastille, where they pledged, "Liberty or Death!" Around 10 A.M., the gathering dispersed; near the Porte Saint-Denis, one group overturned an omnibus and began to erect the first barricade. Many others were constructed over a wide area with astonishing speed; by noon, virtually the whole of eastern Paris, except for the Hôtel de Ville, was in the control of the insurgents.

The construction of barricades was allowed to proceed virtually unmolested, in accordance with a strategy worked out by Cavaignac and accepted by the Executive Commission, which that morning gave him full command of all military forces in Paris. His plan was to treat the insurrection as a military rather than a police problem, and he was determined to avoid the experiences of the army in 1830 and in February of 1848, when contingents had been isolated, demoralized, and disarmed, and the result had been humiliating defeat. Also, again conscious of February, Cavaignac assumed that he must rely on regular troops rather than the National Guard. Instead of seeking to prevent the construction of barricades, the general planned first to concentrate his forces, mostly in the west of Paris near the Assembly, but also at the Hôtel de Ville, after which he would send strong columns against the insurgent positions. The corollary was that he would allow the insurrection to develop instead of trying to forestall it.

Cavaignac's strategy was dictated in part by the relatively small number of troops at his disposal. To combat the esti-

[38] Reproduced in Emile de Girardin, *Questions de mon temps, 1836 à 1856* (Paris, 1858), III, p. 436.

[39] *Compte rendu des séances*, V, pp. 833-834, 25 November 1848.

mated 40,000 to 50,000 active and well-armed insurgents who were morally and materially supported by most of the population of eastern Paris, fighting often from behind formidable barricades in the tangled maze of streets in pre-Haussmann Paris, Cavaignac had only 25,000 regular troops in the city, many of whom had been disarmed in February, together with 2,600 republican guards. He also included the 15,000 Gardes Mobiles in his plan of concentration, but it remained uncertain if, how well, or how long they would fight. As reserves, there were 4,000 regular troops in Versailles and Saint-Germain; in addition, Cavaignac had alerted three brigades of the Army of the Alps to draw near Paris, but as this was in anticipation of trouble expected on July 14, these troops were not available during the fighting.[40]

The expected unreliability of the National Guard was so great that Cavaignac did not even include it in his plan of concentration. Nevertheless, the guard was called out at 8:30 A.M. on June 23, but the response was ominous. In eastern Paris most refused to answer the call, sympathized with the insurrection, or fought as insurgents. Indeed, Gossez found that the "cadres" of the insurrection were the National Guard units of the working-class areas.[41] Even in the central *arrondissements*, only 4,000 Guardsmen answered the summons, while 60,000 remained at home. Only in the predominantly bourgeois west did the National Guard respond very positively, and most of these remained in a defensive posture in their own quarters, only some 12,000 being available for combat.[42]

The Garde Mobile, on the other hand, moved swiftly to the points of concentration along with the regiments of the line; many reached their assigned positions before noon, and vir-

[40] Jean Vidalenc, "La Province et les journées de juin," *Etudes d'histoire moderne et contemporaine*, II (1948), p. 100. See also Ferdinand Boyer, "L'Armée des Alpes en 1848," *Revue historique*, CCXXXIII (1965), 86-87.

[41] "Les Ouvriers de Paris," p. 810. For the call up of the National Guard, see Zaniewicki, "L'Armée française en 1848," I, p. 74, and the register of the Executive Commission kept by Pagnerre, A.N., 67 AP 5.

[42] Louis Girard, *La Garde nationale, 1814-1871* (Paris, 1964), pp. 313-316.

tually all were concentrated by 3 P.M.[43] Some soldiers converging on the Hôtel de Ville crossed barricades without attempting to dismantle them, in accordance with instructions.

Before the fighting began, there were several efforts at conciliation. François Arago made the most dramatic attempt. Appearing with a group of Guardsmen before a barricade across the Rue Soufflot, the venerable scientist and republican asked the insurgents why they had risen against the republic.

"You were at the barricades with us in 1832," protested one insurgent, and another's comment indicated the stark significance of the barricade now separating them: "Monsieur Arago, we are full of respect for you, but you have no right to reproach us. You have never been hungry, you don't know what poverty is."

Arago vainly sought to convince the workers of the good intentions of the government, and soon concluded that "force must decide."[44]

There were other, less dramatic attempts, by mayors and National Guard officers, to persuade the insurgents to disband peaceably. Cavaignac himself authorized one such unsuccessful initiative by sending to calm the Faubourg Saint-Antoine a deputy well known there, Charles Beslay, who later was to be a member of the Commune of 1871.[45]

The place where the first barricade was erected, at the Porte Saint-Denis, was also the scene of the first fighting, which broke out around noon on June 23, when insurgents fired on National Guardsmen who called on them to surrender. At about the same time, Arago's forces went into action near the Panthéon. Other skirmishes involving Guardsmen occurred near the Hôtel de Ville. Even before noon, Cavaignac had begun to send out his regular troops, supported by the Garde Mobile, in three columns. One went to reinforce those at the Hôtel de Ville, which was feared to be the first objective of the in-

[43] Doumenc, "L'Armée et les journées de juin," p. 262; Zaniewicki, "L'Armée française en 1848," I, p. 75.

[44] Stern, *Histoire de la révolution de 1848*, III, pp. 157-158. For a slightly different version of the exchange, see Schmidt, *Journées de juin*, p. 53.

[45] Beslay, *1830-1848-1870: Mes souvenirs* (Paris, 1873), p. 182.

surgents, after which they were expected to attack the National Assembly. Another column was to attack to the north, from Montmartre to the Faubourg du Temple. The third was to operate on the left bank.

General Lamoricière arrived at the Porte Saint-Denis shortly after National Guardsmen had taken the barricade in a fierce battle. Lamoricière was able to take others, but found resistance so strong that he had to call for reinforcements. There was also bloody fighting near the Hôtel de Ville and on the left bank, in which General Bedeau and a republican deputy, Bixio, were wounded. During the afternoon, the insurrection spread to some suburban communes inside the fortifications, in particular to La Villette and Belleville. But the repression also was spreading; acting spontaneously on hearing the news of the uprising, 350 volunteer National Guardsmen from Rouen and Vernon entrained for Paris, where they arrived at about 5 P.M.[46] They were the first wave of what soon would become a massive intervention from the provinces against the Paris workers.

Late in the afternoon of June 23, in response to Lamoricière's pleas, Cavaignac himself decided to lead seven battalions to his aid. The commander in chief then remained in the area of the Faubourg du Temple for several hours, personally directing the assault on one imposing barricade. He did not return to his headquarters in the Palais Bourbon until after 8 P.M., convinced more than ever of the gravity of the situation.[47]

The National Assembly had met in regular session at 1 P.M., shortly after the fighting began, and following a brief attempt to go on with normal business, the Comte de Falloux rose to read his report advocating early dissolution of the National Workshops. Fearing this would enflame the insurgents further, Corbon, as chairman of the Committee on Labor, immediately introduced a proposal for governmental encouragement of workers' producers' cooperatives by a credit of 3 million

46 Vidalenc, "La Province et les journées de juin," II, p. 101.

47 The sources vary somewhat on the precise time of Cavaignac's absence, but it was most probably between 4 P.M. and 9 P.M.

francs, and the Assembly postponed discussion of Falloux's report.

During the afternoon, Victor Considérant and Caussidière sought in vain to persuade the Assembly to make conciliatory overtures. Considérant drew up a proclamation signed by Louis Blanc and twenty other deputies; it called upon the workers to throw down their "fratricidal weapons" because they were "victims of a fatal misunderstanding" and promised that the Assembly would work for "social fraternity."[48] The agitated Assembly refused even to permit Considérant to read it aloud. The reception of Caussidière's suggestion that he lead a delegation to appeal to the insurgents was equally cold. "One doesn't reason with insurgents," shouted one deputy, "one defeats them!" The Assembly declared itself in permanent session, and during the evening heard periodic reports on the fighting. Only at midnight was the session suspended; many deputies slept in the great hall, around which troops were once more massed.

Having given unity of command to Cavaignac, the Executive Commission was unable to function effectively, and members dispersed to various points. During Cavaignac's absence in the Faubourg du Temple, Marie and Ledru-Rollin at the Palais Bourbon were unable to grant the many requests for reinforcements; dissatisfaction increased, all the more since the latter was suspected of sympathy for the insurgents. In fact, however, Ledru-Rollin took the initiative of telegraphing nearby departments for assistance.[49] But some deputies asked for the resignation of the Executive Commission.[50]

During the night of June 23, there were significant developments on both sides. The insurgents, still in command of most of the eastern portion of the city, rebuilt or strengthened many barricades and erected new ones. They were encouraged

[48] For the text, see Stern, *Histoire de la révolution de 1848*, III, pp. 336-337.

[49] Vidalenc, "La Province et les journées de juin," II, p. 101. Zaniewicki argues that Cavaignac did not yet have the authority to issue such a command. ("L'Armée française en 1848," I, p. 77.)

[50] *Compte rendu des séances*, V, p. 819, 25 November 1848.

also by news that Marseille too was in arms, and by rumors that workers from Rouen and Lille were coming to their aid, although in fact the uprising in Marseille had already been suppressed, and the only men to come from Rouen and Lille fought on the other side. Indeed, the June insurrection was almost purely a Parisian affair. There was apparently no connection between the uprisings in Paris and Marseille, and expressions of sympathy for the Paris workers were relatively few, in the Seine valley, at Angers, Dijon, Le Mans and Orléans. The industrial towns of the north were calm, as was, perhaps owing to precautions taken, Lyon.[51] Louis Chevalier found that in six departments near Paris, there was no perceptible echo to the insurrection in workers' milieux.[52] Yet, the fighting in the city was so unexpectedly difficult that Cavaignac found it necessary to send an armed convoy during the night to Vincennes for more ammunition. He visited command posts of the bivouacking troops during the night, and returned after 2 A.M., to sleep on a cot in an office.

Early in the morning of June 24, the fighting resumed, and bourgeois Parisians were awakened by the sound of cannon fire.[53] From their strengthened positions, the insurgents took the offensive, particularly in the center, where they seized the *mairies* of the Eighth and Ninth *arrondissements*, disarmed an infantry battalion in the Place des Vosges, and seemed about to attack the Hôtel de Ville.

Members of the National Assembly, who gathered even before the special session was to resume at 8 A.M., were alarmed at the spread of the insurrection, and as Tocqueville reflected, "it was difficult to believe that it would not end by being victorious, when one remembered that all the great insurrections of the last sixty years had triumphed." As Tocqueville arrived, he found Thiers in an unusual state of agitation.

"I know something of insurrections," said Thiers, "and I tell you this is the worst I have ever seen. The insurgents may be here within an hour, and we shall be butchered one and all."[54]

51 Vidalenc, "La Province et les journées de juin," II, pp. 122-126.
52 Chevalier, "Les Fondements économiques et sociaux," pp. 299-300.
53 Tocqueville, *Recollections*, p. 156.
54 *Ibid.*, pp. 158, 162.

Lamartine also told Victor Hugo that he feared an imminent invasion of the Assembly.[55] Tocqueville nervously sent a message to his wife, telling her to flee to Saint-Germain should the insurgents take control of Paris.

The movement to replace the Executive Commission by Cavaignac also reached a climax on the morning of June 24. Jules Senard, the Assembly's president and an ardent supporter of the general, opened the meeting with a brief speech indicating that the situation was grave, but predicting victory if the suppression were energetically pursued. He praised the leadership of Cavaignac, but was silent concerning the Executive Commission.[56] He then suspended the session for half an hour, during which the change of governments was prepared. Senard himself with a few republican deputies asked the Executive Commission to resign, but they refused, saying that they would retire only if the Assembly willed it. Confident of such a result, Senard began conferring with the general while the *bureaux* of the Assembly also discussed the matter. Also in Cavaignac's favor was a statement from the Minister of the Interior, Recurt, who said that the National Guard lacked confidence in the government, and would no longer fight unless all power were given to Cavaignac and Paris were declared in a state of siege.[57]

The republicans were eager to accept the general; the Rue de Poitiers was less enthusiastic, but preferred him to the Executive Commission. The idea of the state of siege aroused some strong objections, especially from republicans who felt it would violate their principles. When the session resumed at 9:35 A.M., a republican deputy, Pascal Duprat, introduced a motion declaring Paris in a state of siege and concentrating all power in the hands of Cavaignac. Although no one spoke against the general, some deputies spoke against the state of siege. But in the midst of the clamor, Jules Bastide, the Foreign Minister, mounted the tribune and excitedly urged: "In the name of the

[55] See Hugo's *Souvenirs personnels, 1848-1851*, ed. Henri Guillemin (Paris, 1952), p. 79.

[56] *Compte rendu des séances*, II, p. 185.

[57] Stern, *Histoire de la révolution de 1848*, III, p. 187.

fatherland, I beseech you to end your deliberations and to vote as soon as possible, for in an hour perhaps the Hôtel de Ville will be taken."

The Assembly immediately complied. By its declaration, at about 10 A.M. on June 24, Paris was declared in a state of siege, and "all executive powers" were delegated to Cavaignac, who thus became virtually a dictator.[58] "The Assembly knew precisely that this was what it wanted," recalled Tocqueville, who himself supported the dictatorship as "indispensable to the safety of the country."[59] Bastide was so worried that he privately told Lord Normanby, the British ambassador, that no one of them could be confident that they would live to the end of that day.[60]

Indeed, that Saturday was the high tide of the insurrection, the day when "for an instant, the insurgents came close to winning," and when the Garde Mobile fought so crucially on the government side.[61] Anticipating victory, the insurgents began to circulate lists of names for a new Provisional Government, which included not only radicals and socialists such as Barbès, Blanqui, Louis Blanc and Caussidière, but even Louis Napoleon Bonaparte. The insurrection threatened to spread still further, and there were even some attempts, soon thwarted, to build barricades near the Invalides.[62]

Armed with new powers, Cavaignac closed the clubs, sought to disarm National Guardsmen who had not responded, and seized a number of newspapers suspected of fomenting the uprising. He even imprisoned Emile de Girardin, famed editor of *La Presse*, and when he heard that Thiers was advocating that the Assembly be moved out of Paris, Cavaignac was enraged. "The departure of the Assembly would lose everything. If M. Thiers continues to adhere to such a proposal, I'll have

58 *Compte rendu des séances*, II, p. 188.

59 *Recollections*, pp. 163-164. Cavaignac's critics later said that his supporters had spread rumors to precipitate the vote, but curiously enough did not argue that Bastide's appearance was calculated. Tocqueville obviously believed that Bastide was sincere.

60 The Marquis of Normanby, *A Year of Revolution: From a Journal Kept in Paris in 1848* (London, 1857), II, p. 90.

61 Gossez, "Diversité des antagonismes sociaux," p. 447.

62 Report of the police prefect to Cavaignac, Reel 21.

him shot."[63] The general sought to dissuade members of the National Workshops from joining the insurrection by continuing to pay them during the combat. The original idea was that of Lalanne, the director, but Cavaignac supported him, whereas the reaction of Lamoricière was to threaten to have Lalanne shot.[64]

Cavaignac did not use his dictatorial powers to reorganize the government; preoccupied with the fighting, he simply retained the existing ministers, although the Executive Commission itself resigned. He did issue several proclamations, justifying their cause to the soldiers and Guardsmen, and appealing to the insurgents to lay down their arms. Early in the afternoon, he used his new authority to send out to all prefects a request for support from the National Guardsmen of the provinces, an appeal that led to a remarkable and unprecedented provincial "Levée en masse" against the insurgent capital. During the next few days, more than 100,000 men from fifty-three departments were to answer the call. Although their contribution to the fighting was slight—most arrived only after the insurrection was over—the provincials gave powerful moral support to the government side.[65]

Fighting continued throughout the second day, during which the tide turned against the insurgents. The anticipated assault on the Hôtel de Ville did not occur, and most of the region was subdued, as was the left bank, except for the Faubourg Saint-Marcel. But the Faubourgs du Temple and Saint-Antoine remained in insurgent hands.

Sunday, June 25, was viewed by some as the crucial day, for both in 1830 and in February 1848, insurrections that lasted three days had triumphed. This was the day of the bloodiest combats, and of other dramatic events. In the north, the Faubourg du Temple resisted Lamoricière most of the day. In the center, two generals and a colonel were killed in leading efforts to penetrate to the Faubourg Saint-Antoine. On the left bank, the government dominated the entire area except near the

[63] André Lebey, *Louis Napoléon Bonaparte et la révolution de 1848* (Paris, 1907-08), I, p. 322n.

[64] McKay, *National Workshops*, pp. 145-148.

[65] Vidalenc, "La Province et les journées de juin," II, pp. 98-115.

exterior boulevards. At one huge barricade at the Place d'Italie, another general, Bréa, was made prisoner while attempting to persuade the insurgents to surrender. Fearing for the general's life, the officer left in charge of the troops asked Cavaignac for instructions.

"The Republic," replied the commander in chief, "cannot be sacrificed for the life of an imprudent general," and ordered the attack to proceed if the barricade did not surrender in fifteen minutes.[66] Meanwhile, a few insurgents, after hearing rumors that the Garde Mobile was shooting prisoners, killed General Bréa and his aide-de-camp, but the barricade fell soon afterwards.

Sunday, June 25, also witnessed some attempts to end the insurrection peacefully. Accompanied by a delegate from La Chapelle, Caussidière asked Cavaignac to promise amnesty for those who would surrender immediately. The general refused to offer any concessions, but did draw up a conciliatory proclamation:[67]

> Workers, and all of you who still raise your arms against the Republic, for the last time, in the name of everything respectable, holy and sacred to men, lay down your weapons. The National Assembly, the entire Nation ask it of you.
>
> You are being told that cruel vengeance awaits you. It is your enemies, and ours also, who say those things.
>
> You are told that you will be sacrificed in cold blood. Come to us, come as brothers repentant and ready to submit to the law, and the open arms of the republic are ready to receive you.

When the text was read aloud in the Assembly, Louis Blanc cried, "Ah, very good, it is excellent!"[68] A thousand copies

[66] See two undated notes in Reel 21, and another cited in Stern, *Histoire de la révolution de 1848*, III, p. 218.

[67] This incident was reported by Caussidière in debate on August 25, and Cavaignac did not deny it, nor Caussidière's statement that Cavaignac had told him then, "If you weren't also a good republican, you certainly wouldn't be here!" See *Le Moniteur*, 26 August 1848, p. 2171, and *Mémoires de Caussidière*, II, p. 229.

[68] *Compte rendu des séances*, II, p. 204, 25 June 1848.

were sent for distribution in the Faubourg Saint-Antoine.[69]

A more dramatic attempt at conciliation was made by the archbishop of Paris, Monseigneur Affre, who took copies of the general's proclamation on a personal appeal to the insurgents in front of a great barricade closing off the Faubourg Saint-Antoine.[70] The archbishop was talking with some insurgents when firing unaccountably recommenced, and he was struck in the body, the bullet apparently having come from the government side.[71] "May my blood be the last to be shed," he murmured before dying.

Although the insurgents were still masters of the Faubourg Saint-Antoine when night fell, it was increasingly clear to them that defeat was imminent. Some wanted to negotiate, and four delegates discussed terms during the night with Senard and with Cavaignac. The former was conciliatory, agreeing to a few minor conditions, and even joining the delegates in a toast to "la République démocratique et sociale," but Cavaignac, warned by Lamoricière that the army would be humiliated if deprived of a complete victory, insisted on unconditional surrender, agreeing only to prolong the truce until 10 A.M. the following day.[72] Many insurgents were willing to capitulate, but others refused, and when the hour struck, the silence was broken by a chorus of voices rising in a last defiant but mournful challenge, "Death to Cavaignac! Death to the executioner of the people!"[73]

The general commanding the troops waited another ten minutes before opening fire. There was little fight left on the other side; many insurgents fled, some began to dismantle the barricades, some were shot. While General Perrot sent several columns into the Faubourg, Lamoricière arrived after ending the last resistance in the Faubourg du Temple. At 11:20

[69] See the receipt from the mayor of the Sixth *arrondissement* in Reel 21.

[70] Schmidt, *Journées de juin*, pp. 107-109.

[71] See the discussion of the controversy over this affair in Dautry, *1848*, p. 194.

[72] Schmidt, *Journées de juin*, pp. 117-118.

[73] Stern, *Histoire de la révolution de 1848*, III, p. 239; Schmidt, *Journées de juin*, p. 119.

A.M. on June 26, Senard excitedly entered the hall of the National Assembly and announced: "The insurrection is over! . . . Thanks be to God. Vive la République!"[74] The announcement was somewhat premature, but by 4 P.M. it was true. Cavaignac sent a message to all prefects and subprefects: "The insurrection is completely vanquished. . . . The cause of order has triumphed. Vive la République!"[75]

What was the price of victory? Official statements issued shortly after the fighting are probably fairly accurate for casualties on the government side, but even now there are no reliable figures for insurgent casualties.[76] The total number of casualties reported by Cavaignac for the regular army was 708, including six generals killed and six wounded. The Prefect of Police reported a total of 1,460 deaths, but this cannot be accurate for the insurgents, for two-thirds of the total represented the army and National Guard. Parisian hospitals treated 2,529 wounded, but undoubtedly there were many insurgents who preferred to tend their wounds privately rather than risk capture. Deaths among the insurgents may have mounted into the thousands. In any event, it seems clear that the June Days were by far the bloodiest insurrection that Paris had yet experienced. A statistic reported by Cavaignac suggests the scope of the fighting: during the four days, more than two million cartridges were distributed, seven times the number on hand at the outset.[77]

But no figures can convey the atmosphere of fear and hatred that led to atrocities and rumors of atrocities on both sides. Stories spread among the Garde Mobile that the insurgents were decapitating victims were fabrications, but there is no doubt that the victorious forces shot some captive insurgents. Yet the view that such *fusillades* killed thousands is probably a gross exaggeration. One extreme estimate was that of Louis Ménard, an insurgent who published a book in which he claimed that only four or five hundred of his comrades had been

[74] *Compte rendu des séances*, II, p. 209.

[75] S.H.A., F 19, telegram of 26 June 1848.

[76] Pending completion of Gossez's work, the best discussion of the losses is probably that of Stern, *Histoire de la révolution de 1848*, III, pp. 251-255.

[77] *Compte rendu des séances*, V, p. 831, 25 November 1848.

killed on the barricades, but that about 3,000 were executed afterwards.[78] However, the contemporary who was the most impartial and most scrupulously accurate of those who wrote about the revolution, Madame d'Agoult, concluded that only about 150 prisoners were shot, adding, "Nowhere, despite what anyone has said, were these executions carried out by orders, or even with the tolerance of the chiefs."[79] Those atrocities that did occur were the work of Mobile and National Guardsmen; the regular army displayed no vindictiveness, and many officers sought to protect prisoners.[80] Thus, the *fusillades* of 1848 were never, as after the coup d'Etat of 1851 and the Commune of 1871, a matter of policy, but were spontaneous and isolated acts. Even Louis Blanc acknowledged that they were the acts of individuals: "No collective responsibility, no generalized accusations," he wrote. "Thank heavens, there are no classes in France to which one could legitimately impute such excesses; they were the work of madmen whom all the parties could disavow."[81]

In addition to the killed and wounded, thousands of insurgents were imprisoned after the fighting, some of them in appalling conditions, according to Ménard and others. Yet, of the 15,000 originally captured, several thousand were freed almost immediately, and of about 11,000 kept under guard, most were to be released in succeeding months.[82]

[78] *Prologue d'une révolution* (Paris, 1904 [1849]), p. 209. He was able to document a number of these later, but nothing approaching the total; see pp. 247-265. Marx also cites a figure of 3,000, perhaps taken from Ménard, in *The Class Struggles in France*, p. 56. On the *fusillades*, see also Chauvet, *Les Ouvriers du livre*, pp. 200-201.

[79] Stern, *Histoire de la révolution de 1848*, III, p. 251n. For a modern historian's appraisal and acclaim of her methodology, see Jacques Vier, *La Comtesse d'Agoult et son temps, avec des documents inédits*, III (Paris, 1961), pp. 71-118.

[80] Zaniewicki, "L'Armée française en 1848," I, pp. 81-82.

[81] In *Nouveau Monde*, No. 6, 1 March 1851, cited in Stern, *Histoire de la révolution de 1848*, III, p. 251n.

[82] Although in a sense it is pointless to compare atrocities, it may be worth noting that the repression following the Commune of 1871 was far more extensive, bloody and vindictive than that following the June Days. See Frank Jellinek, *The Paris Commune of 1871* (New York, 1965 [1937]), pp. 364-371.

MOTIVATIONS

What were the motives for the rigorous suppression of the insurgent workers? First, and most obviously, it was a matter of a government defending itself against a violent and serious attack; however confused, vague, and contradictory the expressed aims of the insurgents, clearly they were not merely demonstrating or seeking to influence policy, but rather wanted to bring down the government and the National Assembly. The men in power were prepared to take the most drastic measures to prevent this.

Yet the motive of simple defense does not explain the ferocity and tenacity with which both sides fought. The June Days were both a civil and a social war, and there was a marked class character to the repression. But just as the insurgents did not constitute a classic Marxian proletariat, neither were their opponents a classic bourgeoisie. Rather, all of the other social groupings in France, from aristocratic *notables* through the layers of the bourgeoisie and the peasantry, and even some sectors of the urban working classes, vigorously supported the crushing of the insurrection.[83]

There is abundant evidence that the uprising stirred profound social fears. Afterwards the *Journal des Débats* celebrated "The victory which has just been won by the cause of order, of the family, of humanity, of civilization." An important Legitimist provincial newspaper, *L'Echo du Midi*, declared that "French civilization, after having been within an ace of its downfall, has been saved by the unanimous cooperation of upright men. . . . It was a cannabalistic war that was declared on us." Similar remarks abound in the press of the period, in which the insurgents were attacked as socialists, anarchists, communists, and even criminals bent on pillage. "It was crime in revolt against the law, the prison lashing out at society," wrote the *Courrier de Lyon*.[84]

[83] See Gossez, "Diversité des antagonismes sociaux"; Vidalenc, "La Province et les journées de juin," II, pp. 119-120; and Tudesq, *Les Grands notables*, II, pp. 1108-1114.

[84] Tudesq, *Les Grands notables*, II, pp. 1109-1110. See also Vidalenc, "La Province et les journées de juin," II, pp. 129-134. For a similar view expressed in almost hysterical fashion by the English Ambassador, see Normanby, *A Year of Revolution*, II, pp. 49-81.

The resolution adopted by the National Assembly on June 28 illustrates perhaps better than any other statement the almost hysterical fears aroused. It denounced "those madmen who, without principles, without flag, seem to have armed themselves only for massacre and pillage."

> Family, institutions, liberty, fatherland, all were stricken in the heart, and, under the blows of these new barbarians, the civilization of the nineteenth century was threatened with destruction.
>
> But no! Civilization cannot perish! No! The Republic, a work of God, the living law of humanity, the Republic will not perish.
>
> This we swear by all of France, which rejects with horror those savage doctrines in which the family is only a name and property is only a theft. . . .
>
> All the enemies of the Republic were united against it in a violent and desperate effort. They are defeated!

The proclamation went on to state that the greatest of crimes "is to take arms against the sovereignty of the people," but promised that "after having energetically reestablished order and assured a severe justice, we will open our arms and our hearts to all who work and who suffer among us."[85]

But the unanimity in the face of the supposed social peril masked different and even contradictory political attitudes. Defense of the republic was not the principal concern of most of the National Guardsmen who marched on the capital. Rather, in the words of Vidalenc, "they came to defend a society threatened at its base by anarchical doctrines, and to end the insupportable dictatorship which the perpetual insurrection of the Paris workers made possible over the political life of the country."[86] There was thus a strongly counterrevolutionary motivation in the massive provincial response. As the historian of the Paris region put it, "they wanted to

[85] *Compte rendu des séances*, II, p. 238, 28 June 1848.

[86] Vidalenc, "La Province et les journées de juin," II, p. 140. Cf. Rémusat, *Mémoires de ma vie*, IV, p. 346.

strangle the Parisian agitation, without knowing very well, in a great number of cases, what sort of agitation it was."[87]

Hostility to the insurgents was often coupled with hostility to the Executive Commission and to the former Provisional Government, members of which were suspected of being in league with them. In some regions, a significant aspect of the provincial response was the return of Legitimists more openly to political life.[88] In general, the great *notables* sought thereafter to oppose republican policies by reference to the insurrection of June. On July 4, the *Gazette de France* wrote, "No social order without social hierarchy," and another Legitimist publication went so far as to associate June 24 with February 24, July 29, 1830, and even 1789. "The truly guilty ones," said *L'Hermine*, "are the artisans of revolutions, the ideologues of all colors."[89] Aided by the social fears aroused, the great *notables* were regaining an ascendancy that was becoming more openly counterrevolutionary. On July 1, the *Courrier de la Gironde* dared to say, "We have never believed in the possibility of the Republic in a country as vast and as populous as ours."[90] Indeed, many provincial conservatives believed that the crushing of the insurrection was a defeat for the republic.[91] A similar belief was also expressed, for quite different reasons, by some of the socialists; the remarks of Lamennais and of George Sand on the death of the republic are well-known.

The governing republicans disagreed, but they shared to some extent the social fears of the country at large and of the majority in the National Assembly. *Le National* said that the insurrection had aimed at nothing less than "the destruction of the family and of property, that is to say, the destruction of society itself," and it hailed the united effort as an illustration of fraternity. "Rich and poor, workers and bourgeois, republicans and royalists, all forgot their distrust and their old quarrels in the face of the common danger."[92]

[87] Chevalier, "Les Fondements économiques et sociaux," pp. 301-306.
[88] Vidalenc, "La Province et les journées de juin," II, pp. 132-133.
[89] Tudesq, *Les Grands notables*, II, p. 1111.
[90] *Ibid.*, p. 1112.
[91] Chevalier, "Les Fondements économiques et sociaux," p. 308.
[92] Issue of 28 June 1848.

But along with defense of society, the dominant concern of the governing republicans was defense of the republic. The threat to them assumed various forms; most obviously, they saw the insurrection as secretly inspired and financed by partisans of opposing political systems. This attitude was uppermost in the minds of those who were alarmed by the reviving strength of the monarchical factions, and who in the multiple elections of Louis Napoleon three weeks earlier had seen the emergence of a serious Bonapartist threat.

Many republicans, including Louis Blanc and Madame d'Agoult, remarked on the Bonapartist sentiment animating some of the insurgents, and Garnier-Pagès insisted on regarding the insurrection as almost entirely a Bonapartist plot.[93] That thesis is scarcely tenable, but there is little doubt that partisans of Louis Napoleon were active. Pujol was perhaps a Bonapartist, and one of the assassins of General Bréa probably was. Louis Ménard, the poet-insurgent previously cited, estimated that about one-third of his comrades were Bonapartists.[94] Modern scholars have found evidence of considerable Bonapartist activity during the June Days, not only in Paris, but also in the provinces.[95] Louis Napoleon was at that time still in London, having declined his seat in the Assembly, and Persigny was in prison; it is uncertain whether it was the prince's policy to foment insurrection, but his name appeared on some insurgents' lists for a new Provisional Government.

Then there was the strange affair of the letter to General Rapatel. On June 24, Rapatel, who had been among those generals retired by the Provisional Government, gave Cavaignac a letter that he had just received from London, dated June 23 and signed Louis Napoleon Bonaparte. It declared, "General, today a great insurrection will break out in Paris. . . . It will certainly overthrow . . . that incapable and discredited government." The letter went on to appoint Rapatel as Minister of

[93] See his *Histoire de la révolution de 1848*, xi, pp. 447ff.; Blanc, *Histoire de la révolution de 1848*, ii, pp. 176, 178; and Stern, *Histoire de la révolution de 1848*, iii, p. 166.

[94] *Prologue d'une révolution*, p. 160.

[95] See Robert Pimienta, *La Propagande bonapartiste en 1848* (Paris, 1911), pp. 72-74; and Vidalenc, "La Province et les journées de juin," ii, pp. 90-91.

War! Cavaignac thought the matter very serious, but forgot it in his preoccupation with the fighting, and never found the letter again.[96]

The republicans also feared that Legitimists and Orleanists were fomenting insurrection to discredit the regime and hasten an eventual restoration. On the first day, the radical Flocon mounted the tribune of the National Assembly to declare that the uprising had only one aim: "the overthrow of the Republic and the revival of despotism."[97] Some barricades flew the white flag, and there were rumors of royalist agents distributing gold. In the midst of the combat, the government nervously ordered the arrest of an aged Legitimist general and a man who had recently returned to Paris after visiting Louis Philippe in England.[98] Cavaignac refused to give a command to the monarchist General de Castellane.[99] The *Journal des Débats* published a report that 3,000 muskets had been sent to

[96] Details of this curious affair came to light in a recent book by A. Parménie and C. Bonnier de la Chapelle, based on the correspondence of a republican publisher: *Histoire d'un éditeur et de ses auteurs, P.-J. Hetzel (Stahl)*, (Paris, 1953), pp. 305-310. The text of the letter was recalled by Colonel Charras, and was an approximate rendering. Louis Blanc had been the first to call attention to the letter, in his *Révélations historiques, en réponse au livre de Lord Normanby intitulé* A Year of Revolution in Paris (Brussels, 1859), II, pp. 179-181. He offered another, briefer, version of the letter, on the basis of information provided by Hetzel, who had been Cavaignac's secretary during the insurrection, following the appearance of the original English edition of Blanc's work in 1858.

André Lebey, who denied any Bonapartist activity during the insurrection, questioned the authenticity of the letter in *Louis Napoléon et 1848*, I, pp. 332-346, but the evidence provided by Parménie should remove all suspicion that the republicans fabricated the letter. However, recent French biographers of Louis Napoleon, including Dansette and Lucas-Dubreton (who accept the letter as genuine), have neglected the Parménie book; and two recent English biographers erroneously state that Louis Napoleon addressed the letter to Cavaignac! (See J. M. Thompson, *Louis Napoleon and the Second Empire* (New York, 1955), pp. 89-90, and T.A.B. Corley, *Democratic Despot: A Life of Napoleon III* (London, 1961), p. 65.)

[97] *Compte rendu des séances*, II, p. 161.

[98] Letters of 24 June 1848, Reel 21, and 25 June 1848, Reel 23.

[99] Castellane, *Journal*, IV, p. 85.

the Vendée in preparation for a new *chouannerie.*[100] The subprefect of Falaise had warned the government on June 16 that he had learned of "a completely organized Orleanist plot" among some workers attached to National Workshop units outside Paris.[101] In the midst of the fighting, Cavaignac seized, besides socialist newspapers, a Bonapartist one, and several monarchist ones, including the influential *L'Assemblée nationale.*

The republicans were well aware that most of the insurgents were workers, but they believed them to have been instigated by agents of the pretenders, or "misguided" by "anarchists" or false and dangerous doctrines. The republicans in the government and National Assembly displayed varying degrees of sympathy for the misery and despair of the workers, but not even the most radical could defend the armed uprising against the National Assembly. They believed that no insurrection, even by starving workers, was justified against the sovereignty of the people as expressed through universal manhood suffrage. This theoretical point had been stated in the *Dictionnaire politique* of 1842, and the republicans continued to express it in 1848.

Against a democratic government, declared *Le National,* "any insurrection is senseless, an outrage against popular sovereignty, a social crime. . . . They are not democrats who seek to make their will prevail by violence over the general will, freely expressed."[102] *La Réforme* agreed that "insurrection is culpable when universal suffrage is applied, when the people is sovereign," and saw in June such an insurrection.[103] Even the professional revolutionist Blanqui insisted on his respect for "the authority of any National Assembly elected by universal suffrage," and denied sympathy for the May 15 assault on it.[104] Although he was in prison during the insurrection, it is thus possible that even he would have been re-

[100] Vidalenc, "La Province et les journées de juin," II, p. 90.

[101] Letter to the Minister of the Interior, Reel 22.

[102] Issue of 25 June 1848.

[103] Issue of 2 July 1848.

[104] Spitzer, *The Revolutionary Theories of Blanqui,* pp. 150-151.

luctant to lead it.[105] Some of the activists of 1848 believed that the revolutionary populace of Paris represented popular sovereignty better than the votes of provincial Frenchmen, but none of the prominent leaders still at large was willing to act on this assumption in June.

Madame d'Agoult has well expressed the point of view of republicans who took arms against the "people" of Paris in June:

> The most convinced republicans, men who throughout their entire lives had fought for the progress of democratic ideas, the Guinards, the Bixios . . . the Aragos, persuaded this time that the people, in rising against the national representation, would engulf, along with law and justice, the Republic and perhaps the State in their calamitous triumph, proceeded, with grieving hearts but with steadfast spirit, to the encounter with that strange enemy whose liberation had been, for more than twenty years, the goal of their efforts.[106]

Though the republicans were defending "order," it was a republican and revolutionary order, the democratic regime which they regarded as the most precious product of February. Moreover, none of the genuine republicans was content with the mere political form; all thought that the republic must improve the condition of the workers, must to some extent be "social"; the social attitudes of *Le National* had become even more pronounced after February. Following the election of the National Assembly, it expressed a desire for "numerous modifications in the organization of society," and insisted that "the political form must serve as the instrument for social reform."[107] The first duty of the National Assembly, wrote *Le National*, is to "do away with the principal abuse of the old regime by emancipating the proletariat," adding "those who

[105] It is true, however, that in 1868 Blanqui wrote an analysis of the June insurrection which implied his approval, deploring only the lack of organization which he felt caused it to fail. See Sylvain Molinier, ed., "Pages ignorées: Blanqui et les barricades de juin 1848," *La Pensée*, 19 (1948), 9-15.

[106] Stern, *Histoire de la révolution de 1848*, III, pp. 171-172.

[107] Issues of 1 and 2 May 1848.

say that the revolution is much less a political revolution than a social revolution are right."[108] *Le National* emphasized its agreement with Louis Blanc on many points, including the necessity of replacing the wage system with one based on association, and on May 10 even asserted, "we must and will proceed into a new social order, to the triumph of the socialist principle."[109] *Le National's* definition of socialism was very vague, however, amounting to nothing more than mild social reforms. But it insisted that these must come gradually, through the deliberations of the National Assembly, and even if the elections of April did not produce the best possible Assembly, it was wrong to use violence against it. *Le National* argued that the democratic republic must be defended against all of its enemies, and took the position (analogous to that of Robespierre against the "ultra-revolutionaries") that "anarchy is the high road by which reaction arrives."[110] Echoing Louis Blanc and the Provisional Government, *Le National* insisted that "The Republic is founded on order; it can live only through order."[111]

Confronted with the insurrection, *Le National* recognized that, whatever agitators there were among them, many of the insurgents were workers made desperate by hunger. But they could gain nothing from an armed attack on the only kind of regime from which they could hope to win improved conditions. "What purpose will this battle serve, if not to shed precious blood? Who could change the condition of the proletarians in one day? . . . Do they not realize, they who claim to be republicans, that they are the most cruel enemies of the Republic?"[112] Not only was the use of force by a minority against the will of the majority completely unjustified, it threatened to lead to some kind of monarchical restoration. *Le National* expressed compassion for the sufferings of the workers, and promised that the National Assembly would be "fraternally sympathetic," that from calm and peaceful discus-

[108] Issues of 3 and 4 May 1848.
[109] Issue of 1 May 1848, and 10 May 1848, p. 2.
[110] Issue of 1 May 1848.
[111] Issue of 15 May 1848.
[112] Issue of 25 June 1848.

sion would derive "ameliorations, legitimate reforms." It demanded that the leaders should be discovered and punished, and that the insurgents should receive justice but not vengeance.[113]

The attitude of *La Réforme* differed in tone but scarcely in substance. It made no reference to social peril, and its editors were obviously more anguished; from the insurgents, *La Réforme* declared, "we hear only the cry of suffering and of hunger."[114] Yet it could find no justification for the resort to violence; it argued at the height of the insurrection that a new social order could not be founded immediately, but could come about only through "piecemeal experimentation."[115] "We were ardent revolutionaries" under the monarchy, *La Réforme* asserted, but "we are progressive democrats under the Republic, with no other code but universal suffrage."[116] Indeed, not even the socialist intellectuals of 1848 thought that anything of value could come out of the insurrection, and by 1895 Engels himself conceded that experience had shown "how impossible it was in 1848 to win social reconstruction by a simple surprise attack."[117]

Though the bourgeois republicans were obviously touched with social fears, there was nothing consciously counterrevolutionary or reactionary in their suppression of the insurgent workers. They believed that the republic was faced with a mortal threat, and they regarded the defeat of the insurrection as a victory. "The Republic emerges triumphant from this bloody trial," observed *Le National*, ". . . consolidated and strengthened." The lesson learned was that the republic could survive any attack. "Anarchy was to make the bed of we know not what restoration: anarchy has been vanquished and with it all the pretenders, of old or new dynasty, eagle, cock or fleur de lys."[118] Louis Chevalier found that the republican National Guardsmen from the region near Paris were more

[113] Issues of 26-29 June 1848.
[114] Issue of 24 June 1848, p. 3.
[115] *Ibid.*, p. 2.
[116] Issue of 2 July 1848.
[117] Introduction to Marx, *The Class Struggles in France*, p. 16.
[118] Issue of 27 June 1848.

eager to crush the insurgents than were the monarchists, and whereas the latter regarded the outcome as a defeat for the republic, they regarded it as a victory, "the republican order of the Assembly winning over the disorder of the streets and over illegality."[119]

The National Assembly, from extreme right to extreme left, from Legitimists to socialists, from peers to the worker-deputies, had agreed with the necessity to defeat the insurrection, and the Assembly's declaration afterwards that Cavaignac deserved well of the country was unanimous.[120] Indeed, those deputies who were suspected of sympathy with the insurrection vigorously denied it, in particular Ledru-Rollin, Louis Blanc, and Caussidière. During the investigation afterwards, the fiery Caussidière pointed out that if he had wanted to lead or support the insurgents he would have been on the other side of the barricades.[121] Louis Blanc, even when he was safely in England, where he had been exiled by Cavaignac, denied that he had been even "morally sympathetic" with the insurrection.[122] Although some of the republicans thought the bloodshed could have been prevented by different policies or a different military strategy, although the anguish of Caussidière, Blanc, and others was obviously deeper than that of the moderate republicans, once the fighting started none of the socialist or radical deputies went so far as to adopt even a stance of neutrality. The radical Lagrange, who at least said that he would refuse to take sides in a civil war, belied his words by remaining in the Assembly; later he eulogized one of the deputies killed fighting against the insurgents.[123]

119 "Fondements économiques et sociaux," pp. 306-309.

120 There was not an actual vote, but no one protested when the president declared the feeling unanimous. See *Compte rendu des séances*, II, p. 238, 28 June 1848, and the proclamations in *Le Moniteur*, 29 June 1848.

121 See his testimony in the *Rapport de la commission d'enquête*, I, pp. 256-257.

122 The reference is in a letter sent on July 17 to the *Journal des débats*, and published in *Pages d'histoire*, p. 187. Faced with a similar option twenty-three years later, Louis Blanc again would choose the side of order, by opposing the Commune.

123 See the records of the sessions from June 23 through June 26, as reported in *Le Moniteur*, or in the *Compte rendu des séances*, II. La

The absence of any prominent leaders among the June insurgents has often been noted. One reason was undoubtedly that potential leaders such as Blanqui and Barbès were in prison. But another was that all of the socialists and radicals of any prominence, from Louis Blanc to Caussidière to Proudhon, were all in spirit on the other side of the barricades, lending their moral support to the troops and cannon of Cavaignac.[124]

THE ROLE OF CAVAIGNAC

General Cavaignac went about the job of crushing the insurrection with determination, but a scene recorded by Madame d'Agoult suggests that even he was not untouched by terrible doubts. On the first day, Joseph Guinard, a close friend who had fought beside Godefroy on the barricades of 1830, and was now a deputy and colonel in the National Guard, asked the general, "What do you demand of us? Do you even know yourself? We are going to fire on the people, on whose side we have always fought. Can you swear to me at least, swear to me before God, by the memory of your father and your brother, that we are going to die or to conquer for the Republic?" The general gripped his hand sorrowfully. "Can you have any doubt? If it were otherwise, do you believe that I would consent to command so terrible a war, to leave on my name so much blood?"[125]

Cavaignac's behavior in June has aroused criticism and outright condemnation, not only because he was directly responsi-

---

Gorce observes that the radicals made a point of remaining in the Assembly hall to avoid any suspicion of complicity. (*Histoire de la seconde république*, I, pp. 352, 390.)

[124] The radical press in the provinces also refused to defend the insurgents. See Vidalenc, "Les Provinces et les journées de juin," II, pp. 129-130. For Proudhon's *mea culpa*, see *Les Confessions d'un révolutionnaire* (Paris, 1849), pp. 41-42. Shortly after the insurrection, Proudhon did express open sympathy for the insurgents, saying he had misunderstood the significance of the insurrection while it was going on. See his testimony in *Rapport de la commission d'enquête*, I, pp. 336-338.

[125] Stern, *Histoire de la révolution de 1848*, III, pp. 172-173. Madame d'Agoult added that Guinard, thus reassured, thereafter participated in some of the bloodiest of the fighting.

ble for defeating the workers, but also because of the manner in which he did it. His strategy of concentrating his troops without seeking to prevent the construction of barricades has been criticized on several grounds. First, that it was wrong in principle, because early inactivity encouraged the insurgents, thus rendering Cavaignac responsible perhaps for the entire insurrection and at least for its size and consequently for the bitter fighting necessary to suppress it. Secondly, the strategy has been criticized as to motivation; Cavaignac was accused of adopting it either to win personal political power or to serve the bourgeois conspiracy of provocation.

All of the criticisms except the last were raised in 1848, first obliquely in July, during the National Assembly's investigation of the uprising, and more fully and directly in November, during the presidential campaign. The principal critics of Cavaignac were moderate republicans, men associated with the fallen Executive Commission. They argued that he had adopted his strategy over the vigorous protests of members of the commission, who had wanted to avoid bloodshed by preventing the erection of barricades. In addition, he was charged with deliberately delaying the attack for another day, hoping thereby to arouse criticism against the Executive Commission and hasten its fall. Only after the terrified National Assembly had decided to appoint him dictator, on the second day of the insurrection, his critics said, had Cavaignac launched his attack on the barricades, which by that time were so numerous and so strong that bloody street fighting was necessary to capture them.[126] The detailed criticisms included charges that Cavaignac had failed to have sufficient troops in Paris when the insurrection broke out, and that he had disobeyed orders of the Executive Commission while he was still only Minister of War.

[126] For the charges in detail and Cavaignac's refutation, see *Compte rendu des séances*, v, pp. 809-849, 25 November 1848. See also the testimony of Cavaignac, Lamartine, Ledru-Rollin, Garnier-Pagès and other principals in the *Rapport de la commission d'enquête*.

One widely circulated criticism of Cavaignac was a pamphlet by Emile de Girardin, entitled "Le Général Cavaignac devant la commission d'enquête," which was reprinted in his *Questions de mon temps*, iv, pp. 26-80.

During a dramatic debate before the Assembly in November, Cavaignac responded vigorously, meeting the criticism effectively on almost all counts. He denied any ulterior motives for his strategy, which he defended on purely military grounds. Cavaignac based his "system of defense" during June frankly on the belief that an insurrection must not be handled as a police affair, but as a battle. Moreover, on the crucial morning of June 23, it would have been futile to seek to prevent the erection of barricades because they were going up simultaneously all over the eastern half of Paris; also, experience showed that barricades were often rebuilt as soon as the troops had departed. Finally, Cavaignac argued that success justified his strategy.

The French historian Zaniewicki (himself an army officer), has subjected the troop movements of June 23 to an exhaustive examination and concludes that Cavaignac's strategy was the only militarily feasible one.[127] Moreover, the strategy was not personal, but reflected "classic" military thought and specific principles affirmed as early as March 16 in a directive issued by General Subérvie. This directive emphasized three rules for the use of the army in maintaining public order: first, the danger of disseminating troops; second, the necessity for written requisitions by civil authorities; third, unity of command. These principles were accepted by all French officers, who in dealing with disorders in the provinces during 1848 often disputed the desire of civilian officials to use small detachments, and experience demonstrated the efficacy of concentration of forces.[128] Cavaignac's belief in concentration was reinforced as a result of his experience in dealing with street disorders in the weeks preceding the insurrection. On June 10, nearly 7,000 soldiers were required to disperse crowds at a single point in Paris, and after unruly demonstrations in favor of Louis Napoleon on June 12 and 13, Cavaignac decided that

127 "L'Armée française en 1848," I, pp. 72-77, 154-155, with notes in II and maps and charts in III.

128 *Ibid.*, I, pp. 154-160. See also Suzanne Coquerelle, "L'Armée et la répression dans les campagnes," *L'Armée et la seconde république*, "Bibliothèque de la révolution de 1848," XVIII (1955), pp. 147-148.

each soldier must carry four days' supply of food and ammunition. It was largely owing to this foresight, Zaniewicki believes, that the troops were able to fight so well.[129]

Some time before the insurrection, Lamoricière and other generals had endorsed Cavaignac's proposed strategy, and Cavaignac informed the Executive Commission that he would take command against an insurrection only on the condition that he could concentrate his troops instead of dispersing them in small details. On June 20, Cavaignac as War Minister issued a circular reaffirming the principles stated in March, and adding that in dealing with disorders the civil authorities should indicate the objective and leave to the military the choice of means in attaining it.[130]

When champions of the Executive Commission severely criticized his strategy in November, Cavaignac conceded that he could rightly be judged culpable if he had suddenly unveiled it on the morning of June 23, even though the commission still had the option then of replacing him with another Minister of War who would follow another strategy. But Cavaignac argued that the Executive Commission shared responsibility for his strategy because, although reluctantly, it had endorsed it in advance as well as on June 23.[131]

Leaving aside for the moment the charge of personal ambition, it seems clear that in principle Cavaignac's plan reflected the *militaire* more than the republican. Despite their own desires to defend the republic and to quell the insurrection, four of the five members of the Executive Commission believed on the morning of June 23 that it would be possible to avoid bloodshed by preventing the erection of barricades.

[129] "L'Armée française en 1848," I, pp. 69-70.

[130] *Ibid.*, I, p. 159.

[131] *Compte rendu des séances*, V, pp. 827-828, 25 November 1848. See also the minutes of the Executive Commission for June 23 and June 24, which were published in *Rapport de la commission d'enquête*, III, pp. 247-251 (but omitted from the minutes as published in 1950). Among Cavaignac's papers is a rough manuscript for a speech apparently intended for use in November, in which he states clearly an argument that he only implied during the debate: how could they criticize him afterwards since "I executed strictly that which I had announced that I wanted to do."? (Reel 22.)

Only Lamartine had originally sided with Cavaignac. It is impossible, of course, to know whether their plan had much chance of succeeding; probably it did not, in view of the vast extent of the insurrection from the outset. Cavaignac's argument from success carries weight. But obviously the majority in the Executive Commission felt more distress than Cavaignac, and a greater concern to avoid an outright battle. Cavaignac's chief object was to defeat the uprising, and he was convinced that only his strategy of concentration would guarantee victory. Some of Cavaignac's remarks give the impression that he was sometimes more concerned with the "honor" of the army and of himself than even the fate of the republic. At a critical early stage of the fighting, the commander in chief almost hysterically threatened to blow out his brains if a single army battalion was disarmed.[132]

That was the closest allusion to one other consideration that must have worried Cavaignac, the morale of the troops. After the humiliation of February, the regiments disarmed by the victorious insurgents had experienced an "epidemic of desertion," and many others suffered serious disciplinary problems.[133] The French scholar Pierre Chalmin found that morale was "shattered from top to bottom. . . . The French army . . . could not forget that it is only necessary for a riot to be victorious to cause legality to cross from one side of the barricade to the other."[134] On May 15, two infantry regiments had watched impassively as demonstrators entered the Hôtel de Ville to create a new Provisional Government; at

[132] The statement was recalled by Barthélemy Saint-Hilaire and not denied by Cavaignac, who did deny having made another often-quoted statement that the National Guard should "defend its shops." See *Compte rendu des séances*, v, pp. 820, 829, 25 November 1848.

[133] Commandant Pierre Chalmin, "La Crise morale de l'armée française," *L'Armée et la seconde république*, "Bibliothèque de la révolution de 1848," xviii (1955), pp. 46-60.

[134] *Ibid.*, pp. 58-59. See also Chalmin's more recent "Les Crises dans l'armée française, 1830, 1848," *Revue historique de l'armée*, xviii (1962), 45-62. Zaniewicki, however, argues that the crisis of indiscipline was soon over, and that morale was good by June. ("L'Armée française en 1848," i, pp. 45-64.) Yet it is difficult to define a mood on the basis of statistics, and there was much evidence that all was not right with the army.

the *Fête de la Concorde* five days later the sullen silence of the line troops contrasted with the enthusiasm of the National Guard and of the Garde Mobile. Cavaignac as Minister of War had sought to replace with fresh regiments those that had been disarmed in February, but the complicated process was far from complete by June 23. During the fighting, he made a point of proclaiming to the soldiers: "Rest assured, you are not aggressors; this time, at least, you have not been the sorrowful instruments of despotism and of treason. . . . Be faithful to the Republic."[135]

Nevertheless, the regular troops fought with markedly less enthusiasm than the Garde Mobile or even than some units of the National Guard. As Tocqueville observed, "They were weakened and, as it were, dulled by the remembrance of February, and did not yet seem quite certain that they would not be told the next day that they had done wrong."[136] Indeed, Blanqui later argued that in view of the instability of the government and the low morale of the troops, the insurgents had been "almost certain of success," but their lack of organization permitted the disciplined troops to defeat them by concentrated attacks. The lesson drawn by Blanqui for a successful proletarian insurrection in the future ironically could have been used by Cavaignac to justify his own strategy: "Organization is victory; dispersion is death."[137] Not only did Cavaignac refuse to disperse his line troops, he was careful to engage them only when conditions were favorable and they had artillery support.[138] Except for the battalion disarmed at the Place des Vosges, the behavior of the troops was correct if hesitant, even among the twenty battalions that had been disarmed in February.[139]

[135] Proclamation to the soldiers, as published in *Le Moniteur*, 25 June 1848.

[136] *Recollections*, p. 177.

[137] See Molinier, "Pages ignorées: Blanqui et les barricades de juin," pp. 9-15.

[138] Gossez, "Notes sur la composition," p. 80. Gossez's research corroborates Tocqueville's observation.

[139] Zaniewicki, "L'Armée française en 1848," I, pp. 80-82. Although some historians have asserted that the victory in June ended the crisis of morale, Zaniewicki argues that it was followed by a new problem of

One of the specific charges against Cavaignac was that on the first day he had failed to obey an order that might have prevented the entire insurrection. Following the demonstrations on June 22, Barthélemy Saint-Hilaire, as secretary of the Executive Commission, sent Cavaignac during the night an order to dispatch troops early the following morning to disperse the crowds that planned to gather at the Panthéon. The troops did not appear, and the Executive Commission questioned Cavaignac on the morning of June 23. His explanation was sufficiently satisfactory for the commission thereafter to invest him with the supreme command of all the military forces in Paris.[140]

However, Barthélemy Saint-Hilaire raised the issue again in the November debate. Cavaignac explained that he had received different orders on how to deal with the same situation from a higher authority, a member of the commission itself, Marie, who had directed him to protect the government by sending troops to the Luxembourg Palace (situated a few blocks from the Panthéon) and said nothing of dispersal. After the general read aloud the text of the two orders to the National Assembly, Barthélemy Saint-Hilaire said he was satisfied.[141] Zaniewicki exonerates Cavaignac on this issue also. He shows the confusion in the command practice of the Executive Commission, and argues that there was no reason for Cavaignac to view the events of June 22 as any more ominous than those of preceding days.[142]

A more persistent charge was that Cavaignac had not gathered enough troops beforehand. On May 20, the Executive Commission decided that there should be 20,000 in Paris, and later this figure was raised to 25,000. Yet during the insurrection Ledru-Rollin, Lamartine, and others had the impression that there were too few. Indeed, on June 24 Lamartine hinted darkly to Victor Hugo that Cavaignac was responsible for the

---

indiscipline, in particular among troops stationed in uncomfortable conditions in and near Paris. (I, pp. 83-85.)

140 Minutes of the Executive Commission, permanent session of 23 and 24 June 1848, *Rapport de la commission d'enquête*, III, pp. 247-248.

141 *Compte rendu des séances*, V, p. 837.

142 "L'Armée française en 1848," I, pp. 71-72.

paucity of troops that made defeat seem imminent at that time,[143] and Ledru-Rollin in November repeated charges that there must have been fewer than 20,000 on June 23. Actually, the published report of the investigating committee had already revealed that on June 23 there were precisely 25,392 regular troops in Paris.[144] Cavaignac produced additional supporting documents in November, and Zaniewicki demonstrates conclusively that Cavaignac indeed had even more troops on hand than previously stipulated.[145]

The basic reason why many observers had the impression that the troops were insufficient was the sheer massive scope of the insurrection. With many soldiers assigned to defend the National Assembly and other points, there were actually only about 11,500 regular troops and 13,000 Gardes Mobiles available for the attacking columns against half a city in arms. To accede to all of the demands for troops, Cavaignac said he would have needed 180,000 men. Even if he had agreed to disperse his troops in small detachments to dismantle barricades, he simply would not have had enough men to do so effectively.

Another charge against Cavaignac was that he had delayed too long in using his troops, either because of the time required for concentration, or because he deliberately waited until he received dictatorial powers on the second day. On the basis of his minute study of troop movements, Zaniewicki concluded that the forces were concentrated with "remarkable speed" and began serious fighting before noon on the first day.[146] The charge of inactivity on June 23 was patently absurd, for there were numerous witnesses to the fighting during the afternoon, which became so intense that Cavaignac himself had felt compelled to lead a relief column and had personally commanded in the Faubourg du Temple for several hours, incurring the additional criticism that he had deserted his post at the ministry. In the November debate, Cavaignac was able

[143] Hugo, *Souvenirs personnels*, pp. 79-81.

[144] *Rapport de la commission d'enquête*, II, p. 54.

[145] "L'Armée française en 1848," I, pp. 73-77.

[146] *Ibid.*, pp. 75-76. Zaniewicki even calculated that the average speed of movement to the points of concentration was precisely 5.2 kilometers per hour.

to produce statistics to show that army casualties for the first day were proportionately higher than for succeeding days.[147]

Did Cavaignac in June apply techniques that he had learned in Algeria, as some historians have suggested?[148] Perhaps his willingness to wage outright war reflected the Algerian "tradition of military violence,"[149] but there is no reason to believe that either his strategy or his tactics were based on his experience in Africa. We have already noticed that the issue of concentration versus dispersion was a general one; it was not his own experience in Algeria but that of other generals in Paris that was uppermost in Cavaignac's mind. The war of the plains of North Africa had virtually nothing in common with civil war in a great city, and the *Africains* had to learn as they fought. Although it has been suggested that Cavaignac's use of cannon against an entrenched foe derived from his Algerian experience, in fact artillery was not a major weapon against the Arabs, and the *Africains* in June displayed ignorance of its proper use. General de Castellane scornfully observed that Cavaignac and other generals at first employed cannon individually and with poor results, instead of massing them. "They did not know how to wage war against the barricades."[150] Indeed, Cavaignac himself admitted that his inexperience of street fighting had led him grossly to underestimate the time necessary to take a barricade when he personally commanded an assault on the first day.[151] In one detail at least Cavaignac employed an African technique: to carry the extra rations, he issued to each soldier a specially constructed sack of the kind used in Algeria.[152]

[147] *Compte rendu des séances*, v, p. 830.

[148] See, e.g., Schmidt, *Journées de juin*, p. 49, and Wright, *France in Modern Times*, p. 174.

[149] Richter, "Tocqueville on Algeria," p. 371.

[150] *Journal*, IV, pp. 83, 87. He made a similar comment to Normanby about Cavaignac's advance of a single cannon, which was soon captured. (See *A Year of Revolution*, II, p. 109.) For detailed discussions, see Zaniewicki, "L'Armée française en 1848," I, pp. 79-80; and the comparison between European and African warfare in Paul Azan, *Conquête et pacification de l'Algérie* (Paris, 1931), pp. 486-498.

[151] *Compte rendu des séances*, v, p. 830, 25 November 1848.

[152] Zaniewicki, "L'Armée française en 1848," I, p. 70.

Cavaignac's oratorical defense in November was so effective that his critics retreated from the veiled but fundamental charge that his military actions were all calculated to bring him to power. When Cavaignac challenged them to make their accusation explicit, Barthélemy Saint-Hilaire and Garnier-Pagès denied that they had intended to accuse Cavaignac "of having committed treason through ambition," and said they only believed that he had committed "grave errors."[153] They still maintained, however, that he had participated in a "parliamentary plot" to bring down the Executive Commission. Cavaignac acknowledged that he had discussed with some deputies the possibility of his replacing the Executive Commission, but denied that his actions constituted a plot, pointing out that on June 15 he had persuaded the commission not to resign.[154] The moderate republican group, in which Jules Senard played an important role, considered several names, including Lamartine and Ledru-Rollin, before settling on Cavaignac, and approached him formally only on June 22. On the following day, after the barricades were up and fighting had begun, the republican "plotters" sent a delegate to ask the Executive Commission to resign. They refused. But as we have seen, the Assembly on the morning of June 24 invested Cavaignac with dictatorial powers.

Both Louis Blanc and Ledru-Rollin later repeated the charges that Cavaignac's political ambitions had dictated his strategy in June,[155] but there is no real evidence to support the accusation, and in view of the general's personality and later political behavior, it seems unlikely that he would have resorted to such means to win political power. The narrow charge of personal ambition has, for the most part, failed to survive in modern historiography,[156] although some writers

[153] *Compte rendu des séances*, v, pp. 834-839.

[154] There was no substantial disagreement between Cavaignac and his critics as to the facts of his political negotiations, only as to their interpretation.

[155] *Pages d'histoire*, pp. 198-200; Calman, *Ledru-Rollin*, p. 200. Calman finds Ledru-Rollin "unconvincing" in this matter.

[156] A notable exception is Henri Guillemin, who wrote in *La Tragédie de quarante-huit*, p. 322, and repeated in his more recent *La Première*

assimilate his strategy to the thesis of bourgeois provocation.[157]

Cavaignac's victory undoubtedly served the class interests of the bourgeoisie, but he personally seems to have been motivated, beyond the military considerations, above all by a desire to defend the republic. In the proclamations that he issued during the fighting, there were no references to saving civilization and property, nor to the insurgents as madmen or thieves. Cavaignac emphasized the necessity of preserving the republic, and his appeals to the workers were almost as compassionate in tone as those of Considérant.

In the first of several proclamations addressed to the insurgents, on June 24, Cavaignac declared:

> You believe that you are fighting in the interest of the workers, but it is against them that you fight; it is they alone who will suffer from so much bloodshed. If such a struggle were prolonged, we would have to despair of the future of the Republic whose irrevocable triumph all of us wish to assure.
>
> In the name of the blood-stained fatherland,
>
> In the name of the Republic which you are destroying,
>
> In the name of the labor which you ask, and which has never been refused to you, dash the hopes of our common enemies. Lay down your fratricidal arms, and be confident that the government, if it is aware that there are criminal agitators in your ranks, knows also that among you there are brothers who are only misguided, whom it recalls into the arms of the fatherland.[158]

On the following day the general issued the conciliatory proclamation cited earlier. His proclamations to the army and to the National Guard were exhortations to defend the republic, but as victory appeared certain on June 26, he warned, "You must not allow the triumph of order, of liberty, in a word, of the Republic, to be the signal for reprisals which are re-

---

résurrection de la république, 24 fevrier 1848 (Paris, 1967), p. 423, that Cavaignac "wanted" the insurrection, "which he would crush, he alone."

157 See, e.g., Renard, *La République de 1848*, pp. 77-78.

158 *Le Moniteur*, 25 June 1848, supplement.

pellent to your hearts."[159] Cavaignac's final proclamation to the army and National Guard is worth quoting in full:

> The sacred cause of the Republic has triumphed; your devotion, your unshakeable courage, have thwarted culpable schemes, made short work of fatal errors. The fatherland, all mankind, thank and bless you for this necessary triumph.
>
> This morning, the emotions of the struggle were still legitimate, inevitable. Now, be as great in tranquillity as you have just been in combat. In Paris, I see victors and vanquished; cursed be my name if I consent to see victims. Justice will take its course. Let it. That is your wish, it is also mine.
>
> Ready to return to the rank of a simple citizen, I will carry back to your midst the civic memory of never, in these grave trials, having taken anything away from liberty except that which the salvation of the Republic itself required, and to bequeath a precedent to whomever may in his turn be called to fulfill duties as great.[160]

This proclamation was much admired by contemporaries, and Madame d'Agoult observed, "Political passions have sought to deprive General Cavaignac of the immortal honor of having conceived and written this proclamation. History will restore it to him completely. Unimpeachable witnesses saw General Cavaignac write it with his own hand, from beginning to end, with an emotion that could only have resulted from improvisation."[161]

Cavaignac's attitude contrasts sharply with the harshly vindictive attitudes of General Gallifet or even Adolphe Thiers towards the *communards* of 1871. Yet it is not surprising that, *malgré* Madame d'Agoult, history has rendered little honor to Cavaignac, for it must be said that on the whole he did not live up to the generous spirit of his proclamations. Although he was not ruthless, he did suppress the uprising with severity and would accept nothing less than unconditional surrender. Too, he must bear some indirect responsibility for the *fusil-*

[159] *Ibid.*, 27 June 1848.

[160] *Ibid.*

[161] Stern, *Histoire de la révolution de 1848*, III, p. 242n.

lades, for although he warned against reprisals, he did not publicly condemn those responsible for them.

Cavaignac felt sorrow after the battle, but he expressed it privately. "I had them fire on my own," he lamented,[162] and Jules Bastide was astonished to find the general weeping.[163] Yet shortly thereafter Cavaignac freely distributed decorations to soldiers and to Gardes Mobiles, and he opposed efforts to grant amnesty.

Both the insurrection and its repression helped to undermine the republic, but for the moment it emerged strengthened from the Days of June: the most dangerous threat to its existence was crushed, and a strong government was in control. If Cavaignac was a military dictator, he was also a republican who immediately indicated his intention of surrendering his powers. If the workers of Paris were now eliminated as a political force capable of exerting pressure on the government, their defeat was not the triumph of counterrevolution, nor of class interests over political ideals. Although political differences on the side of order seemed insignificant in the common effort, they were not erased. With a few exceptions, the *républicains de la veille* underwent no significant changes in their political or social attitudes after June, but remained essentially what they had been before, inexperienced men of no exceptional abilities, somewhat chastened by the bloodletting, but still determined to launch the great experiment of representative democracy in conditions of continuing political, social and economic crisis.

162 Carnot, MS "Mémorial," dos. 23, p. 5.
163 Stern, *Histoire de la révolution de 1848*, III, p. 344.

VII · The Republic of the Moderates

FROM DICTATOR TO PREMIER

For Jules Bastide and some other republicans, Cavaignac's delegated authority was not enough. As soon as victory seemed certain, Bastide urged him to assume full dictatorial powers and to use them to strike down the "true authors of insurrection," the men of the "reaction," the "enemies" of the republic.

"It's a *coup d'Etat* that you ask," the general replied, "*A coup d'Etat!* I don't want that, I will never do it. France has seen only too many for the last sixty years. We ought to make her lose the habit, instead of imposing still another on her. A dictatorship! You shouldn't dream of it. A dictatorship, when we are standing in blood! That would authorize the first man to come along to kill in order to win power."[1]

Bastide's continued pleas were in vain. Cavaignac admonished him, "Let's not seek to imitate the men of the Revolution. If they were living in our time, even the most ardent of them would understand that it is not boldness that is necessary, but respect for the law, and that one does not found liberty with despotic measures."[2]

Thus, Cavaignac shunned the opportunity to strengthen and continue his personal rule. Maxime du Camp, who had fought as a young National Guardsman, recalled that "On June 26, 1848, he was the master; he could have done everything he wished to do. The entire nation, which proclaimed him its savior, would have followed him unhesitatingly."[3] Yet, immediately after the capture of the last barricade, the general told the National Assembly that he would lay down his powers as soon as they were no longer necessary for "the salvation of the Republic."[4]

[1] Stern, *Histoire de la révolution de 1848*, III, p. 344.

[2] *Ibid.*, p. 345. A slightly different account of the discussion between Bastide and Cavaignac is presented in Du Camp, *Souvenirs de l'année 1848*, p. 302. Cf. also Bastide, *La République française et l'Italie en 1848* (Brussels, 1858), p. 220.

[3] *Souvenirs de l'année 1848*, p. 304.

[4] *Compte rendu des séances*, II, p. 212, 26 June 1848.

To scattered protests that it was too soon, Cavaignac replied, "In my opinion, a Republic must be jealous of its powers."[5] He was confident that the Assembly would retain him in power, but he wanted to receive a new vote of confidence and to change the legal basis of his authority, so that it would derive "not from the kind of proclamation by the Assembly on June 24, but following mature deliberation."[6] Accordingly, on the morning of June 28, Cavaignac formally surrendered the powers accorded him four days earlier. The Assembly voted that he "deserved well of the fatherland," and at Cavaignac's suggestion the army, National Guard and Garde Mobile were included in the accolade. Then, belying any suggestion of mature deliberation, the Assembly almost immediately reinvested the general with the executive powers of the republic. There was a slight but significant change in the wording of the resolution. Whereas the decree of June 24 had given "all the executive powers" to Cavaignac, that of June 28 declared: "The National Assembly entrusts the executive power to General Cavaignac, who will take the title of President of the Council of Ministers, and he will name the ministry."[7]

The general's support in the Assembly was virtually unanimous: a member of the Réunion de la Rue de Poitiers, Bernard Bonjean, first proposed his retention in power, and a staunch *républicain de la veille*, Martin de Strasbourg, offered the formal motion, which was adopted without a word of protest or recorded vote.[8] None of the firebrands of the left, not Louis Blanc or Caussidière or Ledru-Rollin or Proudhon, all of whom later bitterly denounced Cavaignac, cared or dared to vote against him on June 28.

To the cynical eye, the change must have seemed inconsequential: the man on horseback remained firmly in the saddle.

[5] *Ibid.*, p. 237, 27 June 1848.

[6] *Ibid.*, p. 238.

[7] *Ibid.*, pp. 240-241.

[8] The future Communard, Charles Beslay, *Souvenirs*, p. 196, recalled that he was the only deputy to oppose the motion, but the *Compte rendu des séances* does not record such a vote. It is interesting that Beslay opposed Cavaignac not because of his suppression of the workers, but on the principle that "the *militaires* are never for liberty." (*Ibid.*)

Moreover, there was no reduction in the arbitrary police powers that he exercised in Paris. At his behest, in the interests of "public security," the Assembly allowed to stand for an indefinite period the state of siege that it had proclaimed during the insurrection. Yet the political change was to be genuine and profound. If Cavaignac's authority was at first ambiguous, soon a true parliamentary regime would emerge.

In forming his government, Cavaignac turned instinctively to the moderate republicans, who had helped him come to power and whose outlook he shared. But his belief in the supremacy of the National Assembly led him from the first to take into account the other political forces within the Assembly. For all its superficial republicanism and its unanimous support of Cavaignac, the Assembly was split into several important factions. The deputies of the extreme left, the "socialists" and radical republicans, formed a small minority whose influence had been waning since the Assembly convened in May; although they had had no part in the June insurrection, socialism was in bad repute afterwards, and they knew they could expect little sympathy from Cavaignac. The Réunion de la Rue de Poitiers supported Cavaignac out of political necessity rather than choice. According to Falloux, they would have preferred the royalist General Changarnier[9] to the stern son of the regicide, however great the latter's services to the cause of order. Although the monarchists did help to make the nomination of Cavaignac unanimous, their distrust of him broke into the open over the question of how the ministers should be chosen. At first there was merely a parliamentary skirmish, in the guise of a debate over a technicality; in the end Cavaignac was personally empowered to select his own ministers, but the vote was far from unanimous.[10]

The Rue de Poitiers was still hopeful of bringing some of its own men into the government, or at least of influencing Cavaignac's selections. At first the monarchists planned to make a condition of their support the acceptance of their nominees for the most important ministries, former Orleanists such as

[9] Comte de Falloux, *Mémoires d'un royaliste* (3d edn., Paris, 1888), I, p. 350.

[10] *Compte rendu des séances*, II, pp. 240-241, 28 June 1848.

Armand Dufaure, Auguste Vivien and Drouyn de Lhuys, but the more prominent Orleanists and Legitimists, men like Thiers and Berryer, felt that the time was not yet opportune for their own open assertion of power.[11] So confident of success were conservative elements that *The Times* of London published a list of the probable ministry in which only two republicans were included, Jules Senard and Eugène Bethmont.[12] But when the monarchists learned that Cavaignac had already drawn up his own list of republican ministers, they decided to accept most of his nominations and to fight only one: that of Hippolyte Carnot to continue as Minister of Education and of Religion.[13] The monarchists were willing to accept another republican in Carnot's place, but threatened to oppose Cavaignac if he did not remove Carnot, who was abhorrent to them on several grounds: as the only man of February still holding his original position, as the author of some controversial ministerial directives, and, most importantly from the point of view of the Catholics, as the proponent of a radical plan for state secular education.

The conflict over Carnot, which took place on the morning of June 28, was brief but sharp. The Rue de Poitiers sent delegates to Cavaignac and to some of the ministers they were willing to accept. As the proposed ministry could fail of majority support if opposed by the Rue de Poitiers, two republicans, Bastide and Senard, whose places seemed otherwise assured, urged Carnot to step down. He agreed, provided his successor would be a republican without religious connections, and Cavaignac at first accepted the decision; he and the ministerial candidates had already settled on another person when Cavaignac impulsively decided that Carnot must be maintained in the interests of republican unity.

[11] Normanby, *A Year of Revolution*, II, p. 69; Stern, *Histoire de la révolution de 1848*, III, p. 256.

[12] Victor Hugo was to be Minister of Education, and the Comte de Falloux his secretary! See *The Times* (London), 29 June 1848, p. 5.

[13] As Falloux recalls the incident, not a single name was pressed on the general, and all of his ministers but Carnot were accepted without contest. (*Mémoires*, I, pp. 350-351.) But Normanby in his diary speaks of negotiations, in which Cavaignac is "indignant at having any names forced upon him." (*A Year of Revolution*, II, pp. 78-79.)

"You will not part company with us," he told Carnot. "They want to decimate the republican party, and I will not allow it to start with you."[14] Carnot agreed to stay; but the delegates from the Rue de Poitiers had already made known to their associates the virtual certainty that he was out, and the announcement of his name before the Assembly evoked "an explosion of murmurs."[15]

In view of this fait accompli, there was nothing the monarchists could do immediately, for the Assembly had empowered Cavaignac to name whom he pleased.

MEN OF THE EVE ON THE MORROW

Cavaignac had chosen a thoroughly republican government, and he made no clean break with the immediate past; most of his ministers had been closely associated with the previous revolutionary governments. Three simply retained their portfolios: in addition to Carnot, they were Jules Bastide as Foreign Minister and Eugène Bethmont as Minister of Justice. Michel Goudchaux, who had been the republic's first Minister of Finance, resumed that position after several months out of power. Athanase Recurt was shifted to the Ministry of Public Works from the Ministry of the Interior, where he was replaced by Jules Senard, former president of the National Assembly. The new Minister of Commerce and Agriculture was Gilbert Tourret, who had been one of Ledru-Rollin's *commissaires.* To replace himself as Minister of War, Cavaignac chose General Lamoricière, who had been offered the position by the Provisional Government but had refused at that time. As Minister of the Navy and of Colonies, Cavaignac appointed a professional officer, Admiral Leblanc.

[14] Carnot, MS "Mémorial," dos. 17, pp. 10-11. Carnot did not mention Senard or Bastide in a briefer version of this incident published by him in August 1848. See his *Le Ministère de l'instruction publique et des cultes, depuis le 24 février jusqu'au 5 juillet 1848* (Paris, 1848), p. 65, which contains a slightly different version of the quotation given above. For the incident from another point of view, see Falloux, *Mémoires*, I, pp. 352-356.

[15] Falloux, *ibid.*, p. 330. Cf. Carnot, MS "Mémorial," dos. 17, p. 11, and *Compte rendu des séances*, II, pp. 243, 28 June 1848.

Cavaignac's government was soundly republican not only in its close links with the previous revolutionary governments, but in the long devotion of most of its members to the republican cause. Aside from the military appointments, and one partial exception among the civilians, all of Cavaignac's ministers were *républicains de la veille*.

Carnot, whom the monarchists had fought so bitterly, regarded republicanism as a family heritage as did Cavaignac. He fought on the barricades in 1830, then turned against the July Monarchy; in 1839 he was elected to the Chamber of Deputies, where he continued to sit until the revolution. He also was a writer and publicist, who, like his father, took a particular interest in elementary education. Accordingly the Provisional Government appointed him Minister of Education, giving him in addition (incongruously, according to later republican assumptions) jurisdiction over religious matters. Carnot was elected to the National Assembly and retained his ministry under the Executive Commission.

Jules Bastide, the Minister of Foreign Affairs, had a history of genuinely revolutionary activity. A Carbonaro as a youth, he also participated in the July revolution; he won some ephemeral renown at that time for scrambling to the top of the Tuileries, where he was the first to unfurl the tricolor.[16] He shared the disillusionment of most republicans with the July Monarchy, and soon was conspiring against it; he was condemned to death in 1832, but escaped to England and later was acquitted. For a time he was editor of *Le National*, but after a quarrel with Armand Marrast shifted to literary and journalistic collaboration with the proto-Christian socialist, Buchez. Bastide was among the republican journalists who captured the February revolution; as he had written a number of articles on foreign policy, the Provisional Government made him secretary-general in the Foreign Ministry, directly under Lamartine. The occasion gave his old antagonist Marrast an opportunity for a *mot* (which must be given in French): "Bastide est étranger aux affaires, plaçons-le aux affaires étrangères."[17] In the elections to the National Assembly, Bas-

[16] *Dictionnaire des parlementaires français*, I, p. 194.

[17] *Ibid.*

tide was chosen by three departments. In May, he became Foreign Minister in his own right. During the June crisis, he revealed himself to be a firm partisan both of repression and of Cavaignac personally, and seems to have won a place of particular influence with the general. Bastide would remain Foreign Minister until the election of Louis Napoleon in December, and thus would establish a kind of record for continuity in office after February.

The third minister to survive the fall of the Executive Commission, Bethmont, had been one of the lawyers who habitually defended republicans against political charges in the early years of the July Monarchy. In 1842 he was elected to the Chamber of Deputies, where he sat until the revolution. Bethmont was active in the banquet campaign, and was one of the first ministers appointed by the Provisional Government. His first portfolio was that of Agriculture and Commerce; under the Executive Commission he was shifted to Religion and on June 7 became Minister of Justice, the position in which Cavaignac retained him.

Michel Goudchaux was, as Tocqueville observed, the rare combination of rich banker and republican.[18] Under the July Monarchy he wrote articles on financial and economic topics for *Le National* and was otherwise active in republican politics; it was at his home that a few republicans met secretly just before the February revolution to prepare a tentative Provisional Government.[19] Goudchaux became the republic's first Minister of Finance, but he resigned after only a week on the ground that the Provisional Government was hindering his efforts to pursue "sound" financial policies. He failed of election to the National Assembly in April, but succeeded in the by-elections of June 4 in Paris. Goudchaux became a vocal critic of the Executive Commission, and on June 15 made a dramatic appeal for the dissolution of the National Workshops. Thus, in the aftermath of the June insurrection, Goudchaux, the most prominent republican financial expert as well as a determined advocate of republican "order," was a natural choice for the government of Cavaignac.

[18] *Recollections*, p. 165.
[19] Cherest, *Marie*, p. 95.

Recurt, the new Minister of Public Works, had a revolutionary background as colorful as that of Bastide. As a member of the Carbonari, he was involved in several plots; in 1830 he fought on the barricades; later he became one of the leading republican opponents of Louis Philippe, and was several times arrested.[20] A physician, Recurt later settled down in the Faubourg Saint-Antoine, where he won a devoted following among workers, to many of whom he offered free treatment.[21] Recurt had some association with the radical wing of the republican party; in 1845 and 1846 he sat with Ledru-Rollin and Louis Blanc on the directing committee for *La Réforme*.[22] One of the leaders of the banquet campaign, Recurt was a speaker at the Château-Rouge banquet in July 1847. During the February days, when lists of names for a provisional government began to circulate, Recurt's name was one of the most popular,[23] but his first position was only that of assistant to the mayor of Paris. The Provisional Government wanted to make Recurt police prefect, but dared not attempt to oust Caussidière from that sensitive position. After February, Recurt sided politically with *Le National* rather than *La Réforme*, but as chairman of the Central Committee that sought to coordinate the moderate republican campaign for the National Assembly, Recurt reproached provincial committees for the paucity of workers and peasants on their lists.[24] He himself was elected in both his native department and in Paris, and the Assembly chose him one of its six vice-presidents. With the formation of the Executive Commission, Recurt became Minister of the Interior, succeeding Ledru-Rollin. When the barricades began to go up on June 23, Recurt had opposed Cavaignac's starkly military plan, crying, "So it's a battle that is wanted. That's senseless!"[25] Once the battle was joined, however, Recurt supported Cavaignac vigorously, participating personally in the attack on his beloved Faubourg Saint-

[20] *Dictionnaire des parlementaires*, v, p. 102.

[21] Weill, *Parti républicain*, p. 93.

[22] *Ibid.*, p. 146n., and Calman, *Ledru-Rollin*, p. 45.

[23] Calman, *Ledru-Rollin*, p. 41.

[24] Weill, *Parti républicain*, p. 223.

[25] *Compte rendu des séances*, v, p. 813, 25 November 1848.

Antoine.[26] Afterward, Cavaignac replaced Recurt as Minister of the Interior with Senard, whose firmness had never wavered, but retained the doctor of the Faubourg Saint-Antoine as his Minister of Public Works.

Jules Senard's personality and background were quite different. Senard was a Rouennais lawyer who had been active for many years in liberal and then in republican politics in his native city. He was associated with the republican newspaper *Le Journal de Rouen*, and in December 1847, presided over the reform banquet in Rouen.[27] When news of the February revolution reached Rouen, Senard and other republicans took over the city council. The Provisional Government named Senard *procureur général* of Rouen, but the more important position of *commissaire* for the whole department went to a more radical republican and a friend of Ledru-Rollin, Frédéric Deschamps.

Rouen, which was one of the few truly industrialized cities in France at the time, experienced on a smaller scale the political and social strife that embroiled the capital in 1848. Senard took a "moderate" position in defense of bourgeois interests, while Deschamps sought to gain more working-class support. In the elections to the National Assembly, Senard and his associates won a striking victory over the working-class candidates. As soon as the returns were in, some of the workers took to the barricades in protest over the results of democratic suffrage. City officials, including Senard, who hurried back to Rouen immediately after arriving in Paris, suppressed the uprising. In a few brief but bitter street battles, which took place in little more than a day, soldiers and National Guardsmen killed twenty-three workers and wounded at least thirty-six more. The Paris radicals were outraged; although the event was tragic and ominous enough they exaggerated and distorted it into a willful bourgeois monarchist "massacre."[28] Actually,

[26] *Dictionnaire des parlementaires*, v, p. 102.

[27] Jacques Toutain, *La Révolution de 1848 à Rouen* (Paris, n.d.), pp. 33-83.

[28] Blanqui in particular misrepresented the political character of the forces of order. See his comment cited in Seignobos, *La Révolution de 1848*, p. 82, and cf. the recent sober account by Dubuc, "Les Emeutes de Rouen et d'Elbeuf," pp. 243-275.

it was republican officials, including the "radical" *commissaire* Deschamps, who had repressed the uprising, although aided, indeed, by monarchists and bourgeois National Guardsmen. Moreover, Deschamps, Senard and others had first tried conciliation, and had only reluctantly resorted to force. Finally, the Provisional Government, which included Ledru-Rollin and both Albert and Louis Blanc, supported the repression morally and with a special dispatch of troops.[29] Afterward, Deschamps resigned in despair, but Senard was regarded as a hero by the National Assembly, which on June 5 elected him its president.

From his pivotal position at the head of the National Assembly, Senard during the June insurrection gave vigorous support to the suppression. As Senard was also one of the key figures in the political maneuvering that brought Cavaignac to power, it surprised no one that in the formation of his regular government Cavaignac chose Senard for the sensitive position of Minister of the Interior. Of all the members of the Cavaignac government, Senard probably comes closest to the socialist historians' model of the bourgeois republican defending class interests. But the time would soon come when Senard would be adjudged too advanced in his attitude toward social problems, too indulgent toward left republican demonstrations, and would be forced from power by the conservative bourgeois and monarchists of the National Assembly.

Of the civilians in Cavaignac's ministry of June 28, only Tourret was not strictly speaking a *républicain de la veille*. An engineer trained at the Ecole Polytechnique, he early left that profession to pursue his deeper interest in agriculture and to participate in national politics.[30] He was a deputy from 1837 to 1842, associated with the left opposition. Although he was not a member of the republican "party," his relations with the republicans were close and cordial; in the words of Carnot, "When the hour of the left arrives, we will not have difficulty in finding a minister of agriculture: we have Tourret."[31]

[29] *Ibid.*, pp. 261-275.
[30] *Dictionnaire des parlementaires*, v, p. 435.
[31] Carnot, MS "Mémorial," dos. 17, p. 25.

When that hour struck in 1848, the republic found a use immediately for Tourret, although not at first as a minister. He was named by Ledru-Rollin as *commissaire* for his native department of Allier, where he was popular enough to be elected to the National Assembly in April. In the Assembly, Tourret was appointed to the most important committee, that charged with drawing up a proposed text for the constitution of the republic.[32] Tourret apparently felt humble in the presence of such renowned constitutional thinkers as Auguste Vivien and Tocqueville, for he rarely spoke during the committee's sessions.[33] After the June Days, his appointment by Cavaignac as Minister of Agriculture and Commerce fulfilled the hopes of the republicans of ten years earlier.

Lamoricière, the new Minister of War, was a brilliant professional soldier who formerly had been Cavaignac's superior in Algeria. He was born to a Legitimist family, but rallied to the July Monarchy, became a Saint-Simonian, then served as a left opposition deputy from 1846 to 1848. But he had been chosen for the War Ministry in the proposed Thiers-Barrot ministry on February 24; he had demonstrated in the streets on behalf of the regency, and had even been wounded by an insurgent's bayonet.[34] Nevertheless, when the Provisional Government was formed later in the day, it, too, offered Lamoricière the War Ministry. He declined on the ground that he was compromised by his behavior that same morning,[35] but rallied to the republic with some show of enthusiasm and "without mental reservation," as he privately insisted to Cavaignac on February 28.[36] In April, Lamoricière was elected to the National Assembly, and during the June insurrection, he led one of the attack columns with his customary bravado. Afterwards, his pride as a *militaire* assuaged, he had no scru-

[32] Curtis, in *The French Assembly of 1848* erroneously identifies Anthony Thouret as a member of the committee (pp. 127 and 139). The similarity of names is confusing, but there can be no question as to which of the two deputies sat on the committee, because the committee member was from Allier, whereas Thouret was from the Nord.

[33] See the minutes, A. N., C 918.

[34] *Dictionnaire des parlementaires*, III, p. 569.

[35] Crémieux, *La Révolution de février*, p. 454.

[36] Letter to Cavaignac, 28 February 1848, family archives, Reel 28.

ples about accepting the War Ministry in the government of Cavaignac. The British ambassador, Normanby, believed that Cavaignac felt compelled to appoint Lamoricière, who in June had "had all the hard fighting." Within a fortnight rumors began to circulate that Cavaignac was jealous of his former superior and already regretted the appointment;[37] whether or not this was true, Lamoricière would remain with the Cavaignac government until its fall, and their relations remained, publicly at least, cordial.

Admiral Leblanc never assumed the position of Minister of the Navy and of Colonies; indeed, his appointment led Cavaignac to make several temporary and rather mysterious changes in his cabinet. As soon as Leblanc's name was announced, a Legitimist deputy protested that he was not a member of the National Assembly, but the Assembly speedily voted that no such restriction had been placed on the choice of ministers.[38] Nevertheless, Cavaignac privately and peremptorily instructed Leblanc to refuse the portfolio,[39] perhaps to conciliate the opposition on parliamentary grounds. The following day, Cavaignac announced that Admiral Leblanc had declined the appointment and that Bastide would replace him while General Bedeau (who was a deputy) took over the Ministry of Foreign Affairs.[40] General Bedeau was a career officer, no *républicain de la veille*, who, like Lamoricière, had once refused the War Ministry offered by the Provisional Government. Cavaignac apparently gave Bedeau the portfolio out of gratitude for Bedeau's valuable contribution during the June fighting, in which he was seriously wounded. Bedeau eagerly accepted, but the fever resulting from his wound became worse, and on July 17 Cavaignac announced his retirement for reasons of ill health. Immediately after his appointment, Bedeau did approach Adolphe de Circourt, who had served the Provisional Government as emissary to Prussia, but no appointment was actually made, and Bedeau seems not to have played an active

[37] Normanby, *A Year of Revolution*, II, p. 108.

[38] *Compte rendu des séances*, II, p. 244, 28 June 1848.

[39] Copy of a note to Admiral Leblanc, 29 June 1848, Cavaignac archives, Reel 21.

[40] *Compte rendu des séances*, II, p. 246, 29 June 1848.

role as foreign minister. Instead, Bastide, who on July 17 officially resumed the portfolio, appears to have functioned as foreign minister throughout the interim period also, and was even the object of a furtive but vain monarchist attempt to remove him.[41]

For his original ministry, Cavaignac had thus chosen, against some monarchist pressure, men of unquestionable republicanism. Nonetheless, his government differed significantly in composition from that of the Provisional Government and the Executive Commission, both of which had included some radicals—Cavaignac's ministry was uniformly "moderate" republican. Yet the moderate *républicains de la veille* had dominated the revolutionary governments from the beginning, when the Provisional Government was acclaimed by the revolutionary crowds, and thus were in a sense more characteristic products of the revolution than the radicals. The process of political change within the government since February had been the erosion of the left: Louis Blanc and Albert were removed in May, and the remaining radical, Ledru-Rollin, had fallen from power with the Executive Commission in June. Now, with the installation of the Cavaignac ministry, the elimination of the socialists and radicals was complete.

Under Cavaignac, the moderate *républicains de la veille* would hold a monopoly of governmental power for several months. At first, they were preoccupied with the consequences of the insurrection, and some of their policies seemed clearly

[41] For Bedeau's appointment and illness, see Adolphe de Circourt, *Souvenirs d'une mission à Berlin en 1848*, ed. Georges Bourgin (Paris, 1908-09), II, pp. 411-412. None of the scholars who have studied foreign policy in Cavaignac's government mentions any instructions from Bedeau. Bastide sent at least one letter of instruction during the interim (to Tallenay in England, 3 July 1848, Archives des Affaires Etrangères, *Correspondance politique*, *Angleterre*, 670, p. 206), and Normanby, who had an understandably keen interest in the matter, makes no reference to Bedeau as Foreign Minister, asserting instead that Bastide acted as Foreign Minister during the interim. (*A Year of Revolution*, II, pp. 81, 86-87.) Noting monarchist intrigues against Bastide on July 10, Normanby observed that "Cavaignac will not give him up without a struggle." (II, pp. 104-105.) Falloux is silent on the temporary shift of Bastide, as is Bastide himself in his published apology, *La République française et L'Italie*.

reactionary, but in most respects the June Days caused no important change in their outlook. Far from renouncing their ideals, they sought to carry to fruition many republican and democratic initiatives taken in the spring. The tone of *Le National*, which was regarded with some justification as the semiofficial voice of the Cavaignac government, did not change markedly after June; though it no longer approved even rhetorically of socialism, it remained the champion of its old democratic and socially tinged program. Nor was there any repudiation of the workers. In the eyes of Cavaignac and of his government, those who rose in June had been "misguided," and the government continued to make verbal overtures to them afterwards. The government of Cavaignac would sponsor a number of measures reflecting characteristically republican social and democratic principles. But as the policies of the ruling republicans had to take shape within the context of the National Assembly, the mood and structure of forces therein would determine in large measure what the government of Cavaignac could accomplish.

THE NATIONAL ASSEMBLY AS LEGISLATURE

The primary purpose of the National Assembly was to draw up a constitution, but until the election of Louis Napoleon as president in December, it was the sovereign political authority and also functioned as a legislature. Before the June Days, it had been in the process of organization, and although it would live on into 1849, it was relatively unproductive after the election of Louis Napoleon. The period of Cavaignac was the most fruitful one for the National Assembly, for herein it not only elaborated the Constitution, but also considered a great number and variety of bills and adopted much significant legislation.

The experience of the insurrection had an important effect on the Assembly, but the changes were not nearly so drastic as has been suggested. Socialism was discredited, and Louis Blanc and other socialists spoke infrequently; although Proudhon was free to expound his doctrines, which on one occasion he did in a speech lasting four hours, the Assembly almost unanimously denounced them in a formal vote on July 31. Moreover, prominent monarchist politicians, Thiers in particular (who won new fame with a book refuting Proudhon, entitled *De la propriété*), played an increasingly influential role, and some of the *républicains du lendemain* who had rallied more or less sincerely now had strong doubts. "From that moment," recalled Rémusat, "many among us felt more openly inclined to a sceptical defiance of republican and even of simply liberal ideas, to a rather odd return to prejudices and procedures which we had thought outmoded and condemned."[42] The Assembly began an official investigation into the origins of the affair of May 15 as well as of the June Days, and it was soon obvious that Blanc, Caussidière, and even Ledru-Rollin were under strong suspicion.

Although there was a growing mood of reaction in the country, it was not ordinarily antirepublican, and in the Assembly the myth of republican unanimity survived the barricades of June intact. Indeed, in a sense the republic was temporarily strengthened by the proof that it could preserve order, and by the fact that a republican general was in power with a victorious army in Paris. As Madame d'Agoult saw it, the "royalist parties were reduced a second time . . . to feigning acquiescence in the Republic."[43] The dominant mood in the Assembly remained that set by the moderate *républicains de la veille*, whose rhetoric on social as well as on political questions continued to predominate. The monarchists continued to identify themselves as republicans, and none spoke openly of the possibility of a restoration. The ambiguities of the spring persisted. Even Thiers was confused in his assessment of the Assembly. In 1852, he recalled that it had been "sincerely Republican, not as believing a Republic suitable to France, but as seeing that despotism or anarchy were the two alternatives. . . . I was as Republican as the Assembly."[44] His real con-

[42] *Mémoires de ma vie*, IV, p. 344.

[43] Stern, *Histoire de la révolution de 1848*, III, p. 248. She goes so far as to assert that, "There was practically no one in France who did not believe, after the insurrection of June, that the republican government was strengthened for a long time to come." (*Ibid.*)

[44] W. Nassau Senior, *Conversations with M. Thiers, M. Guizot . . . During the Second Empire* (London, 1878), I, p. 44.

version, of course, did not come until the Third Republic; in 1860 he said of the deputies of 1848: "I ruled them, though they hated me as a Monarchist."[45]

The Assembly continued to choose *républicains de la veille* as its presidents, first Marie to succeed Senard, then on July 17, Marrast, who remained in that position; the worker Corbon remained as vice-president. But in the committees, monarchists assumed more prominence. Odilon Barrot as president of the committee investigating the May and June affairs was the most striking illustration of this, but there were many others. Thiers and Berryer each headed one of the fifteen discussion groups, or *bureaux*, into which the Assembly was divided, and other monarchists presided over most of the others.

The most important groupings within the Assembly took the form of loose associations of deputies brought together by past affinities or new common interests. These were usually called "réunions" and designated by their place of meeting. Although their political significance was partially ambiguous, and although they lacked real party structure and means of discipline, two of these were large and influential enough to play significant roles in the Assembly.

One was the *Réunion du Palais National*, sometimes called the *Réunion Démocratique*, a group of about 200 at first, and 256 by late July.[46] This was the most important organization of the *républicains de la veille*, although a few *républicains du lendemain* also were members. During the summer, a small dissident group of republicans, partisans of the fallen Executive Commission and hostile to Cavaignac, split off to form the *Réunion de l'Institut*. The radicals at first gathered in the *Réunion de la Rue de Castiglione*, which later shifted to the Rue Taitbout and called itself the Mountain; it numbered be-

[45] *Ibid.*, II, p. 340.

[46] Seignobos, *La Révolution de 1848*, p. 87, gives the membership at more than 300, which is still much smaller than the 500 moderate republicans he found in the Assembly. But on May 27 *Le National* reported about 200 members, and on July 25 it published a letter from the group's president, Glais-Bizoin, who wrote that his *réunion* was the largest in the Assembly, with 256 members. Although a full list of members does not, to my knowledge, exist, it is known that some members were only *républicains du lendemain.*

tween 40 and 60 deputies, and had little influence. Most of the *républicains de la veille,* of both nuances, were bourgeois, usually professional men and journalists. Of the relatively few working-class deputies in the Assembly, more were associated with the moderate republicans than with the radicals; only five of the twenty-six workers and foremen were radicals.

The most interesting, and sometimes the most effective of the *réunions* was that of the Rue de Poitiers, later to be known as the Party of Order. This group represented the most important implementation of the common policy of Orleanists and Legitimists in 1848 to set temporarily aside political and ideological differences in order to defend conservative interests within a regime that both hoped would be ephemeral. It consisted of a core of about 200 deputies, although on occasion its meetings may have attracted 300 or even 400.[47] About half the membership consisted of "new men," but half were experienced politicians or *notables* of all the monarchist nuances. The president was a general named Baraguey d'Hilliers (who had a reciprocated dislike for Cavaignac), but the most influential members were Legitimists such as Berryer, Falloux, and Larochejaquelein, and Orleanists such as Thiers, Rémusat and Barrot. Tocqueville for a time was associated with the Rue de Poitiers. A tiny minority of six were *républicains de la veille,* men evidently shocked by the events of 1848 into an attitude of strong conservatism. None had been prominent in republican ranks, and one of the most vocal, Joseph Dégousée, would resign in disgust on November 6, after concluding that "The Republic is tolerated there only as a temporary necessity."[48]

Although the Réunion de la Rue de Poitiers was probably no larger in its active members than the republican Réunion du Palais National, it had an added advantage in the prestige and oratorical talents of its leaders. Thiers, Falloux and the

[47] The only membership list known to exist is to be found among the papers of Berryer, A. N. 223 AP 2d.6. It contains 198 names, and may be assigned to early 1849, but there is good reason to believe that the membership was little changed since the period of Cavaignac. Although he does not cite this list, Tudesq offers an excellent discussion of the Rue de Poitiers in *Les Grands notables,* II, pp. 1094-1096, 1141-1144.

[48] *Ibid.,* p. 1144.

Marquis de Normanby thought that the Rue de Poitiers could control the majority in the Assembly.[49] An interesting commentary on the ambiguity of the term "moderate" with respect to forces in the Assembly is to be seen in the opinion of Madame Dosne, the mother-in-law of Thiers, that the Rue de Poitiers represented the "moderates of all nuances," whereas the Palais National represented the "half-red *républicains de la veille*."[50]

Of the approximately 300 unaffiliated deputies, many were former liberal Orleanists who remained aloof from both the republicans of the Palais National and the monarchists of the Rue de Poitiers. Most of the deputies without previous political experience also remained unaligned with the *réunions*.

There was thus no coherent majority in the Assembly, neither in terms of political antecedents nor in terms of the functioning groups of 1848. The Cavaignac government, despite its broad and almost unanimous support at times, did not accurately reflect the political composition of the Assembly. Being *républicain de la veille*, it was to the left of the majority of the deputies, who were *républicains du lendemain*. Cavaignac was retained in power because he had the support of the two most influential groups in the Assembly, the Palais National and the Rue de Poitiers, each of which had its own reasons for maintaining him.

The motives of the moderate republicans were obvious: Cavaignac was one of their own, he had crushed the insurrection, he gave the republic strength and stability, he appointed a moderate republican ministry and furthered moderate republican policies. Why were the monarchists of the Rue de Poitiers willing to support a thoroughly republican government? First, they were grateful to Cavaignac for his services in June. Shaken by the revolutionary upheaval, they

[49] See Senior, *Conversations with M. Thiers*, I, pp. 30-31; Falloux, "Les Républicains et les monarchistes depuis la révolution de février," *Revue des deux mondes*, IX (1851), 393-422; Normanby, *A Year of Revolution*, II, pp. 69, 222. Normanby referred to the group as the "Two Hundred," but it is obvious that he meant the Réunion de la Rue de Poitiers.

[50] Henri Malo, ed., *Mémoires de Madame Dosne, l'égérie de M. Thiers* (Paris, 1928), I, p. 246.

were relieved to find a strong government, even a republican one, emerge at last after four months of turmoil. They would have preferred a monarchist general, and wanted some of their own men in the Cabinet, but they knew that Cavaignac held the reins of power, and was capable of using force against them if they adopted an openly antirepublican stance. Moreover, there was even some advantage to the monarchists in having an unquestionably republican government in power when, as Molé told Normanby, "it will have to take a great many very painful measures." It was convenient to "leave to the Republic the task of undoing what had been done since February."[51] Moreover, with an immediate restoration out of the question, and Cavaignac refusing to appoint monarchist ministers, they knew that to influence policy at all they must seek to do so for the present through a republican government. Their attitude, Madame d'Agoult suggested, was that "Paris is well worth a Marseillaise."[52]

When the Palais National and the Rue de Poitiers had similar or identical policies, they could command huge majorities. But when they were in conflict, neither could form a majority unless it could both maintain unity and win support from a sizable bloc of the unaffiliated deputies. Both groups wooed them in the name of the moderate republic, with different emphases on its nature or on its concern for "order." Neither the republicans nor the monarchists could be sure of the real views of these men who had been elected as republicans and continued to support many republican policies.

Because there were so many new men, the Assembly seemed particularly susceptible to the power of oratory; speakers as diverse in background as Lamartine, Montalembert, and Ledru-Rollin were able to influence important decisions, it seemed, by well-timed and powerful speeches. Tocqueville observed that most of the deputies, although without experience, were "imbued with a new spirit"; more were sincere, honest and courageous than men he knew in the Chambers of the July Monarchy.[53] Thiers, too, was astonished and de-

[51] Normanby, *A Year of Revolution*, II, pp. 146, 153.

[52] Daniel Stern, *Lettres républicaines* (Paris, 1848), letter 2, p. 14.

[53] *Recollections*, p. 114.

lighted by the naiveté of many deputies. They were "honest and intelligent, but ignorant," and "party men . . . were few." Thiers knew that his oratory was effective; it was the only Assembly (before 1871 at least) in which he liked to speak.[54] Seignobos concluded that "This Assembly of honest men, well-intentioned and without *parti pris*, was going to be at the mercy of the atmosphere and speeches during the sessions,"[55] but in fact the Assembly was not nearly so unpredictable. The republican spirit still seemed to animate many of the deputies who had not been republicans before 1848, but beneath the appearance of republican solidarity real political differences continued to exist. The radical republicans, divested of power after the June insurrection, formed a small but important minority, which engaged in continuing quarrels with the moderate republicans. On some significant issues, there was a kind of coalition of bourgeois republicans and bourgeois monarchists against threats to the existing social order. But on other issues, radical and moderate republicans stood together in opposition to the monarchists. The republicans had an advantage in that the conflicts were expressed through republican forms, but the monarchists also had a source of strength in the fact that a majority of the deputies had but shortly before been monarchists or at least nonrepublicans. The conversions of 1848 were numerous enough or the republican myth strong enough to support a variety of republican policies, but on a number of significant issues the skilled *routiers* of the Rue de Poitiers could reach the essentially conservative propensities of most deputies and defeat the republicans.

THE CARNOT AFFAIR

Although the men of the Rue de Poitiers were willing to maintain Cavaignac in power, they sought to exert as much influence on him as possible. Unsuccessful in their initial attempt to divest Cavaignac of a single minister, they immediately prepared another offensive. Their distrust of Carnot increased

[54] Senior, *Conversations with M. Thiers*, II, p. 340.
[55] *La Révolution de 1848*, p. 84.

two days after the installation of the Cavaignac government when the minister formally presented his plan for a sweeping educational reform, providing for free, compulsory, and secular education for all French children. The plan was bitterly opposed by Voltairean Orleanists and Catholic Legitimists alike, for the avowed purpose was not only to provide lay education, but also to republicanize the new generation.

On June 28, Carnot had already recognized "the impatience of the religious party to take possession of the Ministry of Education."[56] In the face of agitation brought forth by the announcement of his appointment, Carnot was prepared then and there to pose the issue of parliamentary confidence. He assumed that he must retire should a majority oppose him and was ready to offer his resignation in open session in order to provoke a vote, but decided against it.[57]

A bitter attack was launched against Carnot, at first outside the Assembly, and he hastened to complete and submit his primary education plan "so that there would remain from our presence at least something that would be difficult to efface."[58] He received many threatening letters; one, signed "some friends of Order and of the Fatherland" and sent on the day he presented the controversial measure, menaced him with death unless he resigned by July 4.[59] Carnot did not resign, but direct pressure was applied on Cavaignac. Carnot noted in his journal: "I know that those gentlemen of the Rue de Poitiers, in negotiating with the new chief of the executive power, made one of the conditions of their support my own retirement. I know that Cavaignac, eager to form a majority for himself in the Assembly, was coming to terms with the reactionaries."[60] Although the general was indeed brought to accept the sacrifice of Carnot, he refused to ask for his resignation. Instead he invited Falloux and other representatives of the Rue de Poitiers to a showdown in the Assembly, saying, "If you want to bring him down, then use your parliamentary weapons against him."[61]

The opportunity for such an attack arose a few days later,

[56] MS "Mémorial," dos. 17, p. 9.
[57] *Ibid.*, pp. 11-12. [58] *Ibid.*, p. 12. [59] *Ibid.*, p. 13.
[60] *Ibid.*, dos. 22, p. 3. [61] *Ibid.*

on July 5, in the discussion of a Carnot proposal to increase the pay of schoolteachers. There was no direct opposition to the proposal itself, but the first speaker, Bonjean[62] of the Rue de Poitiers, immediately attacked Carnot's direction of the ministry.[63]

The strategy was shrewd; instead of criticizing Carnot on religious or political grounds, or even referring to his educational reform plan, Bonjean raised the spectre of "socialism." Carnot had circulated to schoolteachers throughout France writings that, cried Bonjean, were "dangerous . . . detestable." He singled out a handbook entitled the *Manuel républicain de l'homme et du citoyen*, presented in the form of a catechism and containing passages such as the following: "The Pupil: 'Are there at least some means of preventing the rich from being idle and the poor from being eaten up by the rich?' " The schoolteacher replies yes, that the republic will find such means by limitations on property and on the use of capital; he also advocates governmental intervention to regulate working conditions, and even "the organization of labor."[64] Many deputies, still shaken by the insurrection less than a fortnight earlier, were aghast. Bonjean charged that Carnot had not only approved the book, but had had 15,000 copies distributed. He asked the deputies to censure Carnot by adopting a resolution condemning "doctrines which are not accepted by the Assembly."[65]

Carnot replied that the censure of the handbook was just a pretext for an attack on his plans for educational reform, which he took the occasion to defend vigorously. But Carnot was a poor speaker and responded weakly to the criticism of the handbook. It was intended for teachers and not for the pupils, he said, and was moreover only one of many that he had had prepared; but he did not deny that 15,000 copies had been distributed. The beleaguered minister, who later

[62] Who later turned Bonapartist, supporting the *coup d'Etat* and becoming a senator under the Empire. In 1871 he was one of the hostages shot by the Commune.

[63] *Compte rendu des séances*, II, pp. 360ff.

[64] *Ibid.*, pp. 361-362. The author was the philosopher, Charles Renouvier.

[65] *Ibid.*, p. 366.

confessed that he had not even noticed the passages cited and had forgotten about the book itself,[66] offered the weak argument that the book had been published not with his "approval" but only with his "authorization."[67]

Carnot conceded vaguely that parts of the book were blameworthy, and that even he would contest some of its doctrines, but insisted that on the whole it was not "reprehensible." He referred to a few passages indicating a respect for private property, but did not comment directly on those cited by Bonjean. (Privately, Carnot noted that he would have suppressed these passages if he had seen them.)[68]

At any rate, the real issue was elsewhere. As Carnot argued, "it is important for the country to know if public education in France is or is not administered according to truly republican principles."[69]

The debate was brief if pointed, Bonjean's and Carnot's being the only speeches of any length. Bonjean then offered a test "vote of confidence" in the form of a token reduction of 5,000 francs in Carnot's requested appropriation of one million to increase the schoolteachers' pay during the last half of 1848. Bonjean urged representatives to vote for the reduction if the doctrines quoted seemed "antisocial," but both republicans and monarchists recognized that the incident was a disguised attack on the whole principle of republican education, and indeed, on the republic itself. It was also the first open test of strength of the Rue de Poitiers. The division was close, but Carnot lost, 314 votes against 302.[70]

The men of the Rue de Poitiers voted en masse against Carnot, 138 of them, as against five mavericks supporting the ministry. The Legitimists and former governmental Orleanists, most of whom were in the Poitiers group, voted solidly against

[66] MS "Mémorial," dos. 17, p. 15, and Carnot, *Le Ministère de l'instruction publique*, p. 65.

[67] *Compte rendu des séances*, II, p. 363.

[68] MS "Mémorial," dos. 17, p. 15.

[69] *Compte rendu des séances*, II, p. 362.

[70] The announced figures were 314 and 303, but only 302 "contre" votes were recorded. At any rate, it was a close decision. Falloux wrongly recalled the victory as by "a very large majority." (*Mémoires*, I, p. 356.)

Carnot. In addition, about a hundred former liberal Orleanists and 130 of the uncommitted deputies voted against Carnot; finally, twenty-five moderate *républicains de la veille*, perhaps frightened by the "red scare," joined the attack on the ministry.

But, considering the circumstances, the *républicains de la veille*, moderate as well as radical, stood remarkably firm behind the embattled minister: 188 of them, or 88 percent of those voting. In addition, a few former liberal Orleanists and uncommitted deputies supported Carnot. On the whole, the forces against Carnot were monarchist, those defending him, republican. It is inaccurate to attribute the fall of Carnot to a defection of the bourgeois moderate republicans.[71] In fact, despite the sensitive issue of "socialism" raised so soon after the June uprising, the Carnot incident witnessed moderate and radical republicans standing together against the assaults from the monarchist, Catholic, and generally conservative right.

The issue was regarded not as a vote of nonconfidence in the government as a whole, but only in Carnot. Although there was no compulsion to do so, Carnot immediately resigned.[72] The republicans dominating the Committee of Public Instruction in the Assembly promptly chose him their chairman. "It was a kind of protest against the parliamentary vote which had just overthrown me."[73]

Cavaignac, who had uttered no word in defense of Carnot, accepted the resignation, but, as the minister charitably recalled, "he told me in his firm and loyal manner, 'You will be replaced by a minister who will follow the same line, or I will retire with you.' "[74]

Such was, indeed, the tacit agreement: Cavaignac would

[71] For example, Léon Bourgeois, *History of Modern France, 1815-1913* (Cambridge, 1919), I, p. 339, says Carnot was "deserted by the republicans." Georges Renard, *La République de 1848*, pp. 95-96 is less explicit, but leaves the impression that the moderate republicans opposed the socialists on the issue.

[72] He later said that he would have done so even if he had won, had the margin of victory been equally close. (*Le Ministère de l'instruction publique*, p. 67.)

[73] MS "Mémorial," dos. 21, p. 19.

[74] *Le Ministère de l'instruction publique*, p. 67.

surrender Carnot, as he had almost done on June 28, but he insisted that the ministry be held by another *républicain de la veille.* The Rue de Poitiers, content with having demonstrated its strength, was willing to accept such a successor, at least for a time, rather than demand "either a representative or a precursor of the ideas that the majority in the Assembly preferred."[75]

To succeed Carnot, Cavaignac appointed Achille Vaulabelle, a former writer for *Le National,* who later won renown for his *Histoire des deux restaurations.* He had refused the post of ambassador to London, offered by Lamartine, but was elected to the National Assembly and for a time was president of the Réunion du Palais National. Vaulabelle had been one of those who on June 22 had advocated Cavaignac as the successor of the Executive Commission. Like Tourret, Vaulabelle was a member of the Assembly's Committee on the Constitution.

In one sense, the choice of Vaulabelle to be Minister of Education and of Religion was a deliberate insult to the Catholics for, whereas Carnot shared the sympathy for the church characteristic of so many republicans of 1848, Vaulabelle had a reputation as a Voltairean.[76] In the Committee on the Constitution, he had vigorously defended elections by departmental lists as "a question of life or death for the cause of the Republic"; only by this means, he argued, could the influence of the local *notables* and the priests he counteracted.[77] Even *La Réforme* regarded Vaulabelle as a "democrat."[78] Carnot himself pronounced his satisfaction with the choice of Vaulabelle and promised to support him "with all my strength."[79] Vaulabelle was acceptable to the Rue de Poitiers because he lacked oratorical talent, as Falloux recalled, and because "he was inoffensive and rather independent of the

[75] Falloux, *Mémoires,* I, p. 357. This passage is an example of Falloux's belief that the Rue de Poitiers did represent the majority, which he assumed was not republican, although in his explicit statements he expressed the prevailing view of the moderate republican majority.

[76] Victor Pierre, *Histoire de la république de 1848* (2d edn., Paris, 1878), I, p. 443.

[77] A. N., C 918, minutes, p. 62.

[78] Issue of 15 October 1848.

[79] *Le Ministère de l'instruction publique,* p. 67.

yoke of his dangerous friends."[80] Certainly Vaulabelle was individualistic, as he demonstrated by moving into his office accompanied by a trunk, out of which he lived a "practically Spartan life."[81] But this action probably reflected also Vaulabelle's shrewd conclusion that he, too, might soon be ousted from the ministry, whenever he should become unduly offensive to the powerful men who had removed Carnot.

[80] *Mémoires*, I, p. 331.
[81] *Ibid.*, p. 332.

VIII · The Reaction

THE REPRESSION

IN June, the National Assembly had given Cavaignac a free hand to put down the insurrection, and when the fighting was over, the general and the Assembly thought it only natural and sensible to take precautions against any further outbursts of mass violence. The defeat of the revolt was thus followed by a general policy of repression of activities that seemed dangerous to the republic and to "society."

In Paris, Cavaignac ruled with the sabre, by virtue of the siege powers declared by the Assembly. For weeks after the insurrection, the victorious troops rounded up prisoners, adding another 1,700 to the thousands captured during the fighting. Court martial proceedings commenced against the "leaders" of the revolt, and the Assembly ordered the others transported without trial to overseas penal colonies. Army patrols kept order in the working-class areas, making full use of their authority to conduct arbitrary searches and arrests and confiscating thousands of muskets. Against what were considered the twin breeding grounds of the insurrection—the clubs and the socialist press—Cavaignac continued the rigorous policies that he had taken during the fighting. The clubs remained closed; the presses of the eleven newspapers seized on June 25 remained sealed; the editor of *La Presse*, Emile de Girardin, languished in jail until July 5. The regiments of the National Guard that had failed to respond to orders (mostly those from the workers' quarters in the east) were dissolved. Cavaignac concentrated 50,000 troops in and near the capital; when the Assembly formally authorized this strength, Cavaignac expressed his appreciation, but drily observed that he did not need special authorization and had already acted.[1]

A far more important manifestation of what might have seemed the authoritarian habits of a general was Cavaignac's solution of the problem of the National Workshops. The Assembly had been preparing to dissolve them before the insur-

[1] *Compte rendu des séances*, II, pp. 371-372, 7 July 1848.

rection, but was following normal procedures. July 3 was the day fixed for debate on the committee's report advocating dissolution, which had been presented on June 23 by Falloux. But on that day Cavaignac came before the Assembly and announced that he had suppressed the workshops by decree. A republican deputy protested this invasion of the Assembly's prerogatives, and Falloux conceded that the general deserved "a slight reproach," but the Assembly did not seek to oppose the action or to censure Cavaignac in any way.[2]

Nor did *La Réforme* protest the abrupt dissolution; it even had praise for Cavaignac's speech in which he asked for substitute methods for dealing with the needs of the workers. "He speaks of the workers," wrote *La Réforme*, "as a fraternal citizen, and in striking down the National Workshops, he has not forgotten the necessities of the morrow."[3] *Le National* saw in Cavaignac's action additional proof that he was the man of the hour. "In a word, M. Cavaignac has known how to act instead of to talk. In the times in which we live, that is a rare and precious talent which we should praise without reservation." The general, concluded *Le National*, "was born to govern."[4]

The dissolution of the workshops, the continuation of the state of siege and, presently, the imposition of new controls on the press and the clubs, seemed justified not only by the past insurrection, but also by fears of new violence. Cavaignac received a number of threats of assassination, and his mother apparently dissuaded him from taking the Elysée as his official residence by arguing that it was "surrounded with walls from which one could easily fire on her son." The general even took the precaution, during ceremonies on July 6 honoring those who "died for the Republic," of ending the funeral procession at the Madeleine rather than enter the insurgent area to visit the Place de la Bastille.[5]

For two weeks, rumors circulated that a new uprising was being prepared, the expected time being the symbolic date of July 14. Caussidière went personally to warn Cavaignac of

[2] *Ibid.*, pp. 347-348, 5 July 1848.
[3] Issue of 4 July 1848.
[4] Issue of 5 July 1848, p. 2.
[5] Castellane, *Journal*, IV, pp. 88-89.

such a possibility, and the government also investigated reports that workers from the provinces planned to converge on the capital.[6] Although the uprising did not materialize then, fears of another insurrection did not dissipate; nor did Engels regard the June battle as decisive, but believed that the Paris workers would soon rise again in successful revolution.[7]

The government of Cavaignac remained apprehensive, as unemployed workers continued to flock to Paris despite the frantic efforts of the Minister of the Interior to stem the movement by ordering provincial officials to refuse passports to workers.[8] In August, social tensions were so great in Paris that the Assembly's Labor Committee was unable to proceed with the official investigation of labor conditions which had been authorized in May and which was proceeding calmly in the provinces.[9] Yet in the countryside peasant disorders requiring the use of troops continued and in some places intensified during the summer and autumn; the total number of army regulars so employed—about 48,000—would actually be greater than the number required to suppress the June insurrection. During the summer, troops were ordered to Lyon three times to cope with possible disorders; as late as September, Cavaignac was receiving warnings of plots to assassinate him and other prominent figures.[10]

[6] Caussidière, *Mémoires*, II, p. 245. On July 14, the government called the third division of the Army of the Alps to the Paris region. (Boyer, "L'Armée des Alpes," p. 88.) See also General Changarnier's testimony before the committee investigating the June insurrection, *Rapport de la commission d'enquête*, I, p. 260, as well as a report of July 12 from the *procureur général* at Bergerac (Dordogne), in the Cavaignac papers, Reel 23.

[7] "Les Journées de juin 1848," appendix to Karl Marx, *Les Luttes de classes en France (1848-1850)*, (Paris, 1946), p. 126.

[8] Senard sent out five such directives. "The tranquility of the capital depends on this, perhaps," he wrote on October 17, "and that interest must dominate all the others." The circulars are in A.N., F 1A 2097.

[9] Hilde Rigaudias-Weiss, *Les Enquêtes ouvrières en France entre 1830 et 1848* (Paris, 1936), p. 206.

[10] See Coquerelle, "L'Armée et la répression dans les campagnes," p. 122; Cavaignac papers, telegram of 28 September from the Prefect of the Côte d'Or, Reel 22; and note from the Minister of the Interior, 29 September 1848, Reel 23.

In Paris, not only the clubs and the socialist press, but the workers' movement as such suffered from the repression. Forty-five delegates of the corporations were arrested as insurgents, but Gossez suspects that only about nine had actually fought.[11] Yet, although no longer a potent political force, the workers' movement was by no means extinguished after June; with heightened class consciousness, workers continued their efforts to organize, encouraged by governmental benevolence toward producers' cooperatives.[12] The central committee of "delegates of the Luxembourg" was weakened but not destroyed, and began to resume public activity during by-elections to the National Assembly in September; on October 29 it opened a new Paris office, on November 13 it held a banquet attended by 2,000 workers, on December 9 it formed a "permanent committee" that won considerable influence in the provinces. Periodicals aimed at the Paris workers declined drastically after June, but did not disappear, and by September their combined circulation was almost as large as it had been in May.[13] This was despite not only the state of siege, but also despite the new laws on the press and the clubs.

CONTROLS ON THE CLUBS AND ON THE PRESS

The state of siege gave Cavaignac all the police powers he wanted in Paris, but in order to regularize procedures and to extend a measure of control in the provinces, the government on July 11 introduced legislation to place the clubs under strict surveillance, to revive the money bond (*cautionnement*) on the press and to republicanize the laws on seditious libel. Adopted with minor changes in late July and early August, these laws were an unmistakable step away from the full freedom of press and assembly that had been among the most cherished products of the February revolution. Nevertheless, they did not represent a sudden upsurge of blind reaction fol-

[11] "Les Ouvriers de Paris," pp. 806-808.

[12] See pp. 294-299.

[13] Gossez, "Les Ouvriers de Paris," pp. 813-856. For the press see his article, "Presse parisienne à destination des ouvriers (1848-1851)," in *La Presse ouvrière, 1819-1850*, "Bibliothèque re la révolution de 1848," XXIII (1966), pp. 170-188, esp. the charts pp. 184-185.

lowing the June Days, for all had their origins in the preceding months, and the government regarded them as practical necessities for the preservation of the republic, and not as disavowals of their ideals.

Repressive action against the clubs had commenced two months earlier, when three of them were forcibly closed, following the abortive May 15 invasion of the National Assembly. Moreover, on June 7 the Assembly, at the unanimous behest of the Executive Commission, adopted a stringent law prohibiting street gatherings (*attroupements*), a law more severe than that of 1831. Later, as agitation in Paris increased, the Executive Commission planned even more repressive legislation against public meetings, as well as against the press.[14]

In proposing a special law after the uprising, Senard maintained that the government did not question "the right of assembly," but argued that complete freedom "would inevitably lead to excesses that would truly imperil society."[15] Because under the siege powers Cavaignac had already arbitrarily closed those Parisian clubs deemed dangerous, Senard was able to argue without complete sophistry that the proposed law, which would permit them to reopen under surveillance, entailed "the consecration of the right of free and public discussion."[16] The bill proposed to regulate both public and private associations of all kinds. Nonpolitical groups could meet after notifying municipal authorities; the public and political organizations, of the kind usually called "clubs," were subjected to close regulation. They had to be completely public, and free; officers had to submit records of proceedings, and the government could send observers. In addition, clubs were forbidden to associate with one another in any way, and secret societies were flatly prohibited. However, the government explicitly exempted electoral meetings and political banquets from restrictions.[17]

The Assembly sought to render the restrictions even more

[14] See the deposition of Lamartine, *Rapport de la commission d'enquête*, I, p. 306.

[15] *Compte rendu des séances*, II, pp. 419-420, 11 July 1848.

[16] *Ibid.*, p. 697, 27 July 1848.

[17] *Ibid.*, p. 658, 25 July 1848, and p. 727, 28 July 1848.

severe than the government had asked. "In order to respond to the true feeling of the country," declared the committee spokesman, Coquerel, a protestant minister and member of the Rue de Poitiers, "the law ought to have only one article: 'The Clubs are prohibited.' "[18] But the general features of the government bill were maintained, with several additions. First, women and children were forbidden to attend meetings. More importantly, the Assembly adopted, over Senard's protests, an amendment forbidding discussion of "any proposal contrary to public order or to morality."[19] Some deputies wanted to give the government the authority to close any club immediately, but the Assembly adopted Senard's version leaving prosecution to the courts.[20]

The final bill was adopted on July 28 by an overwhelming majority, 629 against 100. The radicals in general voted against it, but they had not opposed the measure in debate. In fact, one of them, Théodore Bac, publicly approved the measure, except for the prohibition on communication between clubs, and Flocon, the former editor of *La Réforme*, a member of a republican secret organization before February, and a friend of Karl Marx, supported the prohibition of secret organizations on the ground that conspiracy against a democratic government was not justified.[21]

In one respect, the Assembly liberalized the government bill by adopting an amendment introduced by the moderate republican Jules Favre exempting "economic (*industrielle*) or welfare associations";[22] this would later be interpreted so as to free the workers' mutual aid societies from surveillance.

The government immediately began to enforce the new regulations. Although many clubs remained closed, and others were prosecuted, the new law by no means forbade political meetings or prohibited the clubs completely. In September, the radicals began a new banquet campaign unmolested, and in November the left-wing Solidarité Républicaine organized

[18] *Ibid.*, p. 616, 22 July 1848.
[19] *Ibid.*, p. 651, 25 July 1848.
[20] *Ibid.*, p. 616, 22 July 1848.
[21] *Ibid.*, p. 653, 25 July 1848, and p. 680, 26 July 1848.
[22] *Ibid.*, p. 702, 27 July 1848.

without interference from the government.[23] In early October, the *procureur général* of the Seine worriedly informed the government that the number of clubs was increasing in Paris and the suburbs, creating "real dangers." The law was "impotent, evaded," and should be strengthened, said the official.[24] But instead of being strengthened, the law soon thereafter was relaxed, as the presidential campaign brought into operation the exemptions on electoral meetings. The clubs born of the revolution of 1848 were not definitely closed until June of 1849, when they were simply suppressed.

As the restrictions on the clubs had their roots in the preceding revolutionary period, so did those on the press. Although the February revolution inaugurated a de facto regime of complete press freedom, the Provisional Government, which acted vigorously and definitively on some matters, such as the abolition of slavery, made only incomplete and temporary changes in the laws governing the press. It abolished the stamp tax, but only for the period of the elections; it only "provisionally suspended" the requirement for a sizable bond (*cautionnement*) that had previously prevented the publication of newspapers lacking considerable financial support.[25] It did abolish the stringent seditious libel law of 1835, but left the earlier one in force until the National Assembly should act.[26] In early June, the Executive Commission authorized officials to demand the payment of *cautionnement* once more, and prepared a bill maintaining the principle of *cautionnement* but reducing considerably the sums required. When this policy was revealed to the Assembly on June 16, many republican deputies were shocked, and promptly moved to abolish *cautionnement.* A few days later, Ledru-Rollin per-

[23] It began to suffer government repression in January 1849. Marcel Dessal, *Charles Delescluze, un révolutionnaire jacobin, 1809-1871* (Paris, 1952), pp. 93, 98.

[24] Letter in "Les Papiers de Marie," *La Révolution de 1848,* I (1905), pp. 186-187.

[25] Collins, *The Government and the Newspaper Press,* p. 102.

[26] As Senard pointed out, the Provisional Government thus took the anomalous position of continuing to outlaw criticism of the principle of monarchy! *Compte rendu des séances,* II, p. 418, 11 July 1848.

suaded the government to shift its ground and to advocate abolition.

The June insurrection interrupted consideration of the proposal, and afterwards the Cavaignac ministry once more took up the question. Although convinced that inflammatory publications had been a root cause of the uprising, several ministers found it difficult as republicans to advocate the hated *cautionnement.* Cavaignac, Recurt and Carnot vigorously opposed it in council, but a majority favored it, and after heated discussions "Cavaignac finally gave in, with considerable ill-humor."[27] The Cavaignac government thus reverted to the position of the Executive Commission a few weeks earlier: it would maintain *cautionnement,* but reduce the amounts. Senard presented the bill on July 11, characteristically proclaiming the principle of liberty in the abstract, while demanding protection against "excesses."[28] Senard sought to soften the reactionary nature of the proposal by presenting it as a great liberalization of the press laws of 1835, which indeed it was. For the Paris dailies, the deposit formerly required was 100,000 francs; now the government proposed 24,000 francs. Much lower figures were set for the provincial dailies, only 6,000 francs for those in the largest cities. Until the Assembly acted, Senard said (repeating the position taken by the Executive Commission), the law of 1830, requiring 48,000 francs in Paris, would be enforced.[29]

Republicans in the Assembly opened a bitter attack on the proposal, as a betrayal of republican principles. Louis Blanc led the assault, speaking for the first time on a bill since the June insurrection. He was joined eloquently by Ledru-Rollin and others of the left, but many of the moderate republicans also vehemently criticized the government proposal. Cried Sarrans: "Do you or do you not want to be republicans? That is the question."[30]

Responding for the government, Marie protested his love

[27] Carnot, MS "Mémorial," dos. 17, p. 34.

[28] *Compte rendu des séances,* II, pp. 416-417, 11 July 1848.

[29] *Ibid.,* p. 417.

[30] *Ibid.,* p. 947, 7 August 1848.

of liberty ("I also have given some proof of that"), but declared that the events of 1848 had taught him the necessity for some limitations, and confessed that he now regarded his previous beliefs in absolute liberty as somewhat unrealistic. He insisted that the law was a temporary necessity provoked by "those frightful excesses of which we have been witnesses and the fatherland the victim."[31]

A group of republicans, joined by some Legitimists, offered a counterproposal requiring authors to sign their articles, as well as other precautions, but ending the bonding practice. The move was defeated, 407 against 342, after which the government's bill was adopted without much difficulty on August 9.

On this significant measure, the republican ministry won its demands only with the support of the Orleanists and the unaffiliated in the Assembly. Most of the republicans, moderate as well as radical, actually deserted the government and remained true to their principles. Even *Le National* bitterly criticized the proposal. For all its "bourgeois" character, *Le National* protested that *cautionnement*, even reduced to 24,000 francs, would make it impossible for many newspapers representing the poor to publish. Anticipating the famous and more pointed cry of Lamennais ("Silence to the poor!"), *Le National* had argued when the bill was introduced, "Now the press will become a privilege that the rich alone will be able to enjoy." When the bill became law, *Le National* lamented, "Do they want it said then that republican society can live only by abandoning principles which gave it hope and victory?"[32] The revived *cautionnement* did have the effect of extinguishing many of the smaller newspapers, notably Lamennais' *Peuple constituant*; but Proudhon's journal survived, thanks to a public subscription, as did a number of other working-class newspapers, including *L'Atelier.*[33]

The Cavaignac government made no attempt to revive the stamp tax, but it did suggest changes in the law on seditious

[31] *Ibid.*, III, pp. 13-15, 8 August 1848.

[32] *Le National*, 13 July 1848 and 9 August 1848.

[33] Collins, *The Government and Newspaper Press*, p. 106; Gossez, "Presse parisienne," pp. 168-188.

libel. Senard presented the bill as a partial implementation of the Provisional Government's decree leaving the pre-1835 legislation in effect until the Assembly could act. The bill left to the Assembly the future enactment of a definitive law; it merely proposed to change provisionally the wording in the existing laws to make them compatible with the republic. Thus, the press was forbidden to incite "hatred or contempt for the republican government" instead of the monarchy, but there was no prohibition on criticism of the chief executive or the ministry.[34]

It was no mere formal change, for Cavaignac was already worried about attacks on the republic in the provinces. Although he seized papers at will in Paris, he was exasperated by his powerlessness in Toulon, Bordeaux and other provincial cities against newspapers "which deny the Republican government about which the law is silent."[35]

The libel bill aroused little opposition, and it was speedily adopted on August 11, two days after the law on *cautionnement*. However, the Assembly introduced a significant addition to the government's bill by outlawing attacks against "the principle of property, and the rights of the family."[36] Furthermore, at the suggestion of one of the most prominent radicals, Lagrange, the forbidden topics were broadened to include offenses against popular sovereignty or universal manhood suffrage.[37]

Although Cavaignac sought to preserve the republic itself from frontal attack, the press remained free to criticize the government and the general himself with impunity. Moreover, the continued vitality and relative freedom of the press were to be revealed during the presidential campaign, when Cavaignac came under vituperative attack. In sum, although Cavaignac's government did retreat from the unfettered freedom

[34] *Compte rendu des séances*, II, p. 418, 11 July 1848.

[35] Letter to Marie, 29 July 1848, published in "Les Papiers de Marie," p. 182.

[36] *Compte rendu des séances*, III, p. 83, 10 August 1848. The amendment provoked the ironical suggestion from Proudhon that the Assembly might as well prohibit all discussion of property, and consequently of the civil code, political economy, etc.

[37] *Ibid.*

following February, the press under Cavaignac was far less restricted than it had been under the July Monarchy or would be later under Louis Napoleon. In 1849, the stamp tax was revived, more sweeping restrictions were imposed, and all were enforced with unprecedented vigor.[38]

At the *coup d'Etat*, all of the leading newspapers were seized; many, such as *Le National*, went out of existence. (*La Réforme* succumbed in 1850.) The Second Empire imposed the most stringent control since 1814 and even under the Third Republic, the *cautionnement* and seditious libel laws remained in force until 1881.[39]

THE STATE OF SIEGE

Although the Assembly favored legal restrictions on the press, many deputies grew increasingly restive over Cavaignac's arbitrary seizures of Parisian newspapers under the state of siege. Few protested his use in general of these powers, but the issue of the press touched all parties directly. Even at the height of the insurrection, Cavaignac had struck right as well as left against newspapers that he believed to be fomenting disorder for political ends. Girardin was freed after a few days, but as weeks passed and the seals remained on the confiscated presses, protests arose from all quarters in the Assembly, from the former liberal Orleanists, from Legitimists, from radicals, from some of the moderate republicans. Although republican newspapers were unmolested, many republicans were pained by the blows dealt against their ideal of freedom of the press.

Cavaignac met the first formal interpellations on July 7 by insisting that the seizures were necessary to assure public order. Conceding that "the state of siege is in fact a terrible weapon in the hands of the power that wields it," he pleaded the "rectitude of my intentions," and asked that the state of siege be continued indefinitely.[40] The Assembly quickly con-

[38] Collins, *The Government and Newspaper Press*, pp. 111-112.
[39] *Ibid.*, pp. 181-182.
[40] *Compte rendu des séances*, II, pp. 372-373.

sented. The government wanted the extraordinary police powers only in Paris, rejecting suggestions that they be extended to the provinces because, as Senard observed, "We do not want it said that men who have consecrated their lives to the defense of democratic principles . . . allowed themselves to be carried away . . . beyond what is strictly necessary."[41]

But the state of siege in Paris remained a source of chronic discontent that was not to be resolved until October. The second attack came on August 1, led mostly by monarchists. A Legitimist deputy denied that the state of siege conferred the power to suspend newspapers; another conservative argued that the state of siege was unnecessary so long after the insurrection. A republican agreed: "The battle is won, so let us be strong enough to return to ordinary law."[42] Victor Hugo, who was a deputy, also protested that the state of siege did not justify arbitrary seizures, and hinted broadly that Cavaignac sought dictatorship. Stung, the general interrupted, "Do not fear, sir, I have no need of so much power. I have enough already, I have too much power. Calm your fears." He denied that he had wielded truly dictatorial powers even during the insurrection, but added proudly: "If there was a dictatorship, I only recall with what patriotic zeal I came to lay it down before the Assembly."[43]

Indeed, the state of siege as Cavaignac interpreted it entailed no assumption of legislative powers, but only of extensive police powers. A juridical device that had originated during the French Revolution, the concept was still in the process of evolution.[44] Cavaignac made his exercise of siege power a question of parliamentary confidence, demanding formal acknowledgment that "nothing in my actions can be considered as blameworthy." This the Assembly promptly voted.[45]

A few days later, on August 6, Cavaignac satisfied the dissident opinion by finally permitting the newspapers seized in

[41] *Ibid.*, p. 425, 11 July 1848.
[42] The debate is in *Compte rendu des séances*, II, pp. 791-801.
[43] *Ibid.*, p. 800.
[44] See Bastid, *Doctrines et institutions politiques*, II, pp. 7-8.
[45] *Compte rendu des séances*, II, p. 801.

June to reappear.[46] But two weeks later, Cavaignac struck at the Paris press once more. He suspended anew four of the more radical newspapers and infuriated monarchist opinion by suspending (on August 24) the *Gazette de France.*

A Legitimist deputy (Crespel de la Touche) hastily introduced a resolution to curb Cavaignac's powers on the press, even under the state of siege. At the same time, a new source of opposition came when republican deputies argued that the Constitution, which was just about to come to the floor, should not be debated while Paris was under a state of siege. The leaders of this move, from the moderate republican Lichtenberger to Ledru-Rollin, conceded that the Assembly's deliberations had been in no way inhibited by the state of siege, but urged that press opinion should also be free during the debates.

Once more, Cavaignac insisted that the state of siege be continued. In one of his most impassioned and controversial speeches,[47] the general developed the thesis that the state of siege was necessary to defend the republic itself. Harking back to the first Revolution for phraseology, as well as for justification, Cavaignac argued that the state of siege was "the law of public safety," a mild counterpart of the Terror. Instead of proscribing men, he proscribed ideas, not "philosophical discussions on questions of a social nature," but political ideas, those overtly hostile to the republic. The ministry itself could be criticized freely, and would respond only by silence or "by better behavior." The Assembly deliberated in complete freedom, free even "from any moral constraint exercised by the government," and by its own decision could lift the state of siege, even if Cavaignac's personal advice was to the contrary. Nor was the freedom to discuss the Constitution infringed, because it would necessarily embody the one principle that must be immune from attack. The state of siege was directed only against published attacks on the republic itself,

[46] *Le Moniteur*, p. 1905. Collins, *The Government and Newspaper Press*, p. 105, errs in asserting that all except *La Presse* were freed in early July, as well as in her dating of other seizures.

[47] The speech is in *Compte rendu des séances*, III, pp. 731-733, 2 September 1848.

whether from left or right. "There is only one thing," concluded the general, "against which we will employ, at our own risk and under our responsibility, all the weapons that the Assembly has given us, and that is any attack against the republican principle."

Although the men of the Rue de Poitiers were alarmed by the uncompromising republican stance of Cavaignac, they still feared to attack him openly or bring down his government by defeat on a major issue. By an overwhelming majority, therefore, the Assembly on September 2 voted to continue the state of siege while the Constitution was being debated, and nine days later gave him another strong vote of confidence on the old issue of press seizures.[48] The state of siege continued in Paris for another month. Because of the changing political situation, the monarchists then began to assert themselves more forcefully, and on October 11 the Cavaignac government was put in a minority position on the issue of the press seizures. As a result, Cavaignac remodeled his ministry, replacing two republicans with former monarchists, and also withdrew his insistence on the state of siege, which in consequence was ended by vote of the Assembly on October 19.[49]

The continuation of the state of siege was a policy of the government, and only tolerated by the Assembly. Cavaignac's attitudes on this issue are revelatory. Clearly the *militaire* in him wanted a free hand in Paris, yet his authoritarian manner crumpled in the face of a hostile parliamentary decision, and he quietly surrendered the powers which a few days earlier he had insisted were still necessary. Although he seems to have exaggerated his desire to protect only the republic, he did use the siege powers against the monarchist press as well as against the socialists. There was an obvious association, moreover, between the state of siege and the rule of the *républicains de la veille*, for the end of the republican monopoly coincided with the end of the state of siege. Cavaignac himself admitted that only a pure republican ministry could have been entrusted with the policies of limiting liberty which the

[48] *Ibid.*, pp. 735, 938.

[49] *Compte rendu des séances*, IV, p. 1008.

situation required.[50] This is not to say simply that the monarchists opposed the state of siege while the republicans wanted to continue it. The issue was never that clear-cut. The government wanted it to continue, but many republicans, and finally a majority in the monarchist-dominated Assembly opposed and ended it. Cavaignac did not employ the siege powers wantonly or harshly; the complaints were solely on principle or against his attacks on the press. Cavaignac's moderate use of the potentially oppressive state of siege was in general regarded as commendable and formed the inspiration for the law of August 9, 1849, which remained the fundamental legislation on the matter in France into the twentieth century.[51] There is scarcely any comparison between his exercise of the siege powers for a few months in Paris, and their extensive application in many departments after the *coup d'Etat* of 1851 and during the early Third Republic.

THE PURGE OF BLANC AND CAUSSIDIÈRE

In addition to the policies of repression, the period of Cavaignac's ascendancy also witnessed a reactionary movement of a more profound nature which struck at the roots of the revolution of February. This movement had its origins in May, and culminated after the June insurrection. It emanated from the nonrepublican majority within the Assembly, but was unwittingly abetted by the government, which did not see its implications until too late.

The movement took the form of an attack on some of the men of February, namely Louis Blanc, Marc Caussidière and Ledru-Rollin. It began following the May 15 invasion of the Assembly, after which three deputies were imprisoned, Albert, Barbès and Courtais. There was also some evidence of the complicity of Caussidière, the revolutionary police prefect and Louis Blanc. The latter had been selected for the new government proclaimed on May 15. (Blanc had almost been carried out of the Assembly triumphantly on the shoulders of

[50] *Ibid.*, pp. 888-889, 16 October 1848.

[51] Clinton L. Rossiter, *Constitutional Dictatorship: Crisis Government in Modern Democracies* (Princeton, 1948), p. 81.

the crowd.) Caussidière, whose conduct also had appeared compromising, resigned as police prefect and as deputy. The attorney general of the republic on May 31 won permission from the Executive Commission to seek the prosecution of Louis Blanc, but Blanc vigorously protested his innocence, and the Assembly by a close vote (369 to 337) refused to lift his parliamentary immunity.[52] Blanc remained in the Assembly, and Caussidière was reelected on June 4, but neither played a prominent role thereafter.

The renewed attack on the two, as well as on other men of February, came after the June insurrection. On the last day of the fighting, the Assembly, at the behest of Senard, had ordered an official investigation into "the causes of the insurrection of June 23, as well as the outrage of May 15, 1848."[53] That Senard and other republicans should desire such an investigation is not surprising, but as it turned out the proceedings fell into the hands of men who sought to discredit some republican leaders and, by implication, much of the revolution itself. This resulted from the political composition of the Assembly as much as from any change in feeling after the insurrection; for of the fifteen-member committee chosen by the Assembly, only six were republicans, the others being Orleanists and Legitimists; and the chairman was Odilon Barrot.[54]

By mid-July, the committee felt that it had enough evidence to prosecute Blanc and Caussidière, and consulted Cavaignac on the matter. Despite the fact that the general's own Police Prefect, Trouvé-Chauvel, a staunch republican and former ally of Ledru-Rollin, demanded the arrest of Caussidière, Cavaignac protested vigorously, but agreed not to obstruct a judicial proceeding nor to oppose a parliamentary debate on the matter.[55] The attorney general opened a parallel inquiry.

[52] *Compte rendu des séances*, I, p. 614, 3 June 1848. La Gorce, *Histoire de la seconde république*, I, pp. 296-297, sees the affair as a political maneuver by Senard and Cavaignac, but cites no evidence except rumor.

[53] *Compte rendu des séances*, II, p. 208, 26 June 1848.

[54] For the membership, see *Le Moniteur*, p. 1504. See also Barrot, *Mémoires posthumes*, II, pp. 275-308.

[55] *Rapport de la commission d'enquête*, II, pp. 321-322, 325-326.

The committee's report, presented on August 3, caused a sensation, for it was clearly tendentious. It singled out for accusation Caussidière, Louis Blanc, Ledru-Rollin and Proudhon, but also cast vague discredit on the entire Provisional Government.[56] The partiality of the report struck even many conservatives as unfair.[57] Ledru-Rollin made effective use of his oratorical talents in an impassioned defense of himself and the Provisional Government. The Assembly was obviously swayed, and Cavaignac himself, no friend of Ledru-Rollin's, left his seat in order to shake the speaker's hand.[58]

The Assembly ordered the publication of all the evidence collected; when this appeared two weeks later in three large volumes, the bias was even more apparent, for the committee had minimized the evidence of Bonapartist and monarchist intrigues and had sought to smear the republicans alone. Even Cavaignac was subjected to criticism, in some of the testimony, for his conduct in June.

The republicans now recognized that they were the victims of a skillful political maneuver on the part of the monarchists. According to Normanby, the government had considered trying to suppress the report, but had decided that this would have been politically dangerous.[59] Knowing that both the attorney general and the committee wanted to prosecute Blanc and Caussidière, and fearful that a long debate could only hurt the republican cause and perhaps stir public disorders, Cavaignac concluded that Blanc and Caussidière must be sacrificed.[60]

[56] *Compte rendu des séances*, II, pp. 844-860. See also *Le National*, 5 August 1848.

[57] Calman, *Ledru-Rollin*, p. 218; and Normanby, *A Year of Revolution*, II, pp. 134-136.

[58] Calman, *Ledru-Rollin*, p. 217.

[59] Normanby, *A Year of Revolution*, II, p. 160.

[60] The Comtesse d'Agoult, a moderate republican who was nevertheless critical of Cavaignac, says that the general let himself be persuaded not to oppose formal accusations, "although with great reluctance." (Stern, *Histoire de la révolution de 1848*, III, p. 262.) But evidence exists that on the day before the debate, Cavaignac was already resolved not to let the accusations against the "representatives who must be prosecuted" consume more than one parliamentary session.

The debate opened on August 25. It lasted from noon until early the next morning, all of those criticized in the report making long speeches in their own defense. It was after midnight that the government dramatically intervened; in the midst of the debate, the president read a letter from the attorney general asking permission to prosecute Blanc and Caussidière. Then Cavaignac himself told the stunned Assembly that the government supported the prosecution, but reluctantly. "Neither I nor any of the members of the council over which I have the honor to preside," said the general, "feel a culpable eagerness to prosecute men who contributed to the proclamation of the Republic. We do it, because it is our duty, but we find in it neither pleasure nor enthusiasm."[61] Cavaignac argued speciously that it was a judicial matter, although the Assembly might regard it as political. He asked an immediate vote lifting the parliamentary immunity of the two men, hinting that he might view delay as a vote of nonconfidence.[62]

Shocked, Representative Grévy, the future president of the Third Republic, pleaded that the Assembly should not judge hastily; but the hour was late, and the Assembly complied with Cavaignac's request. Strong majorities voted to prosecute Blanc and Caussidière for complicity in the May but not in the June insurrection.[63] Caussidière feared that they would be arrested on leaving the Assembly, but Cavaignac reassured him. "If you have need of several days to arrange your affairs, I promise that you shall have them." Reassured also by Marie, with a "gracious and jesuitical smile," Caussidière slipped out of the huge and disorderly Chamber at about 5 A.M., unnoticed

---

Letter of Adolphe Blanqui, 24 August 1848, reporting on a conversation with Cavaignac, published in *L'Amateur d'Autographes*, XXXIX (1906), 6-8.

[61] *Compte rendu des séances*, III, pp. 504-505, 25 August 1848.

[62] *Ibid.*, p. 508.

[63] *Ibid.*, pp. 517-519. The attorney general did not ask to prosecute Blanc for the June insurrection. The Assembly refused to authorize the prosecution of Caussidière for the June insurrection by a vote of 281 to 458, perhaps because he would be required to go before a court-martial rather than a civilian court. The votes lifting parliamentary immunity for the May affair were against Blanc 504 to 252, and against Caussidière, 477 to 278.

by his weary colleagues.[64] By the time the last vote was counted and the session adjourned at 5:45 A.M., Louis Blanc had also disappeared. Although Cavaignac had abetted the political assassination of the two, it seems clear that he purposely permitted their escape; certainly nothing was done to prevent it. Louis Blanc got a few hours' sleep and then, without even seeking to disguise himself, calmly departed by train from Saint-Denis.[65] Both he and Caussidière reached England without difficulty.[66]

Although the two men of February were safe in England, the republican cause had been severely damaged in the whole affair. The republicans were divided and humiliated; the moderates realized too late that they had been duped into inflicting an injury on their own left wing. The Cavaignac government in particular had played "the scarcely honorable role of executor of the vengeance of the majority."[67]

But should it seem astonishing that in the course of a revolution men should turn against or desert their former partners? Rather, it is remarkable that in 1848 the revolution did not devour its own children, if we think of the leaders rather than the thousands who were the casualties of June. For all the bitterness of political conflict, heads rolled only figuratively. The greatest violence against republican leaders occurred not after the June insurrection, but following the much milder May invasion of the Assembly. Then there was no prolonged meditation and weighing of political consequences before acting; three members of the sovereign National Assembly, including a member of the Provisional Government, Al-

[64] *Mémoires de Caussidière*, II, pp. 259-260. Cf. Hugo, *Souvenirs personnels*, p. 94.

[65] Blanc, *Pages d'Histoire*, pp. 261, 302.

[66] Madame d'Agoult said the government helped the two to escape, *Histoire de la révolution de 1848*, III, p. 265. La Gorce says the government failed to act, "from either indecision or indifference," *Histoire de la seconde république*, I, p. 426. Normanby thought it was Ducoux, prefect of police, who let the pair escape, *A Year of Revolution*, II, p. 185. If so, Ducoux was not removed or reprimanded. Blanc believed the government permitted him to flee. (*Révélations historiques*, II, p. 209.)

[67] Bastid, *Doctrines et institutions politiques*, II, p. 28.

bert, were promptly thrown into jail, and the Assembly voted immediately to prosecute them. While Albert languished in the dungeon at Vincennes, his radical colleagues remained at liberty for three more months. When they finally were purged, they were permitted to escape. Only two men were stricken, whereas the monarchist reaction had hoped to have Ledru-Rollin at least, in addition. There were no other political purges in the Assembly; even in the antisocialist atmosphere following the June insurrection, so outspoken a socialist as Proudhon, who also had been accused in the *Rapport*, remained completely free, free even to proclaim his doctrines at length from the tribune.

AMNESTY REFUSED BUT ACCOMPLISHED

Cavaignac had imprisoned thousands of insurgents, about 15,000 in all, but their fate was quite different from that usually depicted by historians. Schmidt, in his influential work, for example, implies that most of these were sent to penal colonies overseas, "without judgment, by arbitrary decision."[68]

Indeed, the National Assembly seemed implacable, as it summarily voted on June 27 to send insurgent "leaders" before courts-martial and to deport all others without trial. A few radicals pleaded vainly for less stringent penalties, but the Assembly refused even to exempt the aged and minors from the prospective voyage to a tropical prison camp.[69]

Moreover, neither the Assembly nor the government was in any mood to consider amnesty. Cavaignac had at first contemplated amnesty as soon as the "terror" of the bourgeoisie was calmed,[70] but opposed any such policy throughout his six months in power. During the fall and winter, several groups of deputies sought a declaration of amnesty from the Assembly, but were unable even to bring the matter to the floor. On November 6, a parliamentary committee noted that amnesty would be "dangerous and inopportune" because doctrines

[68] Schmidt, *Les Journées de juin*, p. 124.

[69] *Compte rendu des séances*, II, p. 235, 27 June 1848. Algeria was excluded in the original law, but as it turned out, Algeria was the only colony to which prisoners were sent.

[70] Stern, *Histoire de la révolution de 1848*, III, p. 260.

preaching the overthrow of the Assembly and the republic were still being disseminated.[71] The issue did not come to a vote until February 1849, when amnesty was defeated by the huge majority of 531 to 167.[72]

If one looks only at the harsh law adopted and the refusal to grant amnesty, the record seems black indeed. But if one considers the policies actually followed, a different picture emerges, a picture not of implacable vengeance but of prudence and even relative lenience toward the prisoners, who seemed to pose a dangerous political problem in a country still undergoing the turmoil of revolution. Cavaignac began immediately the policy of tempering the punishment demanded by the Assembly. The general had personally been opposed to arbitrary imprisonment but had contemplated having all cases considered by military courts. When the Assembly decided that most would be denied trials, at his behest the word "transported" was substituted for "deported," to avoid the stigmatization of the prisoners as criminals, with the attendant loss of civil rights. The amended resolution acknowledged that the treatment of the prisoners was political, "a measure of public safety."[73] Privately, moreover, Cavaignac told his cabinet that he would not execute the law in its full rigor but wanted only to remove the prisoners from Paris, where they constituted a danger and were in some danger themselves.[74]

The policy of mitigation began with the release of more than 3,000 prisoners within days of their capture. The other 11,000 remained for a time in prisons and forts in the Paris area.[75] Thereafter, Cavaignac appointed in succession several

[71] *Compte rendu des séances*, v, pp. 315-316.

[72] *Ibid.*, vii, p. 614. Cavaignac and most of his former ministers, then all merely deputies, voted against amnesty.

[73] *Compte rendu des séances*, ii, pp. 217-218 and 232, 27 June 1848.

[74] Stern, *Histoire de la révolution de 1848*, iii, p. 260.

[75] The figures in this discussion are taken from various reports presented before the Assembly, notably those of 5 October 1848 (*Compte rendu des séances*, iv, pp. 640-643); 25 October 1848 (*ibid.*, v, pp. 514-517); as well as a report of 21 January 1850 before the Legislative Assembly (*Le Moniteur*, 22 January 1850, p. 236). There are a few minor variations in the figures; where these exist, I have used approximations.

committees charged with releasing prisoners deemed deserving of clemency for one reason or another. Although the Assembly had turned the operation over to the military under the state of siege, in practice Cavaignac assigned civilian lawyers and judges to conduct the crucial portions of the investigations. During the summer they and the military committees freed more than half of the remaining prisoners (6,400 in all), sent 255 "leaders" before courts-martial, and designated 4,348 for transportation.[76]

Beginning in August, these remaining prisoners were shifted from Paris to northern ports, such as Le Havre and Brest. Still wishing to release more, Cavaignac created ten new civilian committees "of clemency," which freed 991 additional prisoners. Finally, he appointed a three-member civilian committee to review all the remaining cases.

Meanwhile, many in the Assembly had second thoughts about sending the prisoners to distant colonies, not primarily for humanitarian reasons, but to reduce expenses. On October 25, the government itself proposed Algeria, with the avowed aim of "conciliating . . . the rights of humanity with political necessities."[77] The government had already sponsored a plan to subsidize the colonization of Algeria with free farmers; the prisoners would be placed in separate colonies for ten years, but would receive their own land after three years.

The extreme left in the Assembly continued to protest the lack of legal defense on the part of the prisoners. Cavaignac's Minister of War, Lamoricière, retorted with some justification that if ordinary legal procedures had been followed, the prisoners could not have been released as speedily as they had been. The government had granted "an administrative justice" and had sought to "soften the rigor of the law."[78] Indeed, Cavaignac's final review committee continued to free prisoners, until by the time he left office, of the original 15,000

[76] Whereas Schmidt had implied that 11,000 were transported, this figure of 4,348 is used by Renard, *La République de 1848*, p. 89n., and others. Neither figure is correct for the number actually sent overseas.

[77] *Compte rendu des séances*, v, p. 102.

[78] *Ibid.*, vi, p. 265, 14 December 1848.

only about 2,700 remained in custody, and all of these were still in France.

The gradual release of prisoners was one of the few Cavaignac policies to be continued by Louis Napoleon; the committee appointed by Cavaignac continued to function, freeing an additional 2,200 prisoners during 1849. At last, in early 1850, the remaining insurgents of June were shipped to Algeria: only 459 were left to suffer this fate.[79]

The treatment of the captured insurgents of June was mild in comparison with the treatment of political prisoners after the Commune of 1871 and even after the *coup d'Etat* of 1851. At that time 26,884 were arrested, of whom only 5,857 were freed; the remainder suffered penalties of varying rigor, including 239 deported to Cayenne and 9,581 to Algeria.[80]

In sum, although the decree of June 27 was harsh, it was never fully implemented; although amnesty was formally refused, in practice most prisoners were amnestied by being liberated. Instead of seeking vengeance, Cavaignac treated the defeated insurgents as the political problem that they were. If mass imprisonments are brutal per se, it seems remarkable that in the agitated atmosphere of 1848 so many insurgents were freed so quickly. Nevertheless, the resort to arbitrary power in the state of siege, the restrictions on the freedoms to publish and to assemble, and the imprisonment in makeshift concentration camps of thousands of poor workers who had helped make the revolution, were not deeds expected of the democratic republic in February. It would be by its positive aims and achievements that the government of Cavaignac would show that it was a true if unheroic heir of the revolution.

[79] Marcel Emérit, "Les Déportés de juin," in *La Révolution de 1848 en Algérie*, pp. 64-73. These finally received amnesty in 1859. Of the 255 insurgents sent before courts-martial, a few were freed, but most were sentenced to prison terms ranging from three months to many years. In addition, early in 1849, two of the assassins of General Bréa were executed.

[80] Seignobos, *La Révolution de 1848*, p. 220.

IX · "La République Démocratique . . ."

CAVAIGNAC IN POWER

The government of Cavaignac was the first to achieve stability since February, and the general sought to adjust to his new role as effective head of state as well as president of the council of ministers. He retained much of his habit of aloofness and isolation, but was now in even closer contact with his mother than previously.[1] After considering the Elysée, Cavaignac decided to take up official residence in a large house on the Rue de Varennes in the Faubourg Saint-Germain. He also maintained cordial relations with his uncle the viscount, with whom he dined each Sunday.[2]

The recently published memoirs of Rémusat have brought to light a piece of gossip about a grande dame of Paris who seems to have thrown herself at the savior of society. According to Rémusat, one Madame Kalergi, a vivacious, blonde and persistent niece of the Russian Foreign Minister, Count Nesselrode, "did everything in the world to attract him." Fearing some kind of diplomatic ploy, the general withstood the amorous siege for a time before surrendering—conditionally. "They say that Cavaignac finally granted what she wanted and saw her occasionally in the morning, but he never visited her during the evening, and limited his relations with her to what was strictly necessary."[3]

Starting in late July, Cavaignac held weekly evening receptions attended by the diplomatic corps, deputies and government officials, and many officers of the National Guard.[4] Rémusat was pleased to see the revival of decorum in governing circles after several months of the "casual and uncultivated

[1] It is regrettable that the best source on the intimate thoughts of Cavaignac, the correspondence with his mother, is thus lacking for the entire period when Cavaignac was in Paris in 1848.

[2] Castellane, *Journal*, IV, p. 106.

[3] *Mémoires de ma vie*, IV, p. 352. In September, Hugo noted that Cavaignac had another mistress, a Mlle Plumkett. (*Souvenirs personnels*, p. 101.)

[4] See Castellane, *Journal*, IV, pp. 91-92, 103.

atmosphere which reflected a revolution made in the streets."[5] The proud and taciturn general did not make conversation easily, however, and many continued to look on him with a kind of awe. "One could scarcely approach him," recalled the worldly Count de Rémusat, "without recognizing that one was in the presence of an historical figure." Observing him at one of the official receptions, the aged savant Biot remarked that Cavaignac reminded him of Washington.[6]

Although such a comparison may seem odd, it is true that if Cavaignac did not found the republic, he was dedicated to its preservation. He and his ministers were aware that their own rule was provisional, but they did not regard the republican form of government as provisional. As Goudchaux declared on one occasion, when his policies were under attack by some monarchists, "I want this form to continue. I don't want it to give way to either a consulate, an empire, a restoration or a quasi-restoration."[7] The moderate republicans under Cavaignac shared this preoccupation with all of the men of February; it was only after the election of Louis Napoleon in December that France came into the hands of a completely different team with completely different values and intentions, even though republican government would be permitted to exist for three years afterwards. Although his manner and methods were sometimes authoritarian, Cavaignac was no Bonaparte, no Monk or MacMahon, not even a lesser Cromwell: he was a republican, and he meant the republic to endure.

Militaire that he was, Cavaignac sought in no way to destroy or to subjugate the National Assembly. When he entered the Chamber, it was not to stampede the deputies out the windows, nor to end their "prating" with bayonets, but to remind them that they were his masters. Although there was no stipulation in the resolution of June 28 that the ministry in whole or in part was responsible to the Assembly, Cavaignac him-

[5] Rémusat, *Mémoires de ma vie*, IV, p. 351.

[6] *Ibid.*, pp. 348, 351-352.

[7] *Compte rendu des séances*, IV, p. 260, 25 September 1848.

self was by implication removable at will by the Assembly.[8] As the general told Caussidière, "My power is not at all as strong as you think it. The majority of the Assembly decides everything. I am only an instrument in its hands."[9] Barrot recalled that Cavaignac exhibited "the most humble deference toward the legislative power. He said repeatedly that he was only the arm of the sovereign Assembly, always ready to bow to its will."[10] According to Madame d'Agoult, it was a fatal weakness in Cavaignac that he respected the Assembly "too much"; by failing to take advantage of his situation through a stronger exercise of power, he lost the opportunity to consolidate the republic "for a long period of time."[11]

Actually, although Cavaignac was indeed deferential to the Assembly, and regarded himself as its "agent," his role was far from passive. He acted strongly if arbitrarily in dissolving the National Workshops; there were no other such actions, but despite his political inexperience the general was an energetic premier who had his own policies and who sought to win support for them in the Assembly. Instead of limiting its actions to the maintenance of order while the National Assembly drew up the Constitution, Cavaignac's government took upon itself the role of fostering both laws on contemporary problems and long-range legislation which often involved profound innovations. The general personally played a major role in directing foreign policy, and took a great interest in certain domestic matters; he acted as the head of a Cabinet that provided vigorous leadership.

Cavaignac also was capable of speaking effectively before the Assembly. He was not exactly an accomplished orator, but the deputies always listened to him with respect, and he sometimes moved them deeply. Rémusat recalled that Cavaignac had charmed the Assembly in his first appearance before it in May. "His thin and tired face was pleasing. . . . His bright eyes expressed intelligence, frankness, and courage, with a shadow of sadness and of suffering. His easy and simple manner united

[8] Bastid, *Doctrines et institutions politiques*, II, p. 14.

[9] *Mémoires*, II, p. 246.

[10] *Mémoires posthumes*, II, p. 310.

[11] Stern, *Histoire de la révolution de 1848*, III, pp. 248-250.

the freedom of the camp with the dignity of command. . . . He was not like us and he won us all."[12] According to Barrot, "Never did a minister habituated to parliamentary life practice so skillfully the art of capturing the confidence of an assembly as this soldier, completely inexperienced as he was of the tribune, and of assemblies." Victor Hugo put it more poetically, "This poor assembly is a true soldiers' girl, in love with a trooper."[13]

Yet there was something vaguely disturbing about Cavaignac's political manner. The hesitancy and indecisiveness noted by some colleagues in Algeria also was noticed by the more perspicacious deputies. "He was, one might say," observed Rémusat, "slow and complicated, as are all the personalities that take shape alone. Inexperience and isolation had rendered him defiant. Transported into an unknown world, it is understandable that he was on his guard. He was too fearful of being deceived to trust himself to others, he was too fearful of making mistakes to trust himself. Proud and scrupulous, he hesitated to decide, although, his decisions once taken, he defended them without weakening. It is for that reason above all that he failed in government."[14] The peculiar combination of qualities in Cavaignac was also observed by Tocqueville, who commented on "one of those short addresses which he sometimes delivered, and in which his mind, which was naturally mediocre and confused, reached the level of his soul and approached the sublime. Under these circumstances he became, for a moment, the man of the most genuine eloquence that I have ever heard speak in our Assemblies: he left all the mere orators far behind him."[15]

MINISTERIAL CHANGES

If the Carnot incident had shown that ministers were responsible to the Assembly, within two weeks Cavaignac showed that the ministers were also responsible to him; or at

[12] *Mémoires de ma vie*, IV, p. 317.

[13] Barrot, *Mémoires posthumes*, II, p. 311; Hugo, *Souvenirs personnels*, p. 125.

[14] *Mémoires de ma vie*, IV, p. 350.

[15] *Recollections*, p. 235. The speech referred to was delivered in 1849.

least that he could appoint new men without seeking the permission of the Assembly. On July 17, Cavaignac made some minor changes in his Cabinet. First, the formal change whereby Bastide resumed the portfolio of Foreign Minister and General Bedeau resigned the duties that he had never exercised. At the same time, Bethmont resigned the Ministry of Justice, on the grounds of ill health, and two new men joined the Cabinet. To supplant Bastide as Minister of the Navy and of Colonies, Cavaignac named a professional officer, Vice Admiral Verninac de Saint Maur. The replacement for Bethmont had some political significance: Cavaignac chose one of the most prominent republicans of 1848, Alexandre Marie, who had been a member of the Provisional Government and of the Executive Commission, and who had only recently been elected president of the National Assembly. There were no protests or debates on the ministerial changes, which did not alter the essentially republican character of the government.

Admiral Verninac had no political background; he was a native of Cavaignac's department of Lot and had been undersecretary in the ministry for the Executive Commission. Although his role was purely routine, Admiral Verninac is, ironically, the only member of the Cavaignac government commemorated by a Paris monument; his name is engraved on the obelisk in the Place de la Concorde for having commanded the vessel that brought the obelisk from Egypt in 1835.

In Marie, Cavaignac had added to his government one of the most influential of the moderate *républicains de la veille*. Under the July Monarchy the republicans considered him, together with Jules Favre, as one of their best lawyers; he was the lawyer for *Le National*, and also defended many political prisoners, including the communitarian theorist, Cabet. Elected to the Chamber of Deputies in 1842, he was one of the few republicans to keep a seat in the Chamber down to the revolution. When, on the eve of the February revolution, some republicans drew up a tentative Provisional Government, Marie's name was included, even before he was aware that such a list was being prepared.[16] Although he feared that France was

[16] Cherest, *Marie*, p. 98.

not yet ripe for the republic, Marie was the first of the republican deputies, even before Ledru-Rollin, to reject unequivocally the proposed regency, and to demand instead the creation of a Provisional Government.[17] The revolutionary crowds accepted Marie as a member of the new government, although there were a few shouted protests. Soon Marie found himself in a sensitive position as Minister of Public Works, in charge of the National Workshops.

Long an opponent of Louis Blanc's views, Marie considered the workshops as merely a device to help relieve unemployment, and in time he came to regard them as politically dangerous because of the large numbers of workers they concentrated in Paris. Although Marie did make an effort to find useful work for the unemployed, his distrust of the institution rendered him ineffectual as the leading policy-maker, and he must bear some of the blame for the failure of the National Workshops.[18]

Maintained in the government as a member of the Executive Commission, Marie favored suppression of the workshops in June, but had wanted to proceed prudently, to "open some safety valves and thus to prevent any explosion."[19] On June 22, Marie held the dramatic colloquy with Louis Pujol. The insurrection thoroughly appalled and frightened Marie, who hotly denied that the "people" had risen or that republicans had fought republicans over the barricades. On assuming the presidency of the National Assembly immediately afterwards, he declaimed: "it is barbarism that . . . has dared to raise its head against civilization."[20] This statement, although often cited as an indication of the hysterical bourgeois incomprehension of the June conflict, did not represent the usual moderate republican viewpoint, nor does it adequately characterize Marie's more constant attitudes. In the same speech, Marie evinced an awareness of the class misery that had provoked

[17] Crémieux, *La Révolution de février*, p. 384.

[18] For a good discussion of Marie's responsibility, see McKay, *National Workshops*, pp. 32-33. For a vigorous defense of Marie, see Cherest, *Marie*, pp. 207-209.

[19] Cherest, *Marie*, p. 252.

[20] *Compte rendu des séances*, II, p. 252, 30 June 1848.

the uprising, and pledged "the moderate, but constant development of the principles that the Republic has established."[21]

When Bethmont resigned for ill health two weeks after that speech, Cavaignac chose Marie to replace him. Marie, who found the presidency of the Assembly less trying than his previous executive positions, was reluctant to take up a ministry once more, but was persuaded to do so in the interests of preserving the republican purity of the Cavaignac government. He felt bound to accept when Cavaignac argued, "If our certain friends refuse us, I will be forced to take doubtful friends, and it is not in that manner that we will carry out the business of the Republic."[22] Before the Assembly, however, Cavaignac explained that the Cabinet wanted "to give a new proof of our deference and of our respect for the Assembly, by choosing the one that the Assembly had chosen itself."[23]

THE PARLIAMENTARY REPUBLIC

If Cavaignac thus flattered the Assembly while exercising his prerogative of naming the ministers, the earlier Carnot incident had indicated that the Cavaignac government would be parliamentary. From the outset, Cavaignac assumed that both he and his ministers had to command majority support. The Carnot affair did not engage the Cabinet as a whole, but soon afterwards Cavaignac developed a conception of ministerial solidarity that was thereafter to characterize his relations with the Assembly. He came to regard individual ministers as spokesmen for the entire Cabinet, and even denied the right of deputies to go behind a minister's publicly stated views to seek other views within the ministry: "The men that you have instituted as the executive power cannot be split. They should always form a unity, and present themselves before you in a compact manner."[24]

On August 1, Cavaignac demanded and received a general vote of confidence after some deputies had criticized his arbitrary treatment of Paris newspapers under his siege powers;

[21] *Ibid.*

[22] Cherest, *Marie*, p. 274.

[23] *Compte rendu des séances*, II, p. 539, 18 July 1848.

[24] *Ibid.*, III, p. 368, 22 August 1848.

he won several similar votes of confidence in succeeding months, and when, in October, the government was put at last in a minority position on an important issue, the entire Cabinet resigned and a new Cabinet, including two former monarchists, was confirmed with a formal vote of confidence.

Within the Cabinet, Cavaignac was the dominant figure, although for the most part he allowed the ministers to manage their own departments. Important policies were often decided by the full council, after which the individual minister presented them to the Assembly. Cavaignac used his prestige within the council, too, but if confronted by a majority of contrary views, "I bow either from conviction, or from deference to the opinions of my colleagues."[25] Cavaignac bowed, as we have seen, on at least one important issue, the reimposition of a money bond for newspapers.

Cavaignac and his ministers were very active in presenting proposed legislation to the Assembly. Normally the ministers presented the bills, but Cavaignac often entered the debates or urged speedy consideration. Ministers often appeared before parliamentary committees to explain their policies, as did Cavaignac himself occasionally. A great deal of legislation was adopted by the Assembly during the six months of Cavaignac's administration; many reform proposals were introduced by private members, but few were enacted. The influence of the Cavaignac government may be measured by the fact that the majority of the laws adopted during this period, including most of the important ones, originated as government bills. Some of these were worked out by the ministers in collaboration with the committees, but many resulted almost solely from the initiative of the government. Even where legislation originated within the Assembly, the Cavaignac government usually took a position and effectively used its influence to support, defeat, or change it.

On much of this legislation, there was little conflict between government and Assembly; either it expressed the response of both to the June insurrection and the continuing fears of further disturbances, or it expressed the desire for moderate re-

[25] *Ibid.*, III, p. 365, 22 August 1848.

forms long held by the republicans and was acceptable to a majority in the Assembly for diverse reasons, including the continuing spirit of 1848. But a few government bills of great importance were opposed by the Rue de Poitiers, and as a result were killed, not by defeat in open parliament (for that would have brought down the government of Cavaignac, which the monarchists continued to feel was a necessary expedient), but by delay (as on Carnot's education bill) and emasculation (as on one of Goudchaux's tax reforms). Finally, some government bills that had seemed acceptable to the Assembly were later withdrawn by the government of Louis Napoleon.

On the whole, the relationship between the government of Cavaignac and the Assembly was remarkably cordial, orderly and fruitful. Although the supremacy of the Assembly was never questioned or threatened, the system also provided a strong executive. So satisfied with the functioning of the Cavaignac government was Jules Grévy, then at the start of a career which was to lead to the presidency of the Third Republic, that he sought to perpetuate it by incorporation into the Constitution of 1848.

Provisional as it was, a republican ministry kept in power by a loose coalition of republicans and monarchists, the government of Cavaignac was an effective one, productive of many forward-looking and democratic policies.

THE APPLICATION OF DEMOCRATIC PRINCIPLES

Political democracy was as fundamental to the republicans as the form of government, and under Cavaignac this second great conquest of February was not only preserved, but egalitarian principles were extended to various national institutions. Although democratic suffrage seemed an unquestioned achievement of the revolution, thus far it had been applied only to the election of the National Assembly. In early June, Recurt, then Minister of the Interior, presented a bill extending universal manhood suffrage to local elections, from the departmental to the communal level.[26] The prospective Con-

[26] *Ibid.*, I, pp. 629-631, 5 June 1848.

stitution was expected to do likewise, but the government wanted to hold temporary elections as soon as possible, for the revolution had thrown the councils into disarray. Paris was provisionally excepted because of the delicate political situation. A committee reported favorably on June 15, but before the bill reached the floor the June insurrection occurred.

The uprising did not dampen the democratic ardor of the republicans, nor the willingness of the Assembly to introduce this sweeping democratic reform into every commune in France. The last action of Senard as president of the National Assembly was to place the local elections bill on the agenda for the next day (June 29), and his first speech as Minister of the Interior for Cavaignac was a request for speedy adoption of the measure.[27]

In one important respect, the Cavaignac government's position was more democratic than that of the Executive Commission, for the original bill had merely contemplated partial elections to fill vacancies. Senard now gave "complete support" to a suggestion by the committee that general elections be held instead, and the Assembly swiftly adopted this principle.[28]

Senard also used his influence to help resolve two other issues in a democratic direction. The first was fundamental, for several deputies implicitly questioned the principle of democracy by suggesting that all who owned property in a given commune should be allowed to vote there, even if they lived elsewhere. Senard, in a brief but spirited reply, denounced the double vote, but pointed out that the essential issue concerned the property qualification: "Take care, citizens! . . . If you want to take the tax as the basis of the electoral right, be very careful, for you will accomplish, perhaps without realizing it, a return to the system that you have wished to abandon."[29] After Senard's intervention, the Assembly rejected the amendment attaching the franchise to property, and instead gave it to all male inhabitants twenty-one years of age and over.

The second significant issue was the question of the selec-

[27] *Ibid.*, II, p. 249, 29 June 1848.
[28] *Ibid.*, p. 256, 30 June 1848.
[29] *Ibid.*, p. 268.

tion of mayors, the wielders of local executive authority. The original bill had contemplated leaving nominations to the prefect, and thus to the central government. Some deputies suggested giving the communal councils complete freedom of choice. But Senard advocated an intermediate position, whereby in all sizable towns the prefect could appoint the mayors, but only from the membership of the councils; in communes with less than 6,000 inhabitants, the prefect would have only a suspensive veto of three months on the council's selections.[30] The Assembly adopted Senard's proposal. The state thus retained control over the all-important towns and cities, but two-thirds of the communes benefited from the reform granting local selection of mayors, for of the 37,000 communes in France, 29,611 had less than 1,000 inhabitants.[31] The Assembly made one retrograde change in the bill, by increasing the residence requirement from six months to one year. Although the powers of the local councils remained limited, the law of July 3 introduced the potentially revolutionary force of political democracy into the provincial life of France, as the February revolution had introduced it into national life.

The law provided for elections to be held in all communes within a month, and at the *arrondissement* and departmental levels before September. Pending a special law on Paris, Cavaignac was empowered to appoint a provisional municipal council to replace the old council dissolved by the Provisional Government.[32]

The results of the municipal elections were far more discouraging to the republicans than had been the national elections in April. Although a thorough historical study of these elections is still lacking, they seemed in most regions to have returned conservatives, Orleanist and Legitimist *notables*.[33]

[30] *Ibid.*, pp. 265-266.

[31] Charles H. Pouthas, "Une Enquête sur la réforme administrative sous la seconde république," *Revue historique*, CXCIII (1942), 8, 11.

[32] *Compte rendu des séances*, II, p. 256, 30 June 1848. Cavaignac appointed the new council on July 4.

[33] Tudesq, *Les Grands notables*, II, pp. 1117-1123. Cf. Chevalier, "Les Fondements économiques et sociaux," pp. 314-337, and Vigier, *La Seconde république dans la région alpine*, I, pp. 292-305.

The former monarchist press gleefully reported the return of "men of a very reassuring character,"[34] while *Le National* lamented the victory of "enemies of the Republic."[35] One reason for the results was undoubtedly the fact that the French masses did not seem very eager to exercise the franchise; only about half of those eligible took the trouble to vote. Moreover, in the communes with populations under 6,000, the democratically elected councils in most of France chose as mayors the same men previously appointed by the government of Louis Philippe.[36]

Senard sought to blunt the reactionary results of the elections by exercising vigorously the government's right to appoint or suspend mayors. For the larger communes, he instructed the prefects to appoint men who were "defenders" of the republic; in those with under 6,000 inhabitants, the prefects were ordered to suspend any mayor who was "hostile to the Republic."[37] It is unknown to what extent these instructions were carried out; at any rate, the elections resulted in few changes in council membership. Furthermore, a year later the councils themselves asked the prefects to appoint all mayors. Louis Napoleon's reorganization decrees of 1852 ended the brief experiment in local democracy.[38]

In other spheres, too, the Cavaignac government fostered egalitarian principles. Tourret, in his first circular as Minister of Agriculture and Commerce, called on the prefects to carry out an *arrêté* of June 19, which broadened the participation in the *chambres consultatives des arts et manufactures*. Heretofore these organizations had been controlled by a few important businessmen, but now all businessmen over the age

[34] Paul Bastid, *L'Avènement du suffrage universel* (Paris, 1948), p. 55. Bastid errs in commenting that the elections were held under the state of siege and in concluding that the results constituted a victory for the government (p. 53). The state of siege existed only in Paris, where elections were not held; and the results were generally monarchist rather than moderate *républicain de la veille*.

[35] *Le National*, 7 August 1848, p. 2.

[36] Pouthas, "Réforme administrative," p. 4.

[37] A. N., F 1A 45, circular of 1 August 1848.

[38] Pouthas, "Réforme administrative," pp. 8-12.

of twenty-one were eligible to elect representatives.[39] Later, Tourret introduced a democratic element into his comprehensive plan for agricultural education, as well as into his proposal for the creation of *chambres consultatives d'agriculture.*

Egalitarian principles also were introduced into the chambers of commerce and the commercial courts. The change in the chambers was made by ministerial instruction: Flocon, in his last official act as minister (on June 27, still under Cavaignac's dictatorship), ruled that the membership of these bodies should be chosen by all businessmen instead of just a few of the most important men.[40] The change remained in effect after the departure of Flocon. The reform in the commercial courts required legislative action. On July 26, Marie presented a bill designed to place these courts "in harmony with our new institutions" by granting to all businessmen the right to elect the judges charged with settling commercial conflicts. Previously only the "notable merchants" of the old and established houses had this important privilege. The only real restriction was the requirement of five years' business activity to qualify as an elector.[41] Nevertheless, the new legislation, which was adopted on August 28 with few changes, resulted in a vast extension of the electoral base for these courts. Previously, in some cities there had been only thirty to fifty electors; now, in Paris alone there were 45,000.[42]

The Cavaignac government also sought to preserve and extend reforms in the ordinary judicial system. On May 25, the Executive Commission had proposed introducing the democratic principle into the selection of juries. When the bill came before the Assembly three months later, after the insurrection, it had the moral support of the Cavaignac government,[43] and it was adopted August 7 with a few minor changes. Although the aim ostensibly was to make all electors eligible for jury duty, a number of restrictions deprived the jury reform of a completely democratic character. Property qualifications were

[39] A. N., AD xix D 256, circular No. 19, n.d. but before July 1.

[40] A. N., AD xix D 256, circular No. 18, 27 June 1848.

[41] *Compte rendu des séances,* II, pp. 674-675, 26 July 1848.

[42] *Ibid.,* III, p. 537, 28 August 1848.

[43] *Ibid.,* II, p. 879, 7 August 1848.

abolished, but the minimum age was thirty instead of twenty-one;[44] there was a literacy stipulation, and servants and some other occupations were ineligible. The Assembly also introduced a change giving local authorities considerable power of selection from the general lists. Nevertheless, the reform brought about a considerable expansion at the base of the jury system.

In addition, the Cavaignac government sought to implement in the judiciary an organizational reform that had been one of the earliest objectives of the Provisional Government. A commission had been created on March 2 to draw up such a reform, but it did not complete its work until October. As soon as the Assembly had drawn up the articles of the Constitution pertaining to the judiciary, Marie presented the special commission's detailed proposals in the form of a bill.[45] The changes suggested were minor, consisting essentially in the suppression of courts deemed superfluous, the simplification of civil procedure and other details. Although the Assembly studied the reform carefully, it finally decided (in early 1849) to drop the matter.

The Cavaignac government also sponsored a number of reforms in the administration of Algeria, changes which loosened that colony from the exclusive control of the military and extended to the French colonists at least some of the advantages of civilian and republican government. Since the conquest began, Algeria had been administered by the Ministry of War, through a governor-general with extensive powers. Even in the narrow coastal strip considered the "civil" territory, the French colonists were subject to the military. By 1848, civilian-military conflict was endemic; the revolution gave the civilians hope that they could escape the rule of the generals. The Provisional Government encouraged the colonists by permitting them to elect four deputies to the National

[44] In both the original proposal of the Executive Commission and the enacted legislation. Bastid, *Doctrines et institutions politiques*, II, p. 25, errs in attributing the restrictions only to the Assembly.

[45] *Compte rendu des séances*, IV, pp. 926-935, 17 October 1848.

Assembly and by promising "progressive" assimilation of Algeria to France.[46]

In the National Assembly, the Algerian deputies urged simple annexation and assimilation to France, following the example of Corsica. But the Algerian generals in the Assembly, notably Cavaignac and Lamoricière, resisted vigorously; Cavaignac, who as Minister of War was rapidly growing in influence when the debate took place on June 15, opposed assimilation chiefly on the ground that in the future the Algerian delegation might become large enough to determine French policy.[47] After listening to the generals, the Assembly, which was then facing more pressing problems, proclaimed Algeria "a land forever French," but declined to consider assimilation.[48]

Nevertheless, Cavaignac was not merely a general defending the interests of his kind. We have already seen the vacillations in his policy as governor-general resulting from his ambivalent role as republican and *militaire*. In Paris as Minister of War, although he opposed outright assimilation, it was he in fact who initiated a kind of "progressive" assimilation without the name. He publicly favored restricting the arbitrary powers of the governor-general over civilians[49] and diminished his own powers there as War Minister, for on his urging the Executive Commission extended to the civil territory the authority of the Ministers of Justice and of Education.[50] This policy of "linkage" (*rattachements*) was consolidated in August by three decrees of Cavaignac as chief of the executive power, which also gave the Minister of Religion jurisdiction in Algeria.[51] In August also, Cavaignac by decree extended the democratized communal organization of France to the civil territory. It provided manhood suffrage for French citizens, and also permitted foreign residents and Arabs to vote under certain conditions. This measure had the unfortunate

[46] Boyer, "La Vie politique et les élections à Alger," p. 44. See also the discussion in Julien, *Histoire de l'Algérie*, pp. 342ff.

[47] *Compte rendu des séances*, I, p. 866, 873, 15 June 1848.

[48] *Ibid.*, p. 919, 16 June 1848.

[49] *Ibid.*, p. 743, 9 June 1848.

[50] *Le Moniteur*, 31 May 1848, p. 1211.

[51] Julien, *Histoire de l'Algérie*, p. 351.

consequence of inducing the military to begin a long history of controlling elections, and also of intensifying the hostility of French colonists toward the Arabs.[52]

In September, the government sponsored a program of colonization that immediately swelled the civilian population and was expected to increase the area of civilian self-government. The Constitution of November 4 provided not only for continued representation of the colonists in the French legislature, but also promised the future application of the entire Constitution to Algeria, which would amount to virtual assimilation.[53] Finally, at the end of his administration, in December, Cavaignac by decree divided the civil territory into three departments, each under a civilian prefect, as in France. The decree of December 9 contemplated, moreover, the gradual extension of civilian areas at the expense of the military ones.[54] The *militaires* in Algeria had watched with dismay the process of diminution in their powers; once the election of Louis Napoleon broke the rule of the republicans, an open conflict developed between the generals and the prefects, a conflict in which civilian government quickly succumbed.[55]

REFORMS IN EDUCATION

In the field of education, the Cavaignac government presided over a number of important reforms reflecting the democratic spirit of 1848. The more significant ones were the work of Carnot, and represented the fruition of initiatives taken in the earliest weeks of the revolution. Although Carnot was in office under Cavaignac only a week, his personal fall did not terminate his policies, which continued to be supported vigorously by the Cavaignac government until the very end.

In February, Carnot had created a special committee, under his Saint-Simonian friend, Jean Reynaud, to draw up a general reform of the primary educational system. While this group

[52] *Ibid.*, p. 352. [53] *Ibid.*, p. 353.

[54] Charles A. Julien, "Le Conflit entre les généraux et les préfets d'Algérie sous la deuxième république," *La Révolution de 1848*, XXIII (1926), p. 796.

[55] *Ibid.*, p. 813.

worked, Carnot introduced a number of detailed reforms, such as the creation of small libraries in some rural communes and evening classes for workers in the cities. More dramatic reforms were instituted at the Collège de France, which was then at one of the peaks of its prestige. Because it was independent of the Université, Carnot was able to introduce immediate and drastic changes there. First, by a decree of March 8, he created an entirely new institution, an Ecole d'Administration, inspired by the Ecole Polytechnique but intended to prepare career government administrators; temporarily, it would be attached to the Collège de France. The new school aroused a great deal of public enthusiasm. Nine hundred youths sought places, and after nationwide competitive examinations 152 were selected to compose the first class, but the school had not yet begun to function when Carnot fell from office. His successor, Vaulabelle, soon revealed that Carnot's policies would be maintained: two days after he assumed the portfolio, on July 8, he officially inaugurated the school, accompanied by Jean Reynaud.[56] Vaulabelle declared that the school "was intended to facilitate the access to public employment of capable young men, whatever the social position where fortune may have placed them."[57]

While the students embarked on rigorous training schedules, Vaulabelle busied himself with the consolidation of the school as a permanent institution. He created a board of directors and announced that the competition for the next class would be held in the autumn.[58] On August 31 Vaulabelle asked the Assembly to adopt legislation for the permanent organization of the school, which thus far had existed only by decree. He took pride in the fact that it was a creation of the republic, which needed to train administrators who would make the republic strong and respected.[59] He advocated the

[56] Gabriel Vauthier, "Le Collège de France, école d'administration," *La Révolution de 1848*, x (1913), p. 458.

[57] Albert Louvel, "L'Ecole d'Administration de 1848," *Etudes d'histoire moderne et contemporaine*, II, p. 27.

[58] Vauthier, "Le Collège de France," p. 459.

[59] *Compte rendu des séances*, III, p. 653, 31 August 1848.

three-year curriculum as prepared by Carnot's special commission. The training would be "gratuitous" and students would be exempt from military service. Vaulabelle asked an appropriation of 20,000 francs to support the school in 1848.

The Assembly's committee supported the proposal, but by the time it was reported out on December 16, the Cavaignac government was about to fall, to be supplanted by men dedicated to destroying the Ecole d'Administration, along with other works of the republicans. Louis Napoleon's Minister of Education, Falloux, postponed indefinitely the resumption of classes and retired Vaulabelle's bill.[60] Later in 1849 the Legislative Assembly, heavily dominated by monarchists, suppressed the school at Falloux's request. The students were bitter, but formed a fraternal association which lasted into the twentieth century. Many of these participants in the remarkable educational experiment of 1848 became prominent in governmental administration, where "they remained marked by the principles of 1848."[61]

In addition to the Ecole d'Administration, Carnot introduced in April another ephemeral innovation at the Collège de France: he suppressed five chairs and created eleven new ones. Two of the chairs were eliminated for practical reasons, but the suppression of the others constituted a purge of nonrepublican ideologies: two were held by monarchists,[62] and the third was the chair of political economy, held by the noted economist, Michel Chevalier. (Carnot believed that the doctrines of the laissez-faire school were inimical to the republic.) The new chairs, in part created to provide instruction for the Ecole d'Administration, were dedicated to subjects such as international law, public law, finance, agriculture and the history of administrative institutions. Moreover, in order to assure the proper political tone, no less than four members of the Provisional Government were among the professors-desig-

[60] *Ibid.*, VII, p. 353, 22 January 1849.

[61] Louvel, "L'Ecole d'Administration," pp. 30-32.

[62] Carnot, *Le Ministère de l'instruction publique*, pp. 55-56. Cf. the comments of Jean Reynaud before the Committee on Public Education, minutes, 2 September 1848, A. N., C 926.

nate: Lamartine, Armand Marrast, Garnier-Pagès and Ledru-Rollin.[63] These changes were maintained by the Cavaignac government after the fall of Carnot, but the reorganization never became fully effective. One weakness was the provision that the new professors would teach without remuneration; also, the republican leaders were preoccupied with political affairs. Lamartine on July 22 maintained that he was too busy to prepare a syllabus, and few of the new professors did any actual teaching.[64]

There had been protests from the beginning over the suppression of the five chairs; in November, as political reaction became manifest in the country and in the Assembly, these protests crystallized into an open attack. Léon Faucher, soon to become Louis Napoleon's Minister of the Interior, led the assault, charging that the purge violated the freedom of education and was unjust to the ousted professors.[65] The chair of Michel Chevalier was made the chief issue, Faucher insisting that political economy was a science that could not be declared out of existence by government fiat. Jean Reynaud defended the action of the Provisional Government, but conceded that the change should have been done legislatively. Edgar Quinet, famous for his defense of intellectual freedom, said that on this ground he regretted "profoundly" the suppression.[66] The purge had few vocal defenders besides Reynaud. The Minister of Education was now no longer Vaulabelle, but Pierre Freslon, who had entered the government with the shift to the right in October. Freslon took a neutral position, saying that the Provisional Government had had the right to act, but the Assembly had the right to revoke that action: "You are sovereign: Decide."[67] The Assembly did decide to revoke the purge by voting retroactive pay for the professors, and as soon as Falloux became Minister of Education, he recalled it; he also went beyond the Assembly's action by asking the eleven new professors to resign.[68] Finally, at the same time that it

[63] Louvel, "L'Ecole d'Administration," p. 24.

[64] *Ibid.*, and Vauthier, "Le Collège de France," p. 461.

[65] *Compte rendu des séances*, v, pp. 518-519, 13 November 1848.

[66] *Ibid.*, p. 543, 14 November 1848. [67] *Ibid.*

[68] Vauthier, "Le Collège de France," p. 464.

dissolved the Ecole d'Administration, the Legislative Assembly restored the Collège de France completely to its former organization.

Another reform introduced by Carnot was an increase in the pay of schoolteachers. It was a "public scandal," he said, that 26,000 *instituteurs* received less than 600 francs a year, and he asked an appropriation of one million francs to finance increases for the last half of 1848. It was by a symbolic reduction of 5,000 francs in this appropriation that the Assembly had voted Carnot's downfall. Nevertheless, having defeated the minister, the Assembly granted without protest the bulk of the appropriation on July 7; moreover, by amendment the 5,000 franc reduction was restored together with an additional 100,000 francs for *institutrices.*[69]

But this and even the previous reforms were minor in comparison with the plan for the primary educational system. Carnot had been about to present the long-heralded project, drawn up by his special commission, when the June insurrection broke out. Two days after the regular Cavaignac government was instituted, Carnot at last presented the bill. It was truly revolutionary, for it proposed nothing less than the free, secular and compulsory education of all French children. The application of any one of these principles would have been a major innovation, for even after the Guizot reforms of 1833 the state's system of primary education was free only to indigents, suffused with religion, optional and far from universal. Carnot asked that the state provide education for both boys and girls, up to the age of fourteen.[70] Parents would be obliged to send their children to school to undertake full courses of study including history and geography, and instruction in the basic principles of the republic. Although the republicans of 1848 were relatively free from the uncompromising anticlericalism characteristic of a later generation, Carnot's bill excluded religious instruction from the state schools. Carnot desired but did not demand a complete mo-

[69] *Compte rendu des séances,* II, p. 376, 7 July 1848.

[70] For the text of the bill, see *Compte rendu des séances,* II, pp. 273-277, 30 June 1848. For a general discussion, see Georges Cogniot, *La Question scolaire en 1848 et la loi Falloux* (Paris, 1948).

nopoly of primary education; church schools could exist, but the state would have the right of "surveillance" over them.

Carnot asked that there be created at least one public primary school in every commune with more than 300 residents. Expenses would be shared by the commune and the state; for the first year's operation, he asked an appropriation of 47,360,950 francs. Carnot also sought to increase "the dignity and independence" of the *instituteurs* (on whom he counted to republicanize the new generation) by removing them from the influence of the local *curés* and placing their selection and tenure completely in the hands of public authorities. Moreover, he proposed to raise the minimum salary for men to the 600 francs already accorded by the temporary law and to grant primary teachers for the first time the retirement benefits enjoyed by other state employees. Although the bill dealt only with primary education, which he considered it essential to reform immediately, Carnot planned also to reform the secondary educational system in the future.[71]

The purpose of the sweeping primary reform, Carnot affirmed, was not simply to impart the fundamentals of learning, but "to foster in the hearts of Frenchmen love for the institutions that France adopted in February," in sum, "the republican education of the country."[72]

This aim was all too obvious to the monarchists and Catholics of the Rue de Poitiers, who brought down Carnot less than a week after he presented the plan. They feared, so Carnot maintained, that just one year of such education "would render impossible any return to monarchical doctrines."[73] Although the Cavaignac government, faithful to its pledge to Carnot, continued to sponsor the bill, it was never to become law. A parliamentary committee gave it careful consideration throughout the rest of the year. When its report was finally ready, in January 1849, the Carnot proposals had been revised and mutilated, but not destroyed.[74] By that time, how-

[71] *Compte rendu des séances*, III, p. 362, 5 July 1848.

[72] Carnot, *Le Ministère de l'instruction publique*, p. 55.

[73] Carnot, MS "Mémorial," dos. 17, p. 23.

[74] See the report of Barthélemy Saint-Hilaire, announced on January 4, but not published until April, *Compte rendu des séances*, IX annex, pp. 161-184.

ever, the republicans were out of power and the Ministry of Education was in the hands of Falloux, who withdrew Carnot's proposal, ignored even the revised version, and created his own nonparliamentary committees which fourteen months later produced the celebrated *loi Falloux*, so alien in spirit and content to the Carnot plan. Although it had never even reached the stage of open debate, Cavaignac remained to the end faithful to the Carnot reform. Even when he was seeking Catholic support in the presidential campaign, Cavaignac refused to yield to their demand that he withdraw the Carnot plan.

If the Cavaignac government failed in its efforts to revolutionize primary education, it had more success with less ambitious reforms in some of the large specialized schools. The purpose was to introduce an egalitarian principle in the Ecole Normale Supérieure, the Ecole Polytechnique, the military school at Saint-Cyr and the naval school at Brest, by making the instruction entirely free.

Such a reform was first proposed on June 20 by Cavaignac himself, as Minister of War, to apply to Saint-Cyr and the Ecole Polytechnique. "Under a democratic government," he declared, "public offices should be accessible to all the citizens, without any distinction based on wealth." The First Republic had introduced this principle in the schools but the Empire and Restoration had erected barriers "to exclude children from the poorer classes." Cavaignac asked for legislation to render attendance "completely free," beginning October 1, 1848.[75]

There was considerable latent opposition to so radical an innovation, but Cavaignac was at the peak of his authority when the committee reported on July 3; thus the Assembly heard the Legitimist Comte de Tredern, of the Rue de Poitiers, suggest adoption of the proposal as "a first step made by the Minister of War along the fecund path of equality."[76]

Encouraged, the government on the following day presented a bill proposing to introduce at the Ecole Normale Supérieure

[75] *Compte rendu des séances*, II, pp. 60-61, 20 June 1848.
[76] *Ibid.*, p. 325, 3 July 1848.

"the principle, fecund and democratic, of gratuity." Carnot, who offered the measure as one of his last official acts, asked the same starting date, October 1, 1848. Eleven days later, the government proposed the application of the same principle at the naval school at Brest.[77]

But the monarchist opposition was already becoming manifest. Its tactic was to seek postponement of the reform at Saint-Cyr and the Polytechnique on grounds that it would prejudice the constitutional question of free education. The government opposed this move, and was successful by a narrow margin of only twenty-seven votes. In the course of a turbulent debate, the government was able to win acceptance of the principle only by retreating on the date of its application, to October 1850.[78] The government was successful in winning immediate introduction of "gratuity" at the Ecole Normale Supérieure,[79] but not at the naval school. The Assembly committee advocated delay to 1850, but the measure never reached the floor before the National Assembly went out of existence.

Although the more important educational reforms had been inspired by Carnot, his successor, Vaulabelle, proved to be more spirited than the Rue de Poitiers had anticipated. In addition to defending vigorously the Carnot heritage, he introduced some unspectacular but important innovations of his own. The first was a reform in the territorial organization of the Université. Shortly after entering the ministry, Vaulabelle began an investigation into the functioning of the twenty-seven academic areas into which France was then divided. There were vast disparities in size among them, yet each had the same organization; officials agreed that this caused expensive and needless duplications. After winning the approval of the pertinent parliamentary subcommittee, Vaulabelle by an administrative decree issued on September 7 suppressed seven of the areas, attaching their institutions to the remaining twenty. To the Voltairean minister, this act of rationalization represented the victory of the general interest over local

[77] *Ibid.*, p. 486, 15 July 1848.

[78] *Ibid.*, pp. 536-552, 18 July 1848, and p. 559, 19 July 1848.

[79] *Ibid.*, pp. 871-877, 4 August 1848.

and private ones, "a serious and necessary reform, desired for a long time."[80]

Neither the monarchists nor the Catholics, apparently, felt touched by the reduction in academic areas. But later in September, during the discussion of the Constitution, Montalembert launched the Catholic assault on the principle of state education, and hence by implication against the Carnot plan, which was then still in committee. In a grandiloquent speech, Montalembert openly attacked the Université as having poisoned the mind of the nation. He even argued, to the amusement and consternation of the Assembly, the superiority of the educational system under the Old Regime. Identifying the interests of property with those of the church, he characterized state control of education as "intellectual communism," ultimately responsible for the insurrection of June![81]

Vaulabelle responded with an equally vigorous defense, eulogizing the revolution of 1789, now completed by the revolution of 1848. He scoffed at Montalembert's charge that the quality of education had declined, citing facts and figures in refutation. He took the characteristic republican position of the time that the Université and the church had common interests, but condemned Montalembert's "political friends" who had controlled education to its detriment under the Restoration.[82] The republican position also was ably defended by Jules Simon. The Comte de Falloux, sensing that Montalembert's bombast had irked even many liberal Orleanists, decided the attack was premature. He made a short conciliatory speech, after which Montalembert withdrew his proposal to introduce "the right to teach" in the Constitution.[83]

The men of the Rue de Poitiers did not forget Vaulabelle's eloquent defense of republican and secular education. Three weeks later they would bring about his downfall, as they had eliminated Carnot. But Vaulabelle had time to introduce one

[80] *Ibid.*, v, p. 475, 11 November 1848.
[81] *Ibid.*, iv, pp. 92-99, 18 September 1848.
[82] *Ibid.*, pp. 143-144, 20 September 1848.
[83] *Ibid.*, pp. 146-150, 20 September 1848.

more minor reform. In October, a few days before he left office, he ordered that beginning with the current academic year, all lycées and colleges must teach the history of the French Revolution.[84]

[84] The decree dated October 8 was published in *Le Moniteur* on October 12, p. 2799.

X · ". . . et Sociale"

BETWEEN LOUIS BLANC AND LAISSEZ-FAIRE

MUCH of the writing on the French Revolution of 1848 has asserted or implied a dichotomy between two opposing views on social and economic questions. McKay's distinction between the moderates who favored a purely political revolution and those who sought a "profound reorganization of society" has already been cited.[1] Stated in other terms, the conflict has been variously seen as "blue republicans" against "red republicans," bourgeois against proletarian, "La République" against "La République démocratique et sociale," laissez-faire liberalism against the socialisms then current, the negative against the positive state.

Although the conflict between liberal and socialist ideologies helps to explain much of the history of the revolution, it has been insufficiently recognized that during 1848 there were not merely two, but three competing points of view on social matters. Georges Renard has been virtually alone in emphasizing them; characterizing their exponents as socialists, "pure conservatives," and "interventionists," he observed that while the influence of the socialists was at its height under the Provisional Government and that of the conservatives under the Legislative Assembly of 1849-1851, the "interventionists" dominated the National Assembly.[2] Because of his own socialist predilections, Renard gave but slight notice to interventionist doctrines, and later historians have ignored his valuable insight.

The third point of view, which was approximately intermediate between the socialist and the traditional liberal economic doctrines, may perhaps be more meaningfully called moderate interventionist or moderate social. Unlike the socialist and liberal views, the moderate interventionist point of view was not expressed by any outstanding exponents (with the partial exception of C. B. Dupont-White), nor did it give

[1] *National Workshops*, pp. 3, 155.

[2] See *La République de 1848*, pp. 228-232.

rise to any distinctive formulae or slogans, all of which are probably reasons why so little attention has been paid to it. Indeed, it was not a coherent doctrine at all, but was largely an attitude shared by several different and sometimes conflicting groups. It was the characteristic outlook of the moderate republicans, but similar views had also arisen in Catholic and Legitimist circles under the July Monarchy, and Louis-Napoleon's interest in the social question may perhaps be compared to this point of view.

Beneath the variety of ideas expressed by these different groups may be discerned a number of shared principles that serve to identify the moderate social attitude. First, it recognized the social question as such, that is, as a new problem rather than the traditional problem of indigence. Second, it was critical of the dominant laissez-faire ideology for offering inadequate or even inhumane solutions to the social question, but it rejected as utopian or dangerous the socialist solutions. Third, it proposed instead diverse individual and moderate reforms that presumably would reduce or end social misery but would leave existing capitalist society intact. Finally, the moderate interventionists, as the term suggests, looked to the state as the most important instrument of reform.

It was this moderate social or moderate interventionist point of view rather than a liberal or negative one, that was dominant during the ascendancy of Cavaignac. It was represented most strongly in the government, but also, as Renard observed, prevailed in the National Assembly.

THE SOCIAL CONTENT OF MODERATE REPUBLICANISM

The moderate interventionist point of view was expressed primarily by the *républicains de la veille.* The mildly social outlook of *Le National* has already been discussed; now it remains to consider in more detail the social content of moderate republicanism. In the first place, within the majority wing of the republican party before 1848 there were two distinct versions of a more markedly social, but still nonsocialist point of view. These were the doctrines expressed by Philippe Buchez and by the working-class newspaper, *L'Atelier.* Buchez was a Catholic republican who developed theories sometimes regarded as Christian socialist, but he was more progressist in spirit than revolutionary, and hostilc to real socialists such as Louis Blanc. It was he who initiated the idea of the producers' cooperatives as the prime solution for the social problem, later made famous under a different form by Blanc. Buchez preferred voluntary association for artisans, but advocated governmental support for associations of factory workers.[3] Another group of republican social Catholics was represented by *L'Atelier*, which had been founded by Buchez and later developed a distinctive working-class point of view under the editorship of some worker-journalists. While it rejected socialism, it had a more varied and pronounced set of social and economic demands than *Le National.*

In general, the moderate *républicains de la veille* had failed to develop a coherent social doctrine, but had contented themselves with expressing a desire to improve the condition of the working classes and with the advocacy of a few modest reforms. Nevertheless, one French economist who did develop a positive interventionist theory in the period became a republican because of his views. This was C. B. Dupont-White, who, proceeding from a forthright condemnation of orthodox liberal theory for its social consequences, elaborated an original economic theory regarded as "an authentic precursor" of state socialism.[4] Dupont-White expressed his views notably in an article published in 1846, entitled "Sur l'intervention de l'Etat dans les relations du travail avec le capital." Like the other moderate republicans, Dupont-White was hostile to the socialists, and after a bitter denunciation of Malthusian views and a dogmatic insistence that the state must "correct the vicious work of nature," he suggested but three reforms that were mild in their social content: first, universal manhood suffrage, and then two kinds of "intervention"—public primary education and public assistance to the unemployed

[3] The school of Buchez is viewed as part of a diverse Catholic response to the social question by Duroselle, *Les Débuts du catholicisme sociale*, pp. 80-93.

[4] Daniel Villey, *Charles Dupont-White, économiste et publiciste français (1807-1878)*, (Paris, 1936), p. xix.

workers.[5] Yet Dupont-White has been hailed as an advanced thinker, "entirely isolated" in his time, who "opposed to classic liberalism the economic vocation of the State, emancipator of the individual and creator of progress."[6] In fact, although he was indeed "isolated" as an economic theorist, the moderate republicans, who are often regarded as "purely political" in their views, had offered a similar condemnation of Malthusianism, together with a much broader program of social and economic reforms of an interventionist character.

After the February revolution, the formerly "advanced" views of the moderate republicans seemed mild in comparison with the full-scale renovation vaguely implied by the socialists' vision of "La République démocratique et sociale." Nevertheless, in the political and doctrinal conflicts between socialists or social republicans and moderate republicans, both Buchez and *L'Atelier* sided resolutely with the moderates. *L'Atelier* was acutely conscious of its intermediate position: "We know that some well-dressed men, claiming to be more sympathetic to our cause than we are ourselves, have categorized us, and will continue to categorize us, as bourgeois, and that, on the other hand, other well-dressed men reject us as communists. This is adequately explained by the unvarying position that we have never ceased to maintain between two extremes."[7]

Le National also continued to oppose socialist doctrines while reaffirming its now traditional position that "the political form should serve as the instrument for social reform."[8] *Le National* supported the National Workshops because "It was necessary at any price to give bread to an enormous mass of workers which the suspension of industrial activity was going to leave without resources," but preferred productive public works.[9] The moderate republican social outlook was also expressed by Lamartine, who in his first speech to the National Assembly on May 6 called for "a continuous series of fraternal

[5] *Ibid.*, pp. 409-412, 419, 442-445.

[6] Jacques Droz et al., *L'Epoque contemporaine, I, Restaurations et Révolutions (1815-1871)*, "Clio," (Paris, 1953), p. 53.

[7] Cuvillier, *Journal d'ouvriers*, p. 33.

[8] Issue of 1 May 1848.

[9] Issue of 22 May 1848.

institutions . . . which would abolish the servile term 'proletarian,' and would elevate the laborer to that high level of right, duty and well-being enjoyed by those first-born to property."[10]

The June Days affected the expression of moderate republican social views but little. *Le National* approved the dissolution of the National Workshops as a political necessity, but argued that it would be "an odious crime" now simply to abandon the workers.[11] The state must continue to give direct assistance, but it had a duty to provide productive labor for the unemployed.[12] *Le National* vigorously rejected the Malthusian doctrines and criticized laissez-faire ideas in general.[13] It came out in support of governmental encouragement to workers' cooperatives, the right to strike, workers' housing, progressive taxation, and even "le droit au travail."[14] It also supported various other government proposals of a social and economic nature, and was the most vigorous proponent of the nationalization of the railroads. *L'Atelier*, which had vigorously opposed the June insurrection, afterwards was critical of Cavaignac's repressive policies but remained in general the exponent of the moderate republican point of view, rather than of "the party of La République démocratique et sociale." Moreover, *L'Atelier* flourished under Cavaignac, reaching a height of 896 subscribers, as against less than 550 in 1847.[15]

A good example of the moderate social point of view was expressed in the speech in which Armand Marrast placed the revised draft of the Constitution before the National Assembly on August 30. Reaffirming the republican belief that progressive social amelioration would flow from democratic institutions, Marrast emphasized the social function of the state as an expression of "fraternity": "Placed at the summit of the State, fraternity fosters a concern at once vigilant for the weak, solicitous for the suffering, active for those whom disasters

[10] *Compte rendu des séances*, I, p. 36.
[11] Issue of 4 July 1848.
[12] Issues of 3, 4 and 24 July 1848.
[13] Issues of 6 May, 5 June and 31 August 1848.
[14] Issues of 4 July, 12 July, 4 August, 11 August and 25 August 1848.
[15] Cuvillier, *Journal d'ouvriers*, pp. 23-26, 137-139, 274.

deprive of their work, charitable for the destitute, attentive to the wretched; a concern which embraces all facts of social existence."

Marrast revealed a clear and sympathetic understanding of the social question:

> We are convinced and we assert that a society is badly ordered when thousands of honest, fit, hard-working men, with no property other than their arms, no means of subsistence than their wages, see themselves condemned to the horrors of hunger, the anguish of despair or the humiliation of beggary, when struck by circumstances beyond their control which drive them from the place where they earned a living.
>
> . . . .
>
> If an impassive society averts its gaze, if it replies, "I have nothing to do with your work. Seek or die, die, you and your families," that society is without compassion, without virtue, without morality or security. It outrages justice, it revolts humanity, it runs counter to all the principles which the Republic proclaims.

Marrast argued that when economic crises produce unemployment, the republic "does not harden its heart, it is not content to wail repeatedly, 'Fate!' To the contrary, it musters all its resources in crying 'Fraternity!' "[16]

THE SOCIAL ATTITUDE OF THE CAVAIGNAC GOVERNMENT

The men who comprised the government of Cavaignac shared the moderate social viewpoint of their fellow republicans. As we have seen, the general himself, under the influence of his brother, had been sympathetic with the social orientation of the party. Although he was hostile to the socialists and crushed the worker insurgents, he seems to have altered his social views but slightly if at all following the insurrection. He understood the plight of the workers and believed that the insurgents had been seduced by false doctrines and enemies of the

[16] The speech is in *Compte rendu des séances*, III, pp. 595-601.

republic "speculating on misery."[17] In announcing the dissolution of the National Workshops on July 3, Cavaignac asserted that "help must be continued for the unemployed workers who are enrolled," most of whom "ask only to work."[18]

Cavaignac did provide unemployment relief and took various steps to stimulate economic recovery and create jobs. He was convinced as he told a group of businessmen that he gathered together on July 6 to discuss means of reviving industry, that the workers "have been misled by false doctrines and are themselves the first victims of the stagnation of commerce."[19] Cavaignac also called upon the Académie des Sciences Morales et Politiques to study social problems and disseminate information on them.

One of the resultant pamphlets was Adolphe Blanqui's valuable work, *Des classes ouvrières en France pendant l'année 1848.*[20] Blanqui, the brother of the famed revolutionary, was an orthodox economist whose views were colored with some humanitarian feelings. In August, he discussed his investigations with Cavaignac, who "cried out aloud when I described to him the misery of the workers."[21] Cavaignac's interest in the workers was attested by the numerous proposals offered by his government in their favor, and by the large number of documents concerning social and economic problems that he preserved in his papers.[22]

The most explicit expression of Cavaignac's post-June social views is contained in the manuscript of a speech that he prepared in 1849 but apparently never delivered.[23] Cavaignac

[17] *Ibid.*, p. 732, 2 September 1848.

[18] *Ibid.*, II, p. 315.

[19] A. N., F 12 2337-2338.

[20] Paris, 1849.

[21] Letter to Dussart, prefect of Seine-Inférieure, 24 August 1848, published in *L'Amateur d'Autographes*, XXXIX (1906), 7.

[22] Judging by the amount of material, only foreign policy engrossed him as much.

[23] This is a nineteen-page document in Cavaignac's hand, preserved in his personal archives, Reel 23. Although unidentified, internal and external evidence suggests that it consists of notes for a speech that he planned to deliver around November 12, 1849.

was then supporting a proposal for government-administered and compulsory sickness and old age insurance for workers, a very "advanced" plan at the time. He wrote an introduction for a published version of the proposal, in which he argued that "it is great and worthy of society to watch over and to provide for the needs of those who comprise it."[24] In July 1849, Cavaignac introduced the plan in the Legislative Assembly, one of several considered. In the ensuing debates, Thiers and others assailed the compulsory principle as "this new communism."[25]

Although Cavaignac, for unknown reasons, did not enter the debate, in his speech notes he vigorously defended the compulsory as against the voluntary insurance plan, as well as the general principle of state intervention: "I am far from believing that a nation is wrong to intervene by means of regulation, protection, encouragement, even by prohibition, in the development of its production and of its consumption." He denied that "the idea of compulsory contributions is a socialist, communist, or destructive one," and attacked as truly dangerous those who "preach that deplorable doctrine of immobility. Those who have said, and still say: 'Nothing, Nothing, Nothing.' These are the most dangerous auxiliaries of disorder and of anarchy." Cavaignac agreed that "freedom of work" should be preserved as far as possible, but favored legal maximums in the length of the working day, and the proposed tax on workers and employers to support the social insurance plan. This was necessary, he argued, because industry did not provide salaries sufficient to permit adequate savings, and the partisans of "unfettered production" were indifferent to suffering.[26] Cavaignac's plan for compulsory social insurance was defeated, and the law adopted in 1850 provided for a much less comprehensive and merely voluntary *Caisse nationale des retraites*.[27] The advanced nature of Cavaignac's views may

[24] Camus-Mutuelet and H. Place, *Caisse générale de secours mutuels: pétition présentée à l'Assemblée Nationale* (Paris, 1849), p. 8.

[25] Renard, *La République de 1848*, p. 311.

[26] It is difficult to follow Cavaignac's thought completely, both because of his diffuse style and the difficulty of deciphering his handwriting.

[27] Renard, *La République de 1848*, p. 311.

be judged by the fact that even this timid measure was the first such plan adopted in Europe.[28]

The majority of Cavaignac's ministers shared the social outlook characteristic of the *républicains de la veille.* In addition, some held strongly individual views. Carnot, for example, was a former Saint-Simonian who remained highly critical of liberal economic doctrines.[29] As we have seen, he removed Michel Chevalier from the Collège de France because of the latter's association with that point of view. In justifying this action, Carnot defended the moderate position which was hostile to both extremes, by citing "the dangers inherent in those fallacious doctrines of liberty . . . and other doctrines, no less dangerous, which they engender to a certain extent as a consequence. Socialism, it is well-known, was born among us as a natural reaction to the vices of that too individualistic political economy."[30] Instead of the single point of view expressed by the English school, Carnot wanted the Collège de France to teach the history of all economic doctrines, including the socialist ones.[31] Hostile to the views of Louis Blanc, Carnot warmly defended producers' cooperatives among workers and was willing to accept state monopolies of certain industries, such as mines, canals and railroads.[32]

Jules Bastide had been associated with the social Catholic school of Buchez, as a writer for the Buchezian journal, *La Revue Nationale.* Although a moderate, Bastide was one of the relatively few republicans who had close contact with workers' groups before the revolution, and in 1847 he wrote a book expressing very "advanced" ideas on the education of workers.[33] As Foreign Minister, he had little to do with social

[28] "Social Insurance," *Encyclopedia of the Social Sciences,* XIV, pp. 134-135. The principle of obligation was not introduced until Bismarck's famous legislation in the 1880's.

[29] See his *Le Ministère de l'instruction publique,* pp. 59-60, and his MS "Mémorial," dos. 5, p. 14 and dos. 12, p. 1.

[30] *Le Ministère de l'instruction publique,* pp. 59-60.

[31] *Ibid.,* and MS "Mémorial," dos. 13, pp. 18-19.

[32] MS "Mémorial," preamble, p. 11; dos. 13, p. 35; dos. 14, p. 22; and dos. 16, p. 13.

[33] Georges Duveau, *La Pensée ouvrière sur l'éducation pendant la deuxième république et le second empire* (Paris, 1948), p. 313.

problems, but despite his close identification with Cavaignac, he retained the sympathy of the workers during the Second Empire.[34]

Another minister who had close contact with workers was Recurt, the doctor of the Faubourg Saint-Antoine. As Minister of Public Works, he fostered several reforms in the interest of the workers; afterwards he renounced politics and returned to the practice of medicine, presumably in the Faubourg Saint-Antoine.[35]

Two of Cavaignac's ministers who are usually regarded as thoroughly bourgeois had also taken a pronounced interest in the social question on the eve of the revolution. They were Marie and Goudchaux, who with other republicans and the staff of *L'Atelier* had held in 1847, at the home of Marie, "a series of discussion meetings on the social question."[36] In considering various plans for workers' cooperatives, the future conflict between socialist and moderate republican doctrines was foreshadowed when Louis Blanc's plan was rejected by a large majority. Instead, Marie, Ledru-Rollin, the *L'Atelier* group and others supported a proposal of Goudchaux for voluntary cooperatives fostered by cheap credit.[37] Although Marie regarded the National Workshops as "an expedient imposed by the necessity of circumstances,"[38] he sought to relieve unemployment in the provinces by similar means. In a circular sent to the prefects on March 14, he urged: "Paris offers the example of what you should do . . . open National Workshops to the unemployed."[39] Although Marie's direction of the National Workshops has been justifiably criticized, he did insist in his first report to the National Assembly that he had ordered public works to the limit of the state's financial resources, and asserted that the duty of the republic was "The amelioration of the condition of the workers. . . . The future of the workers is

[34] *Ibid.*

[35] *Dictionnaire des parlementaires*, v, p. 102.

[36] Cuvillier, *Journal d'ouvriers*, p. 31.

[37] Carnot, MS "Mémorial," dos. 16, p. 13, and Cherest, *Marie*, pp. 73-74.

[38] *Ibid.*, pp. 169-170.

[39] A. N., F 1A 45.

the highest, the first question for the Republic."[40] As Minister of Justice for Cavaignac, Marie had little to do with social questions, but in 1863 the worker Corbon recalled that Marie was one of "the friends of popular ameliorations who has shown most effective concern for workers' associations."[41]

Michel Goudchaux, despite his belief in "sound" financial policies, also had a distinct social cast to his outlook. We have already noted his interest in workers' cooperatives. A successful banker, Goudchaux was well received by the business community as the first Minister of Finance for the Provisional Government. Although Goudchaux rarely departed from the prevailing liberal assumptions of his time in his economic views, he was a firm advocate of the construction and operation of the railroads by the state. Moreover, as a moderate republican imbued with the humanitarian ideal of his party, Goudchaux rejected Malthusian views and hoped to use the republic as an instrument of social improvement.[42] Goudchaux had created a sensation on June 15 with his dramatic appeal for the immediate dissolution of the National Workshops, but it is usually forgotten that in the same speech he suggested a comprehensive program of social reforms. He agreed that the revolution was essentially "social," that the republic must remedy "poverty," solve the question of "the organization of labor," or perish. Repudiating the National Workshops as politically dangerous, Goudchaux argued that the state should provide "useful work" instead. While rejecting the kind of revolutionary plans that were emanating from the Luxembourg Commission, Goudchaux advocated state encouragement of workers' cooperatives, tax reforms in the interests of the working classes, further reforms along the line of that already enacted

[40] *Compte rendu des séances*, I, pp. 60-62, 8 May 1848.

[41] Anthyme Corbon, *Le Secret du peuple de Paris* (Paris, 1863), p. 131n.

[42] This discussion is based primarily on Goudchaux's speeches in the National Assembly in 1848 and not on an exhaustive study of his views, a subject that needs independent investigation. Raymond Lazard, *Michel Goudchaux (1797-1862)*, (Paris, 1907), is of little value, being merely a collection of speeches compiled by a grandson.

in the *conseils de prud'hommes,* and free education, all with the avowed aim of improving the condition of the workers.[43]

As Cavaignac's Minister of Finance, Goudchaux's first concern was to revive confidence and conciliate the business community, and for a time his views coincided with the liberal ones dominant in the Committee on Finance. But Goudchaux showed his republican colors on several issues, in particular on tax reform. When one proposal was under attack, Goudchaux excitedly declared that the republic must distinguish itself from the monarchy by establishing a more equitable tax system; his deepest concern was not for the political form but for "the amelioration of the condition of the masses."[44] Like Marie, Goudchaux also was later remembered by Corbon as one of "the friends of popular ameliorations."[45]

Senard, Cavaignac's first Minister of the Interior, had had no such contact with workers' groups, but on the morrow of the February revolution, in a grandiloquent speech on becoming *procureur général* at Rouen, he added his voice to the vogue of eulogizing the workers.[46] In helping to crush the April uprising at Rouen, however, Senard won the reputation as a man of order. Nevertheless, he turned out to be one of the most outspoken opponents of Malthusian doctrines in the Cavaignac government. He had given an indication of his moderate social views before the committee investigating the June insurrection,[47] but his first outburst in the Assembly came on July 31, in the midst of a long speech by Proudhon. Senard having interrupted to ask for an appropriation of two million francs for urgent relief in Paris, several deputies indignantly observed that the request came at a singularly inopportune moment. Stung at the imputation, Senard retorted: "The government, without troubling to find out if socialism is watching, is busy relieving those who are suffering."[48]

[43] The speech is in *Compte rendu des séances,* I, pp. 885-887.
[44] *Ibid.,* II, p. 810, 1 August 1848.
[45] Corbon, *Secret,* p. 131n.
[46] See *Discours prononcé par le citoyen Senard* (Paris, 1848), p. 5.
[47] *Rapport de la commission d'enquête,* I, p. 349.
[48] *Compte rendu des séances,* II, p. 782.

It was during the debate on a maximum hours law, however, that Senard enunciated most clearly a moderate interventionist point of view. The liberal economist Wolowski having moved to repeal outright the Provisional Government's decree setting a ten-hour limit, Senard opposed him with an eloquent defense of the principle of government regulation. Rejecting the classical arguments for complete freedom, Senard invoked "a more powerful reason, one which should dominate all others: the interest of humanity!"[49] Expressly placing his viewpoint "between the socialist and the [classical] economic doctrines," Senard declared: "It is a strange way to understand the liberty and dignity of man to see in them the right to destroy oneself, to sacrifice one's health, to sacrifice one's life in the course of excessive labor. One puts the State in a position that we will never accept, when one would have the State, in the face of such facts, abstain and do nothing but utter the famous formula of political economy: *Laisser-faire, laisser-passer*."[50] Senard's forceful speech influenced the Assembly to adopt an intermediate position on the hours law, retreating on the number of hours but clearly embodying the principle of governmental regulation.[51]

Cavaignac's Minister of Agriculture and Commerce, Tourret, was chiefly interested in agriculture, but he also revealed a considerable sympathy for the workers. As a member of the Committee on the Constitution, Tourret spoke rarely, but his first comment was to express his desire to establish relations between workers and employers "on the basis of perfect equality."[52] Shortly after entering the government, Tourret expressed his views in a long circular to the prefects. Along with a desire to encourage agriculture, Tourret envisaged a vague program of social reforms for urban workers that "will bring to the future of laborers pledges of security denied to them by the shortsightedness of the laissez-faire policy which from now on will be impossible, because it will be no less inhuman than impolitic."[53]

[49] *Ibid.*, III, p. 645, 31 August 1848.
[50] *Ibid.*, III, pp. 749-750, 4 September 1848.
[51] See pp. 299-302.
[52] A. N., C 919, minutes, I, p. 123, 9 June 1848.
[53] A. N., AD xix D 256, circular of 6 July 1848.

Bethmont, who was briefly Minister of Justice, had been one of the earliest advocates in the Provisional Government of public works to relieve unemployment.[54] He had also collaborated with the editors of *L'Atelier* in drawing up legislation reforming the *conseils de prud'hommes.*[55]

Of Cavaignac's original government, even General Lamoricière had a history of interest in social and economic problems, for he had been associated with the Saint-Simonian school. The Cabinet shift of October 13, politically retrograde, was less so with respect to the social orientation of the new men. Pierre Freslon, who became Minister of Education, was a *républicain de la veille* who had taken a somewhat conservative position in the April elections. He spoke out in May against Louis Blanc, but proudly proclaimed himself "son of a worker" and an advocate of gradual social reform.[56] In July, as spokesman for the Thirteenth Bureau of the Assembly, Freslon opposed the article of the constitutional draft that included "le droit au travail," arguing: "The philanthropy of the State destroys private charity in men's souls. We must not go too far in the direction of Malthus, but neither should we fling ourselves into the absolutely opposite system."[57] Although Freslon stopped short of affirming liberal doctrines, he did show more sympathy for them than any of Cavaignac's original ministers. As we have seen, he retreated from Carnot's position on the chair of political economy in the Collège de France. At that time he vaguely acknowledged that this school offered solutions to many problems.[58]

The other two new ministers of October 13, Auguste Vivien and Armand Dufaure, were former liberal Orleanists, but both now expressed the moderate social orientation of the Cavaignac government. Although primarily a constitutional lawyer, Vivien had in July publicly avowed his support for state encouragement of workers' cooperatives,[59] and as Minister of the Interior he took initiatives to improve conditions for workers within his department.

[54] See his circular of 28 February 1848, A. N., F 1A 45.

[55] Corbon, *Secret*, p. 151n.

[56] *Compte rendu des séances*, I, p. 112, 10 May 1848.

[57] A. N., C 918 minutes, II, p. 21, 27 July 1848.

[58] *Compte rendu des séances*, V, p. 542, 14 November 1848.

[59] *Ibid.*, II, p. 478, 14 July 1848.

Dufaure, who had been a Minister of Public Works in 1839, and afterwards was in an independent liberal opposition group of deputies, took an unusually active interest in the reform of public assistance under Cavaignac. He maintained that the Cabinet transformation of October signified the admission into the government of *républicains du lendemain* who had served the previous regime in order to further "social ameliorations."[60] In presenting a series of comprehensive public assistance reforms, Dufaure expressed a desire to avoid political disorders, but he insisted even more strongly on his humanitarian and social motives.

Distinguishing his plans from the former concern only with the weak and disabled, Dufaure argued: "Civilization confronts us with those great oscillations of industry which neither governments nor the calculations of private interests can control. During these inevitable depressions, what will become of the worker and his family when he has been unable to save resources in advance?"[61] Invoking the new Constitution, Dufaure said that France must not "remain coldly impassive in the face of real distress," but must grant "material ameliorations" to the poorer classes.[62] Dufaure's association with the Cavaignac government accounts in part for his new concerns, but the future showed that Dufaure's conversion to republican principles was lasting: although he served in the government of Louis Napoleon before the *coup d'Etat*, he stubbornly defended republicans who still held governmental positions[63] and vigorously renewed his struggle for public assistance reform.

MODERATE INTERVENTIONISM IN THE NATIONAL ASSEMBLY

The moderate social viewpoint had other sources than the doctrines of the *républicains de la veille*. The chief of these was what has been called social Catholicism.[64] Charitable

[60] *Ibid.*, IV, p. 903, 16 October 1848.

[61] *Ibid.*, V, p. 855, 27 November 1848.

[62] *Ibid.*, p. 853.

[63] See Tocqueville, *Recollections*, pp. 244, 247.

[64] This discussion is based primarily on Duroselle, *Les Débuts du*

activities were, of course, a traditional concern of the church, but in the generation before 1848 a number of influential Catholics took cognizance of the social question as a new problem growing out of an industrializing society and advocated new and distinctly social policies to cope with it.

Lamennais is probably the most famous of the social thinkers who started from Christian values, but he was unusual in that he left the church to join the republican movement. Other Catholics, such as Buchez, found the republican party hospitable to both their religious and their social views. *L'Atelier* also represented a fusion of the Catholic and republican as well as the workers' orientation. But not all of the social Catholics associated themselves with the republicans; within the Legitimist party too there developed a minority wing with a distinctly social tinge. As early as 1834, Villeneuve-Bargemont advocated legislation as a means of improving the condition of the working classes, and after 1840 the social question became the subject of lively interest among many Legitimists. The new concern was expressed in the influential Paris newspapers *La Quotidienne* and *La Gazette de France*, which took a sympathetic interest in Louis Blanc's ideas on "the organization of labor."[65] Although the social Legitimists failed to elaborate a consistent body of doctrine, they did vaguely favor workers' cooperatives and some government intervention. One Legitimist writer even suggested a guaranteed minimum wage.[66] Legitimists gave considerable support to the 1841 law regulating the labor of children in factories, and in 1845 Armand de Melun clearly enunciated the new social

---

catholicisme social. See also Gordon Griffiths, "The Vicomte Armand de Melun and the Catholic Social Movement in France, 1848-1851," in Frederick J. Cox, et al., eds., *Studies in Modern European History in Honor of Franklin Charles Palm* (New York, 1956), pp. 141-156; Joseph N. Moody, "French Liberal Catholics, 1840-1875," in *French Society and Culture Since the Old Regime*, pp. 150-171; and Paul Droulers, "Catholicisme et mouvement ouvrier en France au XIXe siècle: l'attitude de l'épiscopat," *Le Mouvement social*, No. 57 (1966), 15-46.

[65] Michel Eon, "Les Questions sociales dans la presse légitimiste sous la monarchie de juillet," unpublished *mémoire* for the *Diplôme d'Etudes Supérieures*, University of Paris, 1948.

[66] Duroselle, *Les Débuts du catholicisme social*, pp. 205-206.

Catholic emphasis on the role of government: "The State alone can alleviate poverty and improve, in a lasting and general way, the condition of those who suffer."[67]

Other notable social Legitimists were Larochejaquelein, Falloux and, close to the republicans in spirit, Lacordaire. Nonrepublican social Catholicism was not a unified movement, but consisted of several small and distinct groups which reflected in different ways the vogue of interest in social problems during the 1840's. Montalembert was an exponent of social Catholicism, and a few other Orleanists such as Billault repudiated the dominant liberal ideology to favor social reforms.[68] On the eve of the revolution, Corbon recalled, undoubtedly with some exaggeration, "The necessity of ameliorating the condition of the people was . . . generally felt,"[69] and in the banquet campaign numerous toasts were made on this theme. The social orientation of the February revolution thus found considerable receptivity in various quarters that were hostile to the socialists. In the elections to the National Assembly, the social mood was almost as strong as the democratic, and many candidates, not content with adopting the republican label, also advocated social reforms and even "the organization of labor."[70] Lacordaire, on the eve of his election to the Assembly, expressed in a sermon at Notre Dame the moderate interventionist attitude in a formula that became famous: "Between the strong and the weak, between the rich and the poor, between the master and the servant, it is liberty that oppresses, and the law that liberates."[71]

In the elections, the extreme laissez-faire ideology went down to defeat along with the old governmental party that had championed it, and the moderate social ideology of the moderate republicans dominated the Assembly. Although the Assembly immediately revealed its hostility to the socialists

[67] *Ibid.*, p. 219.

[68] Zeldin, *The Political System of Napoleon III*, pp. 67-68.

[69] Corbon, *Secret*, p. 195.

[70] Henri Moysset, "L'Idée d'organisation du travail dans la profession de foi des candidats à l'Assemblée Constituante de 1848," *La Révolution de 1848*, III (1906), pp. 27-42.

[71] Henri Lacordaire, *Oeuvres* (Paris, 1884), IV, p. 473. Cf. Labrousse, *Mouvement ouvrier*, p. 134.

by removing Louis Blanc and Albert from the government, it chose Buchez as its first president, and Corbon became chairman of the important Labor Committee. Fears of social revolution did cure some of the social Catholics (notably Montalembert) and the *ralliés* of their sympathy for the workers, but much of the social reformist spirit persisted. The policies of Falloux, for example, may be understood as a reflection of his moderate social outlook. As Duroselle put it, "We believe that in him, as in most of the conservative social Catholics, there coexisted a great hostility towards the system of the National Workshops, together with a sincere desire for social reform."[72]

Even after the June insurrection the moderate social and interventionist spirit continued to dominate the National Assembly, in much the same fashion as did the political ideals of the moderate republicans. Although the socialists were discredited and their speeches received with hostility or ridicule, the Assembly hall did not customarily ring with the phrases of political economy. Expressions of pronounced liberal economic views were relatively uncommon. It is true that the ideal of "liberty" for the economy in general was assumed by all but a tiny group of genuine socialists, and that the rights of private property were vigorously defended. It is true, moreover, that the Finance Committee, where Thiers was the leading influence, reflected strongly the liberal ideology, and that some of the most applauded speeches, such as those of Montalembert against the nationalization of the railroads, and of Thiers against Proudhon, expressed eloquently the hostility toward extensions of governmental activity. Nevertheless, the dominant tone in the Assembly throughout 1848, not only in public debate, but also in the working committees, was quite different.

The note that was constantly sounded was the necessity of "ameliorating the condition" of the working classes. We have already encountered some examples of this appeal; the phrase, and similar ones, were commonplaces in the mouths of orators after the June insurrection. Thiers later recalled how the mood of the Assembly contrasted with his own: "They used

[72] Duroselle, *Les Débuts du catholicisme social,* p. 444.

to say to me, 'Cannot we do something for the working classes?' as if the working classes wanted anything done for them—as if the duties of a Government were not preventive, the averting external and internal war, commercial changes and unnecessary expenditure."[73] The moderate republican Madame d'Agoult, while disparaging the socialism of the "utopians" and the "sectarians," hailed the spirit of the Assembly in July as "the socialism of statesmen," which "is persuaded that society can change the crushing conditions of the life of the proletarians."[74]

Nor was the moderate social spirit mere show, empty harangue. For the Assembly concerned itself with an astonishing number of reform measures of a social and economic character. From the beginning, the Assembly was flooded with proposals, but in the early weeks the huge body was just getting organized, and few reforms were enacted or even debated before the June insurrection. Those that were, such as the reforms in the *conseils de prud'hommes* and the initiation of the nationwide inquiry into labor conditions, were moderate social rather than socialist in nature. Under the regime of Cavaignac, the Assembly devoted serious study to scores of measures calling for various kinds of governmental intervention in the economy. These included efforts to stimulate recovery, create jobs and provide unemployment relief, as well as more long-range innovations such as tax reform, postal reform, partial nationalization of the railroads, state encouragement of workers' cooperatives and agricultural colonies, new agricultural educational institutions, agricultural credit, distribution of communal land, workers' housing, accidents in factories, rudimentary social insurance, and removal of restrictions on labor unions. Although many of the proposals were ultimately rejected, notably the changes in the labor code, they were done so only after careful scrutiny. Moreover, many significant reforms were enacted, in particular those introduced or supported by the government, and the Cavaignac regime was the period most hospitable to the individual re-

[73] Senior, *Conversations with M. Thiers*, II, pp. 340-341.

[74] *Lettres républicaines*, letter 6, 8 July 1848, pp. 10-14.

forms advocated by Buchez and *L'Atelier*, as well as by Armand de Melun. In mid-September, Dufaure took note of the Assembly's accomplishments: "Has there ever been an Assembly in the world which has, in so little time, devoted so much study to the sufferings of unfortunate citizens, shown so much anxious concern, taken so many measures in the spirit of fraternity, as the present Assembly?"[75]

LE DROIT AU TRAVAIL

The Constitution adopted in November reflected the moderate social and humanitarian viewpoint dominant in the Assembly. Indeed, the intermediate position of the moderate republicans and those who followed their inspiration may be seen quite clearly in the transformation of "le droit au travail" into paragraph VIII of the Preamble and Article 13. *Le droit au travail* was one of the formulae that expressed the social nature of the revolution, somewhat less vague than the principle of *fraternité*, less concrete than the idea of association. Originally a Fourierist notion, *le droit au travail* had won a much broader appeal by 1848 and was implicitly endorsed by the Provisional Government in its decree of February 25.[76] Although the proclamation had been wrested forcibly from the newly constituted government by a small group of armed workers, it soon came to be regarded as a sacred promise of the revolution. But the phrase was ambiguous, signifying to some the obligation of the state to provide work for the unemployed, and to others, such as Proudhon, the obligation to provide work for each in his particular trade and thus to initiate a profound change in the social and economic order. Moreover, as social tensions increased, the slogan became for the revolutionary groups a rallying cry, and for conservatives a dreaded symbol of social revolution. The Constitutional Committee

[75] *Compte rendu des séances*, IV, p. 14, 14 September 1848.

[76] Even though the term itself was absent from the decree. The pertinent paragraph reads: "Le gouvernement provisoire de la République française s'engage à garantir l'existence de l'ouvrier par le travail." Henry, "Le Droit au travail," p. 44. Cf. the discussion in Labrousse, *Mouvement ouvrier*, pp. 199-216.

was divided on the question, but a majority finally decided in its favor, and it was included in the draft Constitution presented to the Assembly on June 19.

After the insurrection, a majority of the *bureaux* of the Assembly rejected the formula, and it was deleted from the revised text submitted on August 30. Nevertheless, at that time Marrast insisted that if the formula had been removed because of its ambiguity, "the substance remains the same," because the duty to provide work was imposed on the state.[77] Outraged, the radical republicans attempted to reinsert the slogan into the text. The result was one of the major debates of the Assembly, in which a dozen of its most accomplished orators participated over a period of five days. It brought Tocqueville to his feet to make his only major speech of the session—against *le droit au travail.* The most effective opponent, however, was Thiers, who performed with his usual trenchant brilliance. Several republicans fervently defended the formula, in particular Ledru-Rollin and Lamartine.

If the radical republicans adopted it as a party slogan, the moderate republicans were split: some opposed it as an empty or dangerous formula or merely doubted the practical wisdom of inserting it into the Constitution, but many believed they must remain faithful to this heritage of February. In July the *Réunion du Palais National* had supported it, and *Le National* remained an advocate; they naturally interpreted it in the sense of the state's obligation to provide work for the unemployed. After extensive debate, in which opponents emphasized the implications of social revolution in the formula, the Assembly on September 14 decisively defeated it, by a vote of 596 to 187.

Those who supported *le droit au travail* were the radical republicans, about 44 percent of the moderate republicans, and a few *républicains du lendemain.* The monarchists voted massively against it, joined by 107 moderate republicans, including the Cavaignac ministry. But the result was by no means simply a victory of bourgeois over proletarian, nor of

[77] *Compte rendu des séances*, III, p. 597, 30 August 1848. For a good summary of the "passionate" debate on Article VIII of the Preamble, see Bastid, *Doctrines et institutions*, II, pp. 79-85.

laissez-faire over state intervention. It is not surprising that so many moderate republicans should have rejected the formula, which had appeared vague and dangerous from the time it was forced on the Provisional Government. What seems remarkable is the large number of moderate republicans—84—who were willing to defend it. The opponents included Buchez and Corbon, the latter arguing that the phrase meant "absolutely nothing."[78] Even Proudhon opposed a final effort in November to insert *le droit au travail* in the Constitution, arguing that it was now an empty partisan gesture to which he refused to lend his support.[79]

Although the celebrated formula was deleted from the Constitution, the substance of its moderate interpretation remained, as Marrast had said, along with broader social duties imposed on the state. Article VIII of the preamble declared:

> The Republic must protect the citizen's person, his family, his religion, his property, his work, and must put within reach of everyone the education indispensable to all men; it must, through brotherly assistance, assure the existence of needy citizens, either by procuring work for them within the limits of its resources, or by giving, where their families cannot, aid to those who are unfit to work.[80]

This article was an even broader statement than that in Robespierre's proposed Declaration of Rights, with a similar emphasis on the duty of the state and some identical phrases.[81] The social function of the state was further elaborated in Article 13:

[78] *Compte rendu des séances*, v, p. 251, 2 November 1848. Corbon supported the interpretation that the state should provide jobs for the unemployed; later he argued that it had been a tactical error to make an issue of *le droit au travail* because it gave the party of "reaction" an opportunity to play on the ambiguities of the formula. (See his *Secret*, pp. 134-137.)

[79] *Compte rendu des séances*, v, p. 260, 2 November 1848.

[80] For the full text of the Constitution, see Bastid, *Doctrines et institutions politiques*, II, pp. 325-333.

[81] See Marc Bouloiseau, et al., eds., *Oeuvres de Maximilien Robespierre* (Paris, 1958), IX, p. 456.

> The Constitution guarantees to the citizens freedom of work and of industry. Society promotes and encourages the development of labor by free primary education, professional training, the equality of relations between employer and worker, insurance and credit institutions, agricultural institutions, voluntary associations, and the establishment, by the State, of departments and communes, of public works designed to furnish work for the unemployed; it provides assistance for abandoned children, for the infirm and for the impoverished aged whom their families cannot help.

Some historians wishing to emphasize the reaction that followed the June insurrection point to the deletion of *le droit au travail*—after, as we have seen, an ambiguous retreat from an ambiguous formula—but overlook the significance of the Constitution as it was adopted.[82] The Constitution expressed not only the moderate social interventionist point of view, but also reflected some of the accomplishments and aspirations of the Cavaignac government during the months that it was in power.

[82] But for a good brief appreciation of the social aspect of the Constitution, see Charles H. Pouthas, *Démocraties et capitalisme (1848-1860)*, "Peuples et civilisations" (3d edn., Paris, 1961), p. 111.

XI · The Attack on the *Crise*

BREAD AFTER LEAD

Some books on the revolution of 1848 leave the impression that the workers who arose in June because their bleak alternatives seemed to be "bread or lead," were left after their defeat to starve, sunken in unemployment that a vindictive government did nothing to alleviate. The classic example is that of Charles Schmidt on *Les Journées de juin, 1848*, which concludes by contrasting the "total incomprehension" of the liberal economist Léon Faucher with the dying words of General Duvivier, who was fatally wounded combatting the uprising: "These poor workers need to be brought under control, but we must do something for them. We must give them work; the hand of the fatherland must open."[1]

In fact, it was the attitude of Duvivier rather than of Faucher that characterized the government of General Cavaignac. Not only did the government provide bread for the vanquished workers, it also sought by various means to create employment and to revive the faltering economy. But it did so only partly out of humanitarian concern; perhaps a more compelling motive was the fear that the alternative might be another insurrection. Although these efforts were less dramatic than the National Workshops, the government seems to have acted vigorously within the limits of its strained financial resources, and the total impression resulting from a consideration of the efforts to relieve misery and stimulate recovery is quite different from that of a sterile and vengeful government.

The most immediate problem was the substitution of direct relief for the National Workshops. During the insurrection, Cavaignac had begun the shift by ordering that payments be made at the twelve *mairies* of Paris instead of at the workshops. In addition, on June 25, the National Assembly voted three million francs for "secours extraordinaires." This action, coming at the height of the battle, was obviously an attempt to weaken the enthusiasm of the insurgents by proffering them

[1] P. 127.

the bread for which many claimed to be fighting. It was also a measure of conciliation, and General Bréa had lost his life in seeking, vainly, to use it as a basis of negotiations.

Relief payments continued after the workers had been crushed. In the first ten days after the insurrection, almost one million francs of this special appropriation were distributed in Paris, the largest amounts going to the Eighth *arrondissement*, which included the Faubourg Saint-Antoine, and to the Twelfth, where General Bréa had been killed.[2] This was in addition to another million francs distributed in the same period, representing the remaining funds from the National Workshops.[3]

In mid-July, Cavaignac called a conference of the twelve *maires* of Paris to discuss further relief needs and the means of stimulating recovery. The group decided that relief would be accorded at the rate of 35 centimes daily per person.[4] Despite the government's efforts to end the depression, mass unemployment continued, and Senard as Minister of the Interior came before the Assembly three additional times to request further relief money for Paris, asking two million on July 25, one million on September 1, and three million on October 11. With a staggering unemployment rate of more than 50 percent, the number of persons on relief remained well above 200,000 during the summer, reaching 274,000 in August.[5] During the last half of 1848, the state spent about 8.5 million francs for relief in Paris, in addition to 4.5 spent by the city. The total public outlay of thirteen million francs was only slightly less than the 13.5 million spent so much more dramatically on the National Workshops from February 26 to June 26.[6]

[2] The figures are given in a chart drawn up for the parliamentary investigation of the uprising. See A. N., C 934 dos. 10.

[3] McKay, *National Workshops*, p. 167.

[4] The Cavaignac archives contain a number of documents concerning this meeting in Reel 22.

[5] See the report of Senard to the Finance Committee, 8 August 1848, A. N., C 927, minutes, II, p. 10. For unemployment figures, see Markovitch, "La Crise de 1847-1848 dans les industries parisiennes."

[6] McKay, *National Workshops*, p. 167, gives a total of 14,493,250 francs for the workshops, of which about one million was distributed

So large an amount of state aid was unprecedented, and the government requests aroused considerable opposition in the Finance Committee and among many deputies. Some opponents charged that the workers were lazy or simply refused work, but the principal argument was that the state should leave relief activities to the municipality. The debates, though lively, were brief, and the Assembly always voted the sums requested. Nevertheless, the Minister of the Interior had to make a personal appeal before two parliamentary committees and had to participate in debate in order to win support. The motives of government and Assembly were as much political as humanitarian; faced with a destitute, sullen and perhaps still defiant worker population, few seriously opposed the rendering of the minimal relief that alone was possible with the sums voted. By October, the average distribution was about 12 centimes per person daily, one-third of the figure set in July and perhaps one-tenth of the average dole under the National Workshops.[7] At the level of the *mairies*, the human suffering was evident, and the *maires* sometimes intervened personally with Cavaignac to plead for more funds. Moreover, there is no evidence that former insurgents or their families were discriminated against; rather, some of the *maires* specifically mentioned that aid was being given to insurgents' families.[8] The language of Senard in requesting funds was sober; without overt reference to the insurrection of June, he invoked "the most imperious considerations of public order and of humanity."[9]

---

after the insurrection. The period of the workshops was, of course, considerably shorter than the period of Cavaignac. I do not mean to imply that Cavaignac provided as much relief as did the National Workshops, but wish merely to show that his government did provide something. The work by Ferdinand Dreyfus, *L'Assistance sous la seconde république (1848-1851)*, (Paris, 1907), is unsatisfactory for the period of Cavaignac, failing to distinguish clearly the sums deriving from private charity, the city and the state.

[7] See the debates of 10 August 1848, *Compte rendu des séances*, III, pp. 61-64, and of 9 November 1848, *ibid.*, V, pp. 413-418.

[8] This information derives from a number of reports preserved by Cavaignac, in Reel 22 and Reel 23.

[9] *Compte rendu des séances*, IV, p. 798, 11 October 1848.

Although the attention of government and Assembly was fixed mostly on Paris, they also provided some aid to the provinces. On July 10 the Assembly voted 500,000 francs for distribution to welfare offices, a sum that must have been fantastically inadequate. On September 1, Senard asked and received another million francs for provincial relief, "designated to aid needy workers, pending the revival of employment."[10] In addition, the Assembly in November allotted another million francs for the indigent and infirm of the country, and 600,000 francs to be distributed when the Constitution was promulgated. Finally, many provincial cities were compelled to float special loans in order "to come to the aid of unemployed workers." The National Assembly spent much of its time considering, and usually granting, such requests.[11]

THE APPEAL FOR CONFIDENCE

The government also made a direct, sustained and diversified attack on the economic crisis. Indeed, its first formal action was the presentation to the Assembly on July 3 of a proposed five-point program aimed at stimulating recovery and creating jobs. Cavaignac personally as well as his Finance Minister, Goudchaux, appealed for adoption of the measures, which were designed both to inspire "confidence" and to assure the workers "that we are opening sources of production for them."[12] Three of the proposals concerned the restoration of credit, one was for a tax reform, and one provided a subsidy for the building industry. These were but the first of a series of efforts to help end the depression and the attendant misery.

Goudchaux's most ardent desire was to restore the "confidence" of the affluent classes, a traditional and conservative policy but also a sensible one. First, Goudchaux reassured those who feared radical innovations by renouncing the proposals for state ownership of the entire railroad system. "Rachat" of the railroads had been, indeed, the keystone of

[10] *Ibid.*, III, p. 678. He cited the same motive for the earlier appropriation in his circular of 15 July 1848, in A. N., F 1A 45.

[11] The quotation is from Representative Desmolles on August 10, *Compte rendu des séances*, III, p. 63.

[12] *Ibid.*, II, p. 315.

the financial program of the Executive Commission, and there was much hostility in the Assembly to any such radical measures.[13] Goudchaux also repudiated other measures of his predecessors which he regarded as inimical to the restoration of confidence. Thus, he asked the Assembly to repay in full the treasury bonds and government savings accounts on which his predecessors had partially defaulted.

The Provisional Government, in dire financial straits and faced with mass demands for cash payment of bonds and a run on the *caisses d'épargne*, had resorted to partial payments in deflated *rentes*, inflicting losses of 25 to 30 percent.[14] The *caisses d'épargne* had represented the liberal economists' favorite prescription for economic distress, and although only accounts larger than 100 francs had suffered, the socialist historian Georges Renard believed that the action of the Provisional Government had hurt "the class most in need of money."[15] Goudchaux in July was silent on the social significance of his proposals, invoking only the need to reestablish the state's credit.[16] As a further demonstration of his renunciation of fiscal adventures, Goudchaux asked the Assembly to authorize the borrowing of 150 million francs from the Bank of France. Goudchaux had correctly judged the mood of the Assembly, for it granted all three of his requests within four days.

More realistic than his predecessors, Goudchaux predicted a budgetary deficit rather than a surplus for 1848 because of increased expenses and revenue losses resulting from the revolutionary crisis. The deficit would be met by the Bank of France loan, and also by a new issue of *rentes* worth 177 million that Goudchaux proposed on July 22. He had rejected pleas for a foreign loan, Goudchaux declared, because "It was up to France to prove that she did not fear to make a loan to the Republic."[17] The conservative nature of Goudchaux's

[13] For a fuller discussion of the railroads, see pp. 290-294.

[14] Alfred Antony, *La Politique financière du gouvernement provisoire, février-mai 1848* (Paris, 1910), pp. 102-109.

[15] *La République de 1848*, p. 312.

[16] His speech is in *Compte rendu des séances*, II, pp. 316-324, 3 July 1848.

[17] *Ibid.*, II, p. 641, 24 July 1848.

proposals was recognized and applauded by the Finance Committee, the stronghold of Thiers and others of staunchly orthodox views.

Both the Finance Committee and Goudchaux sought to adopt another traditional policy, that of retrenchment, but with little success. The government departments resisted serious pruning efforts, and the only significant saving was Goudchaux's reduction of ministerial salaries.[18]

Continuing fiscal difficulties hampered the government in its efforts to deal with the economic depression, for although Goudchaux was not hostile on principle to public works and subsidies, he had no theory to justify deficit financing, and assumed that he must balance the budget as nearly as possible.

STIMULATION OF EMPLOYMENT

The renunciation of the "rachat" of the railroads was as much a decision against massive public works as against fiscal innovation. Limited by the budget and concerned to avoid large concentrations of workers for political reasons, the government tacitly rejected the recourse to public works on a large scale as a method of relieving unemployment. Nevertheless, it did make some use of this method, particularly outside Paris.[19] In August, the government proposed to assume ownership of the important railroad line from Paris to Lyon, which was still under construction, on the principal ground that the imminent failure of the company would throw 40,000 men out of work and have a disastrous effect on the economy. The Assembly voted twenty million francs for this purpose, and construction continued.[20]

In the autumn, the government also took temporary control of several other, less important lines in order to assure continued construction and operation; for example, the Bordeaux-

[18] From the 80,000 francs of the July Monarchy to 48,000 francs. Marcel Marion, *Histoire financière de la France depuis 1715*, v (Paris, 1928), p. 295.

[19] Labrousse points out, however, that 1,770 millions were spent on public works in 1848. Such expenditures were reduced by more than 10 percent in 1850 and 1851, despite Article 13 of the Constitution of November 4, 1848. (*Mouvement ouvrier*, p. 217.)

[20] See pp. 292-293.

La Teste line and that from Vierzon to Bec d'Allier. In November, the Minister of Public Works cautioned a parliamentary committee against delay in approving one such request for funds: "It is important to provide work in the shops, and the news of the rejection of this bill would produce the most deplorable effect on the population."[21] In the department of the Sarthe, officials later reported that the 450,000 francs spent on construction of a line to Le Mans "were precious for the working population of the city, who were employed during the entire winter."[22]

The government also won approval from the Assembly for the expenditure of several million francs to support other kinds of public works, with the principal aim of creating employment. The most important of these appropriations were two million francs for maintenance of national roads, and another million for works on the Marne River.[23]

Even after the change of ministers in October, the Cavaignac government sponsored another new request for job-creating public works. On November 8, Vivien asked two million for decorative work to be done at the Louvre. Citing the stagnation in the building industry, he asked aid for artisans of this trade: "The government could not refuse its protection to a class so important and yet so unfortunate today. . . . It would be unjust, impolitic perhaps, to refuse them the assistance which is so necessary to them."[24] This project would be particularly valuable for the workers because almost all of the money could be used for wages, Vivien argued. The Assembly complied with the request.

One of the most interesting public works activities supported by the Cavaignac government was that on the provincial *chemins vicinaux*, the local roads hitherto maintained exclusively by special taxes in each community. In proposing the allocation of six million francs for this purpose on July 22, Senard revealed a mixture of motives—political, social and eco-

[21] A. N., C 298, minutes, Committee on Public Works, p. 120.

[22] Frédéric Lemeunier, *A.-J. Trouvé-Chauvel, banquier et maire du Mans, ministre des finances de la deuxième république* (Le Mans, 1953), pp. 70-71.

[23] *Compte rendu des séances*, IV, pp. 509-511, 30 September 1848.

[24] *Ibid.*, V, pp. 393-394.

nomic—that represented a peculiarly moderate republican and statist response to the social problem. Senard cited the necessity for providing work, particularly in view of the coming winter, but also expressed his desire to inhibit the flow of workers from the countryside to the cities, where they became "a cause of misery for the worker himself, and a dangerous embarrassment" for the government.[25] At first the money was to be diverted from funds for railroad construction, but later Senard requested outright appropriation because any reduction in railroad construction would create unemployment.[26] The Assembly, however, granted only three million, the other three million to be raised locally.

By September, when the law was adopted, Senard's fear of the workers had abated, and in his instructions to the prefects he emphasized social aims:

> This allocation, although its principal purpose is to provide jobs for the workers and to assure them a just remuneration, is intended in addition to serve the interests of agriculture of course and thus to contribute to the permanent improvement of the condition of the rural population. . . . The local roads will constitute an immense workshop in which the worker will find work within reach in times of agricultural unemployment.[27]

Although the Assembly had reduced the amount of state funds by the introduction of a "matching" principle, the law of September 22 nevertheless represented the first instance of state intervention in the maintenance and improvement of the *chemins vicinaux*. Moreover, Senard did not regard the measure as a temporary expedient, but hoped to continue permanently such state aid, "advantageous both to agriculture and to the working population."[28]

[25] *Ibid.*, II, p. 605.

[26] *Ibid.*, IV, p. 196, 22 September 1848.

[27] A. N., F 1A 45, circular of 23 September 1848. In a subsequent circular of 6 October 1848, Senard said simply that the principal object of the law was "to provide jobs for the workers during the winter of 1848-1849."

[28] A. N., F 1A 45, circular of 23 September 1848.

In addition to its modest use of public works projects, the Cavaignac government also sought to stimulate economic revival and relieve unemployment by diverse measures of aid to private business. Although this intervention was also on a modest scale, it showed the government's willingness to use the resources of the state to attack the crisis directly. Moreover, the Cavaignac government not only continued to use the few innovations introduced by the Provisional Government, but acted in a more direct manner than its predecessors. First, the government left in operation the three related institutions that were already helping to ease the commercial crisis in Paris and other cities: the *comptoirs d'escompte*, the *sous-comptoirs d'escompte*, and the *magasins généraux*, all created in March. The *comptoirs d'escompte* provided credit to businessmen on the basis of two signatures only and were financed by the state, the municipality and private subscription, each providing a third of the funds. By May, forty-four of these institutions existed, making capital available even to the smaller businessmen.[29] Although "more than one financier made no secret of his hope that this institution would be as provisional as the government itself,"[30] the *comptoirs d'escompte* were preserved by both the Cavaignac government and by Louis Napoleon, who under the Empire changed their character.

The *sous-comptoirs d'escompte* had been designed to serve those businessmen unable to obtain the second signature permitting them to make use of the *comptoirs d'escompte*. In addition, the Provisional Government had created *magasins généraux*, "huge public pawnshops," where businessmen could get loans on the collateral of products which they deposited. "This innovation was a partial borrowing from the socialist theories of the time . . ." observed Renard, "and it partially democratized credit."[31] All three of these useful institutions were maintained, and in the case of the *sous-comptoirs*, elaborated further by the Cavaignac government.

Perhaps the most interesting and significant economic policy of the Cavaignac government was its attempt to stimulate the

[29] Renard, *La République de 1848*, p. 336.
[30] *Ibid.*, p. 337.
[31] *Ibid.*

recovery of the construction industry of Paris, the one most severely stricken by the depression. During 1848, unemployment rates among construction workers reached 64 percent,[32] and Gossez found that workers from this trade had "formed the mass of the insurgents" in June.[33] Although many industries had been seeking economic aid from the state, Goudchaux on July 3 asked only for assistance to the building industry, because it was best able to employ "a large number of workers from the National Workshops."[34] The minister requested an appropriation of five million francs for this purpose, to be used through the *sous-comptoir d'escompte*; thus far, the builders, having no merchandise to pledge as collateral, had been unable to take advantage of the *sous-comptoir*, and most construction had been suspended. Goudchaux said that no other industry would be able to employ so many workers, and alluding to the costs of direct relief, argued that even if the state should fail to receive reimbursement for its loan, the Assembly should "readily consent to a sacrifice which will occupy in a useful manner so many of the workers now on relief."[35]

Cavaignac also argued that the measure would stimulate general economic revival; indeed, according to a proverb then current, "When the building trade prospers, all prosper."[36] In thus seeking to revive artificially a sensitive industry, the Cavaignac government was taking a kind of direct action that even the earlier revolutionary governments, not to mention the July Monarchy, had failed to do. Opposition on principle erupted in the Finance Committee; one deputy opposed the move as a step along "a fatal road" and another insisted that "the true method of reviving industry consists in strengthening credit."[37] But the Assembly, urged to speedy action by Cavaignac, adopted the bill the day after it was proposed. By

32 Markovitch, "La Crise de 1847-1848 dans les industries parisiennes," p. 257.

33 Gossez, "Diversité des antagonismes sociaux," p. 451.

34 *Compte rendu des séances*, II, p. 322, 3 July 1848.

35 *Ibid.*, p. 323, 3 July 1848.

36 Cited on July 13 by a deputy, *ibid.*, p. 447.

37 A. N., C 927, committee minutes, I, pp. 120-122, 4 July 1848.

virtue of this direct state support, the *sous-comptoir* for the building industry was the most successful aspect of a generally successful experiment.[38]

Still another form of aid to the Paris building industry was adopted a week later, on July 13. This was a measure, introduced by three private deputies but vigorously supported by the government, to subsidize construction by means of tax exemptions. Supporters emphasized that the aim was, in the words of Senard, to "come to the aid of the workers." To encourage immediate construction, the law exempted from taxation for ten years all buildings begun before the end of 1848 and completed by July 1, 1850. The law had another social aspect, vigorously defended by Goudchaux, in that it sought to encourage the construction of workers' housing by granting fifteen-year tax exemptions. To qualify, builders' plans had to meet government approval.[39]

In addition to encouraging the building industry, Cavaignac on July 6 personally called together businessmen from the Eighth and Ninth *arrondissements*, which had been the heart of the insurrection, to discuss "the steps to take to revive commerce in the Faubourg Saint-Antoine."[40] At an informal meeting in the office of Tourret, Cavaignac expressed his "feelings of benevolence . . . for the misguided and unfortunate workers,"[41] and listened to pleas for subsidies and other aid, but in the end acceded to none of the requests.

Instead, Tourret created a special Commission "to inquire into the best means of reviving employment." While rejecting, as had the earlier revolutionary governments, a policy of general subsidies to business, the Cavaignac administration decided to support two of the most important artisan trades of Paris, the cabinetmakers and the bronze-workers.[42] Neither of these trades, because of special circumstances, had been able

[38] Antony, *Politique financière*, pp. 97, 184. See also Rondo Cameron, *France and the Economic Development of Europe, 1800-1914* (Princeton, 1961), pp. 126-127, 196.

[39] For details see *Compte rendu des séances*, II, pp. 429-430, 12 July 1848, and pp. 445-457, 13 July 1848.

[40] A. N., F 12 2337-2338.

[41] *Ibid.*

[42] *Compte rendu des séances*, III, p. 280, 18 August 1848.

to benefit from the *sous-comptoirs d'escompte.* The cabinet-makers, suffering an unemployment rate of 72 percent, were concentrated in the Faubourg Saint-Antoine, where, said Tourret, they and their families, some 50,000 persons in all, were on relief. In addition, some 10,000 bronze-workers in other parts of Paris were left unemployed because of the depression. The government asked 600,000 francs to provide direct loans to the artisans, the system requested by workers' delegates to the commission. A similar plan had been put into effect in 1830, but then only the larger shops had been aided, whereas the intention now was to aid the individual workers.[43] A combination of motives, political and social, was suggested by Tourret, who said the bill would serve the purposes of "order, jobs and humanity.[44] One republican deputy criticized the measure as inadequate and unjustly limited to Paris, wryly pointing out that the state seemed eager to aid the former insurgent areas, but did nothing for destitute workers in other cities, whose conduct in June had been exemplary. But the Assembly on September 1 granted the credits without further debate.[45]

A mixture of motives also was apparent in another government policy, a subsidy to the Paris theaters. On July 11, Senard asked a credit of 670,000 francs for this purpose, arguing that it would cost less to aid the theaters than to pay direct relief to the unemployed theater workers. He said that the theaters had remained open, to their economic detriment, after the February revolution at the express request of the Provisional Government, but had since been forced to close, and would be unable to reopen without assistance. The government would stipulate that most of the money be used for wages.[46]

In committee, deputies approved the measure as following the precedent of five million francs accorded the building industry, and argued that it would help to stimulate general recovery by attracting more money into circulation.[47] Reporting favorably for the committee, Victor Hugo also emphasized

[43] For details, see *ibid.*, pp. 452-453, 25 August 1848.

[44] *Ibid.*, p. 281, 18 August 1848.

[45] *Ibid.*, pp. 368-370.

[46] *Ibid.*, II, pp. 421-424.

[47] A. N., C 926, minutes of the Committee on the Interior, 12 July 1848.

the moral value of the theater, "an efficacious sedative." Although one Legitimist deputy from Ille-et-Vilaine protested that too much money had already been voted, "always in the interests of the workers of the capital," the law was adopted without serious opposition. It stipulated that two-thirds of the money be used for wages.[48]

The army under Cavaignac also sought to provide additional jobs by ordering some of its equipment made by civilian manufacturers. On June 16, such orders were placed for 78,000 shakos and 230,000 republican *plaques*. After the insurrection, large orders for cloth, cans, saddles and other items were deliberately let among numerous manufacturers with this social objective in view; notably, an order for 75,000 blankets was distributed on September 14 among all the workshops of the Twelfth *arrondissement* of Paris "in order to aid the working classes."[49]

The government and Assembly were largely concerned with Paris, but some attention was directed to at least one important provincial city, Lyon. In April, the Provisional Government, in an effort to aid the textile workers there, ordered the manufacture of 43,000 flags and 130,000 sashes, for the use of the towns and communes of France. On June 23, the Executive Commission asked five million francs to pay for the articles, but the Assembly shelved the matter following the insurrection. On September 2, however, the Cavaignac government reintroduced the bill, increasing the amount requested to 6,800,000 francs.[50] Some 30,000 workers were kept on the job by the state's orders; although the government could simply have paid for work already completed, instead it decided to subsidize the two million francs' worth still to be manufactured. The law was adopted on October 14, substantially unchanged.[51]

Although the Cavaignac government thus was willing to give aid where possibilities were greatest for creating jobs, it followed its precedessors in renouncing a more general

[48] *Compte rendu des séances*, II, pp. 513-516, 17 July 1848.
[49] Zaniewicki, "L'Armée française en 1848," I, pp. 131-132.
[50] *Compte render des séances*, III, p. 717.
[51] *Ibid.*, IV, p. 864.

policy of aid to the stricken economy. Duclerc, Minister of Finance for the Executive Commission, on June 20 had opposed a suggestion that thirty million francs be granted in subsidies on the ground that the principle "is vicious, and would not produce any useful result." To meet all requests for aid, he observed, one billion francs would be needed.[52] The suggestion was withdrawn, but a month later a somewhat similar proposal was made by two Alsatian industrialists, who asked that the government aid industry by placing orders worth nineteen million francs for military supplies.[53] Goudchaux opposed the suggestion, citing the poor fiscal condition, and arguing that the government already was aiding industry to the limit of its ability, citing in particular the twenty million francs appropriated for the purchase of the Paris-Lyon railroad.[54]

At the very end of the Cavaignac administration, one more attempt was made to aid a particular industry, and the different reception it received in the Assembly revealed a shift in sentiment away from the interventionism of the summer. On December 12, the government asked an appropriation of 100,000 francs to permit the carriage industry to benefit from the *sous-comptoirs d'escompte*, in the same manner as the building industry.[55] Trouvé-Chauvel, Goudchaux's successor, said the policy would reduce the demand for direct relief, and "provide jobs for several thousand workers."[56] By the time the committee reported on January 5, the Cavaignac government had fallen, and the Orleanist spokesman (Hervieu) contemptuously rejected the proposal with the observation that "the day of the National Workshops, of painful memories, is fortunately past." Policies "of this sort" had been "wrung" from the Assembly during the summer because of "imperious necessities," but now the committee spokesman

[52] *Ibid.*, II, p. 81.

[53] *Ibid.*, II, pp. 838-844, 3 August 1848.

[54] *Ibid.*, III, pp. 160-162, 14 August 1848.

[55] It is not clear why the measure was introduced at this time, but it was badly timed for a maneuver in the presidential campaign because elections were held on December 10 and 11.

[56] *Compte rendu des séances*, VI, pp. 233-234, 12 December 1848.

declared that "the State can and must no longer be regarded in the future as the sleeping partner of private industry!"[57] The Assembly shelved the matter.

THE PLAN FOR COLONIZATION OF ALGERIA

Certainly the most spectacular response to the problem of unemployment was the plan to establish jobless workers in agricultural colonies in Algeria.[58] Deputies from Algeria had advocated state-supported colonies early in 1848, but it was the socialist Pierre Leroux who in mid-June linked Algeria to the social problem by suggesting the implantation of unemployed workers there. After the insurrection, many other voices took up the idea, from radicals like Caussidière to social Legitimists like Falloux. The mayors of Paris formally pleaded for colonization on behalf of the workers "so woefully stricken by the suspension of industry,"[59] and in August, 20,000 families of Paris workers petitioned the Assembly to finance their colonization in Algeria.[60]

The Assembly was drawing up a detailed plan when the government of Cavaignac presented its own, which was adopted virtually unchanged on September 19. The plan called for the establishment of 12,000 colonists in Algeria by the end of 1848, at a cost of five million francs. But the plan was more than a hasty expedient, for it contemplated financing colonization for at least three years, at a total cost of 50 million francs. In presenting the bill, Lamoricière emphasized both social and imperialistic aims; mere relief, while helpful, was "sterile for the future," whereas this plan would strengthen the North African colony. Undoubtedly there was in addition an unstated political motivation—the desire to remove from Paris some of its turbulent working-class population, but if so,

[57] *Ibid.*, VII, p. 83.

[58] The best, though still incomplete accounts of this project are Lucien Genet, "Les Colonies agricoles de 1848," in *La Révolution de 1848 en Algérie*, pp. 107-121, and Julien, *Histoire de l'Algérie*, pp. 362-375.

[59] A. N., C 912 dos. 58.

[60] Société d'Histoire de la Révolution de 1848, *Procès-verbaux du comité du travail à l'Assemblée Constitutante de 1848* (Paris, 1908), p. 112. See also *Le National*, 19 August 1848, p. 4.

thousands of the workers themselves eagerly sought to take advantage of the opportunity.[61]

Under the law, the government paid all the expenses of transporting men and whole families. In Algeria they received 2 to 10 hectares of land, which would become their own property after three years. The government was to provide housing and all expenses for the first three years. In addition, the state sought to encourage colonization by workers unfamiliar with farming by guaranteeing them jobs on public works projects; but they could become farmers and receive free land whenever they wished.

Although the socialists, the workers and social Legitimists such as Falloux wished to establish colonies of a cooperative or "associationist" nature, the government insisted on fostering only individual private farms. Nevertheless, the opposition to "association" was on practical grounds only; Lamoricière affirmed the government's support of the principle of "association," but argued that previous experiments had proved its impracticality in agriculture. Moreover, the law specifically provided for workers' cooperatives on public works projects, a more liberal version of the policy already adopted for France.

Although the plan was drawn up by an Algerian general, Lamoricière, in the ministry of another Algerian general, Cavaignac, it was not, as has been suggested, simply "the reply of the *militaires*" to other plans.[62] If the plan later fell under arbitrary control, a different fate was contemplated by the law. Although the army was to direct the establishment of the villages, they were to attain full civilian status after one year, and the Cavaignac government was taking other steps to free the civil territory from military control. The plan represented the views of no particular individual or group, but was a pragmatic response to the social and political problem posed

[61] For the speeches of Lamoricière, see *Compte rendu des séances*, III, pp. 942-944 and 984-987, 11 and 13 September 1848. Julien's view that the motivations were exclusively political does not take into account some of the evidence presented here, nor my interpretation of the outlook of the Cavaignac government.

[62] Droz, et al., *Restaurations et révolutions*, p. 458.

in 1848, channeled along characteristically statist lines. It contrasted sharply with the previously held views of Lamoricière, who had opposed colonization by the state and advocated exploitation by private capital.[63] Nor did it accord with any of the other widely discussed plans, such as that of General Bugeaud, the champion of military colonization, or of General Bedeau, partisan of free colonization. In outline, it most closely resembled the views of Cavaignac himself, who in 1847 had suggested the implantation at state expense of "poor" civilian colonists who would be legally protected from domination by capitalists. But Cavaignac had also advocated military colonies on the frontiers, and his aim in 1847 was primarily imperialistic rather than social.

Under previous "official" colonization the state had aided only colonists who had at least 1,200 francs of their own; under the law of 1848, all Frenchmen and their families were eligible, subject to selection by a special commission. In practice, only Parisians were accepted in 1848, and the few hundred colonists installed during 1849 before the plan died were mostly from Lyon.[64] The commission was strongly republican: it included Charles Beslay, the future Communard, and the fiery Montagnard Martin-Bernard. Trélat, who had been Minister of Public Works for the Executive Commission, was chairman.[65] In three weeks, 36,000 Paris workers had applied for the 12,000 places.[66] Working hastily, the commission prescribed few formalities, and by October 8 the first convoy was ready to depart. The demand was so great that in mid-November the government increased to 13,500 the number of colonists to depart before the end of the year.[67] The social benefits of the plan were still broader, for it provided jobs for many unemployed workers already in Algeria.[68]

The first colonists departed in ceremony. Lamoricière,

[63] Genet, in "Les Colonies agricoles," was unable to explain Lamoricière's reversal.

[64] Genet, "Les Colonies agricoles," pp. 107, 111.

[65] The members are listed in *Le Moniteur*, p. 2629.

[66] *Ibid.*, p. 2744.

[67] *Compte rendu des séances*, v, p. 684, 18 November 1848.

[68] Emérit, "L'Esprit de 1848 en Algérie," *La Révolution de 1848 en Algérie*, p. 20.

Trélat and other dignitaries made enthusiastic speeches, and a worker led the group in song;[69] on their arrival in Algeria, military bands and more speeches greeted them. But many colonists were soon disillusioned by the long journey under poor conditions, the bleakness of the forty-two "village" sites, and the authority of the military over them. Many of the agricultural colonists were miserable, but the workers fared well on construction jobs.[70] In December, *L'Atelier* was still so enthusiastic that it put the colonization plan beside the creation of the republic as the two most notable events of 1848.[71] Although errors had been made and conditions for many colonists were bad, Lamoricière and his governor-general in Algeria worked diligently, and "at the beginning of 1849, one could still hope for the success of the enterprise."[72]

But the election of Louis Napoleon was followed by a shift in policy. Succeeding ministers of war were hostile to the program; they stifled funds, maintained permanent military control, and harassed the colonists as "enervated men of the capital" and "insurgents of June."[73] After the convoys of 1848, only a few hundred more colonists embarked early in 1849, and soon many embittered colonists began to return to France, while others died of disease. Many contemporaries regarded the venture as a failure, but in long-range terms it was successful. All forty-two villages remained in existence, and some were very prosperous.[74]

[69] *Le Moniteur*, 10 October 1848, p. 2764.

[70] Emérit, "L'Esprit de 1848 en Algérie," p. 21.

[71] Droz, et al., *Restaurations et révolutions*, p. 458.

[72] Genet, "Les Colonies agricoles," p. 113. Julien, however, suggests (p. 369) that Lamoricière struck "a fatal blow" at the colonies in withdrawing agricultural experts for economic reasons.

[73] Genet, "Les Colonies agricoles," p. 115.

[74] Julien, *Histoire de l'Algérie*, p. 375. Cf. Genet, "Les Colonies agricoles," pp. 117-119.

XII · The Reformist Republic

INTRODUCTION

Most of the social and economic activities of the Cavaignac government noted thus far were undertaken to cope with the immediate problems of the depression, and none of the emergency measures gave rise to substantial and organized opposition. Political and ideological differences were submerged in a common desire to take action against the pressing problems of the moment.

But the Cavaignac period also witnessed an efflorescence of projects for reform of a social and economic nature; although some were in part attempts to deal with the *crise*, they also were intended to embody a more permanent solution to some more general social or economic problem. Moreover, many of these reforms derived from doctrines or theories or demands that antedated the revolution, or were elaborations or modifications of reform policies taken or adumbrated during the earlier phases of the revolution. It is true that some plans from the earlier period were scrapped after the June Days, but most of the more dramatic of these had existed only as demands with little chance of success either before or after June. It is also true that a few reforms made in the earlier period were retracted at least partially under Cavaignac. But if there were some retreats, these seem insignificant in comparison with the reforms preserved and the new ones attempted by the Cavaignac government. Because most of the new reforms were long-range in character, affected material interests, and involved principles on which there was wide disagreement, their consideration often resulted in conflicts among the several powerful segments in the Assembly, in particular involving the Réunion de la Rue de Poitiers, which was the bastion not only of the monarchists but also of the conservatives and the partisans of liberal economic doctrines. Some of the measures were accepted as merely expedient, some triumphed over opposition, some were modified in response to the opposition. Nevertheless, in spite of some total defeats the record of the

Cavaignac government in accomplishments in the social and economic spheres seems remarkable in view of its reputation as a government of reaction.

THE STATE AND THE RAILROADS

The retreat of the Cavaignac government from plans to nationalize the railroads is often regarded as evidence of the reaction against socialism.[1] However, although nationalization of important industries has constituted an essential aim of modern socialist movements, the problem was not posed in so clear a fashion in 1848, and it is anachronistic to view it in that light. The problem then was not nationalization but "rachat" of the rail network; it was a complex and already a traditional national problem, in which the 1848 issue of "socialism" offered little more than an ancillary source of conflict. Although the Cavaignac government renounced general *rachat*, it did so mostly on practical grounds and not out of hostility to it as a "socialist" scheme. Indeed, the Cavaignac government never repudiated the principle of nationalization of the railroads, and even embarked on a plan of partial nationalization. In both its ideology and its policies the Cavaignac government was far more statist and less favorable to the private railroad companies than either the July Monarchy or Louis Napoleon.[2]

The principal champion of general *rachat* both before and during 1848 was not socialist but the bourgeois moderate republican organ, *Le National*, which for years had assailed the "financial feudalism" of the railroad companies and urged the state to "buy back" the concessions. The issue became magnified in 1848 not only because the republicans had come to power, but because the economic depression made *rachat* seem desirable to many others. With many railroads foundering and threatening to throw thousands out of work, the Pro-

[1] See, for example, Ponteil, *1848*, pp. 151-153, and Guillemin, *La Tragédie de quarante-huit*, p. 359.

[2] The article by A. Matagrin, "Le Rachat des chemins de fer en 1848," *Revue socialiste*, XL (1904), 417-446, 529-571, is helpful but incomplete for the Cavaignac period.

visional Government saw *rachat* as a solution, and for a time even the companies favored it, as the only way to save their investments.[3] In April, the socialists of the Luxembourg took up the plan as one aspect of a proposed broad reorganization of the economy, and this provoked a propaganda campaign against *rachat* by "the reactionary parties."[4] But the plan presented to the Assembly on May 17 by the Executive Commission was a moderate republican and not a socialist one; Duclerc, the moderate republican Finance Minister, defended it as a republican and as a practical measure.[5] *Le National* vigorously supported the plan, while *La Réforme* and other radical journals paid little attention to it. The prominent Orleanist journals opposed the plan, but on fiscal and practical grounds, not on principle.[6] As late as June 3, most of the companies still wanted "to be bought back"[7] but opposition grew, and on the eve of the insurrection Montalembert scored an oratorical triumph by opposing *rachat* as a socialist scheme.[8]

Le National bitterly attacked Montalembert's views, and continued its strong advocacy of *rachat* after the insurrection,[9] but the Cavaignac government withdrew the plan. Undoubtedly it was motivated in part by its awareness of hostility in the Assembly, but Goudchaux argued simply that *rachat* was incompatible with its hopes of reviving "confidence" and with its other specific proposals. He said the plan would be too costly in the immediate future and would not show a profit until 1850. Moreover, it would entail a huge issue of *rentes* which, released simultaneously with those issued in reimbursement of the savings accounts and treasury bonds, would debase their value and injure the state's credit. But Goudchaux

[3] *Ibid.*, p. 439.

[4] *Ibid.*, pp. 439, 529.

[5] *Compte rendu des séances*, I, pp. 277-283.

[6] *Ibid.*, pp. 535-543.

[7] Statement of Duclerc before the Committee of Finance, A. N., C 927, minutes, p. 62.

[8] *Compte rendu des séances*, II, pp. 148-154, 22 June 1848. Cf. Renard, *La République de 1848*, pp. 359-360.

[9] See the issues of 23 June and 2 July 1848.

proclaimed "emphatically" the state's right to expropriate the railroads.[10] Cavaignac himself arose to explain that the government had weighed *rachat* against the reimbursement plan, and had retired the former when the latter was chosen. "As for the principle," he said, "it has been clearly stated, and we accept it completely."[11] As the government's intentions remained unclear, opponents of *rachat* in the Committee on Finance finally wrested from Goudchaux on July 14 a statement that *rachat* was "inopportune" and that "the present administration" did not intend to propose it.[12]

The government's subsequent railroad policies revealed clearly its continuing interest in state construction and operation to serve both immediate economic and long-range national needs. One of the most important lines, that from Paris to Lyon, was in particular difficulty, and on the eve of the June insurrection the Executive Commission had asked a state subsidy of six million francs, but withdrew the request pending settlement of complete *rachat*.

The Cavaignac government, on June 30, at first merely reintroduced the same proposal, but a month later decided to seek nationalization instead. Recurt sought to avoid controversy by using the term "reprise" instead of "rachat." The principal argument he offered was the necessity of maintaining employment for the thousands of construction workers. He asked credits of twenty million francs to buy the railroad stock and continue construction for the remainder of the year.[13] Goudchaux himself publicly supported the plan, as did other moderate republicans. Victor Lefranc stated the intervention-

[10] *Compte rendu des séances*, II, pp. 316-317, 3 July 1848. Goudchaux took the same position with respect to the much less important proposal for nationalization of the fire insurance companies.

[11] *Ibid.*, p. 324.

[12] *Ibid.*, II, pp. 480-481. Renard and Matagrin incorrectly assert that Goudchaux here "renounced" the principle of nationalization of the railroads. Goudchaux on July 14 made no statement of principle at all. Moreover, on August 16 he reminded the Assembly that he had not abandoned the principle (*Compte rendu des séances*, III, p. 196), and subsequent policies illustrated that this was so.

[13] *Compte rendu des séances*, II, pp. 889-891, 4 August 1848, and III, pp. 151-156, 12 August 1848.

ist issue clearly: "Something must be done to intervene between the impotence of the company and the necessity of providing work, and the state alone can do it."[14]

In the course of debate, the term "rachat" was freely employed, and although some deputies opposed on the basis of respect for property and contracts, the charge of socialism was not raised. Montalembert was absent, and Thiers was silent; against only scattered opposition, the Assembly adopted the plan on August 17. Although writers such as Renard and Matagrin attach little importance to the nationalization of the Paris-Lyon railroad, preferring instead to lament the failure of general nationalization, Louis Girard has recently emphasized its significance as a predecent for state construction and operation of a line "of capital importance."[15]

In late November, as construction neared completion, the government was faced with the problem, left unresolved in the August law, of whether the state should operate the railroad itself or grant a private concession. The Cavaignac government proposed that the state operate the Paris-Lyon road directly. In addition, the Minister of Public Works, now Vivien, suggested that the state begin immediately the extension of the line to Avignon, at a cost of 46 million francs. In summary, the Cavaignac government contemplated permanent state operation of this important north-south railway, and placed no theoretical obstacles in the way of further accretions to the state-owned portion of the network. Vivien even cited the possible "danger" in surrendering so important a national artery to a private company.[16]

The election of Louis Napoleon resulted in an immediate shift in policy in favor of the private companies once more. Léon Faucher, a vociferous opponent of nationalization, withdrew Vivien's proposal; in the spring of 1849 the government

[14] *Ibid.*, p. 202.

[15] *La Politique des travaux publics du second empire* (Paris, 1952), p. 38. This 1848 nationalization is ignored in the recent survey by Mario Einaudi, et al., *Nationalization in France and Italy* (Ithaca, N.Y., 1955). See p. 68 for the far less significant examples given of nineteenth century precedents.

[16] *Compte rendu des séances*, v, pp. 927-933, 29 November 1848. Renard and Matagrin neglect to mention this interesting proposal.

agreed to temporary state operation of the Paris-Lyon railroad, but only until arrangements could be made for a new private concession. In a direct reversal of opinion, another minister now cited the "danger" of permanent state operation.[17]

THE ASSOCIATIONIST EXPERIMENT

The Cavaignac government revealed its statist proclivities in another significant issue in 1848, that of "association," or workers-producer cooperatives. "Association" was one of the ideas for workers' emancipation most popular in the decade before 1848; Buchez and Louis Blanc were exponents of two varieties of the idea, and in 1847, as we have seen, the moderate republicans took a sympathetic interest in the notion. In 1848, many workers' cooperatives formed spontaneously, and shortly before the insurrection of June a moderate republican deputy proposed a modest measure of legal encouragement to the movement. Corbon of *L'Atelier* made a similar proposal on June 23, but nothing was accomplished until after the uprising was quelled.

On July 3, Goudchaux announced the government's support for state aid to the cooperatives,[18] and the following day Corbon introduced a new bill in a mildly "social" speech: "The moment has come, citizens and representatives, to broach frankly and clearly this question of association in labor."[19] The bill provided state encouragement by means of an appropriation of three million francs, to be distributed to cooperatives composed either entirely of workers or of workers and employers. The Assembly adopted it on July 5, without debate on the principle.[20]

In the eyes of many in the Assembly, the law was undoubtedly acceptable only as a sop to the workers or a cynical attempt to discredit the ideal of "association" by a deliberately abortive policy. Thiers, for example, afterwards told Corbon that the conservatives would have appropriated twenty mil-

[17] *Compte rendu des séances*, VI, p. 399, and X, pp. 338-340.
[18] *Ibid.*, II, p. 317.
[19] *Ibid.*, p. 336.
[20] *Ibid.*, p. 358.

lions if necessary "in order to make a dazzling experiment that would cure you of all that great madness."[21]

But the law was much more than that, for it had a great deal of sympathetic support in the Assembly, and represented a real victory for the advocates of "association."[22] Buchez and his followers, Corbon and *L'Atelier* and even Louis Blanc, regarded it as such.[23] Moreover, many of the moderate republicans were sympathetic to workers' cooperatives, and the government's support was forthright. As late as September a minister expressed the government's general desire to "see the principle of association extended" in order to bring to the workers "the benefits which today are exclusively reserved for entrepreneurs."[24] Corbon himself believed in the good faith of the moderate republicans, several of whom he later recalled as among those who had demonstrated "the most effective concern for the workers' associations."[25]

Moreover, the Cavaignac government sympathetically administered the law. It appointed to the administrative council charged with dispensing loans men known for their sympathy for workers' association, including Corbon himself, Alcan, the

[21] Cited by Emile Heftler, *Les Associations coopératives de production sous la deuxième république* (Paris, 1899), p. 70. Another study, *Les Associations ouvrières encouragées par la deuxième république* (Paris, 1915), is by Octave Festy, who also edited the minutes of the council, *Procès-verbaux du conseil d'encouragement pour les associations ouvrières (décret du 5 juillet 1848): 11 juillet 1848—24 octobre 1849* (Paris, 1917). A more recent study is by Yvonne Picq, "Les Associations professionnelles ouvrières en 1848," unpublished *mémoire* for the *Diplôme d'Etudes Supérieures*, University of Paris, 1942. Another recent work is Bernard Schnapper, "Les Sociétés ouvrières de production pendant la seconde république: l'exemple Girondin," *Revue d'histoire économique et sociale*, XLIII (1965), 162-191.

[22] Duroselle, *Les Débuts du catholicisme social*, p. 360, sees the law as "an unexpected triumph" for the school of Buchez.

[23] Armand Cuvillier, *P.J.B. Buchez et les origines du socialisme chrétien* (Paris, 1948), pp. 73-74; Corbon, *Secret*, p. 133; Louis Blanc, *Pages d'histoire*, p. 196. Cf. Gossez, "Les Ouvriers de Paris," pp. 813-839.

[24] The spokesman was Lamoricière, discussing the problem of association in Algeria, *Compte rendu des séances*, IV, p. 123, 19 September 1848.

[25] *Secret*, p. 131n. Goudchaux, Marie and Garnier-Pagès were among those listed.

author of the original proposal, and several other followers of Buchez; one-third of the council were writers for *L'Atelier*.[26] The council immediately adopted a statement, approved by the Minister of Agriculture and Commerce, that was forthrightly social and even socialist: "The National Assembly, imbued with the desire to see the condition of the workers ameliorated, and conscious of its duty to help wage-earning workers transform themselves into voluntary associates, wishes to encourage the spirit of association."[27]

Indeed, the very enactment of the legislation had stimulated the formation of many workers' cooperatives, "an associationist movement as strong if not as tumultuous as the one inspired by the committee of the Luxembourg."[28] By mid-November, 440 associations had appealed for government aid.[29] Many had been formed specifically to benefit from the July 5 law, and some disbanded if the loan was refused. But many others, "infected with the fever of association," disdained even to appeal to the state, preferring to remain "free."[30] In December 1848, a Parisian workers' journal observed jubilantly that cooperatives "are forming everywhere."[31]

The Cavaignac government, far from wishing to undermine the associationist experiment, sought further legislation to make it still more favorable to the workers. In September, Tourret proposed to exempt the cooperatives from certain legal fees and to hold the interest rate to a minimum; more significantly, he wanted to render state encouragement more permanent by creating a revolving fund of loans repaid, in order to continue "for the longest possible time the benefits of the decree."[32] By the time the proposals were debated in November, however, much hostility was expressed in the Assembly to the "socialistic" experiment. A deputy indignantly termed one of the larger cooperatives a "phalanstery." Tour-

[26] Heftler, *Associations coopératives*, p. 109.

[27] Cited in Festy, *Associations ouvrières*, p. 2n.

[28] Picq, "Associations professionnelles," p. 55.

[29] According to the Minister of Agriculture and Commerce, *Compte rendu des séances*, v, p. 570, 15 November 1848.

[30] Picq, "Associations professionnelles," p. 55.

[31] *La Ruche populaire (journal des ouvriers)*, (Paris, 1848), p. 351.

[32] *Compte rendu des séances*, III, pp. 914-915, 9 September 1848.

ret pleaded that preferential treatment was necessary if the associations were to flourish in a hostile business community, but the Assembly rejected all of his proposals except the minor one concerning legal fees.[33]

Meanwhile, the council had been considering the hundreds of requests for aid; as funds were limited, the council sought to encourage only the most viable groups. By November 15, it had granted loans to twenty-six associations, fifteen in Paris and eleven in the provinces.[34] Most were composed exclusively of workers. But the changing mood of the Assembly and opposition within the council discouraged Corbon and other Buchezians; in late November and early December he and four others resigned, and thereafter the council favored the mixed associations. Nevertheless, of the forty-six groups to receive subsidies by the end of 1848, thirty-one were purely worker organizations.[35]

During 1849, only about ten more associations received loans before distribution ended in October,[36] and on January 1, 1850, Louis Napoleon ended the program by decree when 400,000 francs of the original three million remained unused.[37] The experiment was by general agreement a failure; many of the associations foundered within a year or two, and by 1863 only three of the subsidized and eleven of the "free" cooperatives still existed.[38] Internal weaknesses seem to have been the chief cause of the failures.[39]

The July 5 law was the most important but not the only legal encouragement given to workers' associations under Cavaignac. Ten days afterwards the Assembly adopted another

[33] *Ibid.*, v, pp. 570-581, 15 November 1848.

[34] *Ibid.*, p. 570.

[35] Heftler, *Associations coopératives*, p. 145.

[36] Figures varied slightly in the three reports on the council's activities. A preliminary one for the year 1848 has just been cited. A report of December 1849, cited a total of 59, but one published in 1850 listed only 56. See Heftler, *Associations coopératives*, pp. 145-150.

[37] Picq, "Associations professionnelles," pp. 29-30.

[38] *Ibid.*, p. 56.

[39] Festy, *Associations ouvrières*, pp. 158-159, 188; Picq, "Associations professionnelles," pp. 61-66. Schnapper suggests that the council did not exercise sufficient care in selecting associations worthy of support. ("Les Sociétés ouvrières de production," p. 189.)

measure which granted cooperatives preferential treatment in competition with private entrepreneurs for public works contracts. The original bill had been introduced on June 12 by a moderate republican writer for *Le National*, and was adopted on July 15. It met considerable opposition, unlike the law of July 5, but the Assembly finally adopted a brief text stating the principle and leaving the details of administration to the Minister of Public Works.[40]

The regulations as promulgated on August 18 created "conditions very favorable to the associations."[41] The ministerial regulations emphasized the association made up entirely of workers, whereas the original and committee versions spoke of these and the mixed type impartially. Now groups of workers could contract directly with the government, eliminating the entrepreneur. Preliminary bonds were waived, and the government was required to grant preference to workers' groups in competition with entrepreneurs. The regulations also embodied another social feature: the creation of health and accident insurance funds by the associations was mandatory.

Even Vivien, the former Orleanist minister who succeeded Recurt, sought to implement the July 15 law "as broadly as possible." In response to demands from workers' groups, Vivien in November changed the regulations to permit the associations to undertake projects for the communes and departments as well as for the state. He also announced that a number of workers' cooperatives had formed in response to the law and were engaged in railroad and navigation projects.[42]

Despite governmental benevolence, however, relatively few associations were formed, and most of these in practice became "temporary leagues of workers organized by state engineers . . . a prolongation of the National Workshops in the prov-

[40] *Compte rendu des séances*, II, pp. 465-480, 14 July 1848, and II, pp. 487-494, 15 July 1848.

[41] Picq, "Associations professionnelles," p. 28. The regulations were published in *Le Moniteur* of 19 August 1848, p. 2057. They may be compared with those in the original Latrade proposal, *Compte rendu des séances*, I, p. 788, and the committee version, *ibid.*, II, pp. 431-432.

[42] *Compte rendu des séances*, V, p. 867, 27 November 1848.

inces."[43] Nevertheless, one of the associations, that of the *paveurs de Paris*, was a remarkable success. It handled projects worth 200,000 francs, and the associated workers earned more than the going wage in addition to sizable bonuses.[44]

THE MAXIMUM HOURS LAW

One of the most significant social accomplishments of the Cavaignac regime was the effective introduction into French legislation of the principle of regulating the workday for adult males.[45] This was done by the law of September 9, 1848, which established a legal maximum of twelve hours in all "mills and factories" throughout France. In principle this law was more advanced than the famous British "ten-hour" law of 1847, which legally protected only women and children. Georges Renard hailed the September 9 law as "the point of departure of all the legislation which since then, in France and elsewhere, has been elaborated to assure the right of leisure to the working class."[46]

The importance of this law is often overlooked because it is usually represented as a retreat from a decree of March 2 which set maximums of ten hours in Paris and eleven in the provinces. Although the increase in the maximum is obvious enough, in more fundamental respects the later action represented an advance, for it substituted meaningful legislation for an empty political expedient. Direct pressure from the Paris workers wrung the March 2 decree from a fearful Provisional Government;[47] even Louis Blanc opposed the reduction in hours.[48] The difference in maximums for Paris and the provinces illustrated the circumstantial origin of the decree; moreover, it was devoid of sanctions, and when these were added

[43] Picq, "Associations professionnelles," p. 30.

[44] *Ibid.*, pp. 30-31.

[45] Charles Rist, *Réglementation légale de la journée de travail de l'ouvrier adulte en France* (Paris, 1898), p. 25.

[46] *La République de 1848*, p. 297. Marx himself recognized the importance of the French law in proclaiming "as a principle that which in England was only won in the name of children, minors, and women." (*Capital*, Eng. trans., I [Moscow, n.d.], p. 300.)

[47] Rist, *Réglementation légale*, p. 37.

[48] Loubère, *Louis Blanc*, pp. 82-83.

a month later, they applied only to Paris. Finally, although the decree had some moral effect in Paris, the government made no serious effort to enforce it.[49] Nevertheless, some doctrinaire liberals sought to rescind the decree after the June insurrection, and even many deputies and others who were sympathetic to the workers agreed that the reduction in hours had been harmful to the economy and thus to the workers themselves.[50] Corbon and his Labor Committee hastily accepted the proposal for repeal on these grounds.[51]

Instead of bowing to the pressure for repeal, the government opposed immediate consideration of the issue, and when debate finally opened on August 30, it took a characteristically moderate interventionist position, retreating on the number of hours to a uniform twelve, but opposing outright repeal.[52] By this time, there were very few defenders of the original decree; even the workers Corbon and Peupin opposed it.[53]

The real issue was between the advocates of complete freedom and the proponents of a twelve-hour maximum. The government's proposal was not debated as a compromise, but was bitterly attacked and vigorously defended on the principle of intervention. Since Tourret was ill, Senard spoke for the government; many deputies were astounded at his firm and eloquent defense of regulation. Senard vigorously attacked the laissez-faire ideology and affirmed the necessity of intervention on social and humanitarian grounds.[54] Léon Faucher said he

[49] Rist, *Réglementation légale*, p. 36, and Loubère, *Louis Blanc*, p. 83.

[50] Rist, *Réglementation légale*, pp. 38-40. Louis Blanc had offered the same arguments in opposing the original reduction. See Loubère, *Louis Blanc*, p. 82.

[51] *Compte rendu des séances*, II, p. 347, 5 July 1848.

[52] Rist, *Réglementation légale*, p. 41, incorrectly states that Tourret had offered a proposal to abrogate the March 2 decree. See Tourret's comments on 9 September 1848, *Compte rendu des séances*, III, p. 906. Cf. the comment of Charles Dupin on 31 August, *ibid.*, p. 637.

[53] Rist, *Réglementation légale*, p. 42, incorrectly includes the two among the defenders of the original decree. Actually, they favored the twelve-hour version and voted against the motion to retain the ten-hour minimum. See their remarks on 8 September 1848, *Compte rendu des séances*, III, pp. 872-873, 879.

[54] See his speeches of 31 August 1848, *Compte rendu des séances*, III, pp. 645-646, and 4 September 1848, III, pp. 749-750.

was disgusted "to encounter the minister of the interior on the same ground as Pierre Leroux,"[55] and the *Journal des économistes* sneered that Senard "has proved that he understands nothing of these matters."[56]

In view of the government's stand, the Labor Committee repudiated its former support for repeal and advocated the twelve-hour maximum. The government strongly supported an amendment designed to protect the shorter hours that prevailed in some industries from being extended to twelve hours, and the law was adopted on September 9. The government's position in favor of intervention had been decisive.[57] *L'Atelier* was enthusiastic: "We applaud this first intervention of the legislative power in industrial questions; it is a conquest of the Revolution thoroughly in the interest of the workers."[58]

The law provided fines for offenses,[59] and the government sought energetically to assure enforcement. Although it lacked provision for inspection, Tourret contemplated the creation of inspectors if it could not be enforced through existing institutions, such as the *conseils de prud'hommes.*[60] In response to a government investigation, most industrialists indicated their willingness to accept the limitation. The regions most favorable were the most industrialized, where competition and misery were extreme.[61]

Thus, circumstances and the policies of the Cavaignac government favored the serious application of the law and its possible improvement. But the advent of Louis Napoleon brought a change in policy, for Tourret's successor (Buffet) was an outspoken opponent of the regulation that he was called upon to enforce. With one exception, succeeding ministers during the Second Republic were also hostile. Rist concludes that the law was a failure not primarily because of

[55] *Ibid.*, p. 647, 31 August 1848.

[56] Cited in Rist, *Réglementation légale*, p. 49.

[57] Rist and Renard agree on this. See *Réglementation légale*, pp. 46-47, and *La République de 1848*, p. 296.

[58] Issue of 7 October 1848, III, p. 226.

[59] Seignobos, *La Révolution de 1848*, p. 368, wrongly states that the law was "devoid of sanctions."

[60] See his circular of 18 September 1848, A. N., AD xix D 256.

[61] Rist, *Réglementation légale*, pp. 51-54.

inherent weaknesses or because of opposition from business, but chiefly because of this ministerial hostility.[62] The law was usually evaded under the Second Empire also,[63] but it remained the foundation for later regulation under the Third Republic. It was still the basic law in 1898 when Charles Rist wrote its history and pleaded for its strict application and the reduction of the maximum to eleven hours.[64]

OTHER LABOR REFORMS

In other matters relating to labor, the record of the Cavaignac government was uneven. It helped to preserve some reforms and initiated a few, but also supported one retrograde measure. Although it sought to appear progressive in labor matters, it failed to lend its support to some important reforms that were under consideration in the Assembly.

One of the most important reforms that was preserved and extended under Cavaignac was that giving workers equal representation with employers in the labor courts, the *conseils de prud'hommes*. Before 1848 these institutions, charged with settling minor disputes between workers and employers, had been favorable to employers, and one of the most insistent demands of *L'Atelier* had been for their reform. The reform was effected by a law of May 27, and the resulting democratization of the *conseils* was so favorable to the workers that employers began to complain that they were insufficiently represented.[65] Nevertheless, Cavaignac not only maintained the reformed *conseils*, but even broadened their jurisdiction in Marseille.[66] Corbon was so satisfied with the reform in September that he considered the *conseils* to be "new institutions, by which industry will be very well supervised, in the interest of the workers and the improvement of labor."[67] Em-

62 *Ibid.*, pp. 51-52, 56.

63 Georges Duveau, *La Vie ouvrière en France sous le second empire* (7th edn., Paris, 1946), pp. 236-239.

64 *Réglementation légale*, pp. 1-5, 340.

65 Renard, *La République de 1848*, p. 307.

66 See the executive decree of July 10, 1848, A. N., F 12 6714.

67 *Compte rendu des séances*, IV, p. 181, 21 September 1848.

ployers regained some of their former influence in the *conseils* by a law of 1853.[68]

Another policy of the Cavaignac government that favored the workers was its friendly attitude toward the *sociétés de secours mutuels.* Before 1848, such organizations needed special authorization and were regarded with suspicion by the government. Ironically, they received their legal charter of freedom in an article of the law restricting the activities of the political clubs, which exempted certain groups from surveillance. It was Cavaignac's Minister of the Interior who interpreted this article to include the *sociétés de secours mutuels.* In a circular of August 31, Senard forbade the prefects to exercise any kind of surveillance over these associations, which were to enjoy "absolute freedom."[69] New laws of 1850 and 1851 again reimposed controls over the *sociétés de secours mutuels.*

The Cavaignac government also carried out in good faith the vast nationwide inquiry into the conditions of labor and industry that had been decreed by the National Assembly on May 25. Tourret issued a long set of instructions on July 11, calling upon all government officials to aid the justices of the peace who were to conduct the investigations, and emphasizing the social purposes of the inquiry: "It is in making all of those concerned with the labor question understand that all are interdependent that we will be able to open for them a new career of development and of prosperity."[70] Senard also called the prefects' attention to the importance of the investigation from which "must emerge the solution for the vital questions of our time."[71] The inquiry, however, proceeded much more slowly than anticipated largely because of practical difficulties and the indifferent attitude of many workers. Although it has been charged that the investigation was deliberately

[68] Georges Weill, *Histoire du mouvement social en France (1852-1924)*, (Paris, 1924), p. 7, completely overlooks the 1848 reform, and erroneously implies that the 1853 law represented a democratization of the *conseils*. In fact, the 1853 law was retrograde from the point of view of worker representation.

[69] A. N., F 1A 2097.

[70] Circular No. 21, A. N., AD xix D 256.

[71] Circular of 5 August 1848, A. N., F 1A 2097.

"sabotaged," there is no evidence that the Cavaignac government had any such intent.[72] There may have been deliberate delays by the authorities in some areas, but a recent study shows that in the Alpine departments the effort was sincere. Particularly zealous were the bourgeois moderate republicans of the Isère.[73]

Actually, delay was most apparent and significant in Paris where the investigation was not under the jurisdiction of the government, but was conducted directly by the Assembly's Committee on Labor. Although this committee was presided over by Corbon and was sympathetic to the workers, the investigation was obstructed by practical difficulties and the fear of creating disturbances, and in fact was never completed in Paris.[74]

Another reform that was preserved under Cavaignac was the abolition of the most hated form of *marchandage*. The *marchandeur* was a kind of subcontractor, particularly in the building trades, who made his profit by exploiting the workers. This kind of *marchandage* was abolished in the same decree of March 2 that established the ten-hour maximum. Along with the attempt to rescind the legal maximum, "the bourgeois reaction,"[75] also sought to restore *marchandage* by completely abrogating the March 2 decree. Although the government took no position on the matter, the Assembly in adopting the government's maximum hours law defeated a move to repeal the abolition of *marchandage*, which thus remained under legal prohibition.[76]

[72] For this vague charge, see Rigaudias-Weiss, *Les Enquêtes ouvrières*, pp. 204-208, 213, 239. Mme Rigaudias-Weiss herself emphasizes (pp. 210-211) the indifference or hostility of many workers.

[73] Philippe Vigier, "La Seconde république dans la région alpine, étude politique et sociale," unpublished *thèse de doctorat*, University of Paris, 1959, II, pp. 492-493. Vigier expressly contests the view of Mme Rigaudias-Weiss. Cf. Bertrand Gille, *Les Sources statistiques de l'histoire de France des enquêtes du XVIIe siècle à 1870* (Paris, 1964), pp. 213-218.

[74] Rigaudias-Weiss, *Enquêtes ouvrières*, pp. 206-207.

[75] Renard, *La République de 1848*, p. 303.

[76] *Compte rendu des séances*, III, p. 913, 9 September 1848. Renard, *La République de 1848*, p. 303, errs in remarking that "Nothing, however, was decided."

In one matter concerning workers the government took a retrograde position, that involving productive work done in prisons. The Provisional Government, in response to demands from workers, prohibited work in prisons and army installations, and promised vaguely to end the labor in the convents. The decree was never applied in the army or the convents, but it was applied in the prisons.[77] In August, Senard proposed to lift the prohibition on work in prisons on the ground that enforced idleness was harmful to the prisoners and the prison system. He denied that prison work constituted "a disastrous competition" to free labor, as the Provisional Government had asserted, but agreed that competition with free labor should be avoided as much as possible.[78] The issue was not a partisan one; there were no protests from former members of the Provisional Government, and the Assembly agreed almost unanimously that work should be resumed in the prisons.[79] The Cavaignac government would have allowed the pronouncements against army and convent labor to stand, but the Assembly in January voted to restore previous conditions.[80]

The Cavaignac government by administrative action introduced two reforms beneficial to workers on public works contracts. In July, the Minister of Public Works, Recurt, instituted for workers on projects in the Bridges and Highways Department a system of compulsory sickness and accident insurance, in which the state paid for medical treatment and gave disability payments to injured workers or their survivors. He also extended these benefits to workers' associations taking advantage of the July 15 law. In December, this protection was extended to workers on all public works projects.[81] While the Assembly was considering legislation to guarantee the wages of workers in case of an employer's bankruptcy, Vivien ordered such a guarantee introduced into regulations for state contracts.[82] There is some evidence that the government con-

[77] *Ibid.*, p. 302.

[78] *Compte rendu des séances*, III, pp. 265-266, 18 August 1848.

[79] *Ibid.*, VII, pp. 61-62, 5 January 1849.

[80] *Ibid.*, VII, pp. 62-64, 115.

[81] A. N., C 924, dos. 549, letter of 25 July 1848, and F 1A 45, circular of 15 December 1848.

[82] *Compte rendu des séances*, V, p. 866, 27 November 1848.

templated other reforms which it never actually introduced, whether from anticipated opposition, changed circumstances, or a simple change of intention.[83]

Although the Assembly had under consideration several other labor reforms, notably for the abrogation of laws prohibiting strikes and for the creation of rudimentary social insurance, the government failed to give its support, and the plans died with the Assembly.

THE ABORTIVE ATTEMPT AT TAX REFORM

In the field of taxation, the Cavaignac government actually sought more serious reforms than had the Provisional Government or the Executive Commission. Besides a temporary tax on mortgages, Goudchaux proposed two new taxes: one introducing the principle of progressivity in the inheritance taxes, and the other a more ambitious change in the tax structure—the creation of a kind of income tax on the *revenus mobiliers,* a source of wealth previously left virtually untapped by the taxes on property. The Provisional Government had sought no such innovations; indeed, it rejected a tax on the *revenus mobiliers* in favor of a temporary increase in existing taxes, the famous 45-centime tax which, although it appeared to be an innovation, in fact was a traditional and profoundly conservative expedient.[84]

The Cavaignac government continued to collect the 45-centime tax, but Goudchaux announced his progressive plans immediately, in the same July 3 session in which he announced his hopes of reviving "confidence" by a sound financial program.[85] The divergence between the views of the government

[83] See Tourret's circular of 6 July 1848, A. N., AD xix D 256; Tourret's statement on 9 September 1848, *Compte rendu des séances*, III, p. 906; and Goudchaux's statement of 1 August 1848, *Compte rendu des séances*, II, p. 811.

[84] Antony, *Politique financière*, p. 160, and Schnerb, "Les hommes de 1848 et l'impôt," p. 16. Antony is excellent for the period covered; Schnerb is the best treatment of the Cavaignac period, but is still inadequate. See also Gossez, "La Résistance à l'impôt: les quarante-cinq centimes."

[85] *Compte rendu des séances*, II, pp. 316-317.

and the majority in the Assembly soon became evident, for while Goudchaux's "sound" policies were speedily adopted, strong opposition arose to his tax reforms, and in the end all were abortive.

The struggle between government and Assembly first became apparent over the proposed tax on mortgage income. This measure was the least important of the three, for it was to be only temporary. The Goudchaux proposal was a modification of an earlier decree of the Provisional Government; but whereas the Provisional Government had imposed a temporary tax on the capital of the mortgage (thus essentially another land tax), Goudchaux instead wanted to tax the mortgage income, at the rate of one-fifth of the annual interest.[86] The Finance Committee was hostile even to this temporary measure, for it embodied the principle of taxing income that Goudchaux had announced as his aim for a permanent change in the tax structure. In open debate, Goudchaux castigated Thiers personally and the committee that he dominated for opposing his efforts at reform. In accepting his credit policies, Goudchaux declared, they had been friendly "without knowing me." He agreed with them in defending "the family, property, and respect for all agreements," but he was determined to seek "a better fate" for "the suffering masses." Senard pointedly interjected that Goudchaux spoke for the entire Cabinet.[87] Boldly, Goudchaux asserted, "it is the *revenu mobilier* that I want to attack today, and it is the *revenu mobilier* that I propose to attack in the future."[88] By a close vote, the Assembly emasculated Goudchaux's reform by reducing the rate from one-fifth to one-eighth of the interest, and Goudchaux withdrew it in disgust.[89] A few days later, the Assembly rescinded the original decree for a tax on mortgage capital, and the whole matter was dead.[90]

Goudchaux's proposal for progressivity in the inheritance taxes also aroused strong opposition. The proposed rates were

[86] *Ibid.*, pp. 499-500, 15 July 1848.
[87] *Ibid.*, pp. 809-812, 1 August 1848; and pp. 824-828, 2 August 1848.
[88] *Ibid.*, p. 810, 1 August 1848.
[89] *Ibid.*, p. 871, 4 August 1848.
[90] *Ibid.*, III, pp. 40-41, 9 August 1848.

from 10 to 20 percent, above a 500-franc exemption. Members of the Finance Committee bitterly protested. "The progressive tax is communism!" cried one.[91] In open Assembly, Thiers sought to discredit the government bill by associating it vaguely with a revolutionary tax proposal offered by Proudhon.[92] A special parliamentary committee on September 1 rejected the principle of progressivity, and three weeks later, Goudchaux, apparently in an attempt to revive the waning political support of the Rue de Poitiers, dramatically announced that the government had retreated from the principle of progressivity on the ground that the country was not yet ready to accept it.[93] The Cavaignac government fell before the bill was debated. When Louis Napoleon's Finance Minister opposed even the softened version of the tax reform, the Assembly decided to shelve the matter.[94]

The most radical of Goudchaux's proposals was the tax on the *revenus mobiliers*. Such a tax had long been a republican demand, an essential part of a broader program which aimed to establish a more democratic tax structure "by relieving those who have been unjustly taxed until now, and by imposing taxes on those who have thus far avoided taxation."[95] The proposed tax on the *revenus mobiliers* was somewhat similar to the British income tax, and the English term was sometimes applied to Goudchaux's proposal. However, Goudchaux's tax, unlike the British one, was not presented merely as a temporary expedient, but "as the basis of a new tax."[96] The bill, introduced on August 23, proposed a tax on all profits from agriculture, commerce, industry and investments, and on high salaries. It was technically a proportional tax, at 2 percent of taxable income, but Goudchaux proposed minimums that would exempt 90 percent of the working classes, whom "we do

[91] A. N., C 927, minutes, I, p. 130, 8 July 1848.

[92] *Compte rendu des séances*, II, pp. 671-674, 26 July 1848.

[93] *Ibid.*, IV, pp. 260-261, 25 September 1848.

[94] *Ibid.*, VII, p. 607, 1 February 1849.

[95] As Goudchaux proclaimed on August 2. *Compte rendu des séances*, II, p. 827.

[96] *Ibid.*

not want to touch." The tax was to yield the sizable sum of 60 million francs.[97] A parliamentary committee, after a month of careful study, modified the proposal (notably in lowering the minimums) but did not reject it.[98] But before the Assembly took up the discussion, the Cavaignac government had fallen, and in January 1849, Louis Napoleon's government withdrew the bill. Goudchaux, then simply a deputy, immediately reintroduced his old plan, but the matter was obviously closed, and the Assembly never took it up again.[99]

Although the Cavaignac government remained true to the republican program of imposing new taxes on wealth, its record on the other side of that program, the reduction of consumption taxes that weighed most heavily on the poor, was nugatory and essentially conservative, if not hypocritical. Its record, however, was only slightly more conservative than that of the Provisional Government, which had set the example of denouncing the indirect taxes as unjust but deferring serious reductions. The Provisional Government had refused all demands until April, when it introduced two minor reforms, on wine and meat, and made a gesture at ending the most hated of the indirect taxes, the salt tax. The wine tax reform involved only changes in collection procedures, actually hurt consumers,[100] and was rescinded by the National Assembly on June 22. More meaningful was the immediate abolition of the duty on meat entering Paris, granted after the street demonstration of April 16. Superficially the most significant reform was the announced abolition of the salt tax, but this was only a variation on the previous policy of postponement, for the tax was not to end until 1849. Moreover, coming as it did on the eve

[97] *Ibid.*, III, pp. 393-396.

[98] See the long report by Parieu, *ibid.*, IV, pp. 520-531, 30 September 1848. The discussion of this measure in Marion, *Histoire financière*, V, pp. 281-283, is unsatisfactory. Marion himself calls Goudchaux's proposal "dangerous" and says that the Finance Committee reported unfavorably. In fact, the measure did not go to the Finance Committee at all, but to a special committee, and the report modified the bill only in detail.

[99] See *Compte rendu des séances*, VII, p. 244, 16 January 1849.

[100] Antony, *Politique financière*, p. 196.

of the convocation of the National Assembly and the demise of the Provisional Government, the announcement was merely "a decree for the gallery."[101]

Back in office after the insurrection, Goudchaux repeated the stand he had taken as Finance Minister in February, promising vaguely to end the salt and wine taxes "against which I have always fought," but asserting that "hard necessity" demanded their retention in the difficult present.[102] After the Assembly revealed its unwillingness to grant new taxes, Goudchaux felt it all the more necessary to collect existing ones, and in late August he proposed to repeal the decree of April 15 and thus to postpone to an indefinite future the abolition of the salt tax.[103] Ironically, on this issue the Assembly was more progressive than Goudchaux, for it voted to reduce the salt tax by two-thirds beginning in 1849.[104] Consistent to the end, Goudchaux argued that it was unrealistic, in a time of fiscal crisis, for the Assembly to reduce this tax while refusing to accept his new ones which "attack only the wealthy."[105]

The only real reform accomplished by the Provisional Government had been the abolition of the meat *octroi* at Paris. However, it soon became apparent that it did not have the intended effect of lowering the cost of meat to the poor. Because the meat trade was controlled by a monopoly, prices had fallen only on the quality cuts and not on the normal fare of the workers.[106] In consequence, the Cavaignac government proposed to revive the *octroi*, arguing that the loss of municipal income was preventing the execution of public works that would create employment.[107] A few deputies protested this restoration of a tax bad in principle, while conceding that the rich and not the poor had benefited from its abolition. Without serious opposition, the *octroi* was revived.[108]

In sum, the Cavaignac government adhered in principle to

[101] *Ibid.*, p. 202.
[102] *Compte rendu des séances*, II, p. 810, 1 August 1848.
[103] *Ibid.*, III, p. 571, 28 August 1848.
[104] *Ibid.*, VI, pp. 400-430, 27 and 28 December 1848.
[105] *Ibid.*, VI, p. 421, 28 December 1848.
[106] Renard, *La République de 1848*, p. 372.
[107] *Compte rendu des séances*, III, pp. 392-393, 23 August 1848.
[108] *Ibid.*, III, pp. 542-543 and pp. 613-619, 30 August 1848.

the republican ideal of reducing taxes on the poor and placing new taxes on the wealthy, but made serious attempts only to bring about the latter, and these were thwarted by the Assembly or the succeeding government. It is interesting that Goudchaux was a far more radical reformer under Cavaignac than he had been as Finance Minister in the very days of February.

POSTAL REFORM

Postal reform was one of the most significant and permanent achievements of the Cavaignac regime. Its enactment in August well illustrated the continuing vitality of the reforming spirit of 1848. Ever since the creation of the famous British Penny Post in 1840, there had been agitation in France for a similar reform, but the July Monarchy had blocked every such effort. Advocates were to be found in all opposition parties, and arguments of many kinds were offered. Before 1848, however, the chief arguments were economic and fiscal: reform would promote general prosperity and would increase the yield of the postal tax.[109] Postal rates then were commonly regarded as a tax instead of a charge for a public service, and the July Monarchy's resistance sprang from a reluctance to reduce any of the indirect taxes. The revolution, in bringing to power the former opposition groups, cleared the way for postal reform, and the social spirit of 1848 provided a strong new justification for it.

The radical republican Etienne Arago, head of the Post Office, urged the Provisional Government to undertake "this generous and brotherly reform."[110] A private member's bill for postal reform was one of the first introduced in the National Assembly, on May 19, and a week later the Executive Commis-

[109] Simone Pineau, "La Question de la réforme postale en France de 1839 à 1848," unpublished *mémoire* for the *Diplôme d'Etudes Supérieures*, University of Paris, 1958. I am indebted to this excellent study for much of my discussion.

[110] Robert Perotin, "Les Services des postes en France avec Etienne Arago," *1848 et les révolutions du XIXe siècle*, No. 182 (1949), p. 23. Perotin wrongly attributes the reform to Arago, for it was the work of the Assembly, exhorted by the government.

sion introduced its own bill. The June insurrection had no detectable influence on the measure. One of its warmest advocates was the former liberal Orleanist deputy, Saint-Priest, who had led the unsuccessful fight under Louis Philippe. Now, urging passage of the government's bill in August, Saint-Priest reflected the spirit of 1848, for "he emphasized more than before the social aspect of the question."[111] Postal reform was regarded as social in two senses, first as a tax reduction in the interests of the poorer classes, and second, as an aid to communication between workers and their families. Both arguments were offered in the Assembly, and by the republican newspapers, *La Réforme* and *Le National*.[112] The liberal economic arguments, previously predominant, "shifted to the background."[113]

The government of Cavaignac supported postal reform even more vigorously than had the Executive Commission. Goudchaux offered all of the usual arguments except the doctrinaire one deriving from liberal economic theories, but declared, "the question that I will call social is the first to come to mind," and it was this line of argument that he developed most fully.[114] Opposing an attempt by the economic liberals to set the minimum letter weight at 10 instead of 7.5 grams, Goudchaux argued that the higher minimum would benefit only "the rich," whereas the poor could correspond quite easily within the lighter limit. Dramatically, he cried that heavier letters would result from the use of an envelope, "a new fashion . . . thoroughly aristocratic."[115] Goudchaux did not go so far as to advocate the abandonment of the postal tax in favor of a concept of public service, but followed the Executive Commission in viewing postal reform as a reduction in an indirect tax. In the precarious fiscal situation, Goudchaux's attitude was rather daring, for the reform could inflict a loss of revenue, at least temporarily. Thus, postal reform was closely associated with

[111] Pineau, "Réforme postale," p. 141. The speech is in *Compte rendu des séances*, III, pp. 232-240, 17 August 1848.

[112] Pineau, "Réforme postale," p. 147. *Le National*, 21 August 1848.

[113] Pineau, "Réforme postale," p. 143.

[114] See his long speech, *Compte rendu des séances*, III, pp. 431-436, 24 August 1848, as well as comments pp. 442-447.

[115] *Ibid.*, p. 445.

other tax reforms, and Goudchaux admitted that he preferred to enact postal reform immediately, even at the cost of deferring abolition of the salt tax.[116] Probably many in the Assembly viewed the matter as a choice between the same alternatives; indeed, when reduction in the salt tax was voted in December, four representatives angrily demanded the abrogation of postal reform.[117] The law, as adopted on August 24 by an overwhelming majority, embodied the features introduced by the Penny Post: a low, uniform rate, and preliminary stamping. The 20-centime rate was still double that of the British, but it represented an 80 percent reduction in the cost of a letter from Paris to Marseille, and was far lower than any other rate in Europe. Most of the European countries followed France in establishing uniform rates between 1850 and 1863.[118]

THE REFORMS IN PUBLIC ASSISTANCE

The Cavaignac government did not merely provide direct relief for victims of the economic crisis; it sought to reform the entire system of public assistance in France in anticipation of recurrent crises. Although some writers disparage public assistance as mere charity, in fact recourse to the state to relieve economic distress, in particular that of the able-bodied unemployed, was in 1848 an "advanced" and thoroughly "social" reform. Aid to indigents had traditionally been the preserve of the church and of the communes; the French Revolution introduced the notion that it was the proper function of the state, but few of the plans of the Convention were ever implemented or survived the Restoration. With the recognition of a new "social" problem, the question of the role of the state again came to the fore. Some of the social Legitimists, although Catholics, began to argue that the state should assume the burden of the new problem,[119] and it will be recalled that when Dupont-White advocated government intervention as a remedy for the social problem, the forms of intervention that he suggested were free primary education and

[116] *Ibid.*, p. 447.

[117] A. N., C 923 B, dos. 428.

[118] Pineau, "Réforme postale," p. 149.

[119] Duroselle, *Les Débuts du catholicisme social*, pp. 216-221.

public assistance. The advanced cause that he championed was thus "to put charity in the laws."[120]

The importance of public assistance as an issue in 1848 was symbolized by the National Workshops and the controversy over *le droit au travail*, and, as we have observed, the duty of the state to provide assistance was written into the Constitution. The Cavaignac government subsequently sought to translate this aim into viable institutions. Although it succeeded in the least radical of its efforts, the largely administrative reform of public assistance in Paris, the Assembly blocked the attempt to establish a far more comprehensive program of public assistance in the provinces.

The Assembly also thwarted another government effort to reform a traditional institution of public assistance, the *Monts de Piété*, or public pawnshops. Most of these had been founded in 1777 "and may be counted among the social reforms which marked the last phase of the *ancien régime*."[121] But by 1848 they had become corrupt, charging high rates of interest that benefited officials and speculators. Nevertheless, the *Monts de Piété* were often the only resort for the poor, and in 1848 workers formed 70 percent of the clientele.[122] The Provisional Government had returned some articles free, and in August Senard proposed a drastic reform in the institutions: first, to remove the corrupt practices; second, to reduce interest rates from 9.5 percent in Paris (and up to 15 percent in some cities) to a uniform 3 percent, all in the interest "of that part of our urban populations whose sufferings are most real."[123] The Assembly did nothing more than study the proposal, although a much lesser reform was finally adopted in 1851.

The two major plans for public assistance reform were introduced in November, shortly after the promulgation of the Constitution. The magnitude of the proposals, more ambi-

[120] Villey, *Charles Dupont-White*, p. 419. Villey notes (p. 412) that half a century later Léon Bourgeois emphasized the same remedies as Dupont-White's "radical" solutions to the social problem.

[121] Alfred Cobban, *The Social Interpretation of the French Revolution* (Cambridge, 1964), p. 140.

[122] Renard, *La République de 1848*, p. 315.

[123] *Compte rendu des séances*, III, pp. 563-568, 28 August 1848.

tious than anything on the subject since the Revolution, was recognized by the socialist historian Georges Renard.[124] The plan for Paris was essentially a response to the defects exposed in the distribution of relief in 1848; the Provisional Government began to draft a reorganization plan, which was elaborated under Cavaignac and presented to the Assembly by Dufaure in the form of a bill. The most significant feature was a separate administration for outdoor relief.[125] With some modifications, the Assembly adopted the Dufaure plan in January, 1849.

The plan for the provinces envisaged genuine institutional creation on a vast scale and was particularly designed to cope with the problem of recurrent unemployment. Dufaure proposed to coordinate all forms of public assistance in France through an elaborate organization supervised by a central council in Paris. This was the first such attempt at coordination by the state since the Convention.[126] One aim of the centralized administration was to provide assistance to those areas previously too poor to support communal welfare offices. In addition, Dufaure proposed to eliminate any conditions of domicile for temporary relief: proof of need would henceforth suffice. The most significant innovation was the proposal to regularize procedures for providing work relief in times of economic crisis. Whenever and wherever need arose, local committees were charged with creating from public funds *ateliers de travaux* in which the unemployed would be assigned to roadbuilding and other public works projects. "It was," as Georges Renard observed, "the very principle of the National Workshops, more prudently applied, despite the efforts of the minister to avoid that name of ill-repute."[127]

Dufaure's plan revealed the influence of the social Legitimists, in particular of Armand de Melun, who dominated the committee that drew it up.[128] But it was more than a simple

[124] *La République de 1848*, p. 316.

[125] *Compte rendu des séances*, v, pp. 383-385, 8 November 1848.

[126] Dreyfus, *L'Assistance sous la seconde république*, p. 74.

[127] *La République de 1848*, p. 318.

[128] Duroselle, *Les Débuts du catholicisme social*, pp. 446-452. Duroselle implies a greater identity of Melun's views with the Dufaure plan than the evidence would seem to warrant.

adaptation of Melun's program; indeed, Melun was hostile to the important institution of the *ateliers de travaux*. Nevertheless, 1848 represented the most statist phase of Melun's thinking, and the entire Dufaure project was too statist even for the socially conscious National Assembly, which never acted on it. Dufaure as a minister for Louis Napoleon in 1849 again fought unsuccessfully for his plan, and in 1851 Melun retreated to a renewed emphasis on private charity but was still unable to win acceptance for a mild reform. Once the élan of 1848 was dead, charity was barred from legislation and again became the province of the church. The Second Empire and even the Third Republic for its first twenty years were marked "by stagnation with respect to public assistance."[129] Not until the rise of the solidarist and socialist movements in the 1890's were further reforms possible, but the century ended without witnessing another attempt at comprehensive reform comparable to that made under Cavaignac.

INNOVATIONS IN AGRICULTURE

There was one further area in which the Cavaignac government undertook innovations on the grand scale: agriculture. Preceding revolutionary governments had virtually ignored this important concern in a country that was still predominantly rural. Under Cavaignac, however, the government and the National Assembly began to express in agriculture "a meritorious fervor," and it was Tourret who above all "distinguished himself by his initiative."[130] Out of a host of proposals considered by the Assembly, the only ones to reach fruition, either in 1848 or in diluted form later in the Second Republic, were those that emanated from the government of Cavaignac.

Tourret introduced three distinct proposals, each a major reform in itself. These were: first, a vast state system of agricultural education; second, a new set of institutions for the

[129] Vladimir Rys, "Sécurité sociale en France et en Grande-Bretagne," unpublished doctoral thesis, *University of Paris*, 1958, pp. 12-13.

[130] Renard, *La République de 1848*, p. 323. Renard is one of the few writers to appreciate Tourret's role.

economic representation of agriculture; and, finally, a program of cheap state credit for farmers. The creation of the nation-wide system of agricultural education was, though short-lived, one of the most remarkable achievements of the Second Republic. A bill was presented to the Assembly on July 17 and enacted on October 3 by a huge majority, essentially in the form proposed. The plan provided for three levels of instruction, entirely at state expense. At the lowest level were the Fermes-Ecoles, model farms to be created in each of the 361 rural *arrondissements* of France.[131] Young farm "apprentices" would receive three years of instruction at state expense in these "schools." At a second level there were to be at least a score of Ecoles Régionales d'Agriculture, in which advanced students would study both theory and practice for two or three years, with scholarships available for needy students. At the apex was the Institut National Agronomique, a virtual "école normale supérieure d'agriculture," to educate professors for the regional schools. The plan went into effect immediately, but was expected to take six years to reach its full proportions. The statist nature of Tourret's plan represented a radical departure from previous governmental attitudes toward agriculture.[132] During 1849 the plan developed on schedule, even though Louis Napoleon's minister was personally hostile to it, but later the Legislative Assembly severely crippled it by reducing appropriations, and after the *coup d'Etat* Louis Napoleon suppressed the infant *Institut national* itself as too expensive.[133]

The second of Tourret's proposals was for a series of *chambres consultatives d'agriculture*, similar to the chambers of commerce. These were to be created in each of the 361

[131] Renard, *La République de 1848*, p. 323, underestimates the magnitude of the plan by saying that it called for one model farm in each department. That was the goal for the first year only. For a recent appreciation of these, "the most far-sighted agrarian reforms advanced by any French government during the nineteenth century," see Gordon Wright, *Rural Revolution in France; The Peasantry in the Twentieth Century* (Stanford, 1964), p. 9.

[132] Michel Augé-Laribé, *La Révolution agricole* (Paris, 1955), pp. 140-142.

[133] *Ibid.*, p. 184.

rural *arrondissements*, and all heads of families engaged in agriculture were to be involved. Tourret wanted the chambers at this lower level in order to give a voice to small farmers and to local interests. He also proposed to reform the national *conseil général d'agriculture* to render it more representative.[134] The Assembly considered the matter sympathetically, but went out of existence without acting on it; the Legislative Assembly finally adopted a similar plan in 1851, but with the *chambres* at the departmental level.[135]

Certainly the most audacious of Tourret's proposals was that for a *crédit foncier*. It was presented on December 18, as the Cavaignac government was going out of existence, although it had been in preparation for several months. Tourret proposed that the state grant loans to farmers at 3 percent interest, to be repaid in thirty-one years, and asked an appropriation of 10 million francs for this purpose in 1849. Any landowner would be eligible if his property was at least 50 percent free of mortgage.[136]

Although the Assembly had been hospitable to Tourret's previous proposals, strong and doctrinaire opposition arose over this one. "That is to proceed straight to communism!" cried the committee spokesman. Although Tourret denied that his scheme was socialistic, the committee disagreed: "The theories professed by the socialist schools have crept little by little into the general current of opinions, and have obscured some of the most simple truths." Nevertheless, the strength of interventionist sentiment in the Assembly was revealed by the fact that the committee rejected this plan by only one vote.[137] Louis Napoleon's government soon withdrew Tourret's proposal, and the later and famous *Crédit Foncier*, a private corporation, differed from it profoundly.

The government of Cavaignac thus ended as it began, one that, for all its moderation in comparison with the socialists, sought to use the state as an instrument of social and economic reform.

134 *Compte rendu des séances*, VI, pp. 257-259, 11 December 1848.
135 Renard, *La République de 1848*, p. 323.
136 *Compte rendu des séances*, VI, pp. 380-384.
137 *Ibid.*, VII, pp. 525-528, 25 January 1849.

XIII · The Drift to the Right

CAVAIGNAC VACILLATES

As the summer wore on, the fundamental weaknesses in Cavaignac's political position became increasingly apparent. There was an unmistakable current of reaction in France, as evidenced by conservative results in the municipal elections, by the reviving self-confidence of the *notables*, by the strong resistance in many regions to collection of the 45-centime tax.[1] The change in mood also began to reveal the inherent fragility of Cavaignac's parliamentary support. A government of *républicains de la veille* emanating from an Assembly dominated by *républicains du lendemain*, it rested on no firm majority, even if large majorities had accepted most of its policies. United against the socialists, united in the policies of repression, the uneasy coalition of moderate republicans and former monarchists drifted apart when it came to serious republican innovations such as Carnot's plan for primary education and Goudchaux's tax proposals.

Cavaignac had realized from the start that he needed the support of the Rue de Poitiers, but his personality, his political inexperience and his strong republican views made negotiations difficult. He was unable to come to an understanding even with Odilon Barrot, the man who had been closest to the moderate republicans before the revolution. Count Rémusat was designated to improve relations between Cavaignac and Barrot, but his discussions with the general seemed like "conversations between seconds for a duel."[2] Rémusat did not even bother to try to bring Cavaignac and Thiers together. The doughty Orleanist was incensed at the general's failure to approach him and made no overtures himself.[3]

As the fear of social revolution subsided, Cavaignac's popularity declined, and he sought to revive his waning prestige but was unwilling to make a clear bid for support in the Cham-

[1] See Gossez, "La Résistance à l'impôt."

[2] *Mémoires de ma vie*, IV, p. 351.

[3] *Ibid.*

ber either to the radical republican left or the monarchist right. It became increasingly apparent that behind his stern and confident manner, Cavaignac was a man of limited political ability. Firm only in his commitment to the republic and his determination to maintain order, Cavaignac proved indecisive and vacillating in his quest for majorities, alternating between statements of uncompromising republicanism and grudging efforts to conciliate the monarchists, making gestures that won no real friends but only served to further the decay of his influence.

His tactics were sometimes bewildering. In early August, Cavaignac had allowed the newspapers seized during the insurrection to reappear, but on August 21 he delighted the conservatives by closing down some of the more radical newspapers in Paris. Just three days later he struck them with alarm by seizing the venerable Legitimist Paris daily, *La Gazette de France*, on the ground that it contained "incessant attacks against the Republic and incitements tending to destroy this form of government in order to supplant it with the monarchy."[4] But the very next day, on August 25, Cavaignac gratified the Rue de Poitiers and angered many republicans by abetting the movement to purge Louis Blanc and Caussidière.

The following week, another policy of the Cavaignac government seemed clearly reactionary and calculated to appeal to conservatives. This was the support given to the movement to revive imprisonment for debt which had been suspended by the Provisional Government. The Committee on Commerce on July 3 proposed its revival, with some liberalization of the former law.[5] *Le National* was still opposed to imprisonment for debt, but on September 1 Senard announced the Cabinet's support for the revival, although he sought to deny that it was antirepublican by citing similar laws in Switzerland and the United States.[6]

Moreover, it was apparently at this time that Lamoricière,

[4] *Le Moniteur*, 25 August 1848.

[5] A. N., C 926, minutes of the Commerce Committee, p. 15.

[6] *Le National*, 29 August 1848; *Compte rendu des séances*, VI, pp. 689-690. A law reviving imprisonment for debt, somewhat less rigorous than the previous one, was finally enacted December 13.

acting as agent for Cavaignac, arranged for a staged scene between the general and Barrot in the Assembly. Cavaignac was to ask for the support of "all of the liberals and moderates," and Barrot would respond favorably.[7] Instead, in addressing the Assembly on September 2 to defend his newspaper seizures, the general delivered an impassioned speech that seemed to deny any basis of conciliation with monarchists. Recalling that "my father sat in the Convention, and I am happy and proud to be the son of such a man," Cavaignac warned, "whoever does not want the Republic is our enemy, our enemy forever."[8] Barrot remained silent in his seat, and was not convinced when Lamoricière insisted sadly that Cavaignac's "tongue had slipped."[9]

This "unexpected sally of republican vigour," in the words of Lord Normanby, alarmed the monarchists, for it seemed to be "the declaration of a political fanatic, capable of any extremities."[10] They heard rumors of another alarming statement from the general: suspecting monarchist intrigues in the National Guard, he had threatened that if he found the culprits, "I'll have them broken."[11]

In mid-September, the monarchists' fears seemed confirmed when they heard that Cavaignac was about to adopt a policy reminiscent of the Convention: he would send *représentants en mission* with unlimited powers "to energetically rally the provinces to the republican opinion."[12] The rumors were in substance true, for Cavaignac as early as September 5 had planned to send out republican deputies, although their activities were to be merely propagandistic.[13] Many in the

[7] Barrot, *Mémoires posthumes*, III, p. 16.

[8] The speech is in *Compte rendu des séances*, III, pp. 731-733.

[9] *Mémoires posthumes*, III, p. 17. Barrot does not give the date of this incident, and associates it with the impending presidential election, but Normanby also mentions the preliminary arrangements and connects them with the September 2 speech, in which he thinks Cavaignac was carried away by his convictions. (*A Year of Revolution*, II, p. 190.)

[10] Normanby, *A Year of Revolution*, II, pp. 189-193, 198.

[11] *Ibid.*, p. 193.

[12] Falloux, *Mémoires*, I, p. 360.

[13] See the circular of that date, A. N., F 1A 2097.

Rue de Poitiers were so incensed that they determined to bring down the government, but Falloux insisted that they seek only to destroy the scheme.[14]

The attack took the form of a parliamentary interpellation, in which Falloux was the chief spokesman. The criticism was strong but oblique, for the monarchists were still unwilling openly to challenge the republican government. In response to Cavaignac's denunciation of Legitimist intrigues, both Falloux and Baze, a former president of the Rue de Poitiers, insisted that they were moderate republicans, and as such, knew nothing of any such intrigues.[15] The conflict, said Falloux, was not between monarchists and republicans, but between republicans who were moderate and those who were less so. One radical deputy retorted, "You have organized the counter-revolution, and you don't want us to combat it." Opponents made the most of the charge that the government was remiss in failing to consult the Assembly on a matter that concerned it directly.

Although the plan was Cavaignac's own, Senard presented the government's case. At first he declared forthrightly that the aim was to "found the Republic, make it respected and loved," but in the face of the aggressive criticism he retreated, and finally said that the purpose was only to obtain information. Nevertheless, the government surprised even *Le National* by announcing that the issue would be a question of confidence.[16] But during a hastily called recess, the government learned that the opposition was too strong and tacitly accepted "an honorable capitulation."[17] The Assembly adopted a vaguely worded compromise resolution declaring that it left to the government "the judgment on the projected measure,"[18] and Cavaignac thereafter quietly dropped the matter.[19]

14 Falloux, *Mémoires*, I, pp. 361-362.

15 The debate is in *Compte rendu des séances*, IV, pp. 64-73, 16 September 1848.

16 *Le National*, 17 September 1848.

17 Falloux, *Mémoires*, I, p. 362.

18 *Compte rendu des séances*, IV, p. 73, 16 September 1848.

19 Senard, feeling himself compromised, offered his resignation, but the Cabinet refused to accept it. (*Compte rendu des séances*, IV, p. 891, 16 October 1848.)

Rancor remained. The influential *Revue des deux mondes,* heretofore generally amicable toward the government although critical of individual ministers such as Bastide, began to attack Cavaignac openly as contemplating "an irreconcilable war against anyone who will attack the republican principle."[20] In this new atmosphere of mutual suspicion and hostility, by-elections were held on September 17 in a number of departments, including the Seine. The results alarmed the republicans, for none of the governmental candidates was successful. Two radical republicans were elected, but the results in the fourteen other constituencies were clearly conservative or reactionary. Molé and a number of other prominent Orleanists were victorious, but the most striking result was the success of Louis Napoleon, who was elected in five departments. The elections revealed clearly what the government had feared since the local elections of July and those on the departmental level in late August, an unmistakable shift away from the moderate republicans.

Heartened, some of the conservatives sought to persuade Cavaignac to bring some former monarchists into his government, suggesting in particular the liberal Orleanists Armand Dufaure and Auguste Vivien. The general refused at that time, but he publicly acknowledged that there had developed "a cloud" between the Assembly and the Cabinet, and he voiced his hope to "make it disappear." To this end, Cavaignac appealed to the *républicains du lendemain* by saying, "We will not question your origin," but he seemed to counteract this appeal by insisting that "the flag of conciliation" must be "a republican flag."[21]

Cavaignac won a vote of confidence, but the cloud remained. Indeed, on that very day there occurred some incidents that served to deepen the distrust between the government and the majority in the Assembly. It was the anniversary of the founding of the First Republic, and the radical republicans took advantage of the occasion to stage a number of political banquets, ominously reminiscent of the campaign that had been directed against the July Monarchy only seven months earlier.

[20] Issue of 14 September 1848, pp. 947-951.

[21] *Compte rendu des séances,* IV, pp. 206-207, 22 September 1848.

In Paris, Ledru-Rollin roused himself from his temporary torpor to preside over a banquet where he made a vaguely social *profession de foi* and toasted "the Republic consolidated by some social institutions."[22] But it was the banquet at Toulouse that particularly aroused the fears of the right. The monarchist press spoke of crowds in the streets shouting "Vive Barbès! Vive la guillotine!," and reported that at the banquet itself the red flag was waved amid shouts and toasts hostile to the National Assembly and to Cavaignac himself.[23] What particularly infuriated the monarchists was the presence of the prefect and other officials, which seemed to signify governmental sanction of the radical banquet. Senard replied weakly to a formal interpellation on the matter, questioning the reliability of the reports and promising to investigate the affair.[24]

Another incident that revealed a gulf between government and Assembly was the vote in early October to submit the choice of the president of France to popular election rather than to the Assembly itself, as the Cabinet desired. But opposition congealed most effectively around the old problem of the state of siege. As late as September 11 the Assembly had voted by a large majority (515-238) to permit Cavaignac to continue to use the siege powers to seize newspapers if he judged it necessary. But when the issue came to the floor again exactly a month later, the government suffered what it regarded as a parliamentary defeat. The proposal to limit the siege powers emanated from the radical republicans, but it also had the support of many monarchists and even of some moderate republicans. The government stood firm on its previous position, but this time the results were different: the government won, but only by five votes, 339 to 334.[25] As the majority included nine votes of the ministers, Cavaignac believed that his Cabinet was in a minority, and he considered resigning. But the ministers insisted that he remain, while they resigned

[22] Seignobos, *La Révolution de 1848*, p. 113.

[23] *Compte rendu des séances*, IV, pp. 494-499, 30 September 1848.

[24] *Ibid.*, pp. 499-500.

[25] *Ibid.*, pp. 806-808, 11 October 1848.

in a body.[26] The ministerial crisis lasted several days. So erratic had been Cavaignac's recent behavior that it was uncertain whether he would turn to the left or the right for a new combination. Rumors circulated that he might appoint Flocon and even Ledru-Rollin.[27]

THE END OF A MONOPOLY

In the end, Cavaignac turned to the right. Barrot was shrewd enough to recognize that although his reputation and his words would seem to classify him "among the most fanatic partisans of the Republic," the general, habituated to authority, "was essentially governmental."[28] A firm alliance with the radicals was not only repugnant to him in some respects, but even the support of all *républicains de la veille* would not have given him the majority that he believed he must have to remain in power. Since the object was to broaden the government's base, it came down to accepting, in the words of Marie, "some representatives of the ideas of the majority. . . . The difficulty was a matter of replacing certain names, more or less compromised, with other names more or less sympathetic."[29] But in plain language such a shift meant that Cavaignac would finally have to accept some former monarchists, and thus to end the virtual republican monopoly of power that had existed since February. Another motive may have been to improve Cavaignac's position as a potential candidate for the presidency.[30]

Yet, although Cavaignac turned to the right, characteristically he did not turn far enough to be very effective, or even to negotiate directly with the Rue de Poitiers. He finally removed three ministers, and in their places appointed Dufaure and Vivien, both former liberal Orleanists, and Pierre Freslon, a *républicain de la veille* with a vague reputation for conserva-

[26] Cherest, *Marie*, pp. 283-294. The letter of resignation is preserved in the Cavaignac papers, Reel 22.

[27] Calman, *Ledru-Rollin*, p. 236.

[28] *Mémoires posthumes*, II, pp. 456-457.

[29] Cherest, *Marie*, p. 284.

[30] Rémusat, *Mémoires de ma vie*, IV, p. 364.

tism (although he was not a member of the Rue de Poitiers). The central figure was Dufaure, who was acceptable to Cavaignac as an apparently sincere convert to republicanism, but who agreed to enter the Cabinet only if he received the Ministry of the Interior. Dufaure persuaded him to accept Vivien, and also wanted Tocqueville as Minister of Education, but Cavaignac rejected the latter in response to threats of resignation by Marie and another minister.[31] Dufaure replaced Senard, who had long since lost the confidence of the monarchists. The others eliminated were Recurt, who had also been under suspicion for his sympathies for the workers of the Faubourg Saint-Antoine, and Vaulabelle, who had pursued too vigorously the policies of the fallen Carnot. Vivien took over the portfolio of Public Works, and Freslon assumed that of Education. The rest of the Cabinet remained as before.

Explaining the changes before the Assembly, Cavaignac admitted that his previous government had not accurately reflected the majority. He said candidly that he would have preferred to keep his former ministry intact, even in the face of waning support, but the ministers themselves insisted on resigning, and once called upon to form a new government, he was determined to create one that would command majority support.[32] Threatening to resign if defeated, Cavaignac submitted his combination to a formal vote of confidence. Dufaure then spoke for the new government, expressing a point of view scarcely different from what might have been expected from Senard, except that as a *républicain du lendemain* he had to emphasize his adherence to the republic.[33] Indeed, Senard himself affirmed his endorsement of Dufaure's policy statement and of the new Cabinet.[34]

Although some radicals bitterly protested the inclusion of *républicains du lendemain*, the new combination easily won a vote of confidence by a majority of 570 to 155. According to Barrot, this vote "taught the *républicains de la veille* that

[31] See Alexis de Tocqueville, *Oeuvres complètes*, XII (Paris, 1964), pp. 277-278; Cherest, *Marie*, p. 284; and Lacombe, *Vie de Berryer*, pp. 572-573.

[32] *Compte rendu des séances*, IV, pp. 888-889, 16 October 1848.

[33] *Ibid.*, p. 887. [34] *Ibid.*, p. 890.

finally they must resign themselves to share power with the moderates."[35] The only way for a minority to retain power against a majority, mused Barrot, is by "terror," which had been "the basis of the situation since February 24," but this phase was ended.[36] Indeed, a by-product of the ministerial change was the lifting of Cavaignac's mild counterpart of the Terror, the state of siege in Paris. Cavaignac tacitly surrendered on the issue that he had defended so vigorously in the past, and on October 19 the Assembly voted to end the state of siege.[37]

The ministerial change did little to improve Cavaignac's relations with the organized groups in the Assembly. Many republicans recognized the need for conciliation, but others were furious at the admission of the former monarchists. Indeed, Cavaignac avoided a formal announcement of the changes before the Assembly, apparently because he learned that the radicals planned to greet it with shouts of "Vive le Roi!"[38] The Prefect of Police, Ducoux, resigned in disgust, denouncing the new ministry as "the personification of the counter-revolution."[39] Even *Le National*, while agreeing in general terms that the government should represent the majority, criticized the specific appointments of Dufaure and Vivien;[40] it argued that the close vote of October 11 had not been a clear expression of majority sentiment, and that Cavaignac could have waited longer.[41]

Even the group that Cavaignac sought to placate, the Rue de Poitiers, was disappointed. The monarchist press at first was joyful and commended the general for having "broken with the small coterie,"[42] but the leaders of the Rue de Poitiers

[35] *Mémoires posthumes*, II, p. 463.

[36] *Ibid.*

[37] *Compte rendu des séances*, IV, p. 1008.

[38] Normanby, *A Year of Revolution*, II, p. 245. The changes were first announced in *Le Moniteur*, and discussed in the Assembly after deputies raised questions about the announcement. (See *Compte rendu des séances*, IV, pp. 866-867, 14 October 1848.)

[39] *Le National*, 15 October 1848, p. 2.

[40] Issue of 15 October 1848.

[41] Issue of 16 October 1848.

[42] Bastid, *Doctrines et institutions politiques*, II, p. 67.

were dissatisfied.[43] In the first place, one of the new men, Freslon, was a *républicain de la veille*; moreover, Dufaure soon gave indications that his conversion to republicanism was indeed sincere. Falloux was discontented with the behavior of both former Orleanists as members of the Cavaignac government.[44] Moreover, Cavaignac undid much of the goodwill he had won, by appointing another *républicain de la veille* to succeed Ducoux as Police Prefect, and naming the fallen minister, Recurt, as Prefect of the Seine.[45] In addition, only a week after the ministerial shift, Cavaignac stirred the resentment of many in the Assembly, republicans as well as monarchists, by firmly advocating the abolition of *remplacement* in the Constitution.

Dufaure soon revealed that his policies would be scarcely less republican than Senard's had been. Questioned on October 25 concerning another banquet, at Neuilly, Dufaure declared that the government had no intention of prohibiting such banquets, although it would repress any disorders that should arise.[46] Moreover, when some deputies demanded the dismissal of the prefect who had attended the controversial banquet at Toulouse, Dufaure said that the investigation had revealed that the prefect's behavior had been correct. He therefore refused to dismiss him, but because the prefect's authority was compromised, he transferred him to another department, the Vendée. Monarchist deputies from this department protested, but Dufaure stood firm.[47]

In late October, the right mounted another attack against the republicans by demanding an investigation of the financial accounts of the Provisional Government. Goudchaux vigorously opposed the move, arguing that "the time of investigations is past,"[48] and when the Assembly defied him by voting an investigation, he resigned.[49] To replace Goudchaux, Cavaig-

[43] Stern, *Histoire de la révolution de 1848*, III, p. 311.

[44] *Mémoires*, I, pp. 348-349.

[45] La Gorce, *Histoire de la seconde république*, I, p. 463.

[46] *Compte rendu des séances*, V, pp. 93-95.

[47] *Ibid.*, pp. 658-660, 27 November 1848.

[48] *Ibid.*, p. 83, 24 October 1848.

[49] Alfred Antony observes that here Goudchaux proved himself a "well-meaning but awkward" friend of the Provisional Government, for his

nac chose another *républicain de la veille*, Jacques Trouvé-Chauvel, who was reputed to be a friend of Ledru-Rollin, and whose appointment aroused the fears of the monarchists.[50] But Trouvé-Chauvel had become a staunch man of "order" after May 15,[51] and had worked closely with Cavaignac as Police Prefect during the June insurrection. In his first speech as Finance Minister, Trouvé-Chauvel reassured the conservative elements by insisting on the need for a balanced budget and emphasizing the necessity of "confidence."[52]

In summary, during October the republicans lost their governmental monopoly, not because of any irresistible political pressure, but essentially because Cavaignac and his Cabinet chose to respect the parliamentary principle of governing with majority support. But although two former monarchists entered the council, it remained dominated by the moderate republicans, who, under the leadership of Cavaignac, showed themselves unwilling to satisfy either the radical left or the monarchist right.

THE CONSTITUTION

In September and October, the chief object of interest in the Assembly was the debate on the Constitution. A committee to draw up a draft had been created shortly after the convocation of the Assembly in May, and a preliminary text was ready by June 19.[53] Thereafter it was discussed by the fifteen *bureaux* of the Assembly and reconsidered by the committee, which presented its final draft on August 30. The Assembly then debated the draft article by article, devoting Mondays

attitude implied that there was something to hide, whereas in fact the investigating committee subsequently concluded that though errors had been made, there was no evidence of dishonesty. (*Politique financière*, pp. 240-245, 276.)

[50] Bastid, *Doctrines et institutions politiques*, II, p. 68.

[51] Lemeunier, *Trouvé-Chauvel*, pp. 58-59.

[52] *Compte rendu des séances*, v, pp. 181-185, 30 October 1848. Cf. Bastid, *Doctrines et institutions politiques*, II, p. 68.

[53] The Constitution has been frequently analyzed. Some of the best and most useful discussions are in Curtis, *French Assembly of 1848*; Jacques Cohen, *La Préparation de la constitution de 1848* (Paris, 1935); and Bastid, *Doctrines et institutions politiques de la seconde république*.

through Thursdays solely to the Constitution throughout September and most of October. A complete text was adopted on November 4. Despite the crisis of June and all of the other pressing matters that occupied the Assembly, "never before had a constitution been so scrupulously elaborated."[54]

Although the final draft and most of the debates took place while Paris was in the state of siege, the Assembly exercised its constituent powers in complete freedom. The government made it a matter of general policy not to take a stand on constitutional issues, which Cavaignac regarded as the prerogative of the Assembly, but on several issues the general's opinions were solicited. First, the Committee on the Constitution sought Cavaignac's opinion on the method of choosing the president. He advocated election by universal manhood suffrage, but later declared his preference for selection by the Assembly. In addition, Cavaignac out of his own experience as chief executive suggested the creation of special *commissaires* to assist the president in his relations with the Assembly. This useful institution was introduced into the Constitution, and was revived in the "constitution" of 1875.[55]

The most significant intervention of the Cavaignac government concerned the issue of *remplacement*, the traditional practice whereby youths could avoid military service by hiring substitutes. This patent example of class legislation seemed incompatible with the egalitarian principles of 1848, and the original draft of June 19 provided for its abolition. But this issue touched the material interests of the *notables* who comprised the National Assembly; most of the *bureaux* took a somewhat embarrassed stand in favor of maintaining *remplacement* by advocating silence on the subject in the Constitution.[56] As a result, the Committee on the Constitution was about to delete the offending article until abolition received the vigorous support of Cavaignac and his Minister of War, General Lamoricière. It was Cavaignac, in fact, who had first broached the matter officially, for as Minister of War under the Executive Commission he had announced his intention to

[54] Bastid, *Doctrines et institutions politiques*, II, p. 71.
[55] *Ibid.*, p. 53.
[56] *Ibid.*, p. 46.

suppress *remplacement* as part of a general reform of army recruitment practices.[57]

Before the committee on August 12, Cavaignac insisted that *remplacement* must be ended in order to have "a good republican army," which he said should be based instead on universal military conscription for two-year periods. But he was willing, in view of the parliamentary opposition, to abolish *remplacement* through the recruitment law that was still in preparation instead of by a constitutional article.[58] It was Lamoricière, the *rallié* and former Saint-Simonian, who invoked most explicitly the egalitarian issue, in phrases surprisingly reminiscent of Karl Marx: *remplacement* permitted the rich to escape service with "a little money . . . while it obliges the poor man, who has only his arms, to give all that he has. It's an infraction against the law of equality." Lamoricière added the interesting opinion that former *remplaçants*, "bad citizens scarcely fit for working," had made up the majority of the insurgents in June.[59] Impressed by the two generals, the committee decided to maintain the article ending *remplacement*.

But this issue aroused strong opposition in the world of the *notables*, and in response to a strong campaign in the press and a flood of petitions, conservative deputies in the National Assembly were heartened to take a stand in favor of preserving *remplacement*.[60] By the time of general debate in October, the committee had changed its position again, and had deleted the article. The Cavaignac government, having recently decided to admit the two former monarchists, also retreated. While opposing *remplacement* in principle, it no longer demanded its explicit suppression. Thiers and other monarchists defended *remplacement* as a necessary and even "democratic" institution, and hinted at the alarm felt among the bourgeoisie. Lamoricière, in a somewhat excited speech, retorted, "I fear that, when they speak to us in the name of the majority of worried fathers and mothers, it is rather a ques-

[57] *Compte rendu des séances*, I, pp. 740-741, 9 June 1848.
[58] A. N., C 918, minutes, II, p. 71, 12 August 1848.
[59] *Ibid.*, pp. 72-73, 14 August 1848.
[60] Tudesq, *Les Grands notables*, II, pp. 1153-1161.

tion of a majority of francs rather than a majority of votes."[61] As Lamoricière returned to his seat, Cavaignac embraced him, but the Assembly was unimpressed, and defeated by a vote of 663 against 140 the motion to prohibit *remplacement* in the Constitution. On this issue, many of the bourgeois republicans did indeed seem to desert the principle of equality to defend class interests.

As we have seen, many of the republicans also sided with the majority in the Assembly against a much more controversial issue, *le droit au travail.* But although the socialist slogan and prohibition of *remplacement* were deleted, perhaps the most remarkable thing about the Constitution of November 4 was the fact that it retained virtually all of the other essential features of the original draft of June 19. Most of the other changes were slight verbal adjustments, and the Constitution itself is evidence of the survival of republican and democratic influence long after the June Days.

The Constitution of 1848 was by far the most democratic drawn up in France in the nineteenth century. In the first place, it was unambiguously republican. None of the monarchists dared mount a frontal attack on the republican form of government in the Assembly, although some of them made a half-hearted and disguised attempt to avoid formally consecrating the republic by suppressing the entire preamble as unnecessary. Article I of the preamble in the final draft declared that France had adopted the republic as its "definitive" form of government, and Article II asserted, "The French Republic is democratic, one, and indivisible." When the preamble came up for discussion in early September, there was no attack on either of these statements, and in arguing for suppression, several deputies criticized less crucial ones. But none of the prominent figures of the Rue de Poitiers lent his oratorical support to the bid for suppression, and after a stirring speech by Lamartine in favor of the preamble, a majority of 481 to 225 voted to retain it. Thereafter Article I was adopted without opposition. In Article II, Larochejaquelein suggested that the word "democratic" needed definition, but

[61] *Compte rendu des séances,* v, pp. 15-16, 21 October 1848.

did not allude to the republic, and the article was adopted unanimously by a formal vote of 777 to 0.[62] How different from 1875, when another monarchist-dominated Assembly adopted by a single vote the celebrated Wallon amendment embodying the term "republic" in another constitution!

Republican doctrines also found expression in the creation of a unicameral legislature, after a move led by Duvergier de Hauranne to create a second chamber was defeated by a vote of 350 to 289. Thiers, a dogmatic advocate of two chambers, later told Nassau Senior that he and his colleagues of the Rue de Poitiers had attached no great importance to the political institutions created by the Constitution, because they were confident that these would be "ephemeral."[63] In the Constitution, the continuous authority and independence of the Legislative Assembly were assured by the provision for a special functioning committee between sessions, ministerial responsibility and the absence of a power of dissolution. In addition, the demands of the prerevolutionary reform movement were satisfied by a constitutional provision which declared government officials ineligible for election to the Assembly.

In general, the democratic doctrines of the republicans were confirmed as the basis of French political life. The principle of popular sovereignty was proclaimed, to be expressed through the legislature elected by universal, direct and secret manhood suffrage for all Frenchmen at the age of twenty-one. Moreover, all Frenchmen were eligible for election at the age of twenty-five, and the deputies would be paid. Equality of electoral districts was not written into the Constitution, but was assumed, and would be employed in the 1849 elections, as it had been in 1848.[64] The remarkably advanced and demo-

[62] For the debate on these issues, see *Compte rendu des séances*, III, pp. 793-847, 5-7 September 1848.

[63] Senior, *Conversations with M. Thiers*, II, p. 30.

[64] The conservatives did not oppose universal suffrage directly, but argued for the commune rather than the department or the canton as the basic electoral unit. The significance of the debates on this issue has recently been emphasized by R. Balland, in "De l'Organisation à la restriction du suffrage universel en France (1848-1850)," *Réaction et*

cratic nature of the Constitution may be appreciated by the reflection that it embodied five of the six demands of the English Chartists that had been rejected as preposterous a few months earlier, and that would not be fully accepted in England until the twentieth century.[65]

The Constitution provided for the expression of popular sovereignty in still another respect: the election of a strong president by universal manhood suffrage. The presidential executive did not represent the implementation of traditional republican doctrine, but resulted largely from the experience of 1848 as well as from a consideration of American practice. Because of the appearance of Louis Napoleon Bonaparte as a serious candidate, the nature of the executive power and the process of selection were crucial political as well as constitutional issues in the autumn of 1848, and will be examined later in connection with the campaign. In the Constitution, in addition to institutions founded on universal suffrage, other great principles of February were reaffirmed: freedoms of press, assembly and petition; the condemnation of arbitrary procedures (these at least in principle); and the abolition of slavery in all French possessions. The revolutionary nature of the institutional changes created by the Constitution of 1848 contrasts sharply with the results of 1830 or with the compromise and more conservative "constitution" of 1875.

The Constitution was adopted on November 4 by an overwhelming majority of 739 to 30. Those voting against were a few monarchists, including Berryer, Larochejaquelein and Montalembert, and radicals and socialists such as the worker Greppo, Pierre Leroux, Proudhon and Pyat. Barrot abstained, but most of the monarchists voted in favor of the Constitution, including Falloux, Molé, Rémusat and Thiers.[66] The Constitution was promulgated in a ceremony in the Place de la Con-

---

suffrage universel en France et en Allemagne (1848-1850) "Bibliothèque de la révolution de 1848," XXII (Paris, 1963), pp. 84-88.

[65] The provision for triennial legislatures even approached the sixth Chartist demand, that for annual parliaments, which, of course, has never been implemented in Great Britain.

[66] *Le Moniteur*, 5 November 1848, p. 3093, carried the names of those voting. Cf. Barrot, *Mémoires posthumes*, II, p. 474.

corde on November 12, 1848. Armand Marrast as president of the National Assembly presided, with Cavaignac at his right and the Minister of Justice at his left. The solemn ceremony, performed as a cold rain mixed with snow fell from dark clouds, aroused little enthusiasm. The Assembly chosen in the republican spring had produced a republican Constitution, but did France, or even Paris, want a republic any longer?

XIV · The Republic Means Peace

CONTINUITY OF POLICY

ALTHOUGH the government of Cavaignac was concerned primarily with domestic affairs, in a year of continuing revolutionary turmoil in Europe, foreign affairs also occupied its attention. Moreover, from the beginning the general himself had taken a great personal interest in foreign policy, and he played an important role in shaping it throughout his six months in office.

What was the foreign policy that the Cavaignac government inherited? From the first, the French republic had adopted a peaceful posture before monarchical Europe, but at the same time proclaimed its sympathy with the liberal nationalist movements that emerged in the revolutionary ferment of 1848. Although the republican *mystique* had included an aggressive nationalistic element that found vociferous proponents in radical Paris after February, the Provisional Government took a moderate position in foreign affairs, as it had done in domestic affairs. Lamartine was the chief architect of this policy of seeking a kind of peaceful coexistence with the monarchist governments, while attempting to preserve a revolutionary appeal. This ambiguous and contradictory but essentially conservative attitude was expressed notably in Lamartine's grandiloquent "manifesto" of March 4, which denied the legality of the 1815 settlement while accepting it in fact, promised that "the French republic will not start war against anyone," and concluded that the republic signified "peace."[1]

Despite Lamartine's conciliatory attitude, Europe held aloof from the republic; even the poet's efforts to establish an entente with England were greeted with cautious aversion. Some governments were alarmed, that of Russia in particular, and the French republic began immediately to improve its

[1] The famous "manifesto" of Lamartine was actually a circular dated March 2 and issued to all French diplomatic agents but it was also widely published. It is reproduced in *Documents diplomatiques du gouvernement provisoire et de la commission du pouvoir exécutif*, ed. Charles H. Pouthas, I (Paris, 1953), No. 8, pp. 7-11.

military posture by concentrating near the eastern and southeastern frontiers forces that soon would become known as the Army of the Alps.[2] The revolution of March 13 in Vienna brought down Metternich and unleashed powerful new tremors in Central Europe and northern Italy. In Paris, French and foreign radical groups urged the Provisional Government to go to the aid of national movements; Lamartine was willing to intervene in Italy, but the Italians, fearing French aggrandizement, rejected the offer. Thus, republican France remained diplomatically isolated and cautiously peaceful while Europe trembled with revolution.[3]

The moderate and fundamentally conservative foreign policy of the Provisional Government was not displeasing to the National Assembly. Although the Assembly became a forum for the advocates of a more active foreign policy, the majority approved that of Lamartine, which was continued in all essentials by Bastide, who became Foreign Minister for the Executive Commission. The Assembly implicitly endorsed the manifesto of March 4, but on May 24 bowed to the pressure in favor of national movements to the extent of adopting a deliberately ambiguous resolution: "The National Assembly requests the Executive Commission to continue to take for guidance in its conduct the unanimous will of the National Assembly as summarized in these words: A fraternal pact with Germany, the restoration of a free and independent Poland, and the liberation of Italy."[4] The three goals were not so much guides to action as hopes for the future; although the intentions seemed clear, the means of execution were uncertain and largely incompatible with the Assembly's more fundamental desire to keep the peace. When Cavaignac came to power, then, France was, as it had been since February, diplomatically

[2] Boyer, "L'Armée des Alpes," pp. 71-73.

[3] A good recent summary of the diplomatic aspects of 1848 in Europe is A.J.P. Taylor, *The Struggle for Mastery in Europe 1848-1918* (Oxford, 1954), pp. 1-23. See also the article by Charles H. Pouthas, "The Revolutions of 1848," in the *New Cambridge Modern History*, x, pp. 389-415. The treatment by Pierre Renouvin in *Histoire des relations internationales V: Le XIXe siècle, I: de 1815 à 1871* (Paris, 1954), pp. 193-218, is inaccurate in some details on the Cavaignac period.

[4] *Compte rendu des séances*, I, p. 415.

isolated but at peace, expressing sympathy for the national movements but doing nothing concrete to aid them.

Although it has been argued or implied that French foreign policy became reactionary following the June Days, the evidence suggests that the Republic of Cavaignac continued in all major respects the foreign policy of the preceding revolutionary governments.[5]

By retaining Jules Bastide as Foreign Minister, Cavaignac indicated his intention to continue the foreign policy followed by the republic since its inception, for Bastide had been associated with the creation of that policy since February, first as general secretary under Lamartine, then as foreign minister

[5] The conception of reaction in foreign policy has seemed to some writers a natural corollary to that of reaction in domestic policy, but is less frequently asserted, for the facts do not easily fit the pattern. See, e.g., Renard, *La République de 1848*, pp. 86, 142-143. An interesting commentary is George Bourgin's *1848: Naissance et mort d'une république* (Paris, 1948); on p. 157, assimilating foreign policy to the domestic scene, Bourgin observes "with the dictatorship of Cavaignac there began another cycle, that of the republic asphyxiated by reaction," but on p. 162, when he considers foreign policy in detail, he observes that from May to December, while Bastide was Foreign Minister, "there was no real change in French policy."

Of the specialized works on foreign policy, that of D. M. Greer, *L'Angleterre, la France, et la révolution de 1848* (Paris, 1925), detects a change to a more conservative policy after June, but more recent works are free of this argument, although some find a shift in emphasis when Bastide replaced Lamartine in May. See, e.g., A.J.P. Taylor, *The Italian Problem in European Diplomacy, 1847-1849* (Manchester, 1934); the series of articles by Paul Henry in the *Revue historique*, CLXXVIII (1936), CLXXXVI (1939), and CLXXXVIII (1940); and César Vidal, "La France et la question italienne en 1848," *Etudes d'histoire moderne et contemporaine*, II (1948). The most recent student of Bastide, Ferdinand Boyer, in "Les Rapports entre la France et le Piémont sous le premier ministère de Jules Bastide (11 mai—28 juin 1848)," *Revue d'histoire moderne et contemporaine*, V (1958), 129-136, argues that as Foreign Minister for the Executive Commission, Bastide continued the essential policies of Lamartine. Robert J. Hahn, in "The Attitude of the French Revolutionary Government Toward German Unification in 1848," unpublished Ph.D. dissertation, Ohio State University, 1955, speculates that the June insurrection may have influenced to some extent a transitory shift that he finds in French policy during the late summer, but concedes that this "can only be inferred . . . as it left no significant traces in the diplomatic correspondence of the period." (p. 163.)

in his own right. Another source of continuity was Cavaignac's avowed subservience to the National Assembly, of which he considered himself the agent in foreign as in domestic affairs.

Yet there were new conditions which enabled the Cavaignac government to develop its own distinctive, though not reactionary, character within the inherited framework. First, the insurrection of June and the forces required for its suppression weakened the military posture of France. Second, the defeat of the insurgents and the new stability imposed by Cavaignac altered to some extent the attitude of foreign governments toward the French republic. Third, during the six months of the Cavaignac administration, the rapidly changing events of a Europe in ferment posed new problems that demanded new policy decisions. Finally, there were the personality and the views of Cavaignac himself.

THE VIEWS OF CAVAIGNAC

Instead of allowing Bastide complete freedom to conduct his ministry, Cavaignac took a direct and continuing interest in foreign affairs, and French policy was a joint product of the two men. Indeed, although Bastide was an active and resourceful minister who conducted most of the diplomatic correspondence, the general himself seems to have been the ultimate architect of policy.[6] As soon as his government was formed, Cavaignac had Bastide supply him with detailed information on the diplomatic problems facing France, including in

[6] This discussion is based primarily on documents preserved in the Cavaignac archives. The general's interest in foreign affairs is attested by the hundreds of notes, letters, reports, clippings, précis, instructions and diplomatic miscellanea that he preserved; they fill three cartons, and are reproduced on microfilm, Reels 24, 25 and 26. Some of the documents are merely duplicates of letters preserved in the Archives des Affaires Etrangères, but many are not, having been the personal correspondence of the general. Most writers assume, on the basis of official correspondence, together with Bastide's published apology, *La République française et l'Italie en 1848*, that Bastide formulated most if not all of French policy. However, the Cavaignac papers contain several important and comprehensive policy statements which form the basis for many fragmentary views expressed by Bastide and other French diplomats in the official correspondence.

some cases copies of all official correspondence since February. Thereafter he maintained a constant if friendly surveillance over Bastide while sometimes personally explaining the French position to foreign diplomats and to the Assembly's Committee on Foreign Affairs, corresponding with foreign heads of state and sometimes with French agents abroad, and on important issues drafting his own instructions to French envoys. Cavaignac, who had been the colleague of Bastide in the ministry of the Executive Commission, retained him because he was in substantial agreement with his views. Yet Cavaignac's dominance seems clear; the casualness with which the general divested Bastide of the portfolio of foreign affairs for almost three weeks well illustrated the locus of authority. Because Cavaignac combined in himself, moreover, the roles both of head of state and of first minister, he was in a stronger position than even Lamartine had enjoyed to represent France to foreign powers.

It is to the views of Cavaignac that we must turn for full understanding of his government's foreign policy. Although he insisted, and undoubtedly believed, that his task was to carry out the aims of the National Assembly, some policies that he personally formulated and sought to implement differed at least in emphasis from the general principles enunciated by the Assembly.[7]

Following Lamartine and Bastide, Cavaignac made his principal aim not aid to the national movements, but the maintenance of peace. But whereas Lamartine's policy arose largely from his own pacificism and his romantic hopes for a fraternal reorganization of Europe, Bastide and Cavaignac regarded peace as desirable on grounds more related to their political faith. Cavaignac in particular, mindful of the results of revolutionary warfare during the first French Revolution, feared that war would result in a military dictatorship in France, and

[7] This analysis is based primarily on three documents preserved in the Cavaignac archives: the instructions of August 8, 1848, prepared for the special envoy to England, Beaumont; the instructions of September 9, 1848, prepared for the special envoy to Russia, Le Flô; and notes for a major foreign policy speech that Cavaignac never delivered. The Le Flô instructions are in Reel 24, the other documents in Reel 25.

conquest rather than liberation abroad. Cavaignac's foreign policy views were closely associated with his attitudes toward domestic politics, as Bastide discovered very early. His refusal to assume a dictatorship and his desire for peace stemmed from the belief that it was wrong to seek to impose republican principles by force either internally or externally.[8]

Although Cavaignac might have been able to win fame and perpetuate himself in power by going to war, recalled Bastide, he preferred instead "the modest role of the man who founds the liberty of his country through peace."[9] The republic, wrote Cavaignac, "does not want it to appear that the democratic principle can be proclaimed and defended only by the cannon";[10] moreover, there was the danger that "war waged by us might stifle the liberty emerging in other countries."[11]

But though peace was desirable, Cavaignac believed that it would serve the interests of the republic only if she could end her diplomatic isolation by finding allies among the monarchist states—alliances based on material interests despite conflicting political principles. Specifically, Cavaignac followed Lamartine in seeking alliances not only with liberal England but also with autocratic Russia, and he contemplated others. But far more than Lamartine, Cavaignac was prepared if necessary to unleash the full force of the French republic's ideological appeal if no allies could be found. In approaching England, Cavaignac wrote, "If all of Europe were to reply that the principle of her constitution is incompatible with governments as they exist, the Republic could then do nothing other than to support itself abroad on ideas and on the masses. . . . If . . . France remains isolated, she will wage war, she will do it because the peace of isolation would be fatal to her."[12] Although he sought an alliance with Russia, he explicitly warned the Tsar that in case of war, republican France would not hesitate to encourage the revolutionary force of Polish nationalism.[13]

[8] Bastide, *La République française et l'Italie*, pp. 221-222.
[9] *Ibid.*, p. 222.
[10] Beaumont instructions, Reel 25.
[11] Speech notes, Reel 25.
[12] Beaumont instructions, Reel 25.
[13] Le Flô instructions, Reel 24.

Cavaignac expressed this alternative policy of generating revolutionary warfare in secret instructions to his ambassadors to England and to Russia, but he never made it public, not even to the National Assembly.[14] On this and some other issues, Cavaignac was far from frank in advising the Assembly of his thinking; although he always acknowledged the Assembly's supremacy, he sought and obtained from it virtually a free hand to conduct diplomacy with whatever secrecy he wished.[15]

POLICIES TOWARD GERMANY AND POLAND

Within the broad objectives declared by the National Assembly and interpreted by Cavaignac and Bastide, the evolution of events determined in large measure the specific policies adopted. The hopes for a "fraternal pact with Germany" in particular were frustrated by the manifest attitude of the Frankfurt Parliament itself.[16]

The movement for a democratic and unified Germany had, in the spring of 1848, aroused the enthusiastic support of the French republicans, for it seemed to be another step toward the realization of a new Europe consisting of democratic and national states. Lamartine shared this attitude, but by the time he left office in May the nature of the emerging state was still uncertain, and the poet had never had to face the practical problem of developing a genuine diplomatic policy toward it. The situation was much the same when the Assembly made its declaration in favor of a "fraternal pact," for the Frankfurt National Assembly had convened less than a week before, on May 18. Thus it was left to Bastide, first under the

[14] Bastide mentioned the possibility, however, in a dispatch of September 6 to a French agent. (Hahn, "Attitude Toward German Unification," pp. 217-218.) Cavaignac developed the idea originally in his instructions to Beaumont on August 8.

[15] See *Compte rendu des séances*, II, pp. 765-766, 31 July 1848, and IV, p. 555, 2 October 1848.

[16] For details on Germany, I am indebted to Hahn, "Attitude Toward German Unification," although the author's failure to consult the Cavaignac documents weakens his argument. See also Rudolf Buchner, *Die Deutsch-französische Tragödie, 1848-1864: Politische Beziehungen und Psychologisches Verhältnis* (Würzburg, 1965), pp. 19-36, 57-58.

Executive Commission and later together with Cavaignac, to deal with Frankfurt as an existing political entity rather than simply with the abstract ideal of German national unity to which Lamartine and then the Assembly had given their fervent blessing.

Bastide, who shared the emotions of most republicans during the early stages of the German national movement, began in late May to feel irritated with the "exaggerated spirit of nationality" evidenced by the men at Frankfurt.[17] Soon the policies of the Frankfurt Assembly began to bring it into conflict with France and to render the prospects for a "fraternal pact" ever more remote. These conflicts became explicit and serious only after the formation of the Cavaignac cabinet, and provoked a shift in French policy, but the June insurrection was a negligible factor in the change.[18]

The French were disappointed by the cool reception in Frankfurt of the proposal for an alliance; on July 3, the German parliament definitively rejected the offer, thus rendering impossible, at least for the present, the fulfillment of that goal. The attitude of Frankfurt also seriously impaired the possibilities for a restored Poland, for the French regarded the German alliance as a necessary prerequisite.[19] French disillusionment with Frankfurt had already sharpened a few days earlier, with the choice of the Archduke John of Austria as the provisional executive. The selection of a Hapsburg not only dashed hopes that the new Germany would be republican, but also threatened to align the new state with Austria against France in the conflict in northern Italy. By September, it seemed clear that in the event of war there, Frankfurt Germany would fight alongside Austria against France.[20] Thus, the actions of the German parliament served to impede the fulfillment of all three of the goals proclaimed by the French Assembly.

[17] Hahn, "Attitude Toward German Unification," p. 119.

[18] *Ibid.*, p. 163. Hahn finds only one reference to the June Days, in a letter of the French ambassador at Frankfurt, but no evidence that the insurrection influenced the instructions from Paris.

[19] *Ibid.*, p. 162.

[20] *Ibid.*, pp. 176-179.

The aggressive nationalism exhibited by the Frankfurt Assembly with respect to national minorities in peripheral areas was further evidence to the French of its unfraternal and undemocratic spirit. Moreover, in each instance of conflict, the French found themselves on the opposite side from the unifying Germany: in Posen, in Italy, even in eastern France, where the Germans were eyeing Alsace and Lorraine, and finally, in Schleswig-Holstein. In that snarled controversy, which had erupted into open warfare, England and Russia intervened diplomatically in favor of Denmark, and on August 28 Prussia concluded the armistice of Malmoe. France, which also sided with Denmark, eagerly welcomed the armistice, but Frankfurt at first refused to accept the settlement. Militarily powerless without Prussia, however, Frankfurt finally yielded in September, but its attitude had disgusted the French, who had now another reason to fear that in the event of general war Germany would be against them.

In the face of Frankfurt's conduct, French ardor for a "fraternal pact" rapidly cooled. Cavaignac declined to accord diplomatic recognition to the provisional government created by the German parliament; the reason was in part practical, for the status of the component states remained uncertain, but probably the French withheld recognition also in order to weaken the prestige of Frankfurt at a time when war seemed imminent in Italy. Bastide also made some efforts to split Prussia from Frankfurt, again out of fears that Frankfurt would support Austria in Italy. Finally, in September, Cavaignac had departed so far from the ideal of a "fraternal pact" with Germany that he was seeking an alliance with Russia, partly out of the fear that Germany posed a threat to France. Events themselves had dispelled the illusions of the spring that relations between republican France and a unified and democratic Germany would be naturally harmonious. Yet, despite the grounds of conflict with Frankfurt, despite his fears of the power of a strong new state in central Europe, Cavaignac did not seek to obstruct the unification process as such, as he indicated quite explicitly to the Tsar: "As for German unity in itself, the Republic . . . does not intend on any grounds to impede or contest the accomplishment of that unity."[21] The mild measures of opposition to Frankfurt constituted only to a slight extent a return to the traditional French policy of seeking to perpetuate weakness and fragmentation in Germany. For if Cavaignac and Bastide observed Frankfurt with deepening disillusionment and even fear, they never departed from the assumption that a new unified Germany would and should emerge from the revolutionary current of 1848.[22]

With respect to the creation of an independent Poland, a theme dear to the hearts of French radicals, basic French policy was already decided before Cavaignac came to power. The suppression of the May 15 attempt to overthrow the government signified, among other things, the political defeat of the most vociferous French advocates of intervention in Poland. Moreover, a week later, the parliamentary advocates of an active Polish policy suffered defeat in the very debate which ended with the resolution endorsing an independent Poland. The May 24 resolution was a deliberately ambiguous justification for the continuation of French neutrality and was adopted after a more strongly worded resolution had been defeated.[23] Soon the attitude of the Frankfurt Assembly began to render the hopes for a reconstituted Poland even less substantial, for on July 3 it spurned the proposal for a pact with France, and on July 27 it voted to annex part of the Duchy of Posen, a traditionally Polish area. The French agents continued, however, to urge the French position on the govern-

[21] Le Flô instructions, Reel 24.

[22] Hahn, "Attitude Toward German Unification" (esp. Chapter V, pp. 213ff.) argues that for a brief period in the late summer the French government did return completely to the traditional policy and actually sought to "undermine the German unification movement." However, this judgment is based solely on inference from actions such as the overtures to Prussia and to Russia, and not on any statements of policy. In fact, the policy statements from the critical period itself (August and September) indicate no such intention. In his neglect of Cavaignac, Hahn remained ignorant of the most important policy statement, the quotation cited above from the instructions to the envoy to Russia on September 9. Hahn had erroneously interpreted the *démarche* made to Russia as one of the clearest evidences of the attempt to "undermine" German unification.

[23] Seignobos, *La Révolution de 1848*, pp. 292-293.

ment of Prussia, and in October the Prussian Assembly astonished and gratified the French by adopting a resolution highly favorable to Polish nationalism.[24]

In September, however, Cavaignac himself indirectly helped to render almost impossible any early restoration of Poland by his attempts for a rapprochement with Russia. "The Republic does not at all intend," he assured Nicholas, "to cross over all of Germany in order to wage war against Russia in the name of the restoration of Poland, but the Republic is obviously sympathetic to this cause, and she will plead it with all the insistence compatible with amicable relations." Still, in the unlikely event of war between France and Russia, Cavaignac warned that he would not hesitate to arouse Polish nationalism.[25]

The attempted rapprochement with Russia soon foundered, and at the end of his administration, Cavaignac's policy on Poland was still essentially that of the republic from the beginning: expressed sympathy for Polish aspirations, but no serious steps to help realize them.

THE RUSSIAN *DÉMARCHE*

The overtures to Russia had their origins under the Provisional Government. Lamartine's initial attitude toward Russia was cordial; he even went so far as to suggest the possibility of an alliance between the new republic and the autocratic regime.[26] The immediate response of Nicholas to the news of February was the famous: "Saddle your horses, gentlemen: The republic is proclaimed in France!"[27] Nevertheless, before the spectacle of a Europe in ferment and Lamartine's pacific manifesto, the Tsar soon changed his mind. He agreed to receive a representative of the republic (who for reasons unknown, how-

[24] Paul Henry, "Le Gouvernement provisoire et la question polonaise," *Revue historique*, CLXXVIII (1936), 232.

[25] Le Flô instructions, Reel 24.

[26] Mikhail N. Pokrovskii, *Pages d'histoire; la méthode de matérialisme historique appliquée à quelques problèmes historiques concrets* (Paris, 1929), on "Lamartine, Cavaignac et Nicholas Ier," p. 62. Although Pokrovskii's interpretation is predictably narrow, he did use the archives.

[27] Edmond Bapst, *L'Empereur Nicolas Ier et la IIe république française* (Paris, 1898), p. 2.

ever, never left for St. Petersburg),[28] and in May Russia herself, worried over the unification movement in Germany, began making cautious overtures to France.[29] But nothing concrete was proposed, and Russia was still withholding recognition from the French republic when the June insurrection occurred. Nicholas was delighted to see any government, even a republican one, stand firm, for the first time during 1848 against a revolutionary movement. He sent congratulations to Cavaignac for "his victory, won so gloriously over the anarchist party."[30]

During the same period, relations between Russia and France were also improved when they found themselves on the same side diplomatically in the Schleswig-Holstein question.[31] In August, the Tsar intimated that he would be happy to receive an "unofficial" French envoy who could prepare the way for a renewal of normal diplomatic relations.[32] Cavaignac eagerly responded. Mindful of the Tsar's military interests, he sent, instead of an experienced diplomat, an Algerian General, Le Flô, bearing a personal letter to Nicholas.

Cavaignac and Bastide had good reason to welcome a rapprochement with Russia. First, Cavaignac was eager to extract official recognition of the republic from the great autocratic power, the only government that still refused to do so. He particularly insisted on this point, and he did so proudly, not as a suppliant: "We do not ask this recognition as did Louis Philippe, who seemed to want pardon for a usurpation. . . . The republican form is not for France a last resort or an accident. It is the goal towards which she has headed for sixty years. . . . The republican form expresses an idea that must take its place in European relations and diplomacy."[33] A rapprochement with Tsarist Russia seemed to proceed naturally from the fundamental policy decision in favor of a conciliatory peace. But Cavaignac, acting on his belief that France must end its diplomatic isolation, proposed a formal Franco-

[28] Pokrovskii, *Pages d'histoire*, pp. 65-66.

[29] Hahn, "Attitude Toward German Unification," pp. 253-255.

[30] Pokrovskii, *Pages d'histoire*, p. 69.

[31] Hahn, "Attitude Toward German Unification," p. 261.

[32] Bapst, *Nicolas I*, p. 16.

[33] Le Flô instructions, Reel 24.

Russian alliance.[34] At that moment the prospect of danger from the emerging Germany was less immediate than the danger of war against Austria in northern Italy. There was already the likelihood that the Frankfurt Assembly would support Austria; what Cavaignac and Bastide feared most was the entry of Russia into the war on the side of Austria, for in that event France would be faced with a powerful continental coalition.

The French soon discovered that the Tsar was still profoundly distrustful of the republic, even in the hands of a general who had crushed the June uprising. To be sure, Nicholas greeted Le Flô warmly, responded to Cavaignac's personal letter with a cordial personal reply,[35] and gave Le Flô the impression that "a solid alliance is possible," but the talk went scarcely beyond pleasantries.[36] In October, Le Flô was an honored guest at a review of the Russian army, sitting beside the Tsar himself, but he was not amused when several Russian generals jested that the troops marching by "were destined for France."[37] Within a fortnight, the Russian attitude was clear to the neophyte diplomat. If it came to war in Italy, Russia would take the field against the republic: "It is no longer in doubt that the armed intervention of France would provoke that of

[34] Bapst, *Nicolas I*, p. 22, erroneously attributes the offer of the alliance to Le Flô because such instructions are lacking in the official correspondence, and he did not use the Cavaignac documents.

[35] Le Flô, anxious to abide by Cavaignac's instructions to bear himself proudly as a representative of the republic, and to scorn "the obsequiousness and . . . the servility of royal courts," disconcerted the Russian Foreign Minister by insisting that Nicholas reply with a holograph letter matching Cavaignac's: "His Majesty must write the entire letter, holograph for holograph—that is important to the dignity of our governments." Nesselrode said that the Tsar would certainly sign the letter personally, but this was not enough for Le Flô, who refused to hand over Cavaignac's letter until Nesselrode told him that Nicholas had agreed to write the complete letter. (Le Flô to Cavaignac, 26 September 1848, Reel 24.) As it turned out, however, the Tsar of all the Russias merely signed, with his customary flourish, the letter to the upstart general whom revolution had carried to the head of the French state. (The letter from Nicholas, dated 21 September 1848, and written in a neat clerk's hand, is in Reel 26.)

[36] Archives des Affaires Etrangères, *Correspondance politique, Russie,* 202: Le Flô to Bastide, 26 September 1848, p. 104.

[37] Le Flô to Cavaignac, 22 October 1848, Reel 24.

Russia, and would cause a general war."[38] Nicholas remained cordial to Le Flô, but declined even to grant official recognition to the republic, pleading now that he would have to await the presidential elections.

THE PROBLEM OF ITALY

Pressing as were the problems of Poland, Germany and Russia, northern Italy was the pivot of French diplomatic thinking; sooner or later, all other questions related to Italy and to the more fundamental problem of war or peace that the situation in Italy posed.[39] Lamartine was the first to emphasize the importance of Italy in the eyes of the republic, in his manifesto of March 4. Palmerston, who had no desire to see Austrian replaced by French dominance in northern Italy, was pleased with Lamartine's generally pacific posture and with his evident desire to accommodate himself to England. From the beginning of the republic, therefore, fairly amicable relations were established with England; and the British ambassador in Paris, Lord Normanby, was on friendly terms with Lamartine, Bastide and Cavaignac.

The originally peaceful attitude of the French republic was put to a new test in late March when revolution and then warfare erupted in northern Italy, following the revolution of March 13 in Vienna. After successful uprisings in the Austrian provinces of Lombardy and Venetia, Piedmont declared war on Austria on March 25, and enthusiastic contingents of Italian nationalists arrived from other parts of the peninsula. The Provisional Government in France hinted its readiness to lend military support to the liberation movement.

But for the moment Radetzky was on the run, and Pied-

[38] Le Flô to Bastide, 2 November 1848, minute in Reel 24. Hahn, "Attitude Toward German Unification," p. 265, cites the original in the Archives des Affaires Etrangères.

[39] Ferdinand Boyer has shed much new light on Franco-Italian relations in 1848 in a series of articles published since 1950, which recently appeared in revised and expanded form in *La Seconde république et Charles Albert en 1848* (Paris, 1967). Some dispatches from Bastide are reproduced in Armando Saitta, ed., *Le Relazioni diplomatiche fra la Francia e il Granducato di Toscana, III serie: 1848-1860, I (7 marzo 1848—29 dicembre 1850)*, (Rome, 1959).

mont spurned the proffered French sword with the cry, "L'Italia farà da sè!" The slogan represented not only a proud monarch's confidence, but also profound fear of republicanism in northern Italy and of presumed French designs on Nice and Savoy.[40] Moreover, the slogan was not limited to Piedmont, but reflected a deep distrust of French aims common to the entire Italian nationalist movement. Even Mazzini opposed the intervention of republican France. Piedmont, claiming to speak for all of Italy, protested the concentration of French troops near the Alps and threatened to fight if they crossed the frontier. As the French republican ambassador in Turin reported, "The character of the Italian movement is that it is above all Italian. No one intends to substitute France for Austria. They do not want French intervention."[41]

In the face of this attitude, Lamartine declared that France would intervene only if asked by the Italians. The Executive Commission continued this policy, and the National Assembly implicitly sanctioned it in adopting the resolution of May 24 in favor of "the liberation of Italy."[42] Thus, Italian opposition frustrated the French republic in its only serious effort to give military support to a foreign revolutionary movement. The French continued to strengthen the Army of the Alps, however, and to poise it for rapid and friendly intervention should the call come.[43] But in the crisis of late June, Cavaignac detached many units from the Army of the Alps to help deal with disorders in Paris and Lyon, and for weeks thereafter France was incapable of giving military assistance to the Italians. As Bastide put it, "The insurgents of Paris had, without realizing it, come to the aid of Radetzky."[44]

The government of Cavaignac made the Assembly's declaration the basis of its Italian policy, but developed its own distinctive methods of implementing it. Bastide and Cavaignac were distrustful of Charles Albert, and reluctant to help create a powerful monarchy on the flank of the French republic,

[40] Boyer, *La Seconde république et Charles Albert*, pp. 25-53.

[41] Vidal, "La Question italienne," pp. 166-169. Cf. Boyer, *La Seconde république et Charles Albert*, pp. 74-81.

[42] *Compte rendu des séances*, I, pp. 382-399, 415; Boyer, *La Seconde république et Charles Albert*, pp. 71, 94, 102-103.

[43] Boyer, "L'Armée des Alpes," pp. 80-85.

[44] *Ibid.*, p. 88.

yet they gave some support to Piedmont in its leadership of the Italian cause against Austria. The king of Piedmont seemed to believe, said Bastide, that "L'Italie, c'est moi,"[45] whereas they preferred to see a federation of republican states emerge in Italy. Nevertheless, they were willing to accept the annexations of Lombardy and of mainland Venetia as an expression of the will of the people who had voted for annexation almost unanimously, and there was no French attempt to veto the union.[46]

Moreover, once the June crisis was ended the Cavaignac government responded favorably to Piedmont's request to purchase arms. Both England and Belgium refused similar requests, but by July 3, Bastide promised to sell thousands of cannon fuses and 50,000 muskets to Piedmont, and deliveries began within a few weeks.[47] Also in July, General Oudinot, commander of the Army of the Alps, came to Paris to discuss the situation with Cavaignac and reconstituted his forces in preparation for an eventual call from Piedmont. Before the National Assembly's Committee on Foreign Affairs, Bastide denied any intention to annex Nice and Savoy.[48] The French were also exerting diplomatic pressure on Austria to surrender Lombardy and to grant autonomy to Venetia, and on July 18, Bastide asked England to join France in mediating the North Italian conflict.[49]

The situation in Italy abruptly changed after July 25, when Radetzky decisively defeated the Piedmontese armies at Custozza. The event shocked many Italians out of their "farà-da-sèism," but Piedmont was still reluctant to ask for French intervention. The king still wanted to fight on alone, and a special envoy sent to Paris, startled by Cavaignac's frank admission of his hopes for a republican federation in Italy, stopped short of requesting intervention.[50] Moreover, the situation was complicated by the simultaneous appearance in

[45] *La République française et l'Italie*, p. 26. See also Vidal, "La Question italienne," pp. 170-171.

[46] Boyer, *La Seconde république et Charles Albert*, pp. 129-132, 153-154.

[47] *Ibid.*, pp. 166-171. [48] *Ibid.*, pp. 177-178. [49] *Ibid.*, pp. 187-188.

[50] Taylor, *Italian Problem*, p. 138. Cf. Boyer, *La Seconde république et Charles Albert*, pp. 194-200.

Paris of a representative of the former provisional government of Lombardy. At a joint conference on August 3 with Cavaignac and Bastide, the two Italians took contradictory positions, the Lombard asking immediate French military aid, and the Piedmontese insisting that help was not needed or wanted at present. The Lombard envoy, Guerrieri, also observed the subsidiary role of Bastide in French diplomacy. He reported that during the two-hour conference, Bastide spoke hardly at all, adding, "Cavaignac sometimes played the role of the *militaire*, and sometimes the role of the politician, analyzing the problems with a great deal of precision and frankness."[51] The general said he had already ordered one division of the Army of the Alps to return from the Paris region to the southeast as a demonstration of moral support for Piedmont.[52] Explaining the situation before "magnificent military maps," Cavaignac said that France would immediately declare war on Austria if Piedmont itself were invaded, but believed that Austria would not go so far.

Cavaignac was prepared to send an army of 60,000 to help drive the Austrians from northern Italy; he stipulated that the commander in chief of the allied forces must be a French general, but made no territorial demands.[53] Cavaignac listened sympathetically to the plea of the Lombard for immediate intervention, but because Lombardy had already voted to join Piedmont, agreed that only the Piedmontese envoy, Ricci, was empowered to speak officially. Ricci said that French intervention would not be needed for three months, and at the end of the conference, the regular Piedmontese ambassador to Paris, Brignole, murmured to Guerrieri that he "feared French intervention more than he hoped for it."[54]

[51] Boyer, *La Seconde république et Charles Albert*, p. 201.

[52] *Ibid.*

[53] *Ibid.*, p. 202. It was probably at this point that Cavaignac had drawn up a draft of a military alliance with Piedmont along these lines. The draft, preserved in Reel 25, apparently was never shown to the Italians, for no reference to it appears either in the official French diplomatic correspondence or in Boyer's works.

[54] Boyer, *La Seconde république et Charles Albert*, p. 203. Cf. Bastide, *La République française et l'Italie*, p. 82.

Pending an unqualified request for military aid, France continued to seek joint mediation with England. In early August they agreed to ask Austria to renounce its claim to Lombardy and to grant a measure of autonomy to Venetia, and Piedmont expressed its satisfaction with these proposals.[55] Although both England and France favored mediation, however, they did so from different motives. Palmerston had agreed to mediation largely out of distrust of France, in hope of averting unilateral French intervention,[56] whereas Cavaignac and Bastide looked upon joint mediation as a means of implementing the goal of liberating Italy while avoiding a war which they feared might become general.

Mediation did not represent for Cavaignac simply a convenient excuse for inaction. Rather, it formed part of a comprehensive plan expressing the full scope of his foreign policy, which he set out on August 8 in personal instructions to Gustave de Beaumont (the writer who had accompanied Tocqueville to America and to Algeria), whom he appointed ambassador to Great Britain.[57] First, Cavaignac took advantage of the Italian problem to seek a closer association; he hoped that joint mediation would ripen into a firm alliance. "The Republic invites the English government to ally itself with her loyally, firmly and publicly." The general intimated to Palmerston that long-range French interests would best be served by unilateral French intervention, which would result in the creation of a northern Italian federation dominated by France, and would also permit France to annex Savoy and Nice. But the republic's immediate interests in preventing general war and ending its own isolation counseled instead an alliance with England. "The interest of England is to moderate and to oppose French action in the solution of the Italian question." The joint mediation thus served the interests of both.

But whereas for Palmerston the diplomatic mediation was an end in itself, for Cavaignac it was merely the first step of a proposed three-stage Anglo-French policy culminating in joint

[55] Boyer, *La Seconde république et Charles Albert*, pp. 213-218.

[56] Taylor, *Italian Problem*, pp. 140ff.

[57] Beaumont instructions, 8 August 1848, Reel 25.

military action if necessary. Cavaignac was determined that Austria must surrender Lombardy. If the offer to mediate diplomatically was unacceptable to Vienna, then he proposed that the French and British stiffen their position into one of "armed mediation." Should Austria still refuse to bow, wrote Cavaignac, then military action must follow: "French intervention would be imperatively obligatory if the mediation should fail. The restoration of the Austrians at Milan is an impossibility for the republic. France declares clearly, she will intervene if the mediation fails." Cavaignac preferred joint military action with Britain, but if Britain refused, Cavaignac warned, then France must fight alone, embroiling all of Europe, in the process, in ideological warfare.[58]

As it turned out, events did not proceed beyond the joint diplomatic mediation. Anxious to appear conciliatory, Palmerston satisfied Cavaignac by finally granting diplomatic recognition to the republic, but he rejected the offers both for an alliance and for any joint military action, even the "armed mediation." The British prime minister indicated his personal willingness to accept Cavaignac's proposals, but argued that the Cabinet and Parliament would oppose them, holding out only the hope that conditions might change in a month or two.[59] There was, indeed, much opposition in England to the association with France.[60]

The National Assembly's Committee on Foreign Affairs in early August sought information from Cavaignac on his Italian policy, but the general refused to divulge the proposed bases

[58] Presumably Bastide knew of the special instructions drawn up by Cavaignac for Beaumont, but he does not refer to them in his official correspondence or in his book. Beaumont's official correspondence as preserved at the Archives des Affaires Etrangères often reflects Cavaignac's ideas, however. Boyer deduced that Cavaignac had provided special instructions but did not use the Cavaignac papers. For an example of Cavaignac's ideas as expressed by Beaumont, see Boyer, *La Seconde république et Charles Albert*, pp. 225-227.

[59] Beaumont to Cavaignac, 1 September 1848, Reel 25. In addition to his official correspondence with Bastide, Beaumont also reported privately to Cavaignac, and these reports are preserved in the Cavaignac papers, Reel 25. Cf. Boyer, *La Seconde république et Charles Albert*, pp. 227-228.

[60] Taylor, *Italian Problem*, p. 143.

of mediation, invoking the necessity for secrecy while negotiations were in progress. Asked if he was adhering to the Assembly's resolution concerning the "liberation" of Italy, Cavaignac responded, "The will of the Assembly will always be the guide for my conduct," and the committee was satisfied.[61]

But even as the general spoke, events in Italy had already drastically altered the situation. On August 9, Piedmont signed an armistice whereby the triumphant Radetzky was left in possession of Lombardy as well as of mainland Venetia. Both England and France vigorously protested this precipitate action, but they went ahead with the proposed mediation, and on August 15 Piedmont formally accepted it. In the circumstances, Austria resisted the mediation despite intense diplomatic pressure, and France for a few more weeks seemed close to war. From the left there arose a clamor for action, for war if necessary to assure the "liberation of Italy." But this was precisely the time when relations with the Frankfurt Parliament were most critical, and Cavaignac feared that both Germany and Russia would support Austria if France intervened militarily against her.

Cavaignac went before the National Assembly on August 21. "In a country such as ours," he said, "it often requires more courage to plead in favor of peace than to counsel war." Peace, he insisted, was desirable for the consolidation of the republic, but war might become necessary. "Mon Dieu, I have made war," he declared, "and it would be quite easy for me to resume the habits, to obey the instincts of my life as a soldier. . . . But until it is necessary, I will resist with an unshakeable firmness all the pressures which seem to me prejudicial to the future of the Republic."[62] The Assembly enthusiastically approved the general's stand.

Cavaignac and Bastide showed no enthusiasm when Piedmont at the end of August sought Marshal Bugeaud to command its army. Cavaignac "flatly refused to authorize Bugeaud, an opponent of the republican regime, to take command of the army of a monarchical government."[63] He also

[61] Boyer, *La Seconde république et Charles Albert*, p. 230.
[62] *Compte rendu des séances*, III, p. 332.
[63] Boyer, *La Seconde république et Charles Albert*, p. 248.

was now unwilling to sign a military convention with Piedmont; he objected to proposed clauses placing the French army in a subsidiary role and renouncing any territorial compensation, and he argued that such an agreement was unnecessary as well as inopportune while mediation was pending.[64]

Yet the French government was perfectly sincere in its threat to intervene militarily against Austria in North Italy. Cavaignac in late August reinforced the Army of the Alps and kept it poised for action.[65] In the face of apparent Austrian unwillingness to submit to mediation, he and Bastide despaired that they might "be compelled . . . to give the signal for general war."[66]

The tension was finally broken on September 3 when Austria agreed to accept joint Anglo-French mediation. As Austria continued to manifest its reluctance to surrender any territory, however, and delayed in agreeing to a site for the mediation conference, the Army of the Alps remained on the alert. When insurrection in Vienna during October paralyzed Austria for several weeks, France perhaps lost an opportunity to take a fresh initiative, but Bastide pledged that the policy of mediation would remain unchanged. If the imperial government survived, he argued, then it would respond favorably to such evidence of French "sincerity and moderation," and "if democracy wins in Vienna, the question of Italian independence will be settled by that very fact."[67]

After Windischgrätz had crushed the Viennese radicals on October 31, the new Austrian government finally (on November 27) accepted Brussels as the site for the conference, to which Tocqueville had already been appointed to represent France.[68] But with Schwarzenberg in power and France now preoccupied with the impending presidential elections, Aus-

[64] *Ibid.*, pp. 252-256.

[65] *Ibid.*, pp. 275-277.

[66] Hahn, "Attitude Toward German Unification," pp. 226-228; Vidal, "La Question italienne," p. 178.

[67] Boyer, *La Seconde république et Charles Albert*, p. 309. For details on the mediation efforts through the end of the Cavaignac period, see pp. 236-343.

[68] *Oeuvres complètes*, XII, p. 278.

tria was more intransigent than ever. The conference was never in fact to convene.

While the Cavaignac government was giving aid and moral support to Piedmont short of war, it gave more wholehearted support to the new republic of Venice. The province of Venetia had arisen against Austria in the spring along with Lombardy, and had given itself to Piedmont in its time of victory; but after Charles Albert fled in late July, Venice became a de facto republic once more under Daniel Manin. Radetzky had overrun most of the province, but the city itself, although abandoned by Piedmont, refused to surrender, and instead appealed to France. Bastide felt particularly sympathetic toward Venice, partly out of a sense of shame over the earlier treatment of the Republic of Venice at the hands of Napoleon,[69] and one of his first acts as foreign minister in May had been to deliver 20,000 muskets to the Venetian revolutionists.[70]

When Austria threatened to reoccupy Venice following the armistice of August 9, Bastide responded immediately to Manin's plea for aid by dispatching two warships to protect the city. Austria did not dare attack, despite its insistence that the mediation which it accepted did not apply to Venice.[71] In mid-September, when the French ships began to withdraw for supplies, Austrian ships appeared but retired hastily after the French ships put smartly about. The French commander was decorated.[72] Austria was able to impose a partial blockade on the city, but French refusal to recognize it so irritated Austria that she almost broke off diplomatic negotiations.[73]

Cavaignac and Bastide also asked the British to join France in a protective occupation of Venice.[74] While the British hesi-

[69] Bastide, *La République française et l'Italie*, p. 127.

[70] *Ibid.*, pp. 128, 137; Boyer, *La Seconde république et Charles Albert*, p. 98.

[71] Boyer, *La Seconde république et Charles Albert*, pp. 262, 266, 294-295.

[72] Bastide, *La République française et l'Italie*, p. 134.

[73] Vidal, "La Question italienne," p. 182; Boyer, *La Seconde république et Charles Albert*, pp. 310-311.

[74] Boyer, *La Seconde république et Charles Albert*, p. 268. See also Taylor, *Italian Problem*, pp. 156-157.

tated, France late in September dispatched an expeditionary force of 3,000 troops from Toulon, but recalled it after a few days. Cavaignac decided to abandon the expedition because of British objections and perhaps also because of Piedmontese opposition.[75]

As late as November 17, however, Bastide pledged to Manin that he would never surrender Venice to Austria, although he warned that the Cavaignac government might soon come to an end. The election of Louis Napoleon did not change the situation immediately, but when warfare was resumed in the spring of 1849, Radetzky besieged and finally defeated the Venetian republic. A decade later, Bastide argued that if Cavaignac had been elected, Venice would still have been free.[76]

In other parts of Italy, too, the Cavaignac government played an active role. Bastide took a firm diplomatic stand against Austrian penetration into the states of central Italy; he even opposed any restorations in Modena and Parma, but was willing to see them annex themselves to Tuscany or Piedmont, as they wished.[77] In the Kingdom of Naples, the scene of the first revolutionary upheaval of 1848, King Ferdinand II was already regaining control after a royalist demonstration on May 15. But Sicily remained in the hands of the insurgents, and Bastide adopted the policy of deterring reconquest by sending a naval squadron to patrol the straits; the French ships also provided asylum for Neapolitans fleeing the revenge of the royalist reaction.[78] Palmerston also dispatched ships to deter Ferdinand, but in September a Neapolitan expedition eluded both the French and English ships and began to bombard Messina. At the firm insistence of the French and British admirals, however, the Neapolitans withdrew, and French ships remained in Neapolitan waters. Although Ferdi-

[75] Boyer, *La Seconde république et Charles Albert*, p. 270. Cf. Parménie, *Histoire d'un éditeur*, p. 290.

[76] Bastide, *La République française et l'Italie*, p. 135.

[77] Paul Henry, "La France et les nationalités en 1848," *Revue historique*, CLXXXVI (1939), 71; Boyer, *La Seconde république et Charles Albert*, p. 293.

[78] Vidal, "La Question italienne," p. 181.

nand bitterly protested this interference with his rights over Sicily as guaranteed by the treaties of 1815, Bastide took Lamartine's original position that France recognized the 1815 settlement in fact but not in law.[79] The imposed truce remained operative until the end of the Cavaignac period.

THE PROBLEM OF THE POPE

Near the end of his administration, Italy presented Cavaignac with yet another diplomatic problem, one with domestic political and even religious ramifications. This was the flight of the pope from a Rome turbulent with political strife. Earlier in the year, Pius IX had represented for many Italians the hope for liberal and national unification, but he lost most of his nationalist support in late April when he refused to permit his troops to participate in the war against Austria; in Rome itself, political radicalism intensified during the year, bypassing the moderate liberal position of the pope. At first Rome was, for the French republic, merely one aspect of the Italian problem; Lamartine expressed his sympathy for the Roman liberals, and Bastide continued the same attitude. After Radetzky's defeat of Piedmont, Bastide warned both Austria and the pope that France would not tolerate an Austrian occupation of the papal territory, and the threat was heeded.

During August, the Cavaignac government clearly indicated its sympathy with the revolutionary movement in Rome as against the political interests of the pope. On the pretext that he needed to strengthen his defenses against possible Austrian intervention, Pius asked Cavaignac in a personal letter to send him three or four thousand troops. Advised by the French ambassador that the pope wanted to use the troops "much more against his interior than his exterior enemies," Cavaignac refused the pope's request, saying that it would put the French republic in "a situation as embarrassing as it would be unacceptable." But the general did agree to send a small

[79] Bastide, *La République française et l'Italie*, pp. 169-170. See also Prince E. Wilson, "Anglo-French Diplomatic Relations, 1848-1851," unpublished Ph.D. dissertation, University of Chicago, 1954, pp. 120-123; and Boyer, *La Seconde république et Charles Albert*, p. 285.

vessel to safeguard the pope personally, if necessary.[80] As early as August, then, Cavaignac laid down the Roman policy that he would pursue until the end of his administration: Catholic France would protect the person of the Holy Father, but Republican France would refuse to aid the papal monarch in his conflict with the Roman revolutionaries.[81]

Moreover, France would not countenance Austrian penetration into papal territory. Austrian troops advanced into the Legations after the armistice of August 9, but were hastily ordered to withdraw in response to Bastide's warning that Austrian occupation would be a *casus belli.*[82]

In September, Pius irritated both Roman radical opinion and the government of the French republic by appointing as his prime minister Guizot's former ambassador to Rome, Rossi. The crisis, and the appearance of the distinct Roman problem for France, came after November 15 when Rossi was assassinated. The pope was forced to appoint a radical ministry, Austria threatened to intervene, and the pope began to consider flight. The Spanish ambassador urged him to go to Majorca, and the French ambassador, d'Harcourt, acting on his own initiative and without instructions, invited the pope to seek refuge in France. Only by going to Republican France, d'Harcourt believed, could the pope avoid associating the church with political reaction and make it possible "to return one day to Rome as a friend of liberty and of Italy."[83]

When news of the assassination reached Paris more than a week later, Cavaignac dispatched a special representative to the pope, and prepared an expedition of 3,500 men to go to Rome. The envoy, François de Corcelle, was explicitly forbidden to interfere in any political conflicts; his sole mission, as was that of the troops, was to assure the personal safety of the pope. Cavaignac explained his policy before the Assembly.

[80] Gilbert de Chambrun, "Un Projet de séjour en France du pape Pie IX (1848)," *Revue d'histoire diplomatique,* L (1936), 361-362.

[81] Even though the Roman Republic was not proclaimed until after Cavaignac had fallen from power, in February 1849.

[82] Boyer, *La Seconde république et Charles Albert,* pp. 262, 291-292.

[83] de Chambrun, "Un Projet de séjour," pp. 334, 337.

The left feared the expedition would be used to restore the pope; Catholic spokesmen wanted the troops to be used for that purpose. But in the end the Assembly voted overwhelming approval of Cavaignac's policy of simple protection of the pope's person.[84]

Actually, the Cavaignac Cabinet supported d'Harcourt's attempt to bring the pope to France and hinted as much publicly, but avoided an open invitation for fear of compromising the pope's initiative.[85] The pope fled Rome during the night of November 24. On December 1, Cavaignac announced "The pope is proceeding to France." The French public response was enthusiastic. The government feverishly prepared to greet the Holy Father with full honors; the Minister of Religion hurried to Marseille, and Bastide ordered that port city to render the pope a cannon salute, "as for a sovereign."[86] Not even the extreme left newspapers opposed the pope's entry into France, believing that his absence from Italy would benefit the revolutionary movements.[87]

But the hopes of the French were soon proved vain. Although the pope had indicated both to d'Harcourt and to Cavaignac in a personal letter that he would go to France, he proceeded instead to the fortress of Gaeta just across the papal border in the Kingdom of Naples.[88] When he heard this news, Cavaignac demonstrated the sincerity of his motives for dispatching troops to Rome: convinced that the pope was now safe, he ordered the expedition, which had not left Marseille,

[84] For the entire debate, during which Cavaignac introduced the reports from Harcourt and the instructions to Corcelle, see *Compte rendu des séances*, v, pp. 944-963, 30 November 1848. Cf. François de Corcelle, "Souvenir de 1848: Première intervention dans les affaires de Rome," *Le Correspondant*, XLII (1857), 585-590; and Jean Leflon, "La Mission de Claude de Corcelle auprès de Pie IX, après le meurtre du ministre Rossi," *Archivum Historiae pontificiae*, No. 1 (1963), pp. 358-402.

[85] de Chambrun, "Un Projet de séjour," pp. 360-361.

[86] *Ibid.*, pp. 481-483.

[87] *Ibid.*, p. 483.

[88] The papal letter of November 27 is preserved in Cavaignac's papers, Reel 26. As late as November 30, Harcourt thought that the pope would go to France from Gaeta. See G. Mollat, "La Fuite de Pie IX à Gaète (24 novembre 1848)," *Revue d'histoire de l'église*, XXXV (1939), 276.

to remain in port.[89] Nevertheless, in a last effort to persuade the pope to leave the reactionary regime of "Bomba," Cavaignac sent another special envoy, this time an army officer, bearing a personal message urging the mutual benefits of a papal sojourn in republican France: "The Republic, whose existence has already been consecrated by the considered, steadfast and sovereign will of the French nation, will behold with pride Your Holiness giving to the world the spectacle of the wholly religious consecration which your presence would promise, and which the Republic will welcome with the dignity and religious respect worthy of this great and generous nation."[90] But Pius IX, influenced by agents of Austria, remained in Gaeta, putting off the French entreaties with a vague promise to visit France in the future.

The Cavaignac government had had sound reasons for offering asylum to the pope. As Bastide later explained, "a republican government has a duty to be solicitous of the sentiments, the beliefs and even the prejudices of those whom it has the responsibility of governing."[91]

But there was an additional, political motive which undoubtedly accounted to a large extent for the alacrity with which Cavaignac acted: his own presidential ambitions. The elections were set for December 10, less than two weeks after the news of the pope's flight reached Paris. Here was an opportunity for Cavaignac to appeal for the support of the clergy, which was far from enthusiastic about the republican general.[92] Nevertheless, Cavaignac did not seek to exploit the situation as thoroughly as he might have. He issued no public invitation until after the pope had already demonstrated his desire to come to France; moreover, Cavaignac's refusal to consider using French troops to restore the temporal authority of the pope lost him much goodwill from French Catholics.[93]

[89] *Compte rendu des séances*, VI, p. 93, 5 December 1848. Cf. Collins, *Catholicism and the Second French Republic*, p. 161.

[90] See de Chambrun, "Un Projet de séjour," p. 488.

[91] Bastide, *La République française et l'Italie*, p. 199.

[92] Corcelle, in "Souvenir de 1848," pp. 581-586, denied the allegation that Cavaignac had any such motives, but see the discussion in Collins, *Catholicism and the Second French Republic*, pp. 158-165.

[93] Collins, *Catholicism and the Second French Republic*, pp. 163-165.

Despite superficial similarities, the subsequent Roman policy of Louis Napoleon was quite different from that of Cavaignac. Whereas the general had refused to use French troops to restore the power of the pope, Louis Napoleon in 1849 sent a military expedition that crushed the Roman republic and permitted the restoration of Pius IX as a reactionary monarch. But in December 1848, Pius IX could not divine the future policy of Louis Napoleon; rather, distrust of him was one reason for the pope's reluctance to come to France.[94] In addition to the memories of Avignon and his distaste for the republic, the pope had to face the possibility that in a few days a Bonaparte would once more come to power in France.

[94] Leflon, "La Mission de Claude de Corcelle," p. 397.

XV · The Twentieth *Frimaire* of Louis Bonaparte

THE RISING STAR

THERE had been virtually nothing of Bonapartism in the February revolution—the republic had seemed the only demand of the victorious insurgents at that time. Yet, even then there had been a few signs of what would become an irresistible torrent by December: a National Guard officer speaking in favor of Louis Napoleon on the steps of the throne in the Tuileries, the unheeded suggestion that Louis Napoleon be made a member of the Provisional Government, shouts of "Vive l'Empereur!" in the Place Vendôme and "Vive Napoléon!" in the Place de Grève.[1] Louis Napoleon hurried to Paris, but returned to London after his cold reception by the Provisional Government. Even by the time of the elections to the National Assembly in April, Bonapartism was so weak that the prince, fearing defeat, refused to pose his candidacy, although two other Bonapartes and a Murat were elected. After the affair of May 15, growing dissatisfaction with the regime began to manifest itself in support for Louis Napoleon, and he was chosen in four departments on June 4. The movement had been largely spontaneous and popular, and it was only after this success that a strong propaganda campaign began.[2]

Alarmed by his victory and by the mounting tension in Paris, the Executive Commission decided to arrest the pretender if he should return to France, but the National Assembly voted to admit him. The prince sent a letter denying hostile intentions, but pledging ominously, "If the people impose duties upon me, I will know how to fulfill them." When this passage was read in the Assembly, there were shouts of disapproval, and Cavaignac, then minister of war, mounted the

[1] Dansette, *Louis Napoléon*, pp. 219-220. Cf. Crémieux, *La Révolution de février*, pp. 351-352, and André-Jean Tudesq, *L'Election présidentielle de Louis-Napoléon Bonaparte, 10 décembre 1848* (Paris, 1965), p. 35.

[2] Tudesq, *L'Election présidentielle*, p. 62; Dansette, *Louis Napoléon*, p. 223.

tribune and excitedly warned, "in this historic letter, the word Republic is not mentioned."[3] Disturbed by the hostile sentiments aroused, Louis Napoleon decided to resign his seat and await events.

Thus, although there was some evidence of Bonapartism among the insurgents of June, Louis Napoleon was at that time still in England, and he became the only prominent political figure to remain untainted either by direct association with the insurrection or with its suppression. For a time afterwards, Louis Napoleon's agents ceased their propaganda, but he tried his strength once more in supplemental elections on September 17. His victory this time was even more striking than in June, for he won in the same four departments and in one other. This time there was no attempt to prevent the seating of the man who was the choice of so many Frenchmen, although Cavaignac's ambassador in London, acting on his own initiative, delayed the prince's departure for a few days by refusing to issue him a passport.[4] Louis finally left London on September 23, and on September 26 he quietly took his seat in the National Assembly, which accepted him without protest. The issue was now much larger; it was no longer a question of whether Louis Napoleon was acceptable as a deputy, but whether he would be acceptable as president of the republic.

THE PROBLEM OF POPULAR ELECTION

Unlike his uncle, Louis Napoleon was to come to power in a perfectly legal fashion, even if he later used force to maintain his position and to prepare for the Empire. Since it was the men of 1848, and not the least of them Cavaignac, who made possible the election of the man who would destroy the republic, it will be well to consider why and how they did so. First, it should be noted that the original decision to create a presidential executive chosen by universal manhood suffrage was made even before Louis Napoleon seemed a problem, for the

[3] *Compte rendu des séances*, I, p. 893, 15 June 1848.

[4] See the letters from Beaumont in the Cavaignac papers, that of 19 September 1848 in Reel 25 and that of 22 September 1848 in Reel 24.

Constitutional Committee came to this conclusion in late May.[5] The ideal of the single strong executive was widespread at that time, growing out of republican theories, the American experiences, and, negatively, dissatisfaction with the collegial revolutionary governments. Even after Louis Napoleon's June electoral triumphs, the committee by a large majority reaffirmed its decision to submit the choice of this strong executive to popular election.[6] Moreover, in late July all of the *bureaux* favored a strong presidential executive, and despite some expressed fear of Louis Napoleon, most favored popular election.[7] The alternative to popular election was election by the National Assembly; the committee decided to hear the views of the man who was then at the height of his prestige, the Assembly's own favorite and an obvious presidential candidate, General Cavaignac. Appearing before the committee on August 12, Cavaignac disarmed the hesitant by his forthright advocacy of popular election, adding that in his position, "he would regret to see the right of election removed from the entire nation and given to the Assembly."[8] After weighing Cavaignac's words, the committee retained popular election.

At that time, in August, the threat of Louis Napoleon still perhaps appeared distant, for had he not meekly resigned his seat? But when the Constitution came up for general debate in early October, Louis Napoleon had just experienced his second great electoral triumph. Indeed, discussion on the executive power followed immediately upon the reading of a statement from Louis Napoleon opting for Paris among the five departments that had chosen him.[9] The Assembly thus debated *en connaissance de cause*. Although there was spirited opposition from isolated radical republicans, partisans of an all-powerful Assembly, and from some monarchists, the committee reaffirmed its position through a prestigious spokes-

[5] Bastid, *Doctrines et institutions politiques*, I, p. 257. Much of the following discussion is based on this work.

[6] *Ibid.*, p. 274.

[7] *Ibid.*, II, pp. 42-44.

[8] A. N., C 918, minutes, II, p. 71.

[9] *Compte rendu des séances*, IV, p. 650, 5 October 1848.

man, Tocqueville, who argued that the executive would be too weak if chosen by the Assembly.

Then a group of moderate republicans led a determined effort to shift the decision from the mass electorate to the Assembly, despite the fact that their own candidate, Cavaignac, had taken the opposite view. It was the young Jules Grévy who at this point introduced the amendment for which he later became famous. Grévy argued that there should be no president at all, but merely a premier named by the Assembly and revocable by it. The proposal was designed to head off Louis Napoleon and to satisfy both the doctrinaire proponents of the omnipotent Assembly and the partisans of Cavaignac. Indeed, Grévy suggested nothing more than the perpetuation of the system that had developed under Cavaignac, "which reflects so well the essence and the necessities of democracy, that the Assembly has been led to it naturally by force of circumstance."[10] Arguing from the experience with Cavaignac, Grévy said that the proposal would create a strong executive who would at the same time be subject to the will of the Assembly.

At this point, however, Lamartine intervened in favor of popular election with one of his most famous and effective speeches. Sneering at the possibility of a new eighteenth Brumaire, which would require "long years of Terror behind and Marengos, victories ahead," the poet nevertheless ended on a fatalistic note: "Let God and the people pronounce! We must leave something to Providence. . . . And if the people are wrong . . . so much the worse for the people! . . . Yes, whatever may happen, it will be a fine thing in history to have attempted the Republic."[11] Many contemporaries believed that Lamartine's speech was decisive in bringing a majority over to popular election;[12] indeed, as Falloux recalled it, the opposite conclusion seemed assured a few hours before the speech.[13] Instead, on October 7 the Assembly overwhelmingly rejected the Grévy amendment, by a vote of 643 to 158. The

[10] *Ibid.*, p. 669, 6 October 1848.
[11] *Ibid.*, p. 686, 6 October 1848.
[12] Seignobos, *La Révolution de 1848*, p. 123.
[13] *Mémoires*, I, p. 378.

opponents of popular election made one more effort, with a proposal for a president elected by the Assembly. The vote on this amendment (introduced by the moderate republican, Leblond) settled the issue: it was rejected 602 to 211. On this crucial division, Cavaignac and his entire Cabinet voted for election by the Assembly, despite the fact that the general himself had earlier pronounced in favor of popular election.

What is the explanation of Cavaignac's strange reversal? Had he changed his mind now that it was too late, or had he always been opposed to popular election, despite his advocacy of it when his influence might have been decisive? Odilon Barrot, who had been a member of the Constitutional Committee and was to become Louis Napoleon's first minister, believed that Cavaignac had sincerely if foolishly favored popular election in August, being confident of success and wishing to free himself from the control of the Assembly.[14] On the other hand, Barthélemy Saint-Hilaire, no friend of Cavaignac's, regarded Cavaignac's August statement as "a very elegant gesture," by which he injured his own interests.[15] Cavaignac himself said later that he had always been in favor of election by the Assembly, but had supported popular election in August to avoid influencing the committee to his personal advantage.[16] His Cabinet had always favored election by the Assembly, Cavaignac said;[17] he publicly changed his own position, in voting for the Leblond amendment, only after he knew that the amendment would lose.[18]

Cavaignac's explanation seems plausible: in August he may have been confident of popular election, but he was virtually certain of election by the Assembly; moreover, at that point there was no need to free himself from the control of the Assembly, which was offering no serious opposition to Cavaignac's policies. However, by October Cavaignac was clearly

[14] *Mémoires posthumes*, II, pp. 395-396.

[15] Cohen, *La Préparation de la constitution de 1848*, p. 115.

[16] *Compte rendu des séances*, IV, p. 895, 16 October 1848.

[17] *Ibid.* Cf. Senard's remarks, *ibid.*, p. 892. Normanby also confirms this view. (*A Year of Revolution*, II, pp. 223, 226.)

[18] *Compte rendu des séances*, IV, p. 895, 16 October 1848.

worried about Louis Napoleon, who had a good chance of winning a popular election though virtually none of election by the Assembly. Whatever the motives, Cavaignac's behavior in this matter was another example of his indecisiveness and hardly likely to inspire confidence.

The Assembly on October 7 voted to submit the choice of the president to popular suffrage. Although in retrospect it seems inexplicable that the Assembly should thus have opened the way for a man that it evidently feared and despised, it should be remembered that Louis Napoleon's victory was by no means certain, and there were still several safeguards against him. One was the provision throwing the final decision into the Assembly should any candidate fail to receive an absolute majority. Many observers, including undoubtedly Cavaignac himself, believed that the general might yet be elected by this means; moreover, it has been argued that Lamartine had advocated popular suffrage not in poetic fervor but in cunning, hoping that he himself might be chosen by the Assembly after a popular deadlock.[19]

After popular election was decided, there were several other attempts to prevent the election of Louis Napoleon. One was a proposal, offered by the moderate republican Thouret, to exclude members of former reigning families. The amendment brought Louis Napoleon to the tribune in his own defense, but his brief, faltering speech was so ineffectual that Thouret withdrew his amendment in contempt,[20] and Ledru-Rollin muttered, "What an idiot! He is ruined."[21] Shortly thereafter the Assembly, without debate, abrogated the article of the law of 1832 exiling him. Nevertheless, Thouret and others still took the matter seriously, and on November 3 he offered his motion again. At this point, Cavaignac intervened personally against

[19] Falloux records a purported statement of Lamartine's to this effect. (*Mémoires*, I, p. 382.) Seignobos, *La Révolution de 1848*, p. 123, speaks of Lamartine's "calcul" as a fact, but Bastid, *Doctrines et institutions politiques*, II, p. 133, questions this view.

[20] *Compte rendu des séances*, IV, p. 743, 9 October 1848.

[21] Ollivier, *L'Empire libéral*, II, p. 101. Cf. Calman, *Ledru-Rollin*, p. 241. Calman errs in the date, as well as in the content of the Thouret amendment.

the exclusion. Eight months ago, he said, he would have supported such a proposal, but to exclude Louis Napoleon now would negate the previous decision to submit the choice to the people. "I am eager to find out at last where the confidence of the nation lies."[22] The Assembly rejected the proposal.

One final method of preventing or delaying a Bonapartist triumph would have been the postponement of the elections, as many of Cavaignac's supporters urged. Indeed, the Rue de Poitiers, at that time disdainful of Louis Napoleon and favoring Cavaignac, decided to oppose early elections,[23] but on October 26 Cavaignac himself advocated an early election: "To delay beyond what is strictly necessary the solemn decision on which I ask you to be willing to fix the date, would be seriously to compromise the future, the existence of the Republic."[24] Cavaignac's attitude on this matter also aroused contradictory speculations as to his motives. Madame d'Agoult suggested that, anticipating defeat, "he was in a hurry to rid himself of a heavy burden,"[25] but Madame Dosne and Rémusat thought that he did so because he was confident of victory.[26] Undoubtedly Cavaignac believed that his own chances would be improved by an early election, but probably the most important consideration to him was the one he offered, that the country must establish a regular government as soon as possible. He already had evidence that the provisional status of the French government was injuring her diplomatic position, and his statement on October 26 only reiterated a stand taken before the issue of popular election had been decided.[27]

After hearing Cavaignac, the Assembly set the elections for December 10. There still remained other precautions, if not against a Bonapartist victory, at least against the misuse of

[22] *Compte rendu des séances*, v, p. 283, 3 November 1848.

[23] Rémusat, *Mémoires de ma vie*, iv, p. 366.

[24] *Compte rendu des séances*, v, p. 115.

[25] Stern, *Histoire de la révolution de 1848*, iii, p. 284.

[26] *Mémoires de Madame Dosne*, i, pp. 245-247, and Rémusat, *Mémoires de ma vie*, iv, p. 367.

[27] See *Le National* for 7 October 1848, p. 2, and cf. Cavaignac's remark in the Assembly the same day, *Compte rendu des séances*, iv, p. 703.

presidential power. One was the prohibition against immediate reelection, the provision that in fact would become the pretext for the *coup d'Etat.* This decision had been taken in May, on theoretical grounds, but two other measures, adopted at the last moment, were clearly directed against Louis Napoleon. These were the requirement for an oath of office, and Article 68, which provided for the automatic deposition of the president should he dissolve the Assembly. These legalistic precautions would prove illusory.

The crucial decision had been the one for popular election, and the ultimate explanation for that was the continuing force, in the Assembly at least, of the democratic spirit aroused in February. Neither Cavaignac's August declaration nor Lamartine's speech was decisive. From the beginning the Assembly and its committees had favored popular election, even in the face of Louis Napoleon's triumphs. For the republicans, popular election reflected a hallowed principle, even though many of them came to prefer election by the Assembly on the practical ground that it was necessary to assure the triumph of Cavaignac. Moreover, the conservatives and monarchists were afraid to oppose universal suffrage openly, and their fears were assuaged by the conservative or antirepublican trend in by-elections, as well as by the conservative results of the municipal elections. Their first alarm at Louis Napoleon began to decline, and some began to fear him less than the perpetuation in power of Cavaignac. Thus, a week before Lamartine's speech the Rue de Poitiers had decided to oppose election of the president by the Assembly.[28]

The men of the National Assembly, either captivated by the ideal of democracy, or fearful of opposing it, had the will only to offer weak gestures against the threat of Caesarism, refusing to place obstacles in the path of the expression of the popular will. In a profound sense, then, Lamartine's grandiloquent speech reflected with complete reality the mood of 1848, and his speech was influential, not in seducing the Assembly, but in giving it heart to do what it felt it must.

[28] See Tudesq, *Les Grands notables*, II, pp. 1114, 1144, and Tudesq, *L'Election présidentielle*, pp. 102-108.

THE CAMPAIGN

Before Louis Napoleon's electoral victories in September, Cavaignac had seemed to many astute Frenchmen the only possible candidate for the presidency, and this attitude persisted to a great extent even into October.[29] Yet there were inherent weaknesses in his political position in the country that were even more serious than in his relations with the National Assembly. In the first place, his reputation as a man of order who had saved society in June was increasingly compromised in the eyes of many conservatives by continuing evidence of his republican inflexibility. But to seek the votes only of committed republicans would be political suicide because they had been a small minority before February, and there was mounting evidence that many of the conversions of the spring were superficial or insincere. Moreover, the republicans were bitterly divided among themselves, partly because of old quarrels, partly as a result of the divisive events of 1848. Some radicals were willing, though with reluctance, to seek republican unity behind Cavaignac, but most were not.

The radicals, organized in the National Assembly as the Mountain, sponsored Ledru-Rollin and sought to form a popular party under the name of the *Solidarité républicaine*, with the endorsement of *La Réforme*. But Ledru-Rollin was too tame for the socialists, a group of whom sponsored the candidacy of François Raspail, a prisoner at Vincennes since the May 15 affair. Cavaignac did not even have all of the moderate republicans solidly behind him, although many republican deputies took leave of the Assembly to campaign for him. There was a small group of dissidents who had opposed his coming to power in June, and Lamartine also decided to stand for election, hoping that enough of his popularity survived to divide the vote and throw the decision into the National Assembly.

Ledru-Rollin and Raspail had vigorous advocates, but little chance of victory. Lamartine won the support of only a single newspaper, and was scarcely even discussed as a factor in the

[29] See Rémusat, *Mémoires de ma vie*, IV, pp. 354, 364.

campaign.[30] As election day approached, increasing evidence mounted that it was most likely to be a contest between Cavaignac and Louis Napoleon.

Neither of the two was particularly attractive to the world of the *notables*, or to what was recognized as their major national political organization, the Rue de Poitiers. Some Legitimists and Orleanists considered putting forward the Count of Chambord or a son of Louis Philippe, but most realized that such candidacies were still impossible, and moreover would split the Party of Order. Other men considered were Thiers, Marshal Bugeaud and General Changarnier, but it became apparent by late September that none of them would be likely to win a popular election.[31]

The forces of both Cavaignac and Louis Napoleon then made efforts to win the support of the Rue de Poitiers and of conservative groups in general. Cavaignac's first such move was an indirect approach to Thiers, through an official in the Ministry of Foreign Affairs named Hetzel, who allegedly offered Thiers the vice-presidency, adding, "Cavaignac will have the first difficulties of the Republic, and in four years you will succeed him."[32] Thiers was not very receptive, telling Hetzel frankly, "I believe the general will be lured rather toward the reds than toward our side." Thiers admitted that he preferred Louis Napoleon, "who seems to dissociate himself more from the reds and socialists than does General Cavaignac."[33]

On November 5, two days after this interview, the Rue de Poitiers decided, following turbulent debate in which the influence of Thiers was paramount, not to support any candidate.[34] The Cavaignac forces had hoped that, failing outright endorsement, the Rue de Poitiers would name a third candidate, who might split the popular vote sufficiently to throw the election into the Assembly, where Cavaignac had the best

[30] Tudesq, *L'Election présidentielle*, pp. 113-114.

[31] *Ibid.*, p. 122.

[32] Malo, *Mémoires de Madame Dosne*, I, p. 266.

[33] *Ibid.*, pp. 266-267.

[34] Tudesq, *Les Grands notables*, II, p. 1164. Seignobos, in *La Révolution de 1848*, p. 126, errs in saying that the Rue de Poitiers agreed to support Louis Napoleon.

chance. Thus the refusal to endorse any candidate would have the effect, as Thiers acknowledged, of working to the advantage of Louis Napoleon, who clearly was the favorite of the popular classes. The prince, in the view of Thiers, was the lesser of two evils.[35] It was after the refusal of the Rue de Poitiers to sponsor a candidate that Dégousée, one of the few republican members, resigned in disgust.[36] By their failure to take a position, the national leadership of the *notables* revealed their continuing perplexity and political weakness in the face of the democratic revolution, for instead of giving leadership they were content to follow mass opinion.[37]

The refusal to adopt a candidate was not necessarily definitive, however, and it left individuals and the press free to support whom they chose. Indeed, this is what a number of provincial newspaper editors did, after deploring the indecision of the Rue de Poitiers.[38] The Cavaignac forces now appealed to various Orleanist politicians, in particular Barrot, Rémusat and once more to Thiers. Before even agreeing to see Cavaignac, Thiers posed several conditions, such as the withdrawal of Carnot's bill on primary education, "a change of personnel," a definitive law against the clubs, refusal to recognize the Frankfurt Assembly, and support of the King of Piedmont against the republicans of North Italy.[39]

The demands angered Cavaignac. "Didn't I give enough guarantees of order in the days of June?" he grumbled, and said he would refuse any conditions until Thiers had "proved his devotion to the Republic."[40] Disgusted, Thiers remarked of the general, "Unbutton him and you'll see that he is red."[41] Molé agreed. "Cavaignac, *c'est la mauvaise République*; he is always thinking of his father and his brother." Louis Napoleon, added Molé, hates the republic and would pave the way to a

[35] Malo, *Mémoires de Madame Dosne*, I, p. 266.

[36] Tudesq, *Les Grands notables*, II, p. 1144.

[37] *Ibid.*, p. 1164.

[38] Tudesq, *L'Election présidentielle*, pp. 126-127.

[39] Some of these conditions are reported in Senior, *Conversations with M. Thiers*, I, p. 33, and others in Malo, *Mémoires de Madame Dosne*, I, p. 272.

[40] Malo, *Mémoires de Madame Dosne*, I, p. 269.

[41] Dansette, *Louis Napoléon*, p. 245.

restoration; "in short, he will be our instrument, whereas Cavaignac would be our master."[42]

Cavaignac also made an unsuccessful approach to Barrot. They talked only briefly, however, because, as Barrot recalled, it was apparent "from the first words that we did not understand each other on the fundamental conditions of government."[43] General Lamoricière was Cavaignac's emissary to Rémusat, whom he asked to draw up an electoral proclamation. Rémusat declined on the ground that the candidate himself should write so personal a statement, but he was flattered and amused that almost simultaneously the Bonapartist forces also asked him to draw up a proclamation for Louis Napoleon, which he also declined to do.[44]

The general's approach to Dr. Véron, editor of the influential Orleanist newspaper, *Le Constitutionnel*, had a more dramatic result. When Véron chided Cavaignac for approaching the monarchists "unwillingly and grudgingly," the general exploded: "Ah, that's how it is, you wish to have everything. . . . Your party always behaves like this, you are intractable; you are all the same—you have learned nothing and forgotten nothing."[45] Cavaignac warned that he would defend the republic "by every means"; Véron left fearful that the general "was working for a *coup d'Etat*," and shortly thereafter came out for Louis Napoleon.[46]

Indeed, rumors were circulating in mid-November that Cavaignac would attempt a coup in alliance with the "red" republicans. He purportedly planned to arrest Louis Napoleon, his cousins and the editors Véron and Girardin, and purge the Assembly of some prominent monarchists, including Thiers and Barrot. Several deputies nervously slept away from home,

[42] Senior, *Conversations with M. Thiers*, I, pp. 33-34.

[43] *Mémoires posthumes*, III, p. 27.

[44] *Mémoires de ma vie*, IV, p. 374.

[45] Several versions of this interview, differing in details, have been published. See Girardin, *Questions de mon temps*, IV, pp. 186-190; L. Véron, *Mémoires d'un bourgeois de Paris* (Paris, 1853-56), V, pp. 130-136; and Lord Kerry, *Secret of the Coup d'Etat*, pp. 85-86.

[46] Kerry, *Secret of the Coup d'Etat*, p. 88; Castellane, *Journal*, IV, p. 109.

until a conciliatory speech by Dufaure on November 24 dispelled most of the fears.[47]

The general had little success in his negotiations with Catholic spokesmen. Informed that the first condition would be the abandonment of Carnot's bill for free, compulsory and secular primary education, the general refused, saying, "It has already been rather painful to me to sacrifice my friend Carnot to the demands of the right; moreover, I can scarcely abandon his bill since I approve the principle which inspires it."[48] Montalembert broke off negotiations without even mentioning the second condition. Many Catholics also were hostile to the general's principal newspaper support, *Le National*, "that old enemy of religion and the clergy, that implacable foe of Catholicism."[49] Nevertheless, Falloux threw his influence behind Cavaignac, as did the social Catholics of *L'Ere Nouvelle*, some liberal Catholics in the south, and two clerical deputies from the Breton department of Morbihan.[50] Cavaignac also won some Catholic support by his offer of asylum to the pope, but the effect was weakened by his refusal to seek the restoration of the pope's temporal powers. Important groups of Protestants also backed Cavaignac, particularly in the Rhineland.

Cavaignac won a considerable amount of newspaper backing. *Le National* and the moderate republican newspapers of the provinces were his strongest champions, and whereas some of the radicals were as hostile to him as to Louis Napoleon, others championed the general in preference to Ledru-Rollin or Raspail, as the only effective opposition to Louis Napoleon.[51] Cavaignac also had the support of *L'Atelier*.[52] Among

[47] Hugo, *Souvenirs personnels*, pp. 121-123. See also Malo, *Mémoires de Madame Dosne*, I, p. 268; and Rémusat, *Mémoires de ma vie*, IV, pp. 376-377.

[48] R. P. Lecanuet, *Montalembert* (Paris, 1895-1902), II, p. 416. See also A. Trannoy, "Notes et lettres de Montalembert (1848-1852)," *Revue historique*, CXCII (1941), 273.

[49] Collins, *Catholicism and the Second French Republic*, p. 166.

[50] Tudesq, *Les Grands notables*, II, p. 1169, and *L'Election présidentielle*, p. 174.

[51] See, e.g., Toutain, *La Révolution de 1848 à Rouen*, p. 106.

[52] Cuvillier, *Journal d'ouvriers*, p. 35.

the liberal newspapers of Paris, Cavaignac was backed by *Le Siècle* and by the *Journal des Débats.*[53] In November, a new periodical, *Le Crédit,* appeared in Paris with the aim of appealing to the business and financial community on the general's behalf. Cavaignac also had the dubious aid of the humorous periodical, *Le Charivari,* as well as a new *Revue comique à l'usage des gens sérieux.*[54] In the provinces, some of the Orleanist and Legitimist newspapers backed Cavaignac, usually late and reluctantly, particularly in Provence and some of the eastern departments. Some Orleanist newspapers which came out early for Cavaignac later began to favor Louis Napoleon as his victory seemed more imminent.[55]

In addition to newspapers, the Cavaignac forces also relied to a considerable extent on pamphlets and brochures, and even a campaign biography, which appeared in two issues of *Le Moniteur de l'armée.* This ploy was somewhat maladroit, as it recounted to largely nonrepublican officers the story of Cavaignac's refusal to march against republicans in 1832.[56] In general, however, the Cavaignac propaganda laid little stress on his republicanism, or even on his services in June, but instead made a broad appeal as a proven defender of order who could continue to provide political stability and the conditions conducive to economic prosperity.[57] The business community was aimed at in particular, with apparently a good deal of success. The powerful Rothschilds apparently gave Cavaignac their support,[58] as did an official of the Bank of France named Odier (whose daughter Cavaignac would marry in 1851).

But the Cavaignac forces also made special appeals to the peasants, and even to the workers; an *Almanach des campagnes* emphasized the agricultural education plan and postal reform, and an *Almanach des ouvriers* reminded workers of

[53] Tudesq, *L'Election présidentielle,* pp. 166-168.

[54] *Ibid.,* pp. 157-168.

[55] *Ibid.,* pp. 172-176.

[56] See Castellane, *Journal,* IV, p. 109.

[57] These generalizations are based on campaign literature preserved at the Bibliothèque Nationale, LB 54, 1701 to 1887.

[58] See Egon Caesar Corti, *The Reign of the House of Rothschild* (New York, 1928), pp. 250, 253-254.

the various measures taken in their interest by Cavaignac's ministry. One handbill issued on behalf of Cavaignac promised communal land to the peasants, employment for workers, the suppression of the wine tax and the end of the hated 45-centime tax, but Dufaure, who functioned as Cavaignac's chief campaign manager, ordered it suppressed.[59]

In Cavaignac's campaign literature, Louis Napoleon was depicted less as a dynastic threat to the republic than as an adventurer whose victory would leave France a prey to new disorders, economic crisis, and civil and foreign war. Some of the radical newspapers supporting Cavaignac also used similar themes. "With Louis Napoleon," wrote *Le Progrès du Pas-de-Calais*, "no confidence, no security, no commerce, no work. With Cavaignac, work, commerce, confidence, security."[60] Some republican newspapers ridiculed Louis Napoleon as the man of Strasbourg and Boulogne, the dandy, the London constable, the man of uncertain nationality.[61] But as more and more of the monarchist newspapers came out for the prince, the republican newspapers began to emphasize the political theme, representing him, in the words of *Le National*, as "the last hope of the secret partisans of monarchical restorations."[62] Cavaignac was deeply concerned about evidence of growing antirepublicanism in the country, as he confessed to the British ambassador on November 27.

> "Then you do not think the country Republican?" asked Lord Normanby.
>
> "Certainly not," Cavaignac answered, "and never was, and never was."
>
> "And you expect to make it so?"
>
> "It is with that object alone that I seek the presidency."[63]

The Cavaignac forces made some use of the administrative

[59] See *Compte rendu des séances*, v, pp. 791-792, 24 November 1848, and Tudesq, *L'Election présidentielle*, p. 115.

[60] Tudesq, *L'Election présidentielle*, p. 164.

[61] *Ibid.*, pp. 156-157.

[62] Issue of 16 November 1848.

[63] Confidential letter from Normanby to Palmerston, 27 November 1848, cited in F. A. Simpson, *The Rise of Louis Napoleon* (3d edn., London, 1960), p. 316.

machinery that they controlled to further the general's candidacy. On November 2, Dufaure distributed to all prefects a circular which, without naming the general, unmistakably recommended him: "The Nation should, in the choice that it makes, confide itself to a past without reproach, to an incontestable patriotism, to a man of virile, energetic determination which has already been proved in the service of the republic, rather than to empty and deceitful promises."[64] The circular was ostensibly impartial, however, in pointing out that the only role of government officials was to assure honest and free elections. The Minister of Public Works, Vivien, also sent out a thinly veiled instruction to all chief engineers, advising them to assure workers that the government was attentive to their interests, as evidenced by the measures already taken, and to warn workers against "false doctrines."[65]

Cavaignac himself also issued on November 10, in the form of a circular on the promulgation of the new Constitution, what some observers took to be his electoral manifesto.[66] Actually, it was little more than it purported to be, a declaration in favor of the Constitution, couched in the familiar phrases of moderate republicanism, but with a more conservative emphasis:

> Founded on the great principle of universal suffrage, . . . the Constitution removes all pretext for insurrection. . . . Universal suffrage is the entire revolution. . . . The Republic without good order, good order without the Republic, are henceforth two things equally impossible, and whoever would claim to separate them or to sacrifice the one to the other is a dangerous citizen whom reason condemns and the country rejects.

The circular criticized the "senseless plans of a very few" who believed that "everything was to be done over, and that of former society nothing should be preserved." While thus condemning the socialists, Cavaignac urged conciliation of

[64] A. N., F 1A 45; *Le Moniteur*, 4 November 1848.
[65] A. N., circular of 16 November 1848, F 1A 45.
[66] Published in *Le Moniteur*, 11 November 1848.

those who, whatever their past views, would serve the republic faithfully.

Shortly before election day on December 10, Cavaignac became involved in two incidents which undoubtedly influenced some voters against him, and others in his favor. The first, which occurred late in November, involved a verbal attack on him from some disaffected moderate republicans, who accused Cavaignac of having cynically allowed the insurrection of June to spread in order to win power by crushing it. At Cavaignac's request, the issue was debated before the National Assembly in a long session on November 25. Ledru-Rollin forcefully joined the attack, but the general defended himself eloquently and effectively.

"The Assembly listened to him for almost three hours with profound attention," noted Victor Hugo, "always with sympathy and confidence, sometimes with a kind of love. . . . Cavaignac, tall and lithe, in black frockcoat and military collar, with his thick moustache, speaking bluntly and jerkily, with numerous digressions, scowling and gesturing sternly, at times combined the ferocity of the soldier with the ferocity of the tribune. Toward the middle, . . . the harangue became a lawyer's plea, but at the end he recovered with a kind of genuine indignation. He pounded the lectern so hard that it overturned a glass of water, alarming the ushers, and when he concluded . . . the entire Assembly burst into loud applause."[67]

It was commonly acknowledged that the general had won an oratorical triumph. The sophisticated Rémusat in particular was impressed. "The speech of Cavaignac demonstrated not only his superiority in the discussion, but also his capacity in action. It is the historical document on which he should be judged." Morny, then not yet associated with Louis Napoleon, told Madame Rémusat, "I do not know if the republic will establish itself in France, but I know that if it does, it is General Cavaignac alone who can found it."[68] By a huge majority

[67] Hugo, *Souvenirs personnels*, p. 125. The debate is in *Compte rendu des séances*, v, pp. 809-849.

[68] Rémusat, *Mémoires de ma vie*, iv, p. 378. See also Tocqueville, *Oeuvres complètes*, xii, p. 279.

of 503 to 34, the Assembly reaffirmed its declaration of June 28 that Cavaignac "deserved well of the fatherland." The opposition was made up almost exclusively of Montagnards, but there were many abstentions by men of the Rue de Poitiers, such as Thiers and Molé. The debate on November 25 was to be Cavaignac's last triumph.

The other incident, which erupted only four days before the election, was the affair of the "récompenses nationales." At issue was a bill sponsored by the Cavaignac government to offer small payments to needy men who had been republican political prisoners under the July Monarchy, in recompense for their sufferings. However, some of the proposed lists, drawn up by a republican committee in Paris, were found to contain names of relatives of men who had attempted to assassinate Louis Philippe, and even some convicted of ordinary crimes. These were published by *La Presse* (under the heading, "The Pensioners of General Cavaignac"), and angry protests arose in the National Assembly.

The government immediately disavowed the lists and withdrew the bill,[69] but suffered from the incident in several respects. Although the publication was an attempt to discredit Cavaignac and emanated from some partisans of Louis Napoleon, some conservatives regarded it with suspicion as a last-minute appeal by Cavaignac to the left.[70] Moreover, in seeking to counteract the maneuver, the government left itself open to a new charge, that of unwarranted use of administrative powers. The Finance Minister, Trouvé-Chauvel, was forced to admit publicly that he had delayed the mail shipments out of Paris on December 7 in order to permit the news of the repudiation of the lists to reach the provinces at the same time as the insinuation that Cavaignac planned to reward assassination and crime.[71] This incident aroused further suspicions of Cavaignac in the world of the *notables*,[72] and at least one Orleanist provincial newspaper, *La Gazette*

[69] *Compte rendu des séances*, VI, p. 111, 6 December 1848.

[70] Tudesq, *Les Grands notables*, II, p. 1207.

[71] *Compte rendu des séances*, VI, pp. 142-145, 8 December 1848.

[72] Malo, *Mémoires de Madame Dosne*, II, p. 10.

de Cambrai, undecided thus far, came out against Cavaignac over this issue.[73]

Although Cavaignac was distasteful to most of the leading *notables*, he did win some following in this quarter. Besides Falloux, Rémusat, Tocqueville and a number of bishops preferred him to Louis Napoleon. Nevertheless, the support for Cavaignac among the *notables*, Tudesq found, was a minority in two senses; a minority of the *notables*, and a minority within the Cavaignac camp, which in the main was politically *républicain de la veille* and socially drawn from the urban petty and middle bourgeoisie.[74]

If Cavaignac's originally strong position deteriorated, Louis Napoleon's improved as the election date approached. He had mass support from the start, but most of the *notables* were alarmed or amused by him at first. In late October a challenge within the National Assembly to clarify his intentions gave him a public platform in which the prince's moderate and reassuring responses to hostile questioning were given wide publicity, and the *notables* began to consider him as a serious candidate.[75] Almost immediately afterward, Emile de Girardin's influential *La Presse* was the first established newspaper to support him. Girardin hated Cavaignac, but had no enthusiasm for Louis Napoleon. *La Presse* offered a variant of the "lesser evil" argument. "We have attached ourselves to the candidacy of Louis Napoleon as one clings to a branch, the last hope of salvation for a drowning man."[76] Shortly thereafter, other influential monarchist journals such as *La Gazette de France* and *Le Constitutionnel* also went over to Louis Napoleon, and the indecisive stand of the Rue de Poitiers also favored him. Monarchist politicians began to look on the prince as a man whose evident weaknesses would render him harmless and easy to use. Thiers' reputed comment, "He is a cretin whom we will lead," was widely circulated. Late in the campaign, however, one newspaper, *Le Courrier de la*

[73] Tudesq, *L'Election présidentielle*, p. 195.

[74] Tudesq, *Les Grands notables*, II, p. 1168 and *L'Election présidentielle*, p. 238.

[75] Tudesq, *L'Election présidentielle*, pp. 132-135.

[76] *Ibid.*, pp. 183-184.

Gironde, argued hopefully, "when one speaks five languages, one cannot be a cretin."[77]

Louis Napoleon had much greater success than Cavaignac in winning monarchist and Catholic support. After some hesitation, he accepted Montalembert's demand for "liberty of education," and thereby won the influential ecclesiastic to his cause. He also outbid Cavaignac on the issue of the pope by advocating restoration of his temporal authority, a pledge that was to be fulfilled in the Roman expedition of the following spring.[78] In his negotiations with the Orleanists, Louis Napoleon seemed at first "very decorous, very meek."[79] As Thiers recalled it, "He was suppleness itself, compared with Cavaignac. There was no sacrifice that he would not make, no engagement that he would not enter into. His highest ambition was to be a mere instrument of the Parti de l'Ordre."[80] But the prince, in his own indirect and baffling way, proved to be as stubborn as Cavaignac had been. Thiers acidly dismissed his proposed electoral manifesto as "detestable, full of socialism and bad French,"[81] and had another drawn up by a committee. But Louis Napoleon politely declined to accept it despite angry threats to abandon him. He even rejected another manifesto written by Thiers himself, except for a few words and phrases that he inserted in his own manifesto which he published on November 27.[82]

The prince began by emphasizing that his name symbolized "order and security." He sought to dispel fears by proclaiming, "I am not an ambitious man who dreams sometimes of the Empire and war, sometimes of the application of subversive theories." He promised on his honor to respect and sustain the republic and to leave office after four years with "liberty in-

[77] *Ibid.*, p. 193.

[78] Dansette, *Louis Napoléon*, p. 248, and Collins, *Catholicism and the Second French Republic*, pp. 176-178, 183-185.

[79] Malo, *Mémoires de Madame Dosne*, I, p. 283.

[80] Senior, *Conversations with M. Thiers*, I, p. 35.

[81] Seignobos, *La Révolution de 1848*, p. 126.

[82] Tudesq, *L'Election présidentielle*, p. 179. For an amusing account of the negotiations, see Malo, *Mémoires de Madame Dosne*, I, pp. 280-300. See also Dansette, *Louis Napoléon*, p. 246.

tact."[83] The man who had sought an accord with Proudhon and who later would call himself a socialist solemnly invoked "religion, family and property, the eternal foundations of any social order," and in general made a strongly conservative appeal. Even more than Cavaignac, Louis Napoleon sought to minimize the revolutionary implications of his point of view, and to present himself primarily as a man of order. Pimienta argues that Louis Napoleon was in December an open candidate of the right, contrary to his demagogic appeal earlier in the year.[84] However, the prince also made discreet allusion to the nationalistic implications of his name and promised to reduce taxes, to favor "industrial laws" for the workers, and even to amnesty the June insurgents.

Despite Thiers' misgivings, the conservative press in general greeted the manifesto favorably, and there were many further adhesions to his cause. Few editors changed their personal opinions of the prince, but supported him in opposition to Cavaignac, increasingly regarded as the "incarnation" of the February revolution whose success would mean further unwanted reforms.[85] As one Legitimist newspaper put it, "the candidacy of M. Louis Bonaparte, although full of disadvantages, is less deadly than that of General Cavaignac."[86] Thiers himself took this position. A week before the election, he finally endorsed Louis Napoleon formally, in a widely published letter: "Without stating that the election of Monsieur Louis Bonaparte would be a good thing, it appears to all of us moderate men as a lesser evil."[87]

Many other prominent *notables* also came out publicly for Louis Napoleon, including Molé, Bugeaud and Baraguey d'Hilliers, the president of the Rue de Poitiers. Montalembert and other Catholic figures also supported the prince, and some who did not, such as Veuillot in *L'Univers*, indirectly favored

[83] The text is published in full in Louis Napoleon's *Oeuvres*, III (Paris, 1869), pp. 24-28. It may be compared with Thiers' proposed manifesto in Malo, *Mémoires de Madame Dosne*, I, pp. 297-300.

[84] *La Propagande bonapartiste*, pp. 95-98.

[85] Tudesq, *L'Election présidentielle*, pp. 190, 196.

[86] *Ibid.*, p. 191.

[87] Seignobos, *La Révolution de 1848*, p. 217.

him because of their even stronger hostility to Cavaignac.[88] With respect to newspaper endorsements, early calculations gave Cavaignac a substantial lead, but in view of the equivocal attitude of many conservative organs and the numerous last-minute endorsements or shifts, estimates of contemporaries varied considerably. By December 7, *Le Crédit* conceded 91 provincial newspapers backed Louis Napoleon as against 117 for Cavaignac, but *L'Ere Nouvelle* on December 9 listed 190 for Cavaignac and only 103 for Louis Napoleon. Cavaignac may have had the majority of the newspapers behind him, but these included many small republican publications; most of the important newspapers of the monarchist "Party of Order" favored Louis Napoleon at the end.[89] In sum, in addition to his popular support, Louis Napoleon also had that of the majority of the monarchist *notables*, although a minority sustained Cavaignac and others either abstained or doggedly continued to advocate Changarnier.[90]

Despite the laws controlling the press and the clubs, the electoral campaign was spirited and proceeded in an atmosphere of almost complete freedom. The revived bond had largely stifled newspapers of the extreme left, but both Ledru-Rollin and Raspail had vigorous press support, although not on the same scale as the two major candidates. Opponents were free to attack Cavaignac severely and with impunity. In Paris, *La Réforme* was most vigorous in its criticism of the general, and in the provinces he was the focus of varied and vituperative attacks. From the left, Cavaignac was called a deserter from democracy, a dictator, the enemy of the socialists and the executioner of the workers. In the Nord, the radical Delescluze founded a new journal that violently assailed Cavaignac as "the true author of the bloody insurrection of June, the ambitious accomplice of the royalists of all

[88] Tudesq, *L'Election présidentielle*, pp. 190-191. Barrot claims to have remained neutral. (*Mémoires posthumes*, III, p. 27.)

[89] Tudesq, *L'Election présidentielle*, pp. 129, 189, 209. Cf. Dansette, *Louis Napoléon*, p. 249, and Lucas-Dubreton, *Le Culte de Napoléon*, p. 454, who say that Cavaignac had only 100 of 380 provincial newspapers.

[90] Tudesq, *Les Grands notables*, II, p. 1180.

nuances."[91] From the right, Cavaignac was attacked as a republican sympathetic to the socialists, as a collaborator of Ledru-Rollin, and even as "the candidate of M. Proudhon," as a man whose election would pose the threat of a new revolution and of "a return to the guillotine."[92] In the Gironde, monarchists revived against Cavaignac the "terrible memories" of his father as a *représentant en mission.*[93] Several newspapers warned openly of an impending *coup d'Etat* by Cavaignac.[94]

Political clubs also flourished openly during the campaign, for they could escape surveillance simply by calling themselves electoral meetings; although Cavaignac was well aware that many of the disbanded clubs had reappeared in this guise, he scrupulously honored this exception granted in the August law on the clubs.[95] Moreover, the government made no effort to apply the law on "attroupements" against opposition demonstrations, even when groups paraded the streets shouting "Down with Cavaignac!"[96] Some ministers and prefects made some use of their office to favor Cavaignac, but these efforts were relatively mild.[97] Cavaignac in a proclamation published on election day called upon each citizen to vote freely and conscientiously, and thereafter "to bow respectfully to the nation's choice, whatever be the name that it will have pronounced."[98]

[91] Dessal, *Charles Delescluze*, p. 77.

[92] Tudesq, *L'Election présidentielle*, p. 184, and Armengaud, *Populations de l'Est Aquitain*, p. 363n.

[93] Albert Charles, *La Révolution de 1848 et la seconde république à Bordeaux et dans le département de la Gironde* (Bordeaux, 1945), pp. 177-178.

[94] See the remarks of Dufaure, *Compte rendu des séances*, v, p. 795, 24 November 1848, and also Rémusat, *Mémoires de ma vie*, iv, pp. 376-377.

[95] See the statement by Dufaure in *Compte rendu des séances*, v, pp. 792-793, 24 November 1848, and the announcement in *Le Moniteur* of 13 December 1848, p. 3546, that following the election the law would be enforced.

[96] See Dufaure's comments, *Compte rendu des séances*, vi, pp. 184-189, 9 December 1848.

[97] See Vigier, *La Seconde république dans la région alpine*, i, p. 312, and Ollivier, *L'Empire libéral*, ii, p. 117.

[98] *Le National*, 10 December 1848.

THE ANTICIPATORY PLEBISCITE

Although a victory for Louis Napoleon seemed "certain" to Barrot[99] and likely to most observers, it was by no means a foregone conclusion. The popular election of a head of state was unprecedented in France, and Cavaignac could not be written off in advance. In the fortnight before the election, the perspicacious Madame Dosne fluctuated almost daily in her assessment, until on December 4 she wearily concluded that "sometimes the wind is for General Cavaignac, sometimes for Prince Louis."[100] Even if the general should lose the popular election, there remained the real possibility that Louis Napoleon also would be denied a majority and later be defeated in the Assembly. Thiers confessed afterwards that he had "miscalculated most grossly" in thinking that Ledru-Rollin would receive between two and three million of the more than nine million possible votes.[101]

However, hope was fading in the Cavaignac camp. The general himself was nervous and irritable; to General de Castellane he "seemed drunk, not from wine, for he is very sober, but from nervous agitation."[102] Rumors of an impending coup cropped up again; Cavaignac was said to have plotted secretly with General Lamoricière; the prefect of police allegedly sought in vain at a night-long conference on December 1 to persuade Cavaignac to arrest Louis Napoleon and to assume power as a dictator.[103]

Voters went to the polls on December 10 and 11 in beautiful, sunny weather; participation was about 75 percent, an increase over the by-elections, but still less than the 84 percent of April. As early as December 12, enough returns had been counted to indicate, in the doleful words of *Le National*, that "M. Louis Bonaparte will have a sizable major-

[99] See *Mémoires posthumes*, III, p. 26.

[100] Malo, *Mémoires de Madame Dosne*, II, p. 7.

[101] Senior, *Conversations with M. Thiers*, I, p. 32.

[102] Castellane, *Journal*, IV, p. 121. See also Rémusat, *Mémoires de ma vie*, IV, p. 379, and Hugo, *Souvenirs personnels*, pp. 130-131.

[103] Maxime du Camp, *Souvenirs d'un demi-siècle. Au temps de Louis-Philippe et de Napoléon III, 1830-1870* (Paris, 1949), I, pp. 97-98.

ity."[104] By December 14, the results for Paris were proclaimed: Louis Napoleon had won 58 percent of the votes cast to 28 percent for Cavaignac. But the results for the whole of France were still more astonishing. The prince had collected 5,534,520 votes, a majority of 74 percent of the 7,449,471 cast. Cavaignac was in second place, but he trailed far behind, with 1,448,302, or 19.5 percent. Instead of two or three millions, Ledru-Rollin had garnered only 371,431, and the other candidates received derisory numbers of ballots. Raspail had 36,964, and Lamartine's popularity had plunged so low that he attracted only 17,914 votes.[105] The prince had won in every department except four, two in Brittany and two in Provence, where Cavaignac triumphed.

What was the significance of Louis Napoleon's great victory, and of Cavaignac's defeat? There is as yet no comprehensive study of the election, but recent research has deepened and broadened our understanding of it.[106] Although much information is still lacking, particularly on the sources of Cavaignac's strength, and although voting patterns sometimes varied widely from region to region, some generalizations may be offered.

The triumph of Louis Napoleon was a victory first of all for the peasantry, as many contemporaries acknowledged; Karl Marx called it the "coup d'Etat of the peasants." Most of the population was rural, and the prince's majorities were consistently higher in rural than in urban areas. In April, when

[104] Issue of 13 December 1848.

[105] The "definitive" results for the 86 metropolitan departments were published December 22 in *Le Moniteur*, p. 3647. In addition to the figures given above, there were 4,687 votes for Changarnier, 12,434 votes for diverse unnamed candidates and 23,219 blank or spoiled ballots.

[106] The outstanding student of the elections is André-Jean Tudesq whose article, "La Légende," and two books, *Les Grands notables* and *L'Election présidentielle*, have already been cited. In addition, see Tudesq's "L'Election du président de la république en 1848 dans l'Hérault," *Annales du Midi*, LXVII (1955), pp. 331-340. Other regional studies previously cited are valuable for December, and there have been other studies of single departments, notably that of Roger Marlin, "L'Election présidentielle de Louis-Napoléon Bonaparte dans le Doubs, le 10 décembre 1848," *Annales littéraires de l'université de Besançon*, II, (1955), fasc. 3, pp. 33-46.

confusion and hopes were high, the peasants had voted for candidates of the republic; by December, they had turned against a regime which not only did little to assuage their chronic grievances, but imposed a 45 percent increase in property taxes. Not only did the National Assembly endorse the tax, the government was grimly collecting it, employing military force on a large scale against this and other forms of peasant unrest. The Creuse, where much blood flowed over the 45-centime tax, gave Louis Napoleon one of his largest majorities. To the strong emotional Bonapartism in the country was now added hope that the new Napoleon would end the tax and appease other economic and class grievances.[107] Finally, while the name of Cavaignac was unknown to many of the unlettered peasants, or even confused with that of Polignac, the name of Napoleon was familiar and esteemed.

But the victory of Louis Napoleon was not simply one for the peasantry, for all of the other classes also gave the prince the majority of their votes. Although Cavaignac did much better in the cities and towns than he did in the countryside, Louis Napoleon still defeated him in most of the cities, albeit with lower majorities than in rural regions. In Paris, his majority was 16 percent below the national average. He also won in four of the seven largest provincial cities, but always with smaller majorities than in the corresponding departments.[108] The victory of Louis Napoleon was a popular or national victory in a broad sense, and Louis Napoleon was the elect of no single class nor of any political party. The majority of the *notables* had supported Louis Napoleon, but only reluctantly, and an important minority had thrown their influence behind Cavaignac, in some cases successfully, in others to be defeated by the mass of popular votes.[109]

Politically, the election of Louis Napoleon was a defeat not

[107] See Soboul, "La Question paysanne en 1848," *La Pensée*, No. 20, pp. 48-50; Gossez, "La Résistance à l'impôt," p. 104 and passim; and Coquerelle, "L'Armée et la répression dans les campagnes (1848)."

[108] Tudesq, *L'Election présidentielle*, pp. 210-211.

[109] See Tudesq, *Les Grands notables*, II, pp. 1162-1211; Chevalier, "Les Fondements économiques et sociaux," pp. 295, 357; and Vigier, *La Seconde république dans la région alpine*, I, pp. 312-326.

only for Cavaignac, but for the *républicains de la veille* who had been in power since February, and in a sense for the February revolution itself.[110] "Will they understand this lesson?" asked the *Revue des deux mondes*; it was the "condemnation of the men of February," observed *Le Courrier du Gard*, and many provincial newspapers took the same view.[111] For them, Cavaignac represented the republic, but from the point of view of many radicals and socialists, the general had betrayed the revolution, and they voted for Raspail or Ledru-Rollin, or even Louis Napoleon, in preference to him.[112] The workers of Paris also understandably gave much support to the opponent of the Butcher of June, but the hostility to Cavaignac from the left was an attitude expressed by only a small minority of the population. Ironically, in view of his reputation as the "savior of society," and in view of his appeal as a man of order during the campaign, a majority of voters seemed to have regarded Cavaignac as too revolutionary, as the symbol of the revolution that had brought violence and disorder. This was the attitude of those conservatives who thought that Cavaignac was too sympathetic toward the reds. On December 9, the *Gazette de France* had declared, "Between M. Cavaignac and Louis Napoleon, let us not hesitate. . . . M. Cavaignac represents the insurrection; Louis Napoleon represents universal suffrage."[113] Indeed, Louis Chevalier found that in the region near Paris the pattern of massive support for Louis Napoleon suggested a repetition of the "provincial mobilization" against the June insurrection.[114] Thus Cavaignac, as the only serious republican contender, had come to symbolize the very insurrection that he had crushed! As the head of the regime that had emanated from the February revolution, Cavaignac was the focus for all of the discontents associated with it, from the disorders of Paris and the 45-cen-

[110] See Tudesq, *L'Election présidentielle*, p. 222, and *Les Grands notables*, II, p. 1162.

[111] *Revue des deux mondes*, 14 December 1848, 1027, and Tudesq, *L'Election présidentielle*, p. 225.

[112] Tudesq, *L'Election présidentielle*, pp. 220, 228.

[113] Lebey, *Louis Napoléon et 1848*, II, pp. 185-186.

[114] "Les Fondements économiques et sociaux," pp. 297, 309, 352.

time tax to the continuing economic crisis. The general who had assuaged the pride of the army in June proved unable to carry the army with him against the Bonapartist tide; Louis Napoleon won even in most of the units in Algeria, but with smaller majorities than in France.[115]

Although the general results seemed clear enough, there were interesting class and regional complications. The prince won strong majorities in all regions except the Northwest, parts of the Midi, and some departments in the east and north. Cavaignac won with majorities of up to 60 percent in two Breton departments (Finistère and Morbihan), and in two departments of Provence (Bouches-du-Rhône and the Var). In addition, neighboring departments in both areas, as well as in the East gave Cavaignac minorities of more than 30 percent; the Nord gave him 42 percent of the vote.

It was ironic that Cavaignac found some of his strongest support in regions where Legitimists were dominant. This was particularly true of Brittany, and Legitimists were also strong in the two departments that Cavaignac won in Provence. Moreover, Louis Napoleon won large majorities in many departments which would support the "red" democratic-socialists of Ledru-Rollin in 1849, and would thereafter remain strongholds of the left.

But it would be erroneous to conclude that Louis Napoleon reflected the revolution and Cavaignac the counterrevolution. Actually, the Legitimists and conservative forces in general gave more backing to Louis Napoleon than to Cavaignac, and local factors account for the unusual electoral pattern. This was certainly true for Cavaignac's Breton victories, for Louis Napoleon won easily in adjoining and equally conservative departments such as the Côtes-du-Nord, and won some of his

[115] See Gossez, "Notes sur la composition et l'attitude politique de la troupe," pp. 102-104. Gossez observes that most of the documentation for military votes has disappeared from the National Archives. In the Hérault, Tudesq found that the most specialized and "more politically progressive" services such as engineering and artillery had supported Cavaignac: "L'Election du président de la république en 1848 dans l'Hérault," p. 339. See also Jean-Paul Charnay, *Société militaire et suffrage universel en France depuis 1789* (Paris, 1964), pp. 155, 185, 199, 201.

largest majorities (80 to 95 percent) in the Vendée, the old Chouan areas, and in the strongly conservative southwest. Part of the explanation, as Tudesq suggests, may be that here Cavaignac seemed the candidate of the revolution because of the hated memories of Cavaignac *père*.[116] There is evidence that in the Gironde, many monarchists opposed Cavaignac for these reasons,[117] but Cavaignac won one of his largest minorities in the Loire-Inférieure, another conservative department where his father had also been active as a *représentant en mission*. Moreover, another such department (Charente-Inférieure), had demonstrated its support for Louis Napoleon as early as June 4, long before Cavaignac was a factor.

In the Breton departments where he won, Cavaignac had only a small amount of direct Legitimist support, and he benefited largely from the weakness of the Napoleonic Legend there. Most Legitimists were critical of both leading candidates, but indirectly aided Cavaignac by attacking the prince more vigorously, thus permitting the small minorities of republicans and of some Orleanists, to work more effectively for Cavaignac. Sometimes the Catholics supported Cavaignac "against the directives of the Legitimists."[118]

The Legitimists were similarly divided in their attitude in the Midi, but here the candidacy of Ledru-Rollin was another important factor; indeed, in Bouches-du-Rhône, where Cavaignac won 56 percent of the vote, Ledru-Rollin was second with 24 percent. The Mediterranean region including the Var, where Cavaignac also won, had powerful republican as well as Legitimist traditions. Moreover, in Marseille, the name of Napoleon was associated with memories of war and economic privations resulting from the Continental System. Ledru-Rollin had a strong following among the workers, but Cavaignac, supported by two republican newspapers and also by some Orleanist and Legitimist *notables* who regarded him as the preferable man of order, won in all quarters of the city.[119] Cavaignac had other sources of strength. In the areas

[116] Tudesq, "La Légende napoléonienne," pp. 81-82.

[117] Charles, *La Révolution de 1848 à Bordeaux*, pp. 178-181.

[118] For this discussion, see Tudesq, *Les Grands notables*, II, pp. 1167-1172.

[119] *Ibid.*, pp. 1170-1172.

around Strasbourg and Boulogne, memories of the prince's adventures benefited the general, who received one of his largest minorities in the Bas-Rhin. Eastern business interests led by the industrialist Jean Dollfus backed Cavaignac as a guarantee of stability and prosperity.[120] In various regions, Cavaignac also won the votes of Protestants, sometimes out of opposition to the candidate supported by the Catholics, sometimes because Cavaignac seemed to represent the *juste-milieu* tradition.[121]

In the cities, the clusters of republicans supported Cavaignac, but he had other partisans. Cavaignac was the preferred candidate of a sizable minority of the great bourgeoisie and also had a strong following among the business and commercial classes. Tudesq observes that although the press in general did not exert a great influence in the election, it was of some importance in swaying opinion in the cities, in particular when it supported Cavaignac. The general's victory in Marseille, where not a single newspaper backed the prince, was the most notable example.[122]

The urban working classes were by no means uniform in their choice of candidates. Ledru-Rollin sought their support most assiduously, and in some cities, such as Marseille and Lille, pulled strongly in working-class areas. But Louis Napoleon also won the sympathies of a considerable number of workers. In Paris, he received his largest majorities in the workers' districts, defeating not only the hated Butcher of June, but also Ledru-Rollin and Raspail, who together won only 12.4 percent of the vote.[123] Not only the impressions of contemporaries but also recent scholarly studies on several regions in France indicate that Louis Napoleon had strong support among workers in many towns and cities. This was the case in the region around Paris, in the Alpine region and in East Aquitaine.[124] But it is also significant that Cavaig-

[120] *Ibid.*, p. 1176.

[121] *Ibid.*, p. 1173.

[122] Tudesq, *L'Election présidentielle*, pp. 212, 217.

[123] *Ibid.*, p. 210.

[124] Chevalier, "Les Fondements économiques et sociaux," pp. 353-365; Vigier, *La Seconde république dans la région alpine*, I, pp. 317-324; and Armengaud, *Les Populations de l'Est Aquitain*, pp. 362-365.

nac too won the votes of many workers, at least in some provincial cities. The evidence is as yet only fragmentary, but it is undeniable that in some cities with large concentrations of workers, Cavaignac won important minorities of workers' votes. In both Reims and Troyes, for example, Louis Chevalier found that Cavaignac won much more support from workers than did Ledru-Rollin or Raspail, and he confesses his inability to fully explain why so many workers would vote for the man of June.[125]

Part of the explanation is undoubtedly that some workers, as did other supporters of Ledru-Rollin and Raspail, opted for either of the leading candidates in order not to waste their votes; many of these votes went to the prince, but others obviously went to Cavaignac as the representative of the republican cause. There was also some positive worker backing for Cavaignac; *L'Atelier* campaigned for him, and in Rouen, the newspaper that had inspired the insurrection of April also campaigned for Cavaignac in December.[126] Industrial workers in provinicial cities did not necessarily identify their interests with those of the Paris insurgents, and undoubtedly there was also some gratitude to Cavaignac for his advocacy of maximum hours legislation. In one industrial city, Lille, Cavaignac actually won a large plurality of votes, almost as many as Louis Napoleon and Ledru-Rollin together.[127]

In general, the victory of Louis Napoleon was a victory for the Napoleonic legend and a defeat for the republicans. It was also a victory for the popular classes, in many regions against the influence of the *notables*, and also against the regime symbolized by Cavaignac. Louis Napoleon made skillful use of the ambiguous Bonapartist appeal, winning popular support which in turn brought him the grudging approval of a majority of the *notables*. The massive triumph of the prince, cutting across political, class, religious and regional lines, suggests that the issue was not precisely the republic, or Cavaignac, but the vaguer and more inclusive question, "Do you

[125] Chevalier, "Les Fondements économiques et sociaux," p. 361.

[126] Toutain, *La Révolution de 1848 à Rouen*, p. 106.

[127] A. M. Gossez, *Le Département du Nord sous la deuxième république (1848-1852)*, (Lille, 1904), p. 332.

want Louis Napoleon Bonaparte to rule, *oui ou non*?" Nor was the issue posed clearly between tendencies of movement and stability, revolution and counterrevolution. Both principal candidates represented different aspects of the revolutionary tradition, both offered themselves primarily as men of order. In turning out the republicans, Frenchmen indicated not only a preference for "order," but also a desire to follow a different and perhaps more dynamic aspect of the revolutionary tradition. As Guizot shrewdly observed, "It is a great deal to be simultaneously a national glory, a revolutionary guarantee, and a principle of authority."[128] The narrow republicanism of Cavaignac, even when mitigated by his broader appeal as a proved champion of order, was no match for a candidacy that "dated from Austerlitz."

THE REPUBLIC WITHOUT REPUBLICANS

As the first electoral results came in, suggesting an impending victory for Louis Napoleon, Cavaignac reportedly was urged for the last time to carry out a *coup d'Etat*. Now it was the republican Colonel Charras who pressed Cavaignac to take action.

> "Are you going to resist?" he asked.
>
> "What? Do you want me to go back on my word?"
>
> "But then *we* will resist."
>
> "No, you will not resist," said Cavaignac. "I will surely be able to prevent you."
>
> "But you are compromising the Republic!"
>
> "It is possible that it will succumb," conceded the general, "but it will rise again, whereas the republic would be lost forever if the one who represented it should give the example of revolt against the will of the country."[129]

Even before the complete electoral returns were in, Cavaignac decided to step down. He was hastened in this decision by

[128] Dansette, *Louis Napoléon*, p. 252.

[129] This incident is reported by Lacombe; his source was a national guard officer who lunched with Cavaignac on December 11, when Charras arrived and the colloquy took place. See *Vie de Berryer*, II, pp. 580-581.

indications of possible disorders, ranging from rumors that an imperial restoration would be attempted on December 15, the anniversary of the return of Napoleon's remains, to rumors that the socialists would burn Paris rather than see a Bonaparte as president.[130] On December 20, in a ceremony in the chamber of the National Assembly, the historic transfer of power was effected. Pale but calm, Cavaignac mounted the tribune, where in a brief and moving speech he thanked the Assembly for "its confidence and its kindness toward me," and offered the resignation of himself and of his Cabinet. The general spoke "with a simplicity and a dignity that cannot be surpassed, . . ." recalled Rémusat. "It is easier to state than to make comprehensible what there was of grandeur in those few words and in the manner in which they were spoken. Whoever heard them will never forget them. It was one of those rare moments which make public life worth prizing."[131]

As the deputies applauded, General Cavaignac left the tribune and strode to the rear of the chamber to resume his seat as one of them. The dignified departure of the erstwhile military dictator won the admiration of contemporaries. "It was a noble example given for the first time in our country," observed Hippolyte Carnot.[132] The general's peaceful surrender of power was also apparently the source of much of Tocqueville's admiration for the general.[133]

After Cavaignac had taken his seat, Armand Marrast, president of the Assembly, proclaimed Louis Napoleon Bonaparte president of the republic. Mounting to the tribune, the prince took the prescribed oath to remain faithful to the republic and made a brief speech in which he included praise for his pred-

[130] Cherest, *Marie*, pp. 285-286; Corkran, *History of the National Constituent Assembly*, II, p. 270.

[131] Rémusat, *Mémoires de ma vie*, IV, pp. 384-385.

[132] MS "Mémorial," dos. 23, p. 12.

[133] Tocqueville had high praise for a speech of Cavaignac's a few months later in which the general indignantly denied that he had fallen from power. "That is not true: I retired voluntarily. The national will does not overthrow; it commands, and we obey. I add—and I want the republican party always to be able to say so with justice: I retired voluntarily, and, in so doing, my conduct did honour to my republican convictions." (Cited in Tocqueville, *Recollections*, pp. 235-236.)

ecessor's "uprightness and devotion to duty." On leaving the tribune, he walked over to where Cavaignac was seated, his hand extended. The general did not stand, but with obvious reluctance permitted the president of the republic to shake his hand.[134]

Even before his investiture, the president-elect had been negotiating with potential members of his Cabinet, most of whom were Orleanists. Thiers was the key figure; while declining to enter the ministry himself, he suggested Odilon Barrot for president of the council, and other Orleanists for the various ministries. But Louis Napoleon also made some attempts to approach the republicans. He evaded a suggestion from Carnot that he offer Cavaignac the presidency of the council,[135] but did persuade a moderate *républicain de la veille*, Alexandre Bixio, to take the portfolio of Commerce. More significantly he sought, in a dramatic night-time interview, to persuade Lamartine to join his government. The poet agreed after some hesitation, but only on condition that Barrot should refuse, and Barrot had already accepted.[136]

The formation of a ministry under the man who had been the last premier of the foundering July Monarchy on February 24 dramatized the antirepublican significance of the election of Louis Napoleon. The ministry was almost exclusively Orleanist, the sole Legitimist being Falloux, who had reluctantly accepted the Ministry of Education and Religion only after the Abbé Dupanloup had persuaded him that it would be in the interests of Catholicism. As for Bixio, the republican, he had accepted largely out of "curiosity" in the opinion of Rémusat, and resigned a week later in protest over Louis Napoleon's demand for documents concerning his intrigues under the July Monarchy.[137]

[134] There is some dispute concerning the incident of the handshake. Odilon Barrot said that Cavaignac refused to shake hands. (*Mémoires posthumes*, III, p. 29.) Carnot, on the other hand, remembered a handshake "in good taste." (MS "Mémorial," dos. 23, p. 11.) *Le Moniteur* notes that the handshake did occur, and other witnesses also observed it. See the discussion in Lebey, *Louis Napoléon et 1848*, II, pp. 325-328.

[135] MS "Mémorial," dos. 23, pp. 10-11.

[136] Dansette, *Louis Napoléon*, pp. 261-262.

[137] Rémusat, *Mémories de ma vie*, IV, p. 387, and Dansette, *Louis Napoléon*, p. 264.

The announcement of the Barrot ministry served to enhance the antirepublican and counterrevolutionary significance of the election in the eyes of the *notables*. "It is a verdict of condemnation against the February revolution," observed *Le Courrier de la Gironde*. "At that time, France suffered a surprise attack by a few political adventurers."[138] Even the monarchist newspapers that had supported Cavaignac now accepted his elimination from power with equanimity, for the disorders feared in connection with Louis Napoleon did not arise, and the composition of the ministry indicated the president's desire to govern through the Party of Order.

Indeed, Falloux, who had voted for Cavaignac, thought that the Party of Order was now officially in power, and "if previous professions of faith were only a game, we are going to throw off the mask. . . . The voters of December 10 did not conceal their sentiments. Why should we still conceal our own?"[139] Moreover, the fact that Louis Napoleon was the choice of the whole people rather than of the Orleanists or Legitimists made possible their continued union in the Party of Order, against not only the threat of socialism, but now against the republicans who had governed France since February.

The monarchist *notables*, whose power had been profoundly shaken by the February revolution, now sought to use the election of December 10 to regain their old dominion. Not only did they comprise the president's first ministry, they also launched a campaign against the remaining stronghold of republicanism, the National Assembly. Newspapers and petitions demanded the dissolution of the Assembly, since they claimed it had completed its work and had lost its representative character. The prince-president agreed on the need for dissolution, but the Assembly resisted. Immediately before the election, the National Assembly had pledged not to dissolve itself until it had adopted ten important "organic laws," including those on elections, the Conseil d'Etat, departmental and communal organization, primary education, and the reorganization of public assistance.

[138] Tudesq, *L'Election présidentielle*, p. 223.
[139] *Mémoires*, I, p. 389.

The ministry sought to persuade the Assembly to enact only two of the organic laws, and while this proposal was being considered, General Changarnier, the new commander of the National Guard and of military forces in Paris, suggested that the Assembly be dissolved by force. Although both Louis Napoleon and leaders of the Party of Order rejected this solution, the Assembly itself seemed stricken with torpor; sessions became much briefer, committees virtually ceased to function and many deputies went on leave. In the end, many of the projected reforms of the Cavaignac government were either retired by the new one or were permitted to die in committee. The demoralized Assembly finally agreed to end its existence in May 1849, after having adopted only two of the organic laws, those on elections and on the Conseil d'Etat.

The elections for the Legislative Assembly in May completed the rout of the moderate republicans. The monarchist *notables* of the Party of Order won some two-thirds of the seats, an unquestioned majority. For the rest of its brief life, the republic was to be securely in the hands of its enemies.

XVI · Conclusions

THE defeat of Cavaignac in December was followed by the collapse of the republicanism of 1848. Thereafter, although the general and many of the republicans remained active in politics for a time, the movement itself underwent a series of transformations. The first was a dramatic shift to the left in the spring of 1849, when radicals and socialists formed a new "democratic-socialist" coalition that assiduously propagandized the workers and more significantly the peasantry. Some of the former moderate republicans joined the coalition, which was remarkably successful in the elections of May 1849—it won some 200 seats while the former *Le National* faction, now called that of the "constitutional republicans," won only about seventy seats in the Legislative Assembly which was dominated by a large majority representing the Party of Order.[1] Some of the republicans of 1848 left politics afterwards in disillusionment or despair; among them were Recurt and Tourret. More sought election in 1849 but were defeated in the general rout of the moderates by the left and the right; of the members of his former government, only Cavaignac himself won reelection as a deputy in 1849.

The democratic-socialist movement was short-lived, however; many leaders were purged, imprisoned or exiled after the demonstration of June 13, 1849 in Paris, and by 1850 republicans of all varieties were seeking an accord in the struggle against both the government of Louis Napoleon and the monarchist majority in the Assembly. *La Réforme* succumbed in January 1850 to a rigorous campaign against the republican press, but *Le National* shifted to the left to support the democratic-socialists.[2] In the partial elections of 1850 in

[1] For the significance of these elections, see Seignobos, *La Révolution de 1848*, pp. 135-136; Jacques Bouillon, "Les Démocrates-socialistes aux élections de 1849," *Revue française de science politique*, VI (1956), pp. 70-95; Tudesq, *Les Grands notables*, II, pp. 1212-1226; and Theodore Zeldin, "Government Policy in the French General Election of 1849," *English Historical Review*, LXXIV (1959), 240-248.

[2] Weill, *Parti républicain*, p. 245.

Paris, the constitutional republicans and the democratic-socialists sponsored a single list, consisting of Carnot, the socialist Vidal, and, in the most dramatic sign of reconciliation, a former insurgent of June, Paul de Flotte. All were successful, and the alarmed response of the Assembly was the adoption of the law of May 31, 1850, which excluded many workers from suffrage.[3]

Cavaignac in his proud and aloof way remained a figure of renown among republicans, but he was still anathema to many of the radicals and socialists, and declined to offer vigorous leadership. He spoke out on a number of important issues in parliament, however, most notably against the law of May 31, 1850, and against the movement in 1851 to revise the Constitution.

The *coup d'Etat* of December 2, 1851 took the republicans by surprise. Among those arrested in Paris during the night was General Cavaignac, who was aroused from sleep by a group of police officers.[4] He protested angrily, but then went with his customary dignity to a cell in the fortress of Ham. The *coup d'Etat* also interrupted Cavaignac's private life, for he was about to marry. A few days later, after the general contemptuously indicated his intention to have the ceremony performed in his prison cell, Morny hastily arranged for his release in late December.[5] Afterwards, the forty-nine-year-old bachelor finally married the young Mademoiselle Odier; he then asked to be retired from the army, a move which he considered the only policy compatible "with my honor and my devotion to liberty."[6] The request was hastily granted.

The large-scale proscriptions that followed the *coup d'Etat* struck mostly at the radicals and socialists, but also at many of the moderate republicans. *Le National* expired with the *coup d'Etat*, and afterwards the rigorous surveillance of the

[3] *Ibid.*, p. 250. For details on the campaign to restrict suffrage, see Balland, "De l'Organisation à la restriction," pp. 114-142.

[4] Deschamps, *Eugène Cavaignac*, II, pp. 347-348.

[5] Kerry, *Secret of the Coup d'Etat*, pp. 206-210. Some correspondence on this subject is preserved in the papers of Morny, A. N., 116 AP 1, dos. 1.

[6] Letter of 13 January 1852, Cavaignac dossier, S.H.A., 1207 G.D.

republicans imposed what Weill called "the years of silence" in which the republicans also practiced a policy of political abstention. In the first elections to the Legislative Body in 1852, three republicans were chosen without having campaigned: Carnot and Cavaignac in Paris, and one Hénon at Lyon.[7] All three were denied their seats, however, because they refused to take the oath to Louis Napoleon.

The *coup d'Etat*, the massive repression and the authoritarian nature of the regime led the republicans under the empire to an obsessive concern for liberty, whereas in the relatively liberal atmosphere of the July Monarchy they had aspired more toward democracy and social justice. Although many republican leaders remained in exile, and those in France were hounded by the imperial police, republicanism nevertheless survived as a potent force in French political life; there were few republican conversions to the empire, and the *républicains de la veille* were joined by a growing cohort of men permanently touched with the democratic spirit of 1848. *La Presse* was sympathetic to the republicans, as was another important Parisian newspaper, *Le Siècle*; Madame d'Agoult maintained an influential republican salon, and cashiered professors covertly indoctrinated the young generation.[8] That the republicans still had a considerable following, even among the workers of Paris, was evident in the crowds that appeared at funeral processions for prominent republicans, such as those for Marrast in 1853 and for Lamennais in 1854.

As for Cavaignac, his personal fortunes improved in 1855, when he inherited half the fortune of his uncle; he bought a château near Le Mans, where he lived in retirement. However, he was among those republicans who helped prepare for the elections of 1857. He and several other republicans were victorious, but once again he resigned his seat. A few months afterwards, on October 28, 1857, General Cavaignac died unexpectedly of a heart attack while hunting near his château. His death brought expressions of sorrow not only from republicans, but also from others whom he had impressed while in

[7] Weill, *Parti républicain*, p. 308.
[8] *Ibid.*, pp. 310-313.

power in 1848. It was on this occasion that Tocqueville offered the opinion that he "would remain great in history," and *Le Constitutionnel* also expressed grief at the death of a political enemy who nevertheless "will hold an honorable place in the history of his country."[9]

The general's young widow insisted on bringing his body to Paris for a public funeral, accompanied by their young son, Godefroy.[10] Large, respectful crowds followed the procession. The pallbearers were his former colleagues, Bastide and Goudchaux; Guinard, whose doubts the general had assuaged in the Days of June; and a worker named Bayard;[11] but there were few *blouses* among the spectators.[12] At the cemetery of Montmartre the body of the general was laid in the family sepulchre near that of his brother Godefroy.

The death of Cavaignac had no profound affect on the republican movement in itself, but 1857 did witness the emergence of an important new policy; some republicans were willing to reject the sterile attitude of abstention in favor of participation in the parliamentary politics of the empire. When Cavaignac, Carnot and Goudchaux resigned their seats rather than take the oath, they were succeeded by others who formed the famous group of "Five" republican opposition deputies. Emile Ollivier and his colleagues soon demonstrated the fruitfulness of this role, and a few other republicans followed Ollivier into acceptance of the liberal empire in 1870.[13] A closely related trend with a better future was the drift of Thiers and other Orleanists toward the republicans, and the formation of a "democratic-Orleanist coalition" which became

[9] Issue of 31 October 1857.

[10] Godefroy also was reared in the family tradition of republicanism, as he demonstrated in 1867, when after winning a lycée contest, he publicly refused to accept the prize for Greek translation from the young prince imperial. (*Dictionnaire des parlementaires*, VI, p. 619.) Cavaignac *fils* also went into politics, and in the end his reputation suffered from his anti-Dreyfusard attitude as Minister of War in the famous *affaire*.

[11] Weill, *Parti républicain*, p. 317.

[12] P.-F. Dubois, "Le Général Cavaignac," *Revue bleue* (5 September 1908), 302.

[13] See Zeldin, *Emile Ollivier and the Liberal Empire.*

the basis for the conservative republic that emerged after the fall of the empire.[14]

The empire also witnessed a new flowering of republican theoretical works, anticlerical, positivistic and less statist than before 1848, with particular emphasis on the theme of liberty.[15] The loosening of political restraints in the 1860's fostered the emergence not only of a strong workers' movement, but also of a new generation of radical republicans who were often contemptuous of veterans of 1848. Yet, while the empire was introducing social and economic policies beneficial to the workers, the new radicals remained preoccupied with political issues, and even Gambetta's Belleville program of 1869 was almost exclusively political, with only brief references to the "social problem" which was expressly subordinated to political change.[16]

The revolution of September 4, 1870, was made in the name of "La République" rather than "La République démocratique et sociale," and the infant Third Republic, already in the hands of monarchists by the spring of 1871, crushed the insurgent Communards more rigorously than Cavaignac had done in 1848. Some of the republicans of 1848 who survived to serve the Third Republic were more moderate than they had been in 1848, but even for the new generation of republicans the political struggle with the monarchists and the religious issue seemed more pressing than social questions. The political institutions accepted by the Opportunists in 1875 were far more conservative than those defended and elaborated in 1848, and those converted monarchists who called themselves "moderates" were far more conservative in their outlook than the moderate republicans of 1848. Indeed, not until the 1890's, and the Radical Ministry of Bourgeois, was France again to witness a government which, while clearly antisocialist, was as seriously determined as the government of Cavaignac "to introduce into governmental policy an effective concern for the underprivileged groups in France."[17]

[14] Girard, "Political Liberalism in France," pp. 124-129.

[15] Weill, *Parti républicain*, pp. 329-354.

[16] See Kayser, *Les Grands batailles du radicalisme*, pp. 39-42, 318-319.

[17] L. Arthur Minnich, Jr., "The Third Force, 1870-1896," in E. M.

In conclusion, what can be said of the French republic under Cavaignac? First, that in certain important respects the traditional picture is correct. The elimination of the Paris workers as a political force, the discrediting of the socialists, the policies of repression, all bespoke reaction. Yet, in more fundamental respects the regime may be better understood as a positive and significant phase of the revolutionary current of 1848. If the moderate republicans crushed the workers, they were acting not only out of class fears, but also in defense of the democratic republic born of the February revolution. In the long run, the June Days undoubtedly dealt the republic a mortal wound, but under Cavaignac the republic was assuredly not dead. In June it was the insurgents who proved themselves bad democrats and republicans, unwilling to accept the political consequences of February. It was the uprising itself, more than its suppression, that undermined the republic. It is undeniable that all the conservative elements enthusiastically joined in crushing the workers, but it is too often forgotten that all of the prominent socialists as well, including Louis Blanc, lent their moral support to Cavaignac rather than to the embattled workers. Finally, the insurrection more than any other event led to the vast shift of opinion away from the republican euphoria of March and April; June demonstrated the instability as well as the strength of the republic, and the lesson of instability seems to have been best learned, particularly by the peasant masses who turned to Bonaparte in December.

However, immediately after the June Days, the strength of the republic seemed most apparent; it had triumphed over a more formidable insurrection than the one which toppled

---

Earle, ed., *Modern France: Problems of the Third and Fourth Republics* (New York, 1964 [1951]), p. 120. The comparison between the Cavaignac and Bourgeois ministries is my own rather than Mr. Minnich's. His comparison of the Bourgeois ministry to the New Deal in the United States and the Popular Front in France also has some validity, *mutatis mutandis*, for the Cavaignac ministry, which after all saw only the beginnings of the social problems accompanying modern industrialization. It is interesting also that the Bourgeois ministry was in existence approximately as long as that of Cavaignac but was even less successful in getting its program accepted by the Chamber.

the July Monarchy; its potential foes on the right, the Orleanists and Legitimists who had ostentatiously rallied to the republic in March, as well as Louis Napoleon and his growing band of adherents, continued to express themselves in the rhetoric of republicanism. Moreover, it was only after the threat of insurrection had been removed that the National Assembly was able to function as a sovereign body and to draw up the Constitution that the republicans hoped would perpetuate the new democratic order. In Cavaignac, inherited political convictions prevailed over class fears, personal ambition, or even military temperament; given dictatorial powers during the insurrection, he insisted on surrendering them immediately afterwards. Although he remained in power, it was as the responsible premier of France's first true parliamentary democracy, and in December he meekly bowed to the will of the French people by stepping down in favor of a Bonaparte without an army. In his cabinet, the moderate *républicains de la veille*, who had dominated the revolutionary governments since February, held virtually unchallenged authority.

The repression during and after the June Days was severe and violated the republicans' avowed liberal ideals, even though Cavaignac sought with some justification to invoke a higher revolutionary principle, that of "le salut public." Cavaignac had none of the vindictive attitude that Thiers later displayed toward the defeated Communards; by the end of 1848, he had freed most of the prisoners, and less than 500 ever reached exile in Algeria.

Under Cavaignac, besides imposing restrictions on the press and the political clubs, the government did force Louis Blanc into exile, but most of the socialists were unmolested though discredited and shorn of influence. Some of the accomplishments and aims of the earlier phase of the revolution were repudiated after June, but many were preserved, and the moderate republicans put forward their own program of positive democratic and even mildly social reforms. Although some were successful, many were thwarted by the National Assembly, which was dominated by *républicains du lendemain*, provincial *notables* and erstwhile monarchists rather than committed democrats.

The political accomplishments of the Cavaignac period are the best known, and although regarded by some historians as superficial, were in a certain sense the most important. At a time when political democracy was still a revolutionary doctrine in Europe, France under Cavaignac preserved and consolidated the democratic institutions that derived from February. The republic of Cavaignac extended political democracy to local government, introduced egalitarian principles into jury panels and institutions such as the commercial courts, and drew up the most democratic constitution since the abortive one of 1793, one more democratic than that of the Third Republic. Cavaignac's government also sought, with less success, to democratize the educational institutions of France. It was able to introduce egalitarian principles into some of the special schools and to organize an Ecole d'Administration to train administrators who would serve the new regime loyally as well as efficiently. The most ambitious educational reform offered by the Cavaignac government was that for universal, free, secular and compulsory primary education, but it was frustrated by the National Assembly. It reemerged as one of the most insistent demands of the early Third Republic, reaching fruition only after the republicans had won control of the regime a decade after its birth.

But the Cavaignac government did not concern itself solely with democratic and liberal reforms. The conception of democracy held by the moderate *républicains de la veille* included a distinct social aspect, even if it fell short of "la République démocratique et sociale" as understood by some of the men of 1848. It is inaccurate to regard the Cavaignac regime as a return to the laissez-faire attitudes of Thiers and Guizot after a brief interlude. It is true that after the June insurrection Thiers himself and some others openly advocated the chill liberal doctrine of the negative state in social and economic matters, but the government of Cavaignac rejected laissez-faire as explicitly as it rejected the various socialist prescriptions for a total renovation of society. Instead, it took an intermediate position, defending the principle of governmental intervention and offering some mild reforms beneficial to workers, but without seeking to destroy capitalism. To be sure, Cavaignac dismantled the National Workshops, but in this he was simply implementing a policy adopted before the June Days. Moreover, his government did not leave the workers and their families to starve, but offered direct relief in lieu of the workshops, and even revived the principle if not the name of the National Workshops in the less politically sensitive provinces. Although the government fearfully avoided large-scale public works projects in Paris, it sponsored them to a considerable extent elsewhere in an attempt to relieve unemployment, and it experimented on the grand scale with the project for the colonization of Algeria by unemployed workers at government expense. In addition, the government sought to stimulate economic recovery and create jobs artificially by subsidizing various industries, particularly those in which unemployment was most severe, such as the building trades in Paris and the textile workers of Lyon. Altogether, these policies and others constituted a remarkably positive governmental response to social and economic crisis. This response was not merely ad hoc, but reflected the moderate social views of the government, which were written into the Constitution, the first since 1793 to state explicitly the social obligations of the state.

The retreat from plans to nationalize the railroads was made not on doctrinaire but on practical grounds, for the moderate republicans were themselves the strongest advocates of nationalization; moreover, the Cavaignac government did nationalize one important line and contemplated further expansion of the state railroad system. Ironically also, it was under Cavaignac that the demand of Louis Blanc and other socialists for government aid to producers' cooperatives first won implementation, though in a limited form. The government also successfully sponsored maximum hours legislation for adult male factory workers. Although the law was weak, it remained as the foundation for subsequent legislation more than a generation later. The government of Cavaignac also preserved other labor reforms from earlier in the year, such as the abolition of *marchandage*, and introduced several minor labor reforms of its own, including sickness and accident insurance for workers on public works projects. The Cavaignac government also introduced important reforms in the field of public assistance, and advocated several forms of aid to agriculture, the most notable being a plan for an elaborate nationwide system of agricultural training. In the field of taxation, the government of Cavaignac sought to innovate more profoundly than had the earlier provisional governments of 1848 by introducing an income tax bill, but the National Assembly thwarted it, and the income tax remained an advanced cause down to its final implementation in the twentieth century. Postal reform was probably the most enduring accomplishment of the Cavaignac regime; all major groups in the National Assembly supported it for various reasons, but the Cavaignac government characteristically advocated it as a democratic and even a social reform because it involved the reduction of an indirect tax and facilitated communication between workers and their families.

The social and economic policies of the Cavaignac regime have received little attention in the past, perhaps because they seemed trivial or false or fence-straddling to the opposing ideologues in 1848, and also undoubtedly because the generation of republicans that emerged after 1870 was so concerned with political problems that it minimized or ignored the moderate social heritage of 1848, which itself went back ultimately to 1793. The moderate republicans of the Cavaignac regime were not very avid social reformers, but they did recognize the existence of the social question and sought to deal with it through governmental action, mild as it was. But the undoctrinaire, pragmatic, moderate reformist attitude of the Cavaignac government appears from the perspective of the twentieth century at least as relevant to concrete social problems as any of the competing socialist programs of 1848. Maximum hours legislation, far more than social workshops, constituted the wave of the future.

The republic of Cavaignac reflected most clearly the viewpoint of the moderate *républicains de la veille*, who, both bourgeois and republican, were also men of 1848, sharing the weaknesses as well as the generous spirit of their time. When their fury against the insurgents was spent, when the threat of social revolution was dissipated, there remained hope in the republic, faith in democracy and—along with lingering fear—a genuine desire to improve the lot of the workers. That their attempts were modest in comparison with the dreams of total renovation, that many of their reforms were abortive, should not obscure the fact that they were sincerely made. The moderate republicans believed that social problems would be solved gradually through the functioning of political democracy, and their own efforts in that direction suggest that they may have been the best hope of the republic, had it endured. But committed republicans were a minority in 1848, and shortly after the socialists and the workers of June went down to defeat so also did the republic of Cavaignac and the moderate republicans. It was the election of Louis Napoleon that most clearly ended the revolutionary movement of 1848, for it swept the republicans from power and put the republic for the first time in the control of men who did not share its democratic ideals, and who set about deliberately to undo the accomplishments of February.

Bibliography

MANUSCRIPT SOURCES

ARCHIVES DÉPARTEMENTALES DE LA SARTHE, LE MANS

Documents des archives privées de M. Eugène Cavaignac, concernant la famille Cavaignac, XVIIIe-XIXe siècle (archives privées de M. Cavaignac, chez Mme Paul-Dubois, Château d'Ourne, Flée). Microfilms de complément, 1 Mi 2:

- Reel 16—Letters of Godefroy Cavaignac
- Reel 19—Papers of Eugène Cavaignac in Algeria
- Reel 20—Papers concerning Algeria and the Ministry of War
- Reel 21—Papers concerning the June Days
- Reels 22 and 23—Papers concerning the June Days and subsequent period to December
- Reels 24-26—Papers concerning foreign affairs
- Reels 27-28—Letters of Eugène Cavaignac

ARCHIVES DES AFFAIRES ETRANGÈRES

Correspondance politique:

- Angleterre—670-672
- Autriche—435-437
- Rome—988
- Russie—202
- Sardaigne—321-322

ARCHIVES NATIONALES

AB xix 2842—Cours et notes de Charles Seignobos: MS *mémoire* for the *Diplôme d'Etudes Supérieures*, University of Paris, n.d., by J. Tournan, "Etat des partis en France au commencement de la seconde république d'après les élections du 23 avril 1848"

AD xix D 256—Circulars, Minister of Agriculture and Commerce

AD xix J 1—Circulars, Minister of Justice

AD xix N 2—Circulars, Minister of Public Works

67 AP 5—Register of the Executive Commission

108 AP 3—MS "Mémorial" of Hippolyte Carnot

116 AP 1 dos. 1—Papers of Morny

223 AP 2d.6—Papers of Berryer, *fils* (1790-1868), "Liste des membres de la Réunion des représentants conservateurs dite 'Comité de la rue de Poitiers' "

C 912-928—Minutes of Committees and other Papers of the National Assembly

C 929-942—Papers of the *Commission d'enquête sur l'insurrection qui a éclaté dans la journée du 23 juin et sur les événements du 15 mai*

F 1A 45—Circulars of Ministers of Agriculture and Commerce, Interior, and Public Works

F 1A 2097—Circulars of the Minister of the Interior

F 1C III—5–Elections, April 1848, Lot

F 12 2337-2338—Commerce and Industry, Miscellaneous

F 12 6714—Commerce and Industry, Miscellaneous

BIBLIOTHEQUE THIERS

Papiers Jules Baroche—MSS Thiers 1241

SERVICE HISTORIQUE DE L'ARMÉE, CHATEAU DE VINCENNES

F ^{1}9—Correspondance générale, 16-29 juin 1848

G ^{6}1—Armée des Alpes, correspondance, 1848

1207 G.D.—Dossier of General Louis Eugène Cavaignac

H 210—Journal d'Orléansville, "Historique d'Orléansville, mois de juin 1844"

H 263–5—Correspondence, Minister of War, 1848

X^{d}386—Insurrection de Paris, 1848

PUBLISHED OFFICIAL SOURCES

Comité national du centenaire de 1848. Charles Pouthas, ed. *Documents diplomatiques du gouvernement provisoire et de la commission du pouvoir exécutif*. 2 vols., Paris, 1953-54.

———. *Procès-verbaux du gouvernement provisoire et de la commission du pouvoir exécutif, 24 février-22 juin 1848*. Paris, 1950.

Compte rendu des séances de l'Assemblée nationale; exposés des motifs et projets des lois présentés par le gouvernement; rapports de MM. les représentants. 11 vols., Paris, 1849-50.

Le Moniteur universel, 1848.

Rapport de la commission d'enquête sur l'insurrection qui a éclaté dans la journée du 23 juin et sur les événements du 15 mai. 3 vols. in 1, Paris, 1848.

Société d'histoire de la Révolution de 1848. *Procès-verbaux du comité du travail à l'Assemblée Constituante de 1848.* "Bibliothèque de la révolution de 1848." Vol. I, Paris, 1908.

BIBLIOGRAPHY

NEWSPAPERS AND PERIODICALS

The *Annual Register*, 1848.

L'Atelier, 1848.

Le National, 1848.

La Réforme, 1848.

La Revue des deux mondes, 1848.

La Ruche populaire, 1848.

The Times (London), 1848.

PUBLISHED WRITINGS BY CONTEMPORARIES

Alton-Shée, Le Comte d'. *Souvenirs de 1847 et de 1848 pour faire suite à mes mémoires (oeuvre posthume).* Paris, 1879.

Ambert, Jules. *Portraits républicains: Armand Carrel—Godefroy Cavaignac—Armand Marrast—Le Colonel Charras.* Paris, 1870.

Audebrand, Philibert. *Nos Révolutionnaires: pages d'histoire contemporaine, 1830-1880.* 3d edn., Paris, 1886.

Babaud-Laribière, F.S.L. *Histoire de l'Assemblée nationale constitutante.* Paris, 1850.

Bapst, Germain. *Le Maréchal Canrobert. Souvenirs d'un siècle.* 7th edn., Vol. I, Paris, 1909.

Barrot, Odilon. *Mémoires posthumes de Odilon Barrot.* 4 vols., Paris, 1875-76.

Bastide, Jules. *La République française et l'Italie en 1848.* Brussels, 1858.

Beslay, Charles. *1830-1848-1870: mes souvenirs.* Paris, 1873.

Blanc, Louis. *1848: Historical Revelations: Inscribed to Lord Normanby.* London, 1858.

———. *Histoire de dix ans, 1830-1840.* 11th edn., Paris, 1848.

———. *Histoire de la révolution de 1848.* 2 vols., Paris, 1870.

———. *Pages d'histoire de la révolution de février 1848.* Paris, 1850.

———. *Révélations historiques, en réponse au livre de Lord Normanby intitulé A Year of Revolution in Paris.* 2 vols. in 1, Brussels, 1859.

Blanqui, Adolphe. Letter to Dussart, prefect of Seine-Inférieure, 24 August 1848, *L'Amateur d'autographes*, XXXIX (1906), 6-8.

Camus-Mutuelet and H. Place. *Caisse générale de secours mutuels: pétition présentée à L'Assemblée nationale.* Paris, 1849.

Carnot, Hippolyte. *Le Ministère de l'instruction publique et des cultes, depuis le 24 février jusqu'au 5 juillet 1848.* Paris, 1848.

Castellane, Comte Boniface de. *Journal du maréchal de Castellane, 1804-1862.* Vol. IV, Paris, 1897.

Castellane, Comte Pierre de. "La Vie militaire en Afrique," *Revue des deux mondes,* IX (1851), 1056-1081.

Castille, Hippolyte. *Histoire de la seconde république française.* 4 vols., Paris, 1854-56.

Caussidière, Marc. *Mémoires de Caussidière, ex-préfet de police et représentant du peuple.* 3d edn., 2 vols., Paris, 1849.

Cavaignac, Louis Eugène. *De la Régence d'Alger (notes sur l'occupation).* Paris, 1839.

Cavaignac, Louis Eugène and Jacques Marie Cavaignac. *Les Deux généraux Cavaignac: souvenirs et correspondance, 1808-1848.* Paris, n.d. [1899].

Cavaignac, Julie Marie. *Les Mémoires d'une inconnue, publiés sur le manuscrit original, 1780-1816.* Paris, 1894.

Circourt, Adolphe de. *Souvenirs d'une mission à Berlin en 1848, publiés pour la Société d'histoire contemporaine.* Ed. Georges Bourgin. 2 vols., Paris, 1908-09.

Corbon, Anthyme. *Le Secret du peuple de Paris.* Paris, 1863.

Corcelle, François de. "Souvenir de 1848: première intervention dans les affaires de Rome," *Le Correspondant,* XLII (1857), 577-599.

Corkran, J. F. *History of the National Constituent Assembly from May 1848.* 2 vols., London, 1849.

De Lord, Taxile. *Histoire du second empire.* 6 vols., Paris, 1869-76.

Dictionnaire politique: encyclopédie du langage et de la science politiques, rédigé par une réunion de députés, de publicistes et de journalistes, avec une introduction par Garnier-Pagès. 2d edn., Paris, 1843.

Du Barail, Le Général. *Mes Souvenirs.* 15th edn., 3 vols., Paris, 1908.

Du Camp, Maxime. *Souvenirs de l'année 1848.* Paris, 1876.

———. *Souvenirs d'un demi-siècle. Au temps de Louis-Philippe et de Napoléon III, 1830-1870.* 2 vols., Paris, 1949.

Duvergier de Hauranne, Prosper. *Histoire du gouvernement parlementaire en France, 1814-1848.* Vol. x, Paris, 1871.

Engels, Friedrich, "Les Journées de juin 1848," annex (pp. 111-126) to Karl Marx, *Les Luttes de classes en France (1848-1850).* Paris, 1946.

Estre, Henry d', ed. *Mémoires du général Changarnier, campagnes d'Afrique, 1830-1848.* Paris, 1930.

Falloux, Comte de. *Mémoires d'un royaliste.* 3d edn., 2 vols., Paris, 1888.

———. "Les Républicains et les monarchistes depuis la révolution de février," *Revue des deux mondes*, IX (1851) 393-422.

Garnier-Pagès, Louis Antoine. *Histoire de la révolution de 1848.* 11 vols., Paris, 1861-72.

Girardin, Emile de. *Questions de mon temps, 1836 à 1856.* 12 vols., Paris, 1858.

Hugo, Victor. *Souvenirs personnels, 1848-1851.* Ed. Henri Guillemin. Paris, 1952.

Hugonnet, Ferdinand. *Français et arabes en Algérie.* Paris, 1860.

Jacquot, Félix. *Expédition du général Cavaignac dans le sahara algérien en avril et mai 1847.* Paris, 1849.

Lacordaire, Henri. *Oeuvres.* Vol. IV, Paris, 1884.

La Hodde, Lucien de. *Histoire des sociétés secrètes et du parti républicain de 1830 à 1848.* Paris, 1850.

Lamartine, Alphonse de. *Histoire de la révolution de 1848.* 2 vols., Paris, 1849.

Malo, Henri, ed. *Mémoires de Madame Dosne, l'égérie de M. Thiers.* 2 vols., Paris, 1928.

Marie, Alexandre. "Les Papiers de Marie," *La Révolution de 1848*, I (1905), pp. 151-158, 181-193.

Marx, Karl. *The Class Struggles in France (1848-50).* "Marxist Library," Vol. XXIV, New York, 1935.

Ménard, Louis. *Prologue d'une révolution.* Paris, 1904 [1849].

Mirecourt, Eugène. *Eugène Cavaignac.* Paris, 1857.

Montagnac, F.J.L. de. *Lettres d'un soldat, neuf années de campagnes en Afrique.* Paris, 1885.

Montalivet, Comte de. *Fragments et souvenirs.* Ed. Georges Picot. 2 vols., Paris, 1899-1900.

Napoléon III [Louis Napoléon Bonaparte]. *Oeuvres.* 5 vols., Paris, 1869.

Normanby, The Marquis of. *A Year of Revolution: From a Journal Kept in Paris in 1848.* 2 vols., London, 1857.

Ollivier, Emile. *L'Empire libéral, études, récits, souvenirs.* 18 vols., Paris, 1895-1918.

Paris révolutionnaire. 4 vols., Paris, 1838.

Pellissier de Reynaud, E. *Annales algériennes.* New edn., 3 vols., Paris, 1854.

Proudhon, P. J. *Les Confessions d'un révolutionnaire.* Paris, 1849.

Quentin-Bauchart, Alexandre. *Etudes et souvenirs sur la deuxième république et le second empire (1848-1870): mémoires posthumes publiés par son fils.* 2 vols., Paris, 1901-02.

Rémusat, Charles de. *Mémoires de ma vie.* Ed. Charles H. Pouthas.

Vol. IV: *Les Dernières années de la monarchie, la révolution de 1848, la seconde république (1841-1851).* Paris, 1962.

Senard, Jules. *Discours prononcé par le citoyen Senard.* Paris, 1848.

Senior, W. Nassau. *Conversations with Distinguished Persons During the Second Empire, from 1860 to 1863.* 2 vols., London, 1880.

———. *Conversations with M. Thiers, M. Guizot, and Other Distinguished Persons during the Second Empire.* 2 vols., London, 1878.

———. *Journals Kept in France and Italy, from 1848 to 1852.* 2 vols., London, 1871.

Stern, Daniel [the Comtesse d'Agoult]. *Histoire de la révolution de 1848.* New edn., 3 vols., Paris, 1878.

———. *Lettres républicaines.* Paris, 1848.

Tocqueville, Alexis de. *The Recollections of Alexis de Tocqueville.* Trans. Alexander Teixera de Mattos, ed. J. P. Mayer, New York, Meridian, 1959.

———. *Oeuvres et correspondance inédites d'Alexis de Tocqueville.* Ed. Gustave de Beaumont. 2 vols., Paris, 1861.

———. *Oeuvres complètes.* Ed. J. P. Mayer. Vols. III and XII, Paris, 1962-64.

Véron, Dr. L. *Mémoires d'un bourgeois de Paris.* 6 vols., Paris, 1853-56.

OTHER BOOKS

Actes du congrès historique du centenaire de la révolution de 1848. Paris, 1948.

Alméras, Charles. *Odilon Barrot, avocat et homme politique, 1791-1873.* Paris, 1950.

Antony, Alfred. *La Politique financière du gouvernement provisoire, février-mai 1848.* Paris, 1910.

L'Armée et la seconde république. "Bibliothèque de la révolution de 1848." Vol. XVIII, La roche-sur-Yon, 1955.

Armengaud, André. *Les Populations de l'Est-Aquitain au début de l'époque contemporaine: recherches sur une région moins développée (vers 1845-vers 1871).* Paris, 1961.

Aubert, R. *Le Pontificat de Pie IX (1846-1878).* Paris, 1952.

Augé-Laribé, Michel. *La Révolution agricole.* Paris, 1955.

Azan, Paul. *Conquête et pacification de l'Algérie.* Paris, 1931.

———. *Les Grands soldats de l'Algérie.* Orléans, 1931.

Bapst, Edmond. *L'Empereur Nicholas Ier et la IIe république française*. Paris, 1898.

Bastid, Paul. *L'Avènement du suffrage universel*. "Collection du centenaire de 1848." Paris, 1948.

———. *Doctrines et institutions politiques de la seconde république*. 2 vols., Paris, 1945.

———. *Les Institutions politiques de la monarchie parlementaire française (1814-1848)*. Paris, 1954.

Beau de Loménie, Emmanuel. *Les Responsabilités des dynasties bourgeoises*. 3 vols., Paris, 1943-54.

Bertaut, Jules. *1848 et la seconde république*. Paris, 1937.

Bertier de Sauvigny. *La Restauration*. 2d edn., Paris, 1963.

Bouloiseau, Marc, et al., eds. *Oeuvres de Maximilien Robespierre*. Vol. IX, Paris, 1958.

Bounoils, Gaston. *Histoire de la révolution de 1848*. Paris, 1918.

Bourgeois, Emile. *History of Modern France, 1815-1913*. "Cambridge Historical Series." 2 vols., Cambridge, 1919.

Bourgin, Georges. *1848: Naissance et mort d'une république*. Paris, 1948.

Boyer, Ferdinand. *La Seconde république et Charles Albert en 1848*. Paris, 1967.

Buchner, Rudolf. *Die Deutsch-französische Tragödie, 1848-1864: Politische Beziehungen und Psychologisches Verhältnis*. Würzburg, 1965.

Calman, Alvin R. *Ledru-Rollin and the Second French Republic*. New York, 1922.

Cameron, Rondo E. *France and the Economic Development of Europe, 1800-1914: Conquests of Peace and Seeds of War*. Princeton, 1961.

Campbell, Peter. *French Electoral Systems and Elections since 1789*. 2d edn., Hamden, Conn., 1965.

Chalmin, Pierre. *L'Officier français de 1815 à 1870*. Paris, 1957.

Charles, Albert. *La Révolution de 1848 et la seconde république à Bordeaux et dans le département de la Gironde*. Bordeaux, 1945.

Charléty, S. *La Monarchie de juillet*. Ed. Ernest Lavisse. "Histoire de France contemporaine." Vol. v, Paris, 1921.

———. *La Restauration (1815-1830)*. Ed. Ernest Lavisse. "Histoire de France contemporaine." Vol. IV, Paris, 1921.

Charnay, Jean-Paul. *Société militaire et suffrage politique en France depuis 1789*. Paris, 1964.

Chauvet, Paul. *Les Ouvriers du livre en France de 1789 à la constitution de la Fédération du livre*. Paris, 1964 [1956].

Cherest, Aimé. *La Vie et les oeuvres de A.-T. Marie*. Paris, 1873.

Chevalier, Louis. *Classes laborieuses et classes dangereuses à Paris pendant la première moitié du XIXe siècle*. Paris, 1958.

———. *La Formation de la population parisienne au XIXe siècle*. Paris, 1950.

Clough, Shepard B. *France: A History of National Economics, 1789-1939*. New York, 1939.

Cobban, Alfred. *The Social Interpretation of the French Revolution*. Cambridge, 1964.

Cogniot, Georges. *La Question scolaire en 1848 et la loi Falloux*. Paris, 1948.

Cohen, Jacques. *La Préparation de la constitution de 1848*. Paris, 1935.

Collins, Irene. *The Government and the Newspaper Press in France, 1814-1881*. London, 1959.

Collins, R. W. *Catholicism and the Second French Republic (1848-1852)*. New York, 1923.

Corley, T.A.B. *Democratic Despot: A Life of Napoleon III*. London, 1961.

Corti, Egon Caesar. *The Reign of the House of Rothschild, 1830-1871*. New York, 1928.

Crémieux, Albert. *La Révolution de février, étude critique sur les journées des 21, 22, 23 et 24 février 1848*. Paris, 1912.

Curtis, Eugene. *The French Assembly of 1848 and American Constitutional Doctrines*. New York, 1918.

Cuvillier, Armand. *P.-J.-B. Buchez et les origines du socialisme chrétien*. "Collection du centenaire de la révolution de 1848." Paris, 1948.

———. *Hommes et idéologies de 1840*. Paris, 1956.

———. *Un Journal d'ouvriers: L'Atelier (1840-1850)*. Paris, 1954.

Dagnan, J. *Le Gers sous la seconde république: la réaction conservatrice (février 1848—2 décembre 1851)*. Auch, 1928.

Dansette, Adrien. *Louis Napoléon à la conquête du pouvoir*. Paris, 1961.

Daumard, Adeline. *La Bourgeoisie parisienne de 1815 à 1848*. Paris, 1963.

Dautry, Jean. *1848 et la deuxième république*. 2d edn., Paris, 1957.

Deschamps, Auguste. *Eugène Cavaignac*. 2 vols., Brussels, 1870.

Dessal, Marcel. *Charles Delescluz, un révolutionnaire jacobin, 1809-1871*. Paris, 1952.

Dictionnaire des parlementaires français, comprenant tous les membres des assemblées françaises et tous les ministres français depuis le 1er mai 1789 jusqu'au 1er mai 1889. Eds. Adolphe Robert, Edgar Bourloton and Gaston Cougny. 5 vols., Paris, 1889-91.

Dominique, Pierre. *Les Journées de quarante-huit.* Paris, 1948.

———. *Les Journées de juin.* Paris, 1966.

Dreyfus, Ferdinand. *L'Assistance sous la seconde république (1848-1851).* Paris, 1907.

Droz, Jacques, Lucien Genet and Jean Vidalenc. *L'Epoque contemporaine, I, Restaurations et révolutions (1815-1871).* "Clio." Paris, 1953.

Dupeux, Georges. *Aspects de l'histoire sociale et politique du département de Loir-et-Cher, 1848-1914.* Paris, 1962.

Duroselle, J. B. *Les Débuts du catholicisme social en France (1822-1870).* Paris, 1951.

Duveau, Georges. *1848.* "Collection Idées." Paris, 1965.

———. *La Pensée ouvrière sur l'éducation pendant la deuxième république et le second empire.* Paris, 1948.

———. *La Vie ouvrière en France sous le second empire.* 7th edn., Paris, 1946.

1848: Le livre du centenaire. Ed. Charles Moulin. Paris, 1948.

1848: Révolution créatrice. Paris, 1948.

Einaudi, Mario, et al. *Nationalization in France and Italy.* Ithaca, 1955.

Eisenstein, Elizabeth L. *The First Professional Revolutionist: Filippo Michele Buonarroti (1761-1837).* Cambridge, Mass., 1959.

Emérit, Marcel. *L'Algérie à l'époque d'Abd-el-Kader.* Paris, 1951.

Evans, David Owen. *Social Romanticism in France, 1830-1848.* Oxford, 1951.

Festy, Octave. *Les Associations ouvrières encouragées par la deuxième république.* Paris, 1915.

———, ed. *Procès-verbaux du conseil d'encouragement pour les associations ouvrières (décret du 5 juillet 1848): 11 juillet 1848-24 octobre 1849.* Paris, 1917.

Gargan, Edward T. *Alexis de Tocqueville: The Critical Years, 1848-1851.* Washington, D.C., 1955.

Gille, Bertrand. *La Banque et le crédit en France de 1815 à 1848.* Paris, 1959.

———. *Les Sources statistiques de l'histoire de France des enquêtes du XVIIe siècle à 1870.* Geneva, 1964.

Girard, Louis. *Etude comparée des mouvements révolutionnaires en France en 1830, 1848 et 1870-71 (1830-1848).* "Les Cours de Sorbonne." Paris, n.d.

———. *La Garde Nationale, 1814-1871.* Paris, 1964.

———. *Le Libéralisme en France de 1814 à 1848: doctrine et mouvement.* Part II. "Les Cours de Sorbonne." Paris, 1967.

———. *La Politique des travaux publics du second empire.* Paris, 1952.

Girardet, Raoul. *La Société militaire dans la France contemporaine (1815-1939).* Paris, 1953.

Godechot, Jacques. *Les Institutions de la France sous la Révolution et l'empire.* Paris, 1951.

Gossez, A. M. *Le Département du Nord sous la deuxième république (1848-1852).* Lille, 1904.

Gouault, Jacques. *Comment la France est devenue républicaine: les élections générales et partielles à l'Assemblée nationale, 1870-1875.* Paris, 1954.

Greer, D. M. *L'Angleterre, la France et la révolution de 1848.* Paris, 1925.

Guillemin, Henri. *La Première résurrection de la république, 24 février 1848.* Paris, 1967.

———. *La Tragédie de quarante-huit.* Paris, 1948.

Heftler, Emile. *Les Associations coopératives de production sous la deuxième république.* Paris, 1899.

Ibos, Le Général. *Le Général Cavaignac, un dictateur républicain.* Paris, 1930.

Jellinek, Frank. *The Paris Commune of 1871.* New York, 1965 [1937].

Johnson, Douglas. *Guizot: Aspects of French History, 1787-1874.* London, 1963.

Julien, Charles A. *Histoire de l'Algérie contemporaine: la conquête et les débuts de la colonisation (1827-1871).* Paris, 1964.

Kayser, Jacques. *Les Grands batailles du radicalisme, des origines aux portes du pouvoir, 1820-1901.* Paris, 1962.

Kent, Sherman. *Electoral Procedure under Louis Philippe.* New Haven, 1937.

Kerry, Lord. *The Secret of the Coup d'Etat.* New York, 1924.

Kindleberger, Charles P. *Economic Growth in France and Britain, 1851-1950.* Cambridge, Mass., 1964.

Labrousse, Ernest, ed. *Aspects de la crise et de la dépression de l'économie française au milieu du XIXe siècle.* "Bibliothèque de la révolution de 1848." Vol. XIX, Paris, 1956.

———. *Le Mouvement ouvrier et les théories sociales en France de 1815 à 1848.* "Les Cours de Sorbonne." Paris, n.d.

Lacombe, Charles de. *Vie de Berryer.* 3 vols., Paris, 1894-95.

La Gorce, Pierre de. *Histoire de la seconde république française.* 4th edn., 2 vols., Paris, 1904.

Lazard, Raymond. *Michel Goudchaux (1797-1862).* Paris, 1907.

Lebey, André. *Louis Napoléon Bonaparte et le ministère Odilon Barrot, 1849.* Paris, 1912.

———. *Louis Napoléon Bonaparte et la révolution de 1848 (avec des documents et des portraits inédits).* 2 vols., Paris, 1907-08.

Lecanuet, R. P. *Montalembert.* 3 vols., Paris, 1895-1902.

Ledré, Charles. *La Presse à l'assaut de la monarchie, 1815-1848.* Paris, 1960.

Lemeunier, Frédéric. *A.-J. Trouvé-Chauvel, banquier et maire du Mans, ministre des finances de la deuxième république.* Le Mans, 1953.

Leroy, Maxime. *Histoire des idées sociales en France.* 3 vols., Paris, 1946-54.

Levasseur, E. *Histoire des classes ouvrières et de l'industrie en France de 1780 à 1870.* 2d edn., 2 vols., Paris, 1903-04.

Lhomme, Jean. *La Grande bourgeoisie au pouvoir (1830-1880).* Paris, 1960.

Lorwin, Val R. *The French Labor Movement.* Cambridge, Mass., 1954.

Loubère, Leo A. *Louis Blanc: His Life and His Contribution to the Rise of French Jacobin-Socialism.* Evanston, Ill., 1961.

Lucas-Dubreton, J. *Le Culte de Napoléon, 1815-1848.* Paris, 1960.

Maitron, Jean, ed. *Dictionnaire biographique du mouvement ouvrier français.* Part I, 3 vols., Paris, 1964-66.

Marion, Marcel. *Histoire financière de la France depuis 1715.* 6 vols., Paris, 1914-31.

Martin, Gaston. *La Révolution de 1848.* "Que sais-je?" Paris, 1948.

Marx, Karl. *Capital: A Critical Analysis of Capitalist Production.* Eng. trans., Vol. I, Moscow, n.d.

McKay, Donald C. *The National Workshops: A Study in the French Revolution of 1848.* Cambridge, Mass., 1933.

Michel, Henri. *L'Idée de l'Etat.* 3d edn., Paris, 1898.

Namier, Lewis. *1848: The Revolution of the Intellectuals.* Oxford, 1946.

Parménie, A. and C. Bonnier de la Chapelle. *Histoire d'un éditeur et de ses auteurs, P.-J. Hetzel (Stahl).* Paris, 1953.

Perreux, Gabriel. *Au Temps des sociétés secrètes: la propagande républicaine au début de la monarchie de juillet*. Paris, 1930.

Pierre, Victor. *Histoire de la république de 1848*. 2d edn., 2 vols., Paris, 1878.

Pimienta, Robert. *La Propagande bonapartiste en 1848*. Paris, 1911.

Pinet, G. *Histoire de l'école polytechnique*. Paris, 1887.

Plamenatz, John. *The Revolutionary Movement in France, 1815-1871*. London, 1952.

Pokrovskii, Mikhail N. *Pages d'histoire; la méthode du matérialisme historique appliquée à quelques problèmes historiques concrets*. Paris, 1929.

Ponteil, Félix. *1848*. 3d edn., Paris, 1955.

———. *Les Institutions de la France de 1814 à 1870*. Paris, 1966.

Pouthas, Charles H. *Démocraties et capitalisme (1848-1860)*. "Peuples et civilisations." 3d edn., Paris, 1961.

———. *La Population française pendant la première moitié du XIXe siècle*. Paris, 1956.

———. *La Révolution de 1848 en France et la seconde république*. "Les Cours de Sorbonne." Paris, 1952.

Rémond, René. *La Droite en France de la première restauration à la Ve république*. New edn., Paris, 1963.

———. *Les Etats-Unis devant l'opinion française, 1815-1852*. 2 vols., Paris, 1962.

———. *The Right Wing in France from 1815 to de Gaulle*. Trans. James M. Laux. Philadelphia, 1966.

Renard, Georges. *La République de 1848*. Ed. Jean Jaurès. "Histoire socialiste." Vol. IX, Paris, n.d. [1906?]

Renouvin, Pierre. *Histoire des relations internationales*. Vol. V: *Le XIXe siècle, I: de 1815 à 1871*. Paris, 1954.

La Révolution de 1848 en Algérie: mélanges d'histoire. Paris, 1949.

Rigaudias-Weiss, Hilde. *Les Enquêtes ouvrières en France entre 1830 et 1848*. Paris, 1936.

Rist, Charles. *Réglementation légale de la journée de travail de l'ouvrier adulte en France*. Paris, 1898.

Robertson, Priscilla. *Revolutions of 1848: A Social History*. Princeton, 1952.

Rossiter, Clinton L. *Constitutional Dictatorship: Crisis Government in Modern Democracies*. Princeton, 1948.

Saitta, Armando, ed. *Le Relazioni diplomatiche fra la Francia e il Granducato di Toscana, III serie: 1848-1860*. Vol. I: *7 marzo 1848—20 dicembre 1850)*. Rome, 1959.

Schmidt, Charles. *Des Ateliers nationaux aux barricades de juin.*

"Collection du centenaire de la révolution de 1848." Paris, 1948.
———. *Les Journées de juin, 1848.* Paris, 1926.
Schnerb, Robert. *Ledru-Rollin.* "Collection du centenaire de la révolution de 1848." Paris, 1948.
Scott, John A. *Republican Ideas and the Liberal Tradition in France, 1870-1914.* New York, 1951.
Sée, Henri. *Histoire économique de la France.* 2d edn., Vol. II, Paris, 1951.
———. *La Vie économique de la France sous la monarchie censitaire (1815-1848).* Paris, 1927.
Seignobos, Charles. *La Révolution de 1848-le second empire (1848-1859).* Ed. Ernest Lavisse. "Histoire de France contemporaine." Vol. VI, Paris, 1921.
Simpson, F. A. *The Rise of Louis Napoleon.* 3d edn., London, 1960.
Soltau, Roger Henry. *French Political Thought in the Nineteenth Century.* London, 1931.
Spitzer, Alan B. *The Revolutionary Theories of Louis Auguste Blanqui.* New York, 1957.
Taylor, A.J.P. *The Italian Problem in European Diplomacy, 1847-1849.* Manchester, 1934.
———. *The Struggle for Mastery in Europe 1848-1918.* Oxford, 1954.
Tchernoff, I. *Le Parti républicain au coup d'Etat et sous le second empire, d'après des documents et des souvenirs inédits.* Paris, 1906.
———. *Le Parti républicain sous la monarchie de juillet: formation et évolution de la doctrine républicaine.* 2d edn., Paris, 1905.
Tersen, Emile. *Quarante-huit.* Paris, 1957.
Thompson, J. M. *Louis Napoleon and the Second Empire.* New York, 1955.
———. *Robespierre.* 2 vols., Oxford, 1935.
Thureau-Dangin, Paul. *Histoire de la monarchie de juillet.* 4th edn., Vol. VII, Paris, 1914.
Toutain, Jacques. *La Révolution de 1848 à Rouen.* Paris, n.d.
Tudesq, Andre-Jean. *Les Conseillers generaux en France au temps de Guizot, 1840-1848.* Paris, 1967.
———. *L'Election présidentielle de Louis-Napoléon Bonaparte, 10 décembre 1848.* "Kiosque." Paris, 1965.
———. *Les Grands notables en France (1840-1849): étude historique d'une psychologie sociale.* 2 vols., Paris, 1964.
Vier, Jacques. *La Comtesse d'Agoult et son temps, avec des documents inédits.* Vol. III, Paris, 1961.

Vigier, Philippe. *La Monarchie de juillet.* "Que sais-je?" Paris, 1962.

———. *La Seconde république.* "Que sais-je?" Paris, 1967.

———. *La Seconde république dans la région alpine: étude politique et sociale.* 2 vols., Paris, 1963.

Villey, Daniel. *Charles Dupont-White, économiste et publiciste français (1807-1878).* Paris, 1936.

Wallon, Henri. *Les Représentants du peuple en mission et la justice révolutionnaire dans les départements en l'an II (1793-1794).* 5 vols., Paris, 1889-90.

Wassermann, Suzanne. *Les Clubs de Barbès et de Blanqui en 1848.* Paris, 1913.

Weill, Georges. *Histoire du mouvement social en France (1852-1924).* Paris, 1924.

———. *Histoire du parti républicain en France, 1814-1870.* 2d edn., Paris, 1928.

Wood, Anthony. *Nineteenth Century Britain, 1815-1914.* London, 1960.

Wright, Gordon. *France in Modern Times, 1760 to the Present.* Chicago, 1960.

———. *Rural Revolution in France: The Peasantry in the Twentieth Century.* Stanford, 1964.

Zeldin, Theodore. *Emile Ollivier and the Liberal Empire of Napoleon III.* Oxford, 1963.

———. *The Political System of Napoleon III.* London, 1958.

ARTICLES

Aguet, Jean-Pierre. "Le Tirage des quotidiens de Paris sous la monarchie de juillet," *Schweizerische Zeitschrift für Geschichte,* x (1960), 216-286.

Amann, Peter. "The Changing Outlines of 1848," *American Historical Review,* LXVIII (1963), 938-953.

———. "*Du neuf* on the 'Banquet of the People,' June, 1848," *French Historical Studies,* v (1968), 344-350.

———. "The Huber Enigma: Revolutionary or Police Spy?," *International Review of Social History,* XII (1967), 190-203.

———. "Prelude to Insurrection: The Banquet of the People," *French Historical Studies,* I (1960), 436-444.

———. "Writings on the Second French Republic," *Journal of Modern History,* XXXIV (1962), 409-429.

Balland, R. "De l'Organisation à la restriction du suffrage universel en France (1848-1850)," *Réaction et suffrage universel en France et en Allemagne* (*1848-1850*). "Bibliothèque de la révolution de 1848." Vol. XXII, Paris, 1963, pp. 67-173.

———. "Une Interprétation du Dictionnaire politique de 1842," *Actes du soixante-seizième congrès des sociétés savantes, Rennes, 1951*. Paris, 1951, pp. 244-261.

Baughman, John J. "The French Banquet Campaign of 1847-1848," *Journal of Modern History*, XXXI (1959), 1-15.

Bécarud, Jean. "La Noblesse dans les chambres (1815-1848)," *Revue internationale d'histoire politique et constitutionnelle*, new series, No. 11 (1953), 189-205.

Bonnardot, J. "La Presse algérienne sous la seconde république et le second empire," *1848 et les révolutions du XIXe siècle*, No. 180 (1948), pp. 21-38.

Bouillon, Jacques. "Les Démocrates socialistes aux élections de 1849," *Revue française de science politique*, VI (1956), 70-95.

Boyer, Ferdinand. "L'Armée des Alpes en 1848," *Revue historique*, CCXXXIII (1965), 71-100.

———. "Les Rapports entre la France et le Piémont sous le premier ministère de Jules Bastide (11 mai-28 juin 1848)," *Revue d'histoire moderne et contemporaine*, V (1958), 129-136.

Boyer, Pierre. "La Vie politique et les élections à Alger," *La Révolution de 1848 en Algérie*. Paris, 1949, pp. 43-61.

Busquet, Raoul. "L'Affaire des grottes du Dahra (19-20 juin 1845)," *Revue africaine*, LI (1907), 116-168.

Calmette, A. "Les Carbonari en France," *La Révolution de 1848*. IX (1912-13), pp. 401-417, and X (1913-14), pp. 52-73, 117-137, 214-230.

Cavaignac, Godefroy. "Le Général Cavaignac (1802-1857)," *Carnet de la sabretache*, No. 100 (1901), pp. 210-231.

Chaboseau, A. "Les Constituants de 1848," *La Révolution de 1848*, VII (1910), pp. 287-305, 413-425, and VIII (1911), pp. 67-80.

Chalmin, Pierre. "La Crise morale de l'armée française," *L'Armée et la seconde république*. "Bibliothèque de la révolution de 1848." Vol. XVIII, Paris, 1955, pp. 28-76.

———. "Les Crises dans l'armée française, 1830, 1848," *Revue historique de l'armée*, XVIII (1962), 45-62.

———. "Une Institution militaire de la seconde république; la garde nationale mobile," *Etudes d'histoire moderne et contemporaine*, II (1948), 37-82.

Chambrun, Gilbert de. "Un Projet de séjour en France du pape Pie IX (1848)," *Revue d'histoire diplomatique*, L (1936), 322-364, 481-508.

Cobban, Alfred, "Administrative Pressure in the Election of the French Constituent Assembly, April, 1848," *Bulletin of the Institute of Historical Research*, xxv (1952), 133-159.

———. "The Influence of the Clergy and the 'Instituteurs Primaires' in the Election of the French Constituent Assembly, April, 1848," *English Historical Review*, LVII (1942), 334-344.

———. "The 'Middle Class' in France, 1815-1848," *French Historical Studies*, v (1967), 41-52.

Coquerelle, Suzanne. "L'Armée et la répression dans les campagnes," *L'Armée et la seconde république*. "Bibliothèque de la révolution de 1848." Vol. XVIII, Paris, 1955, pp. 121-159.

Daumard, Adeline. "Les Relations sociales à Paris à l'époque de la monarchie constitutionnelle d'après les registres paroissiaux des mariages," *Population*, XI (1957), 445-466.

———. "Une Source d'histoire sociale: l'enregistrement des mutations par décès: le XIIe arrondissement de Paris en 1820 et 1847," *Revue d'histoire économique et sociale*, XXXV (1957), 52-78.

Doumenc, General. "L'Armée et les journées de juin," *Actes du congrès historique du centenaire de la révolution de 1848*. Paris, 1948, pp. 255-265.

Droulers, Paul. "Catholicisme et mouvement ouvrier en France au XIXe siècle: l'attitude de l'épiscopat," *Le Mouvement social*, No. 57 (1966), 15-46.

Dubois, P. F. "Le Général Cavaignac," *Revue bleue* (Sept. 5, 1908), 300-303.

Dubuc, André. "Les Emeutes de Rouen et d'Elbeuf," *Etudes d'histoire moderne et contemporaine*, II (1948), 243-275.

Duchon, Paul. "Les Elections de 1848 (d'après les correspondances inédites du prince Louis Napoléon et de M. de Persigny)," *Revue de Paris*, CCLIII (1936), 30-61, 381-411.

Emérit, Marcel. "Les Déportés de juin," *La Révolution de 1848 en Algérie*. Paris, 1949, pp. 63-73.

———. "L'Esprit de 1848 en Algérie," *La Révolution de 1848 en Algérie*. Paris, 1949, pp. 13-28.

Fasel, George W. "The French Election of April 23, 1848: Suggestions for a Revision," *French Historical Studies*, v (1968), pp. 285-298.

Geffroy, Gustave. "Les Journées de juin 1848," *La Révolution de 1848*. Vol. I (1904), pp. 22-29.

Genet, Lucien. "Les Colonies agricoles de 1848," *La Révolution de 1848 en Algérie*. Paris, 1949, pp. 107-121.

Gershoy, Leo. "Three French Historians and the Revolution of 1848," *Journal of the History of Ideas*, XII (1951), 131-146.

Girard, Louis. "Political Liberalism in France, 1840-1875," *French Society and Culture Since the Old Regime*. Trans. Joseph N. Moody, eds. Evelyn M. Acomb and Marvin L. Brown, Jr. New York, 1966, pp. 119-132.

Gossez, Rémi. "Diversité des antagonismes sociaux vers le milieu du XIXe siècle," *Revue économique*, VI (1956), 439-458.

———. "Notes sur la composition et l'attitude politique de la troupe," *L'Armée et la seconde république*. "Bibliothèque de la révolution de 1848." Vol. XVIII (1955), pp. 77-110.

———. "Presse parisienne à destination des ouvriers (1848-1851)," *La Presse ouvrière, 1819-1850*. "Bibliothèque de la révolution de 1848." Vol. XXIII (1966), pp. 123-190.

———. "La Résistance à l'impôt: les quarante-cinq centimes," *Etudes*, "Bibliothèque de la révolution de 1848." Vol. XV (1953), pp. 89-132.

Griffiths, Gordon. "The Vicomte Armand de Melun and the Catholic Social Movement in France, 1848-1851," *Studies in Modern European History in Honor of Franklin Charles Palm*. Eds. Frederick J. Cox et al. New York, 1956, pp. 141-156.

Haury, V. "Les Commissaires de Ledru-Rollin en 1848," *Lae Révolution française*. Vol. LVII (1909), pp. 438-474.

Hawgood, J. A. "Liberalism and Constitutional Development," *New Cambridge Modern History*. Vol. X, Cambridge, 1960, pp. 189-196.

Henry, F. "Le Droit au travail," *1848: Révolution créatrice*. Paris, 1948, pp. 43-77.

Henry, Paul. "La France et les nationalités en 1848," *Revue historique*, CLXXXVI (1939), 48-77, and CLXXXVIII (1940), 234-258.

———. "Le Gouvernement provisoire et la question polonaise," *Revue historique*, CLXXVIII (1936), 198-240.

Higonnet, Patrick L. R., and Trevor B. Higonnet. "Class, Corruption, and Politics in the French Chamber of Deputies, 1846-1848," *French Historical Studies*, V (1967), 204-224.

Houtin, Albert. "Le Clergé et la noblesse d'Anjou aux élections de l'Assemblée nationale constituante de 1848," *La Révolution de 1848*. Vol. VIII (1911-12), pp. 149-161, 208-218, 289-299.

Julien, Charles A. "Le Conflit entre les généraux et les préfets d'Algérie sous la deuxième république," *La Révolution de 1848*. Vol. XXIII (1926), pp. 794-813.

Labrousse, Ernest. "1848–1830–1789: Comment naissent les révolutions," *Actes du congrès historique du centenaire de révolution de 1848.* Paris, 1948, pp. 1-20.

Langer, William L. "The Pattern of Urban Revolution in 1848," *French Society and Culture Since the Old Regime.* Eds. Evelyn M. Acomb and Marvin L. Brown, Jr. New York, 1966, pp. 89-118.

Leflon, Jean, "La Mission de Claude de Corcelle auprès de Pie IX, après le meurtre du ministre Rossi," *Archivum historiae pontificiae.* No. 1, 1963, pp. 385-402.

Levy, Claude. "Les Journées parisiennes de juin 1848 d'après des études récentes," *Bulletin de la société d'études historiques, géographiques et scientifiques de la région parisienne,* xxxv (1961 [1963]), 19-26.

Lévy-Schneider, L. "Les Préliminaires du 15 mai 1848: la journée du 14, d'après un document inédit," *La Révolution de 1848.* Vol. VII (1910), pp. 219-232.

Loubere, Leo A. "The Emergence of the Extreme Left in Lower Langudoc, 1848-1951: Social and Economic Factors in Politics," *American Historical Review,* LXXIII (1968), 1019-1051.

Louvel, A. "L'Ecole d'Administration de 1848," *Etudes d'histoire moderne et contemporaine,* II (1948), 19-36.

Marcilhacy, Christianne. "Les Caractères de la crise sociale et politique de 1846 à 1852 dans le département du Loiret," *Revue d'histoire moderne et contemporaine,* VI (1959), 5-59.

Markovitch, T. J. "La Crise de 1847-1848 dans les industries parisiennes," *Revue d'histoire économique et sociale,* XLIII (1965), 256-260.

Marlin, Roger. "L'Election présidentielle de Louis-Napoléon Bonaparte dans le Doubs le 10 décembre 1848," *Annales littéraires de l'université de Besançon,* II (1955), fasc. 3, pp. 33-46.

Matagrin, A. "Le Rachat des chemins de fer en 1848," *Revue socialiste,* XL (1904), 417-446, 529-571.

McKay, Donald C. "Le Vicomte de Falloux et les ateliers nationaux," *La Révolution de 1848.* Vol. XXX (1933), pp. 30-42.

Minnich, L. Arthur, Jr. "The Third Force, 1870-1896," *Modern France, Problems of the Third and Fourth Republics.* Ed. E. M. Earle. New York, 1964 [1951], pp. 109-123.

Molinier, Sylvain, ed. "Pages ignorées: Blanqui et les barricades de juin 1848," *La Pensée,* No. 19 (1948), 9-15.

Mollat, G. "La Fuite de Pie IX à Gaète (24 novembre 1848)," *Revue d'histoire de l'église,* XXXV (1939), 266-282.

Molok, A. I. "Problèmes de l'insurrection de juin 1848," *Questions d'histoire*, II, Paris, 1954, pp. 57-100.

Moody, Joseph N. "French Liberal Catholics, 1840-1875," *French Society and Culture Since the Old Regime*. Eds. Evelyn M. Acomb and Marvin L. Brown, Jr. New York, 1966, pp. 150-171.

Moysset, Henri. "L'Idée d'organisation du travail dans la profession de foi des candidats à l'Assemblée constitutante de 1848," *La Révolution de 1848*. Vol. III (1906), pp. 27-42.

Pinkney, David H. "The Crowd in the French Revolution of 1830," *American Historical Review*, LXX (1964), 1-17.

———. "The Myth of the French Revolution of 1830," in *A Festschrift for Frederick B. Artz*. Durham, N.C., 1964, pp. 52-71.

———. "A New Look at the French Revolution of 1830," *Review of Politics*, XXIII (1961), 490-506.

Perotin, Robert. "Les Services des postes en France avec Etienne Arago," *1848 et les révolutions du XIXe siècle*. No. 182 (1949), pp. 17-24.

Pouthas, Charles H. "Une Enquête sur la réforme administrative sous la seconde république," *Revue historique*, CXCIII (1942), 1-15.

———. "The Revolutions of 1848," *New Cambridge Modern History*. Vol. x, Cambridge, 1960, pp. 389-415.

Richter, Melvin. "Tocqueville on Algeria," *Review of Politics*, XXV (1963), 362-398.

Saurin, Marcel. "L'Ecole d'Administration de 1848," *Politique. Revue internationale des idées, des institutions, et de la vie politiques*, Nos. 25-32 (1964-65), 105-195.

Schnapper, Bernard. "Les Sociétés ouvrières de production pendant la seconde république: l'exemple girondin," *Revue d'histoire économique et sociale*, XLIII (1965), 162-191.

Schnerb, Robert. "La Côte d'Or et l'élection présidentielle du 10 décembre 1848," *La Révolution de 1848*. Vol. XX (1924), pp. 376-411, and XXI (1924), pp. 74-93.

———. "Les Hommes de 1848 et l'impôt," *1848 et les révolutions du XIXe siècle*. No. 176 (1947), pp. 5-51.

Soboul, Albert. "La Question paysanne en 1848," *La Pensée*, No. 18 (1948), 55-66, No. 19 (1948), 25-37, and No. 20 (1948), 48-56.

Spring, Elsbeth. "Tocquevilles Stellung zur Februarrevolution," *Schweizer Beiträge zur allgemeinen Geschichte*, XII (1954), 50-98.

Stearns, Peter N. "Patterns of Industrial Strike Activity in France during the July Monarchy," *American Historical Review*, LXX (1965), 371-394.

Trannoy, A. "Notes et lettres de Montalembert (1848-1852)," *Revue historique*, CXCII (1941), pp. 253-289.

Tudesq, A. J. "La Crise de 1847, vue par les milieux d'affaires parisiens," *Aspects de la crise et de la dépression de l'économie française au milieu du XIXe siècle*. Ed. Ernest Labrousse. Paris, 1956, pp. 4-36.

———. "L'Election du président de la république en 1848 dans le Hérault," *Annales du Midi*, LXVII (1955), 331-340.

———. "La Légende napoléonienne en France en 1848," *Revue historique*, CCXVIII (1957), 64-85.

Vallès, F. "Le Suffrage universel dans le département du Lot," *La Révolution de 1848*. Vol. II (1905), pp. 97-106, 146-160.

Vauthier, Gabriel. "La Journée du 15 mai 1848," *La Révolution de 1848*. Vol. XXV (1928), pp. 242-251.

———. "Le Collège de France, école d'administration," *La Révolution de 1848*. Vol. X (1913), pp. 451-470.

Vidal, César. "La France et la question italienne en 1848," *Etudes d'histoire moderne et contemporaine*. II (1948), 162-183.

Vidalenc, Jean. "A Propos de la campagne des banquets," *Actes du quatre-vingt-unième congrès national des sociétés savantes*. Paris, 1956, pp. 679-689.

———. "La Province et les journées de juin," *Etudes d'histoire moderne et contemporaine*. II (1948), 83-144.

Wright, Gordon. "A Poet in Politics: Lamartine and the Revolution of 1848," *History Today*, VIII (1958), 616-627.

Zeldin, Theodore. "Government Policy in the French General Election of 1849," *English Historical Review*, LXXIV (1959), 240-248.

UNPUBLISHED *MÉMOIRES*, THESES AND DISSERTATIONS

Amann, Peter. "A French Revolutionary Club in 1848: *The Société Démocratique Centrale*: A Document from the Archives nationales, Edited and Translated." Unpublished Ph.D. dissertation, University of Chicago, 1958.

Baughman, John J. "The Political Banquet Campaign in France, 1847-1848." Unpublished Ph.D. dissertation, University of Michigan, 1953.

Chevalier, Louis. "Les Fondements économiques et sociaux de l'histoire politique de la région parisienne, (1848-1870), tome

I (février 1848-décembre 1851)." Unpublished doctoral thesis, University of Paris, 1950.

de Luna, Frederick A. "The Republic of Cavaignac." Unpublished Ph.D. dissertation, University of Iowa, 1962.

Eon, Michel. "Les Questions sociales dans la presse légitimiste sous la monarchie de juillet." Unpublished *mémoire* for the *Diplôme d'Etudes Supérieures*, University of Paris, 1948.

Fasel, George W. "The French Moderate Republicans, 1837-1848." Unpublished Ph.D. dissertation, Stanford University, 1965.

Gallaher, John G. "An Evaluation of the Revolution of 1848 by American Diplomats." Unpublished Ph.D. dissertation, Saint Louis University, 1960.

Gossez, Rémi. "Les Ouvriers de Paris, 1848-1851. Livre premier: l'organisation ouvrière." Unpublished *thèse de troisième cycle*, University of Paris, 1963.

Hahn, Robert J. "The Attitude of the French Revolutionary Government Toward German Unification in 1848." Unpublished Ph.D. dissertation, Ohio State University, 1955.

Michiels, Jeanne. "Le *Journal des débats* et la seconde république." Unpublished *mémoire* for the *Diplôme d'Etudes Supérieures*, University of Paris, 1955.

Picq, Yvonne. "Les Associations professionnelles ouvrières en 1848." Unpublished *mémoire* for the *Diplôme d'Etudes Supérieures*, University of Paris, 1958.

Pineau, Simone. "La Question de la réforme postale en France de 1839 à 1848." Unpublished *mémoire* for the *Diplôme d'Etudes Supérieures*, University of Paris, 1958.

Rys, Vladimir. "Sécurité sociale en France et en Grande-Bretagne: étude sociologique." Unpublished doctoral thesis, University of Paris, 1958.

Sweet, James. "France during the Last Two Years of the July Monarchy: The Climate of Opinion, 1846-1848." Unpublished Ph.D. dissertation, University of California, Los Angeles, 1955.

Vigier, Philippe. "La Seconde république dans la région alpine: étude politique et sociale." Unpublished doctoral thesis, 3 vols., University of Paris, 1959.

Wilson, Prince E. "Anglo-French Diplomatic Relations (1848-1851)." Unpublished Ph.D. dissertation, University of Chicago, 1954.

Zaniewicki, Witold. "L'Armée française en 1848. Introduction à une étude militaire de la deuxième république (22 février-20 décembre 1848)." Unpublished *thèse de troisième cycle*, University of Paris, 1966.

Index